BITTER FRUIT

BITTER FRUIT

*The Story of the American Coup
in Guatemala*

STEPHEN SCHLESINGER

AND

STEPHEN KINZER

Revised and Expanded Edition

Published by
Harvard University
David Rockefeller Center for Latin American Studies

Distributed by
Harvard University Press
Cambridge, Massachusetts
London, England

TO THE PEOPLE OF GUATEMALA

Second David Rockefeller Center for
Latin American Studies Edition 2005
Harvard University

Library of Congress Cataloging-in-Publication Data
Schlesinger, Stephen C.
  Bitter fruit
  Bibliography: p.
  Includes index.
  1. Guatemala—History—Revolution, 1954.
  2. Guatemala—Foreign relations—United States
  3. United States—Foreign relations—Guatemala
  4. United Fruit Company
  I. Kinzer, Stephen. II. Title.
F1466.5.S34   972.81'052   80-1728
AACR2
ISBN 0-674-01930-X

CONTENTS

ABOUT THE AUTHORS

STEPHEN SCHLESINGER is Director of the World Policy Institute, a foreign policy think-tank, at the New School in New York City. After the publication of *Bitter Fruit*, he lectured extensively around the United States on the findings of the book and helped to rally opposition to U.S. policy in Central America. In 1990, he served as an election monitor in the Guatemalan presidential election. He has since continued to urge the release of all the still-secret CIA documents on the coup. He started this effort in 1977 with a Freedom of Information request made on the agency, followed by an unsuccessful Federal court battle and thereafter with a public campaign which put maximum pressure on successive CIA Directors to place the documents in the public arena.

STEPHEN KINZER spent 13 years writing about Latin America, first as a contributor to leading magazines and then as a correspondent for the *Boston Globe* and *New York Times*. From 1983 to 1990, while the Sandinista government was in power in Nicaragua, he was the *Times* bureau chief there. As he was completing that assignment, Columbia University honored him with the Maria Moors Cabot Award, a prestigious journalism prize that had also been given to the murdered Nicaraguan newspaper editor Pedro Joaquin Chamorro. In 1991 Mr. Kinzer published *Blood of Brothers: Life and War in Nicaragua*. Since then he has been a *New York Times* correspondent in Europe, covering the Yugoslav wars and the emergence of post-Communist states, and in Istanbul, from which he has covered Turkey as well as the new nations of the Caucasus and Central Asia.

JOHN H. COATSWORTH is Monroe Gutman Professor of Latin American Affairs at Harvard University, where he also serves as

Director of the David Rockefeller Center for Latin American Studies. He taught at the University of Chicago from 1969 until he joined the Harvard faculty in 1992. He was elected president of the American Historical Association for 1995. Professor Coatsworth's research has focused on the comparative economic history of Latin America and the economic and international history of Mexico and Central America. His most recent books include *The United States and Central America: The Clients and the Colossus* (New York: Twayne, 1994), a history of U.S.-Central American relations, and *Latin America and the World Economy Since 1800* (Cambridge: Harvard University Press, 1998), a volume of essays co-edited with Alan M. Taylor.

JUNE CAROLYN ERLICK, publications director of the David Rockefeller Center for Latin American Studies, is the author of *Disappeared, A Journalist Silenced* (Emeryville, CA: Seal Press, 2004). Erlick is also the editor-in-chief of *ReVista, Harvard Review of Latin America*. A graduate of the Columbia Graduate School of Journalism, Erlick worked as a correspondent in Latin America and Germany for almost two decades. She teaches journalism at Harvard Extension and Summer Schools. A special investigator for the Inter American Press Association's Unpunished Crimes Against Journalism Project in Guatemala, Erlick became involved with the organization when she received an IAPA scholarship to study in Bogotá, Colombia, in 1977. Erlick also has received two Fulbright Fellowships to teach journalism and do book research in 2000 and 2005.

RICHARD A. NUCCIO is Director of International Programs at the California-based Center for Civic Education. He received his doctorate in political science, with a special interest in Latin American politics, in 1977 from UMass Amherst. His involvement in Guatemala began in the mid-1980s when, as director of Latin America and Caribbean programs at the Roosevelt Center for American Policy Studies, he helped to secure U.S. funding for efforts to rebuild civilian research institutions that later contributed key personnel to the peace process. From 1991 to 1993 he was a staff consultant to Robert G. Torricelli, chairman of the Western Hemisphere Subcommittee, House Foreign Affairs Committee. Between 1993 and 1997 Dr. Nuccio served as senior policy adviser in the Inter-American Affairs Bureau of the State Department, as U.S. coordinator in the Guatemalan peace process, and as special adviser to the president and secretary of state for Cuba. He is a former Visiting Fellow at Harvard University.

INTRODUCTION
TO THE 2005 HARVARD EDITION

Stephen Kinzer and Stephen Schlesinger did not set out to write a classic. They set out to write a fast-paced and highly readable narrative of the overthrow of Guatemala's democratic government by the United States in 1954. They also hoped to convince their readers of the need for what Harrison Salisbury in his 1982 introduction called "a basic reappraisal of American policy in the Western Hemisphere."[1]

When *Bitter Fruit* first appeared in bookstores in 1982, Guatemala was plunging into yet another round of terror and death. On March 9, the Guatemalan president General Romeo Lucas García, perennial star of international reports on human rights abuses throughout the world, declared his own hand-picked candidate the winner of yet another fraudulent election. Rioting erupted in Guatemala City. The government diverted troops from fighting guerrilla insurgents to suppressing the protests. The military high command fretted and worried, and consulted with powerful friends domestic and foreign. On March 23, Lucas García was packed off to exile. The country's military leaders installed a former general turned Christian fundamentalist, Efraín Ríos Montt, as the new president. The army got back to the business of killing insurgents, along with suspected insurgents, suspected supporters of the insurgents, peaceful dissidents of all kinds, and indigenous villagers in zones where subversives were known to be or suspected of operating.[2]

The Ríos Montt era lasted a little over 16 months, until he, too, fell in a military coup on August 8, 1983. Between early 1982 and the end of 1983, the Guatemalan army destroyed some 400 towns and villages, drove 20,000 rural people out of their homes and into camps, killed between 50,000 and 75,000 mostly unarmed indigenous farmers and their families, and violently displaced over a million people from their homes (of whom 150,000 fled into neighboring Mexico). As the atrocities escalated, the U.S. government gave repeated and dramatic evidence of its support of the Ríos Montt regime. Economic aid resumed in October. President Reagan praised Ríos Montt and his government on a state visit in December. In January 1983, the U.S. government lifted its embargo on the sale of arms to Guatemala and sent $6.3 million in spare parts for helicopters, the same helicopters that had already begun to appear in accounts of army massacres of entire villages. Reports based on eye-witness accounts were dismissed by U.S. officials as "unconfirmed."

Unlike the 1950s, Guatemala did not suffer alone in the 1980s. Including the 50,000 or so deaths in the Nicaraguan revolution against the Somoza dictatorship (1977–79), the 80,000 or so killed in the Salvadoran civil war (1981–90), another 50,000 in the contra war waged by the United States against the Sandinista government in Nicaragua (1983–90), and the several thousand victims kidnapped and executed by the security forces in Honduras and Panama, the Central American dead by 1990 equaled the number of U.S. soldiers killed in all of World War Two (about 300,000). By that date, one out of every 150 or so Central Americans had been killed. Refugees (internal as well as external) numbered over two million by 1990 in a region whose total population did not exceed 29 million.

For a generation of U.S. citizens and countless college students, *Bitter Fruit* helped to place the bitter conflicts of the 1980s in historical context. Walter Lafeber's history of the U.S.-Central American relations, aptly titled *Inevitable Revolutions,*[3] provided a much needed critical survey, but *Bitter Fruit* provided the depth that only a case study can offer. Had it not been for the passage of the Freedom of Information Act of 1966, however, this book could never have been produced. Kinzer and Schlesinger used its provisions to secure the declassification of thousands of documents, including many sensitive CIA reports and memos. They also painstakingly accumulated a wealth of additional detailed information through interviews and additional research.

Since *Bitter Fruit's* publication, important new sources of information have become available to researchers. Piero Gleijeses's masterful 1991 book, *Shattered Hope: The Guatemalan Revolution and the United States, 1944–1954*,[4] shed new light on many of the crucial events in Guatemalan history in this decade, from the assassination of Francisco Arana in 1949 to the decision by Jacobo Arbenz to give up and flee the country. Gleijeses interviewed many of the key figures of this era, including Arbenz's widow María, his close collaborator Manuel Fortuny, secretary general of the communist *Partido Guatemalteco de Trabajo*, and his principal military aides and betrayers. More recently, the C.I.A. finally declassified a large quantity of materials hitherto withheld that added much new detail about the agency's organization and implementation of what it called "Operation PBSuccess."[5] While these and other works have added considerably to knowledge about U.S.-Guatemalan relations during the Arévalo and Arbenz presidencies, this new information tends to confirm rather than alter *Bitter Fruit's* account of events.

Even with the new sources now available, parts of the Guatemalan story still remain obscure because the necessary documentation has either been destroyed or buried. Little is known about the "sizable U.S. military mission in Guatemala City" nor have the official documents released to date revealed much about "in-country CIA connections with Guatemalan individuals and groups."[6]

Bitter Fruit helped to inspire debate among scholars and practitioners about the motivations or causes of the U.S. intervention to overthrow the Arbenz government. An important contribution to this debate was published in the same year as *Bitter Fruit*. In his book entitled *The CIA in Guatemala*,[7] Richard H. Immerman argued that U.S. policymakers were driven by the "cold war ethos" of anti-communism to overreact to evidence of communist "infiltration" in Guatemala. Jorge Domínguez has recently made a similar argument, suggesting that ideological blinders led U.S.

policymakers to act "irrationally" toward Guatemala in the 1950s.[8] This view is amply confirmed, in a sense, by every serious work on Guatemala in the 1950s, all of which conclude that while the Arbenz government was reformist or progressive the probability of a communist regime coming to power was virtually nil.[9]

This is not to say that Guatemala's communists lacked influence or power. Ironically, much of the new work on the internal politics of Guatemala in the early 1950s suggests that the *Partido Guatemateco de Trabajo* (PGT—Guatemalan Party of Labor), as it called itself, exerted more influence in the Arbenz administration and became more deeply embedded in the country's social and political life than the U.S. government knew at the time. Gleijeses showed that "the PGT leaders—[Manuel] Fortuny foremost—were Arbenz's closest advisers and constituted his kitchen cabinet, which discussed all major decisions."[10] Fortuny became President Arbenz's most trusted advisor and confidant. The two men shared a vision of a modernizing and democratic Guatemala, inevitably capitalist for many years to come because its social structure and geographic location gave it no choice, but with a government committed to improving human and civic rights along with living standards and access to education and health. It was this vision, along with their implacable honesty and commitment, that brought them together.[11]

The links between the Arbenz government and Guatemala's communitsts extended beyond the president's office and the reform legislation drafted there. As Greg Grandin has shown in *The Last Colonial Massacre*, the Guatemalan communist movement, though small in numbers, young in age, and lacking in experience, nonetheless managed to inspire, organize, mobilize and form alliances with other groups in many parts of the country. Though numbering no more than 5,000 in 1954, Guatemala's communists were succeeding on a scale that made it possible, for the first time in the country's history, to imagine Guatemala as a future democracy. The Guatemalan communists formed a small part of a much larger democratic movement, but "there would not have been a significant expansion of democracy in Guatemala were it not for the PGT."[12] The 1954 intervention and its aftermath crushed prospects for a social democracy in which communists would have participated actively; a communist regime on the East European or Asian model, was never in prospect.

Thus, even if they had been better informed about President Arbenz's collaboration with the PGT and the significance of the party in Guatemala's democratic reforms, the evidence of the era makes it difficult to believe that U.S. policymakers could have been worried about an imminent "Communist takeover," as they professed themselves to be. Actions that are irrational with respect to their explicit goals may, however, make perfect sense in some other context. For example, reviews of *Bitter Fruit* often mentioned the emphasis that Kinser and Schlesinger gave to the close ties between the U.S. administration and the United Fruit Company (UFCO), principal victim of the Arbenz government's agrarian reform and other policies.[13] Indeed, as the authors point out, every U.S. policymaking official involved in the decision to overthrow the Guatemalan government, except for President Eisenhower himself, had a family or business connection to UFCO.[14] The access of key UFCO officials to decision makers in the U.S. government, the sympathy of the U.S. administration toward UFCO interests, and the established U.S. view that hostility toward U.S. companies constituted a key symptom of communist penetration all gave UFCO and its anti-Arbenz campaign in the U.S. media considerable influence. If prior U.S. policy is any guide, the United States would probably not have intervened only to save UFCO, but that is scarcely the point. The interpretive issue is just how much more reasonable this irrational intervention seemed to key policymakers because of UFCO.

Most accounts of the 1954 Guatemalan intervention, including *Bitter Fruit*, have also emphasized the historic U.S. dominance of the Caribbean basin and the U.S. record of continuous direct or covert intervention in the internal affairs of the small states in this region to maintain that dominance. As the reviewer for the *Times Literary Supplement* summed it up, "Clandestine operations, by the KGB and MI6 no less than the CIA, suit the post-colonial global system which emerged in 1945, the Cold War being more a pretext than a serious cause."[12] This view is closer to my own (and to Gleijeses) than to others, though it is consistent with the *Bitter Fruit* narrative.

What was at stake in Guatemala in the 1950s was less the imagined Soviet threat to the security of the United States than the historic U.S. threat to the sovereignty of Guatemala. The Guatemalan government could not accomplish its objectives without recovering more freedom of action than the United States saw as consistent with its customary dominance. It did Arbenz no more good than it did the Sandinistas in Nicaragua a quarter century later to demonstrate his country's independence of the Soviet Union. Whatever U.S. policymakers said to each other and to the public in 1954, this seems never to have been the real issue.

Most historical accounts of the events that brought down the Guatemalan government in 1954 have emphasized the pivotal role of the United States. Like *Bitter Fruit*, they have noted the relative ease with which the United States achieved its objective of overthrowing the Arbenz government and contrasted it to the unsuccessful effort of the United States to achieve the same results in Cuba only seven years later.[13] Since U.S. goals, methods, and capabilities did not change, explanations for the difference in outcomes have tended to point to internal factors. Some early accounts criticized Arbenz for cowardice in failing to put up a fight; Gleijeses rebutted this view by showing that the army's defection left him little to fight with.[14] In the Cuban case, in contrast, the counter-revolutionaries at the Bay of Pigs in 1961 faced an army that had no ties to the old regime, no worries about communism, and no hesitation about defending its leaders to the end. The United States encountered a similar difficulty when it launched its "contras" against the Sandinista government in Nicaragua in the 1980s.

The differences between the Guatemalan military establishment in 1954 and the armed forces of revolutionary Cuba after 1959 and Sandinista Nicaragua in 1979–90 mirrored differences in two societies. Deborah Yashar's comparative analysis of Guatemala and Costa Rica demonstrates that in Guatemala a powerful class-based opposition arose to challenge the Arbenz government, oppose its reforms and support rebellion.[15] The United States intervention served "as a catalyst" in an already polarized political environment in which the Guatemalan elite fiercely and nearly unanimously opposed the government while urban workers and growing numbers of peasants and rural laborers supported it. In Cuba and Nicaragua by contrast, polarization did not occur until after revolutionary governments supported by broad multi-class coalitions had effectively destroyed the pre-revolutionary state as well as the old regime's armed forces and replaced them with institutions loyal to the new order.

Most accounts of the Guatemalan events, like *Bitter Fruit*, assume that the U.S. role was decisive. The United States organized, financed, trained, and equipped the invasion forces. U.S. personnel flew the rebel aircraft and filled the airways with bogus transmissions suggesting a much larger force had invaded. Unrelenting U.S. diplomatic and political pressure encouraged treason and demoralized supporters. CIA assets in the officer corps and the administration worked actively to undermine President Arbenz's authority and block efforts to move against the rebels. Only the bombing and radio transmissions could have been accomplished without willing and enthusiastic Guatemalan collaborators. Operation PBSuccess would have failed, as Yashar suggests, had it not been for divisions within Guatemalan society and the Guatemalan military.

Though the U.S. intervention would have failed without powerful Guatemalan allies, it is not so clear that Guatemala's powerful conservatives could have brought down the government and the democratic regime created by the 1944 "Revolution" without U.S. intervention. Were Guatemalan conservatives—"a united oligarchy, the Catholic Church, and parts of the middle class," according to Yashar—sufficiently powerful despite majority support for Arbenz to overthrow the government and install an authoritarian regime on their own?[16] Growing tensions within the military preceded the 1954 overthrow, but these tensions were deliberately exacerbated by U.S. pressure and U.S. agents. *Bitter Fruit* had it right, I think, in arguing that Arbenz could have survived had the United States not sought to overthrow him, though historians and political scientists will continue to debate this issue far into the future. What seems unquestionable, from the evidence in *Bitter Fruit* and in all the more recent books, is that divisions within Guatemala made overthrowing its government even easier and cheaper than U.S. policymakers had calculated.

Had Arbenz served out his term, the opposition might well have been strong enough to contest and even win the 1955 elections.

Although a distinct minority, the conservative opposition had both money and organized religion on its side. Divisions within the army were strong enough to make it risky for Arbenz to rig the election of his successor. Guatemalan voters, or even Arbenz himself, might have opted for calm and consolidation, as Mexican President Lázaro Cárdenas did in 1939 when he chose a successor more conservative than himself. In short, the democratic option—however uncertain its results—was still open to Guatemalan conservatives in 1954. The U.S. intervention gave them an opportunity to win by opting instead for the security of authoritarian repression. In taking this path, they condemned their country to four decades of unremitting brutality and violence.

Written in the post-Vietnam war era, *Bitter Fruit* raised questions that were still hotly debated in the early 1980s when it appeared. U.S. policy in Central America in that decade returned to the dogmas of the High Cold War, ignoring the lessons taught by *Bitter Fruit* and a generation of critics of U.S. interventions in the Caribbean. Though the Cold War itself ended nearly a decade ago, the lessons Bitter Fruit sought to convey are just as relevant as they were when Stephen Kinzer and Stephen Schlesinger first set out to write about the tragedy that befell Guatemalan democracy in 1954.

～

In his Afterword to this edition of *Bitter Fruit*, Stephen Kinzer, now a foreign bureau chief for the *New York Times*, summarizes the 35-year history of repressive government and endemic civil warfare that followed the 1954 events. He concludes by citing the 3,600-page report of the United Nations Commission for Historical Clarification (CEH) presented to Guatemalan president Alvaro Arzú on February 25, 1999. The CEH was created by the peace agreement signed in December 1996 between the Guatemalan National Revolutionary Unity (URNG) guerrillas and the Guatemalan government. Headed by German jurist Christian Tomuschat, the CEH was forbidden by the terms of the peace agreement to name the perpetrators of the massacres, extra-judicial executions, tortures, and other abuses it investigated. The U.S. government aided the Commission's work by providing massive documentation from the files of the State Department and other agencies, though the C.I.A., according to press reports, directly provided little of value. U.S. official documents, the CEH report stated, demonstrated conclusively the continuous support provided by the C.I.A. to the Guatemalan Armed Forces, even in periods when U.S. officials were receiving confidential reports of massacres and other human rights violations on a massive scale.

The U.N. Commission's findings came as no surprise to Richard Nuccio, whose Foreword to this volume provides an insightful summary of the U.S. role in the Guatemalan peace process. Nuccio served as foreign policy adviser to Congressman and later Senator Robert G. Torricelli and in senior policy positions in the State Department and the White House during the Clinton Administration. He was a key player in the events he summarizes. It was Nuccio who exposed the C.I.A.'s misconduct in concealing from congressional oversight committees the fact that one of its Guatemalan "assets" had been involved in the murder of Michael DeVine, an American citizen, and in the extra-judicial execution of a guerrilla leader, Efaín Bámaca, married to U.S. citizen Jennifer Harbury. Nuccio reported the C.I.A. deception to Torricelli, who went public with the information in circumstances Nuccio describes in his account. The C.I.A. demanded that Nuccio's highest-level security clearance (for "sensitive compartmented information" or SCI) be withdrawn as punishment and when the president declined to intervene in the matter, Nuccio resigned from the administration, in February 1997.

As Nuccio's "Foreword" and Kinzer's "Afterword" make clear, the United States has yet to undertake that "basic reappraisal," so much needed and so long overdue that *Bitter Fruit* called for when first published in 1982.

JOHN H. COATSWORTH

Notes

1. Harrison Salisbury was senior military affairs analyst for the *New York Times* when *Bitter Fruit* was first published. His brief "Introduction" was notable for its tone of foreboding and its anticipation of the U.S. interventions of the 1980s. "If the Guatemala model is to be applied today to other countries . . .," he wrote, "we will simply sink ourselves deeper into the mud of militaristic adventurism."

2. For accounts of the Ríos Montt era, see George Black et al., *Garrison Guatemala* (New York: North American Congress on Latin America, 1984); Jennifer Harbury, *Searching for Everardo: A Story of Love, War, and the CIA in Guatemala* (New York: Warner Books, 1997); Susanne Jonas, *The Battle for Guatemala: Rebels, Death Squads, and U.S. Power* (Latin American Perspectives Series, No 5, Boulder, CO: Westview Press, 1991); Deborah Levenson-Estrada, *Trade Unionists Against Terror: Guatemala City, 1954–1985* (Chapel Hill, NC: University of North Carolina Press, 1994); Beatriz Manz, *Refugees of a Hidden War: The Aftermath of the Counterinsurgency in Guatemala* (Albany, NY: SUNY Press, 1988); Victor Montejo, *Testimony: Death of a Guatemalan Village* (Willimantic, CT: Curbstone Press, 1987); Jennifer G. Schirmer, *The Guatemalan Military Project: A Violence Called Democracy* (Philadelphia: University of Pennsylvania Press, 1998). Between 1979 and 1998, Amnesty International published at least 15 reports on human rights abuses in Guatemala; other reports were published by the International Commission of Jurists and a number of U.S., European, and international organizations. The now classic work on the brutal aftermath of the 1954 coup is Richard N. Adams, *Crucifixion by Power; Essays on Guatemalan National Social Structure, 1944–1966* (with chapters by Brian Murphy and Bryan Roberts, Austin: University of Texas Press, 1970). See also Carol Smith, ed., *Guatemalan Indians and the State, 1540–1988* (Austin: University of Texas Press, 1990) and Kay Warren, *The Symbolism of Subordination: Indian Identity in a Guatemalan Town* (Austin: University of Texas Press, 1978).

3. The full title is *Inevitable Revolutions: The United States in Central America* (New York: W. W. Norton, 1983).

4. Princeton: Princeton University Press, 1991.

5. Nick Cullather, *The C.I.A.'s Classified Account of Its Operations in Guatemala, 1952–1954* (Stanford University Press, forthcoming in 1999). An earlier version was made available by the CIA. The Stanford edition has a new introduction by the author and an "Afterword" by Piero Gleijeses.

6. See John F. McCamant, "Review Essay: Intervention in Guatemala: Implications for the Study of the Third World," *Comparative Political Studies*, 17:3 (October 1984): 373–407; the quotes are from p. 374.

7. Austin: University of Texas Press, 1982.

8. Jorge I. Domínguez, "'U.S.-Latin American Relations During the Cold War and Its Aftermath" in *The United States and Latin*

America: The New Agenda (Cambridge, MA: Harvard University David Rockefeller Center for Latin American Studies and University of London Institute for Latin American Studies, forthcoming, 1999).

9. See all of the works cited in this introduction. In addition, see Cole Blasier's pioneering comparative study of U.S. intervention in Latin America, *Hovering Giant: U.S. Responses to Revolutionary Change in Latin America* (Pittsburgh: University of Pittsburgh Press, 1976).

10. Gleijeses, *Shattered Hope*, 182

11. Ibid., 141–3.

12. Greg Grandin, *The Last Colonial Massacre: Latin America in the Cold War* (Chicago: University of Chicago Press, 2004), p. 52.

13. See the discussions of this issue in the reviews by McCamant cited above ("Review Essay," 379–80) and Whitney T. Perkins in *Journal of American History*, 70:1 (1983): 198–99. For a recent work on UFCO in Guatemala, see Paul J. Dosal, *Doing Business with the Dictators: A Political History of United Fruit in Guatemala, 1899–1944* (Wilmington, Del.: SR Books, 1993). For a recent account of the Arbenz agrarian reform and its impact, see Jim Handy, *Revolution in the Countryside: Rural Conflict and Agrarian Reform in Guatemala, 1944–1954* (Chapel Hill: University of North Carolina Press, 1994).

14. See chapters 5 and 7 below; this issue is also discussed in John H. Coatsworth, *The United States and Central America: The Clients and the Colossus* (New York: Twayne, 1994), chapter 3.

15. Leonard Bushkoff, "Set piece operation," *Times Literary Supplement*, December 17, 1982, p. 1391.

16. For a careful and systematic effort to compare the two cases, see Cole Blasier, *Hovering Giant*, cited above.

17. Gleijeses, *Shattered Hope*, chapter 14. Note also that it would have been impossible to organize and arm a militia in time to do any good once the army had defected.

18. In *Demanding Democracy: Reform and Reaction in Costa Rica and Guatemala, 1870s–1950s* (Stanford: Stanford University Press, 1997). In the case of Cuba, virtually the entire business class and most of the leaders (and many followers) of the middle class professional and political organizations opposed to the revolutionary government flew off to Miami after U.S. hostility intensified in mid-1960 to await (or participate in) the U.S. intervention they expected to come; see Jorge Domínguez, *Cuba: Order and Revolution* (Cambridge: Harvard University Press, 1978), chapter 5.

19. See *Demanding Democracy*, 200.

FOREWORD
TO THE 2005 EDITION

The CIA and the Guatemalan Peace Process

At the dawn of the 1990s the United States Government had an opportunity rarely granted in politics of righting a wrong. Having launched the Cold War in the Western Hemisphere with the Central Intelligence Agency-organized coup against Jacobo Arbenz, the United States might now through its support for a peace process contribute to the ending of four decades of civil conflict unleashed by that intervention.

Some of the signs were auspicious. The global conflict with the Soviet Union was over. Cuba, the remaining reservoir of Communist dogma in the Americas, was viewed as irrelevant to the politics of the region. The Bush Administration had reversed the destructive policies of the Reagan years in El Salvador and Nicaragua and accepted political settlements in both countries. Although Guatemala's civil war was nearly invisible on Washington's radar screen, veteran officials knew that failure to resolve Guatemala's conflict could reverse Central America's emergence from a decade of war and revolution.

Nevertheless, the United States had to overcome its perceived and actual alliance with Central America's right if it was to play a constructive role in Guatemala's peace process. In the Salvadoran negotiations, the United States had not been able to overcome its identification with the Salvadoran government and military.

Parties to the United Nations-brokered Salvadoran peace talks were referred to as the "Four Plus One," signifying that, unlike the Four (Mexico, Spain, Colombia, and Venezuela), the United States had relations only with the Salvadoran government. Assistant Secretary for Inter-American Affairs, Bernard Aronson, riding an elevator at UN headquarters in New York during the talks, was confronted with a classic diplomatic dilemma when the doors opened at one floor and Joaquín Villalobos, a senior guerrilla commander, entered. The two senior officials rode to the lobby in silence without acknowledging the existence of the other. They would only shake hands and exchange war stories after the final peace accord was signed. Aronson knew that his inability to deal directly with guerrilla leaders was a liability. But politically it was impossible until the guerrillas had laid down their arms for the United States to build relations with an illegal organization responsible for killing American Marines.

Despite the end of the Cold War, in the early 1990s the United States faced a similar situation in Guatemala. The Reagan Administration had restored military aid to Guatemala, and the guerrilla front known by its Spanish acronyms as the URNG was considered a mortal enemy of the United States. Indeed, one of the senior URNG commanders was alleged to have assassinated a U.S. ambassador in 1968.

However, the 1990 death of an American citizen, Michael DeVine, began a process that would shift Washington away from identification with the government and the military. DeVine's murder—he was taken from his rural lodge by a Guatemalan military patrol for interrogation about a stolen rifle and later found nearly decapitated from a machete blow—shocked Bush's college friend and ambassador to Guatemala, Thomas Stroock. Determined to get to the bottom of the DeVine murder, he confronted his CIA station chief and demanded to know whether any CIA "assets" in the Guatemalan military were involved. Assured that they were not, Stroock was nevertheless convinced that the military had at least tried to cover-up its role. He called his friend the President and recommended the suspension of military aid to Guatemala. George Bush listened.

Guatemala's new civilian president, Jorge Serrano, was dismayed that Bush had severed military aid. An ardent member of one of

Guatemala's evangelical sects, Serrano expected more sympathetic treatment by a Republican Administration. Frustrated with his inability to get his "message" across in Washington, Serrano hired the lobbying firm of Patton, Boggs, and Blow to seek out new friends. One of the Washington power centers courted was the Subcommittee on Western Hemisphere Affairs of the House Foreign Affairs Committee and its new chairman Robert G. Torricelli. When Torricelli decided to make a trip to Mexico in the spring of 1992 and include a stop in Guatemala, Patton, Boggs and Blow convinced their client to give special attention to the visiting Democrat. Torricelli and Stroock spent a day with President Serrano, lunching at his Caribbean vacation home, helicoptering to a jungle hot springs, and cruising down the Rio Negro in the President's yacht. Substantively the trip was more exciting. Serrano wanted Washington's aid not to resist change in Guatemala but to advance it. He asked Torricelli to carry a personal message to the URNG guerrillas for him. He was committed to peace and would do what was necessary to secure it, including reform of Guatemala's notorious army. But, he needed to know the URNG's bottom line—were they prepared for serious negotiations?

A few days later Torricelli met with Pablo Monsanto, one of four senior URNG commanders, in the bar of the María Isabel Sheraton Hotel next to the U.S. embassy in Mexico City. This first meeting ever between a member of the U.S. Congress and the URNG produced an exchange of documents between the URNG and Serrano that formed the basis for the peace process agenda a year and a half later. For U.S. policy it created a breakthrough that was followed up intelligently by the Bush Administration. Torricelli's State Department control officer took on a new assignment as liaison to the URNG. Back in Washington the State Department worked with Torricelli's office to ensure political support and began issuing visas for travel to New York and Washington to the URNG's political diplomatic commission. First lower level political appointees and then senior officials met with URNG representatives. By the end of the first year of President Clinton's term three of the four commanders had visited Washington, the first time they had ever been on U.S. soil.

The payoff for the United States of this investment in developing relations with a guerrilla organization still in active conflict with a friendly government came in early 1994. The Guatemalan government and the guerrillas each asked the United Nations to take a direct role in mediating their protracted and thus far unproductive negotiations. In a variation on the Salvadoran model, each party, rather than the UN itself, invited six countries to form a "Group of Friends" of the peace process. Unsurprisingly, Mexico, Spain, Colombia, and Venezuela were again asked to accompany the process as in El Salvador. Invitations to two others were less expected. The Guatemalan government requested Norway's involvement, a distant country with peace process experience and a Guatemalan connection dating back to the devastating 1976 earthquake. Most surprising of all, the *guerrillas* also asked for the participation of the United States, a clear signal that the extraordinary Executive/Legislative coordination of the previous two years had made a difference.

The Clinton Administration quickly took advantage of this breakthrough. The State Department appointed a U.S. coordinator to the peace process and began the complex task of convincing each side, and some of the skeptical members of the "Group of Friends," that the United States Government could be an "honest broker" in the process.

But neither the White House nor the State Department knew that in another part of the Executive Branch a very different approach to Guatemala continued. For the Central Intelligence Agency had not told Ambassador Stroock the truth about its involvement in the murder of Michael DeVine. One of their "assets" was indeed connected to the murder, a fact that they had not reported to Congressional intelligence oversight committees as required by law.

The "friends" and "enemies" of U.S. policy for the previous forty years were switching roles. For the sake of peace, the United States needed to work with the URNG guerrillas and distance itself from the repressive apparatus of the army. But despite changes in the world and in Guatemala the Central Intelligence Agency was determined to maintain the battle lines first drawn in 1954.

From 1990 until 1995 the cover-up of the CIA's involvement in an American citizen's murder held firm. But just as the peace process began making progress, a dedicated lawyer named

Jennifer Harbury came forward to make claims on the Guatemalan government and then on her own country's officials. She wanted the truth about her missing guerrilla husband, Efraín Bámaca, who used the nom de guerre of "Everardo." According to the Guatemalan government's version of events Everardo had disappeared in a firefight with the army. Or, perhaps, he had committed suicide under interrogation. Or, maybe, he was buried namelessly as another casualty of a dirty war. An answer to the whereabouts of a guerrilla commander did not, after all, seem like such an important matter to the Guatemalan government.

That was not an adequate answer for Ms. Harbury. She pressed more and more successfully for Congressional and media attention to her case. She asked rhetorically what kind of peace process this was if it could not find a solution to such a prominent case as hers. State Department and National Security Council officials provided the same answer to Ms. Harbury's queries that they had since 1993: nothing more was known about her husband's case than the inadequate explanations offered by Guatemala's government. Ms. Harbury found it hard to believe that the U.S. Government's associations with the Guatemalan military provided it no information about the capture of such a prominent guerrilla commander.

Until June 1994 the association of U.S. intelligence agencies with Guatemalan "assets" engaged in murder, torture, kidnapping and other systematic human rights abuses might have been shortsighted or, as the President's Intelligence Oversight Board concluded, unnecessary since these informants actually provided little if any information. But in June 1994 the Guatemalan parties negotiated a human rights accord that went into immediate effect calling on all sides to end such abuses. The U.S. ambassador to Norway, the site of the talks, signed on behalf of his government as a "Witness" to the accord and pledged his government to do all it could to see that it was fulfilled. From that moment on every agency of the U.S. Government should have made that commitment its highest priority. One did not.

Instead the CIA made its priority in Guatemala the protection of its human intelligence network, even those removed from the payroll for such egregious abuses as the murder of an American citizen. As Ms. Harbury pressed her case and State Department officials demanded more details from their CIA "colleagues" they encountered a strange reluctance to use the Agency's vaunted contacts for the Harbury case.

In 1995 the rest of the U.S. Government began to learn why. That January a member of the Guatemalan CIA station reported to his chief that one of his contacts had identified the Guatemalan officer who had ordered Bámaca's execution. The station chief instructed his colleague not to report the information to the U.S. ambassador, Marilyn McAfee, and to delay informing CIA headquarters in Langley, actions for which the station chief was subsequently fired. The identity of Bámaca's alleged assassin was such a dangerous secret because it was the very same individual who had earlier been involved in the murder of Michael DeVine, and whose actions had never been reported to the Congressional oversight committees. What knowledgeable CIA agents in Washington and Guatemala feared had now come true: Harbury's pressure on her case had unmasked the earlier cover-up.

The Agency would have preferred to keep these details within the family of the Executive Branch and the House and Senate Intelligence Committees. But Rep. Torricelli believed that the truth about her husband's case might convince Ms. Harbury to end a "hunger strike-to-the-death" that she was conducting in front of the White House. He sent an angry letter to President Clinton denouncing the Agency, and called Harbury to his office to share what he knew.

The result was worse than Langley had imagined. After first trying to defend the Agency the White House quickly shifted and declared that "heads would roll" at the CIA if the President had been misled. The President's Intelligence Oversight Board (IOB) conducted a year-long review and concluded that,

> . . . several CIA assets were credibly alleged to have ordered, planned, or participated in serious human rights violations such as assassination, extrajudicial execution, torture, or kidnapping while they were assets—and that the CIA's Directorate of Operations (DO) headquarters was aware at the time of the allegations.

The report also concluded that,

Out of a general concern for the protection of its sources, out of neglect, or for other reasons, the CIA informed neither State Department officials, at the embassy or in Washington, nor National Security Council officials of alleged abuses by assets until late 1994 and early 1995.

The "good news" of the IOB report was its conclusion that CIA's local employees had killed no U.S. citizens, "only" Guatemalans.

The consequences for an Agency that is accustomed to reward its malefactors with promotions were unusual: two former Guatemalan station chiefs fired and eight other members of the Operations Directorate disciplined. The CIA was also forced to review the conduct of its assets worldwide and dismissed hundreds of them. However, it immediately took steps to insulate itself from future scrutiny by punishing those responsible for disclosing its conduct to the Congress and by declaring that any Congressional attempts to legislate access to classified information were unconstitutional.

The impact on the U.S. role in the peace process was devastating. The CIA's treachery destroyed the careful work of years to establish the United States as an honest broker in the peace process. No one—not Ms. Harbury and her allies in the human rights community, nor the Guatemalan military, nor the guerrillas—believed that the State Department and the White House could have been so deceived by their own intelligence service.

The consequences for the peace process itself were more complex. The political victory for the URNG guerrillas represented by the Guatemalan army's misdeeds and the embarrassment for Guatemala's government delayed the peace process for nearly a year until a new civilian government was elected. However, the scandal undermined the most hard-line elements of the Guatemalan military. Those within the military supporting the peace process and their civilian allies in the government moved to push aside the dinosaurs. The new government of Alvaro Arzú on taking office felt empowered to dismiss a raft of senior generals and to make the concessions necessary to sign a final peace settlement in December 1996.

And so, in the end, the United States did make its contribution to peace in Guatemala. By protecting its Guatemalan "friends" from the Cold War era, the Central Intelligence Agency had conducted its own Guatemalan policy and destroyed the attempt of official policy to play the role of an honest broker in the peace process. Yet, paradoxically, through this betrayal of the U.S. national interest the CIA undermined the political power of the murderers, torturers, and kidnappers with whom it had been aligned since 1954 and helped to create the conditions for the peace that the vast majority of Guatemalans have sought for decades.

RICHARD A. NUCCIO

REFLECTIONS IN 2005

In July 1954, a Guatemalan teenager named Irma Flaquer was gazing out of the window with her younger sister. Just before the "American coup," discussed so eloquently by Stephen Schlesinger and Stephen Kinzer in this book, overthrew the progressive government of Jacobo Arbenz, Irma had returned to Guatemala after several years in Mexico with her theater director father and her younger sister Anabella.

American planes were flying overhead and bombing the city. And the teens' uncle, Antonio Barrutia, a congressional representative under the Arbenz government, was jailed and later deported to El Salvador. Khaki-dressed soldiers sometimes came to the girls' grandmother's house late at night, pounding loudly on the door and searching for weapons that the uncle might have left behind.

That was Irma's introduction to Guatemalan politics and, when she grew up to be one of the country's most noted reporters, the coup would mark her political and moral vision in a column entitled "What Others Don't Dare Write."

I first heard of Irma Flaquer in 1996 when I was assigned to her case for the Inter American Press Association's Unpunished Crime Against Journalists Project. The reporter had been kidnapped from the Guatemalan streets in October 1980, her son shot to death before her eyes; she was never seen again; her body was never found, and her murderers have never been identified.

I didn't quite know where to start, so before I took off for Guatemala, I asked Stephen Kinzer, the co-author of this book and a former newspaper colleague in Central America, if he had heard of Irma.

"I envy you for your trip to Guatemala, for which I have always had such a special love," he wrote back in a March 25, 1996, letter. "The coexistence of such unspeakable beauty and horror may be unique in the world."

He told me that he indeed had known Irma, observing, "Irma Flaquer was a real dissident who saw the world the way people in normal countries see it, and talking to reporters was part of that. I suspect she had a very unpleasant death. She is someone I really admire because her goal was to bring Guatemala out of the pit."

I often thought of Kinzer's words as I investigated Irma's kidnapping, becoming fascinated with her intrepid commitment as a reporter and columnist. I found that Irma Flaquer was an ordinary citizen with extraordinary talents. That is why she chose to do what ordinary citizens often do in what Kinzer calls "normal" countries: observe, reflect and dissent.

These actions would lead to her still unresolved 1980 disappearance, but not before more than twenty years of speaking out, of trying to ferret out the truth in Guatemalan politics, a truth made muddy by the insidious and persistent legacy of the 1954 coup with its fierce anti-communism, militarized violence and an enduring culture of fear. And perhaps directly because of this legacy, Irma constantly underscored in her writings the rule of law, an end to impunity, and a relentless search for some sort of objective truth and normality.

In 1961, the Guatemalan Congress passed the Law for the Defense of Democratic Institutions, giving stiff jail sentences to communists and communist collaborators. For weeks, Irma had railed against the bill in her columns. If Guatemala prohibited the study of Marxism, she'd written in a February 9, 1961, column in *La Hora*, no one would really be qualified to say who was a communist and who wasn't. Among the law's provisions was a one-year prison sentence for anyone "distributing books, pamphlets, posters, records, tapes, and any type of printed or recorded mate-

rial that advocates Communism or the establishment of any entity of a communist type in Guatemala." Irma wrote in her column:

> My eyes read, but my poor brain can't take in what this bill spells
> out. Because only in the era of the Holy Inquisition would such a
> document have been possible.
>
> This bill effectively institutes a branch of government in which
> Guatemalan citizens would be 'properly' classified. Communists and
> communist sympathizers, duly registered in this archive, would not
> be permitted to assume public office, carry arms, own radios or
> transmitters or printing presses or photocopying machines, to join
> political parties or organizations or belong to any kind of civic
> group. . . .
>
> That is, intellectual freedom is taken away from us, and we are not
> free to know, to study all the doctrines and ideologies to come to our
> own conclusions. Who can establish what we ought to think? This is
> unheard of.
>
> There is no human power that can stop people from reading what
> they wish; we are human beings who have a capacity to think and
> analyze and, therefore, to try to stifle freedom of thought is an
> incredible offense in our times against human dignity.
>
> And on the other hand, who is going to establish who is a com-
> munist? I don't believe that there are many people in this govern-
> ment capable of distinguishing between communism, socialism or
> existentialism.
>
> Everyone talks about communism; government officials are all
> willing to do anything to avoid it. But the bad thing is that they don't
> even understand the nature of the doctrine, they end up committing
> even greater injustices and intolerable abuses to stamp it out. . . . If
> the (government) doesn't want communism to arrive here, the most
> effective arms a thousand times over are to give the people bread,
> clothing, education and social justice. Because it is (the president)
> who is sowing the bad seeds of totalitarianism to maintain the
> Guatemalan people hungry, poorly clothed and ignorant.
>
> Guatemala belongs to Guatemalans; and it is not the property of
> don Miguel [the president Ygídoras Fuentes] and his collaborators.
> We all have the right to think and to express ourselves freely.[1]

As John Coatsworth points out in his introduction to *Bitter
Fruit*, opposition to Arbenz—even within a polarized society—
could have still accomplished its goal by exercising a democratic

option. Through a series of U.S.-bolstered military regimes, Irma Flaquer railed against what Coatsworth calls "the security of authoritarian repression," occasionally linking it directly to the 1954 U.S. intervention: "We have already suffered *en carne propia* [directly and personally] the unfortunate policy that has offended us with its gifts and denigrated us with its interference."[2]

For Flaquer, as for many Guatemalans, 1954 was a watershed year. She understood that its impact stretched beyond issues of intervention and authoritarianism, that it had accustomed Guatemalans to a climate of constant polarization, a world of black and white. Flaquer wanted to see the world in terms of grays, in terms of the possibilities of finding solutions through democratic means and above all, truth-telling without regard to special interests. She explains to her readers:

> Many people believe that the journalist ought to oppose the regime in power, whatever the circumstances might be . . . A completely impartial attitude isn't understood in this environment, where political and personal interests play such an important role. Nevertheless, I believe—and I will always believe—that the obligation of the honorable journalist is to tell the truth to his or her readers. It doesn't matter if the truth affects the left or the right, or if this truth makes the government look bad or favors the opposition . . . I believe that my obligation is to tell the truth, no matter whom it hurts.[3]

The 1954 coup was carried out through a mesh of lies and deceptions, and truth-seeking in the years to come was never an easy task. By the time Kinzer and Schlesinger wrote *Bitter Fruit*, much of the horror experienced in Guatemala had already been disclosed in the foreign press, by human rights organizations and in the halls of the U.S. Congress. It would more than a decade, though, before the UN-sponsored Historical Clarification Commission and a church-led truth commission put numbers on the atrocities, more than two hundred thousand deaths, with the military responsible for ninety-three percent of them.

Flaquer protested the abuses committed in the name of anti-communism and anti-terrorism and documented them. However, she often writes as if the country was on the brink of civil war, rather than plunged into bloody turmoil, as we can see more clearly now. And while she saw the chaos, she continued to plea for democratic institutionality.

In 1970, a colonel—who had been responsible for so much death and torture in a fierce anti-guerrilla campaign in the 1960s that he was called "the Butcher of Zacapa"—was elected president of Guatemala. Flaquer had written extensively about the abuses, and had nearly lost her life to a bomb planted in her car in 1969.

Yet, upon his election, Flaquer wrote him an open letter, again defending the democratic process. Citing his virulent anti-terrorist platform during the electoral campaign, she wrote with perhaps quiet irony:

> It's possible that I am not precisely the indicated person to be giving you advice. During the electoral campaign that brought you to the presidency, I was one of your fiercest opponents. I think no one attacked you like I did. But, in spite of my best efforts, you won the elections. In my opinion, this incident (the bombing) is not going to stop me from saying what I think. Are we in agreement?
>
> Many people advised me to shut up a bit now that I've had the good luck to be a survivor. But you have to understand that to live without the freedom to say what I think is, for me, the same as being dead. I consider it my obligation to try to find solutions to the country's problems. And it's absolutely impossible for me to maintain my pen inactive.
>
> That's why I'm addressing you today, hoping that my commentaries won't be misinterpreted. I'm very well aware of all the gossiping that goes on in presidential circles, and after all, a president is simply a human being.
>
> So, with your permission. . . .
>
> You, Colonel Arana, might have had your own very original ideas during the campaign, but now you are the constitutional president of the Republic. You aren't just the representative of the MLN and the PID (the rightist political alliance), but of the entire nation.
>
> That's why you shouldn't be swayed by the passions of the rightists or the leftists . . . You have to be the representative of national unity. If you just listen to both sides—like the good father of the Guatemalan nation—it just might be possible to find a formula for reconciliation.
>
> Lamentably, for both tendencies, ideas cannot be fought with

arms or with terror. One can capture a man and torture him; one can cut out his tongue, kill him, burn him, and reduce him to dust, but somewhere, the Idea will survive, eternal and unvanquished. The only way of combating ideas is with other ideas.

And this is one of the problems that you are called on to resolve—to guarantee complete freedom of expression for ideas. That each and every Guatemalan, independently of his or her ideology, can express beliefs without fear—except perhaps for the fear of making a fool of themselves.

Every time an idea is repressed, it comes back stronger, more insistent, more dangerous. If ideas cannot flow, they emerge wherever and whenever possible. And that leads to the problem we are all so worried about: *violencia*.

And who is responsible in Guatemala for the violence? The right, in its most crude and primitive form, has caused the problems of exploitation of man by his fellow man. Since, for the right, capital does not have a social purpose, it becomes an instrument of domination to obtain power. . . . So then a theory emerges in opposition to this one, that capital ought to have a social function . . . a more just and humanitarian position. . . .

But, unfortunately, this fraternal and disinterested doctrine got caught up in its own instruments of domination. Some saw the doctrine as a way of achieving power. At least, that is what happened in Guatemala, which is what interests us here.

The left got carried away and the right, seeing its privileges threatened, armed to the teeth and began the battle. So now the militants from both positions are killing each other in the streets. And in the name of whom do you think they're doing it? In the name of peace and progress for Guatemala. What do you think about that?

I don't think the problem can be resolved calling each other names and even less by machine gunning each other. And while everyone is caught up in heated discussions, the common people continue in their daily tragedy of hunger and frustration.[4]

Killing and disappearances, repression and torture, continued and indeed escalated. In 1976, two teenage boys in a fish restaurant after a soccer game on a quiet Sunday afternoon were gunned down by members of the ambulatory police working as a bodyguard for a powerful businessman. The businessman, Jorge Köng, said the boys were making too much noise. The boys had refused to quiet down, saying that they "lived in a free country."

Flaquer took up the cause of sending the businessman who had ordered the shootings to jail. The contradictions between what was being said about democracy and justice and what was actually being done profoundly worried her. Along with her fellow Guatemalans, she yearned for a *estado de derecho*, a constitutional state in which the laws would be obeyed. She set out to prove that democracy could function by following the case closely through the court system.

In prolific and frequent columns, she had advocated Köng's arrest and trial. She considered impunity one of Guatemala's basic problems: people literally getting away with murder. She observed:

> If we cannot believe in the courts, we are sowing the seeds of violence. The first consequence is that many will decide to take justice into their own hands, since they cannot count on those who are in charge of administering the system to do so impartially. The rich and influential have gone free for their crimes, while the poor are fatally destined to rot for stealing a piece of bread for their children. The belief that there is no justice is the true mother of all violence.[5]

Köng was eventually sentenced to eight years and eight months in jail. It felt for once that the pen was mightier than the sword, and that due process would win out, just as it had failed in 1954. Shortly thereafter, however, Köng walked free, the verdict overturned. The one case that Flaquer had pointed to as a Guatemalan victory for the rule of law became the one that convinced her that justice in Guatemala was truly an illusion.

As I investigated the case of Flaquer's disappearance, I became more and more intrigued by her outspoken attitude in a culture of silence. The investigation evolved into a biography (*Disappeared: A Journalist Silenced*, Seal Press 2004), and I asked Kinzer to write a foreword since he had personally known the journalist.

Until then, I had only seen Flaquer's words as powerful testimony to the harsh legacy of the "American coup." Kinzer's observations made me see my own research in a new way.

During the holocaust that descended on Guatemala during the

1970s and '80s, government-sponsored death squads roamed the country with impunity. Anyone who protested, anyone who organized, anyone who challenged the established order was liable to be killed. The lucky victims met sudden death in street corner assassinations. Others were made to 'disappear,' often suffering through long periods of unspeakable torture before being murdered. All of this was done with the collusion of the country's leaders and at least the tacit approval of their supporters in Washington and other foreign capitals.

In such a climate, the person of conscience faces a stark choice between safe submission and dangerous activism. Irma Flaquer chose the latter. Her passion for justice and her deep sense of patriotism, however, led her to use her talents to confront the brutal system under which Guatemala was suffering. Ultimately she became another of its victims.[6]

I had long understood Flaquer's role in denouncing the bitter fruits of the 1954 coup. Reading Kinzer's foreword, I understood for the first time that Flaquer—with her kidnapping and disappearance never resolved and never punished—had herself become another of the era's bitter fruits.

JUNE CAROLYN ERLICK

Notes

1. Column, *La Hora*, Guatemala, February 9, 1961, translation June Carolyn Erlick.
2. Column, *La Hora*, Guatemala, February. 20, 1961, quoted in Erlick, June Carolyn, *Disappeared, A Journalist Silenced*, p. 55, Emeryville, CA: Seal Press, 2004.
3. Column, *La Hora*, Guatemala, April 6, 1962, quoted in Erlick, June Carolyn, *Disappeared, A Journalist Silenced*, p. 60, Emeryville, CA: Seal Press, 2004.
4. Column, *La Hora*, Guatemala, February 4, 1971, quoted in Erlick, June Carolyn, *Disappeared, A Journalist Silenced*, p. 131, Emeryville, CA: Seal Press, 2004.
5. Column, *La Hora*, Guatemala, September 14, 1977, quoted in Erlick, June Carolyn, *Disappeared, A Journalist Silenced*, p. 212, Emeryville, CA: Seal Press, 2004.
6. Kinzer, Stephen, in Erlick, June Carolyn, *Disappeared, A Journalist Silenced*, p. 212, Emeryville, CA: Seal Press, 2004, p. xiii.

PREFACE

Numerous individuals and institutions were helpful in the writing of this book. We would like to thank the congressional authors of the Freedom of Information Act (FOIA), who provided us with an indispensable tool to review the inner workings of United States foreign policy. The FOIA enabled us to obtain documents from the State Department, the National Archives, the Naval Department and the Federal Bureau of Investigation which described many details of American policy and conduct in Guatemala.

Pursuant to our FOIA request, the State Department released to us over 1,000 pages of material. Three individuals serving on the Information/Privacy Staff in the State Department's Bureau of Administration were particularly helpful: Deborah M. Odell, Mary Spruell and Kathleen Siljegovic. At the Department of the Navy, Rear Admiral USN (Ret.) John Kane, Jr., director of the Naval Historical Center, was most cooperative in retrieving papers from the Navy's archives explaining the movement of U.S. ships, submarines and planes during 1954. At the National Archives, Gibson Smith of the Modern Military Branch of the Military Archives Division provided important documents from the Defense Department.

In addition attorney Mark Lynch of the American Civil Liberties Union's National Security Project provided us continuing legal counsel in our attempt to win release of documents from the Central Intelligence Agency.

Our experience with American libraries was at all times worthwhile. Of special value for our research purposes were: the Eisenhower Library and its director, John E. Wickman, and his assistant director, Martin M. Teasley, who were most cooperative in providing us with important documents from the Eisenhower collection; the Princeton University Library, which houses the John Foster Dulles' papers, and the Seeley G. Mudd Manuscript Library, at the same university, containing Allen Dulles' papers; the Boston Public Library; and the New York City Public Library, which harbored a significant trove of materials on the coup. As well, the New York Public Library provided a research office in the Frederick Lewis Allen Memorial Room. In Guatemala, the Biblioteca Nacional offered important sources.

We also wish to thank Richard Harris Smith, who generously permitted us to quote from his forthcoming biography of CIA Director Allen Dulles, called *Spymaster's Odyssey: The World of Allen Dulles* which will be published in 1983.

Among special friends who read and commented upon the manuscript, we want to make mention of Judy Elster, Mrs. Ilona Kinzer, and Arthur Schlesinger, Jr., all of whom spent several days reviewing the manuscript.

The authors take full responsibility for all information contained in the book.

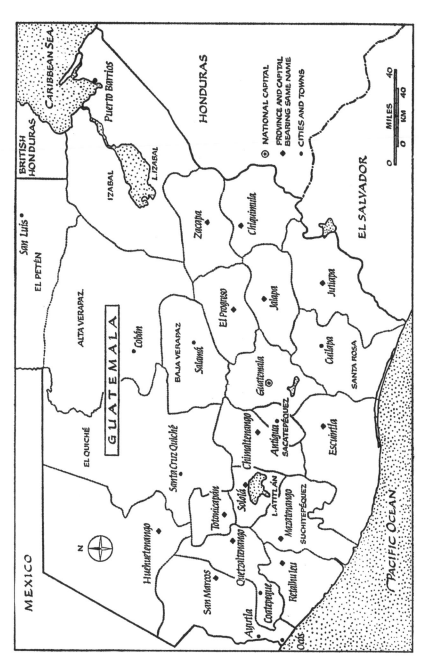

Guatemala

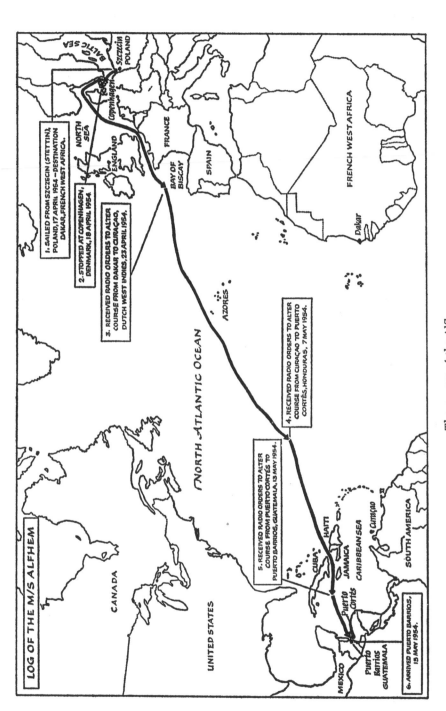

The voyage of the Alfhem.

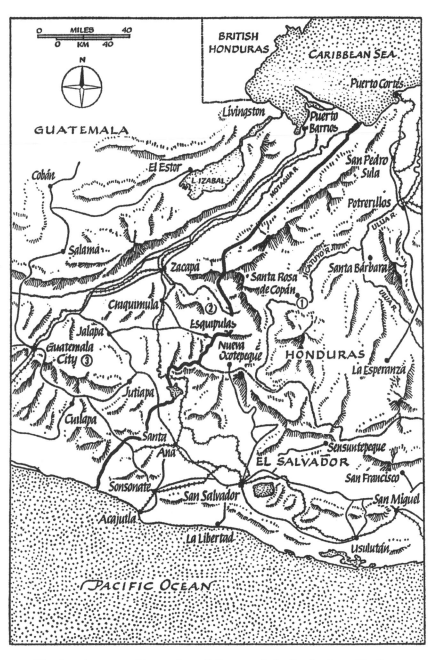

*The invasion route. Guatemalan rebels crossed the border from Honduras
(1) and set up headquarters in Esquipulas (2). Clashes between rival
forces took place at Chiquimula. Rebel planes also bombed the Guatemalan
capital (3) and Zacapa.*

1

THE BATTLE BEGINS

As dawn broke over Guatemala City, a C-47 transport plane lumbered low in the sky, flying from the south over nearby mountains. It was still early on the morning of June 18, 1954. The sun's rays were weak in the east. The weather was cool and hazy.

The plane steered a direct course for the sleeping capital. As it reached the outskirts, the aircraft abruptly dove from its flight path toward the capital's center where the stately National Palace stood. It swooped over the plaza facing the Palace, then swerved upward again, suddenly spewing thousands of small leaflets into the air. It veered away and sped out of the city, disappearing beyond the horizon.

The leaflets fluttered in the wind and gradually floated down,

settling onto city streets, market stalls, store roofs, courtyards
and gutters. Passersby scooped some up; Guatemalan police re-
trieved others. The printed notices, in large block letters, carried
a bold demand: Guatemala's President, Jacobo Arbenz, must resign immediately. They warned further that the mysterious
plane would return that afternoon and blow up the city's main
arsenal to assure Arbenz's swift departure. If he had not quit by
then, the circulars added, the aircraft would also bombard the
Palace. The leaflets were signed "National Liberation Forces."[1]

News of the craft's morning visit spread quickly. The event
deeply rattled an already shaken city. Every eleven days for the
past month a plane—usually a U.S.-made Beechcraft—had
made similar raids, first on May 26, next on the night of June 6
and then today. Each time, the ghost ship had descended like a
hawk from the sky, scattered its leaflets and vanished. The messages grew more ominous with every call. In the earlier trips, the
circulars had addressed the Guatemalan Army, warning its
officers about a supposed secret plan by President Arbenz to replace the military with a citizens' force and urging soldiers to
rise up against the President. This latest leaflet was the first to
demand that the President surrender.[2]

A great fear was overtaking Guatemala. Ominous and mysterious events had multiplied over the past few months. On May
Day, traditionally a festive workers' celebration in Guatemala, a
new radio station suddenly appeared on the air broadcasting
from "somewhere in Guatemala"; it demanded Arbenz's overthrow. Most Guatemalans already knew enough to link the
"Voice of Liberation" with the exile forces of Carlos Castillo
Armas, a forty-year-old former army colonel and longtime
enemy of President Arbenz who had been plotting against the
government from neighboring Honduras. In recent days, Castillo
Armas had grown bolder and issued appeals, declaring, "I am
certain that 90 percent of the people of Guatemala are thoroughly ready to rise up and fight against the government."[3]

Meantime Guatemalan newspapers printed reports of Castillo
Armas' men walking down the streets of Tegucigalpa, the Honduran capital, talking openly of a forthcoming invasion of Guatemala. Some of the "troops" admitted they were receiving handsome wages, usually paid in American dollars. Many were not

Guatemalans, but foreign mercenaries. Several times Guatemalan President Arbenz had demanded that Honduras round up Castillo Armas and his followers, but nothing had happened. Foreign correspondents and photographers, especially from the United States, began to converge on Tegucigalpa, apparently aware that a battle was imminent.[4]

The Guatemalan government was understandably jumpy. It had survived more than thirty attempted coups by right-wing Guatemalans in the past nine years under Arbenz and his predecessor, Juan José Arévalo. Now the incidents were accelerating. Recently, the unknown dissidents had been scrawling the slogan "32" on city walls, referring to the constitutional clause prohibiting any political party from having a foreign affiliation and thus protesting the existence of a Communist party in the country. Raiders had tried to blow up Guatemala's main railway to the Atlantic Ocean. At the end of May, the Guatemalan police uncovered a secret conspiracy to overthrow Arbenz. They arrested several plotters, and others quickly took refuge in foreign embassies.

On June 8, President Arbenz invoked the constitutional provision allowing him to suspend civil liberties for thirty days during an emergency. Six days later, an unmarked plane parachuted arms on the Pacific coast of Guatemala, and villagers, who recovered some of the rifles, noticed Soviet markings suggesting that somebody was trying to frame Arbenz as a Soviet puppet, or that the Russians were somehow involved in a bizarre espionage stunt. The President now sent his children out of the country to Mexico City. He began to call for loyalty from around the country. Everyone could feel tension in the air; a confrontation appeared imminent.[5]

As the breakfast hours passed on June 18, President Arbenz strode tight-lipped along the underground tunnel that led from his living quarters via an elevator to the presidential office on the second floor of the National Palace. A vigorous forty-one, he was in the fourth year of his six-year term. He was only Guatemala's second President elected under a democratic constitution in 133 years of independence.[6]

Arbenz arrived at his suite. Grim-faced, he heard fresh news from aides: a plane or planes had just attacked the Pacific port

of San José, strafing buildings and puncturing holes in the sides
of some gas storage tanks; the aircraft also hit the inland city of
Retalhuleu. Worse, Honduran newspapers had reported that
chartered DC-3s were airlifting troops loyal to rebel leader Castillo Armas from Tegucigalpa to camps near the Guatemalan
border. Some of these insurgents had that morning crossed into
Guatemala and overrun the frontier post at La Florida, advancing into the country under a banner of "God, Fatherland and
Liberty" ("Dios, Patria y Libertad"). Arbenz and his advisers
recognized that the long-promised National Liberation offensive
led by Castillo Armas heralded by the morning leafleting was
finally underway along the Honduran border.[7]

The reports were still sketchy. President Arbenz talked at
length with his military commanders, Foreign Minister Guillermo Toriello and various political advisers. Acting as befitted a
former commander of the armed forces, Arbenz decided to place
his 6,000-man army and 3,000-man police force on alert, but he
determined to hold the army strength in reserve, confining most
troops to their barracks until further notice. As the midday conference thrashed out different alternatives, Foreign Minister
Toriello, a liberal landowner-turned-diplomat and spokesman for
his country's cause abroad, urged an immediate appeal to the
United Nations Security Council. He also suggested that Guatemala send a message to the Inter-American Peace Committee
of the Organization of American States (OAS) requesting a
fact-finding mission to set up a truce.[8]

Toriello argued that Guatemala must first consider how its actions might be seen overseas before it took any military action.
His small country was in an extremely delicate position. A
month earlier, an international outcry had arisen over Guatemala's purchase of arms from Czechoslovakia. The United
States had leaked the story to the press as the weapons were
being unloaded at a Guatemalan seaport. Arbenz's government had reluctantly acknowledged the accuracy of the American report but defended its need to re-equip its army.

At a press conference on May 19, President Dwight Eisenhower had escalated the verbal jousting between the two nations
by castigating Guatemala for accepting the Czech weapons,

warning of a possible Communist "outpost on this continent."
Soon afterward, Eisenhower publicly authorized large airlifts of
military aid to Honduras and Nicaragua, Central American dictatorships closely allied with the United States. The U.S. press
began to print accounts of mass arrests and tortures allegedly
perpetrated by the Arbenz regime. On June 15, Secretary of
State John Foster Dulles declared that Guatemalans were living
under a "Communist-type reign of terror" while carefully adding
that only they themselves possessed the "capability of cleaning
their own house."[9]

Hoping to show the world the untruth of the U.S. assessments,
Foreign Minister Toriello did not wish Guatemalan troops to en-
gage the invaders that morning, either on the ground or in the
air. He wanted to make clear that the Guatemalan government
was not the cause but the victim of the invasion. Nor did
Toriello, a shrewd former ambassador to Washington, want to
give the United States an opportunity to capitalize on any inad-
vertent frontier infraction to accuse Guatemala of aggression
against Honduras. Instead, Toriello recommended that Guatemala indict its neighbors, from whose territory the unmarked
planes and invading soldiers were apparently coming. Honduras
never seriously denied the obvious: that its territory was the
jumping-off point for the men crossing the border. And Honduras
or Nicaragua seemed the most likely base for the mysterious aircraft, since the small planes had limited range and could only
have flown from close by.

Toriello and Arbenz, with the assent of the other participants,
quickly agreed to single out Honduran President Juan Manuel
Gálvez and President Anastasio Somoza García of Nicaragua,
the latter a longtime foe of Arbenz's, for measured denunciations. Toriello began to draft stern diplomatic notes demanding
that Honduras and Nicaragua prevent any further border incur-
sions by Castillo Armas' followers. He also prepared a protest to
the United Nations accusing both countries of aggression against
Guatemala.[10]

But the divisions between Guatemala and the United States
ran too deep and were too advanced for Toriello's overnight
repair. The Arbenz government had embarked on a land reform
program that included expropriation of some of the vast acreage

belonging to the United Fruit Company. The land reform was not popular either in the company's Boston boardrooms or in Washington, where the firm had enormous influence. United Fruit controlled directly or indirectly nearly 40,000 jobs in Guatemala. Its investments in the country were valued at $60 million. It functioned as a state within a state, owning Guatemala's telephone and telegraph facilities, administering its only important Atlantic harbor and monopolizing its banana export. The company's subsidiary, the International Railways of Central America (IRCA), owned 887 miles of railroad track in Guatemala, nearly every mile in the country.[11]

The Eisenhower administration had taken action in early March 1954—weeks before the much-publicized Czech arms shipment—to give Guatemala a final warning of its displeasure over the land seizures. At the Tenth Inter-American Conference in Caracas, Venezuela, Secretary of State Dulles had exerted heavy pressure on Latin states to endorse a resolution condemning "Communist" infiltration in Latin America. It was directly aimed at Guatemala, though no nation was named. Only Guatemala voted in opposition to it, with two others abstaining in meek protest.

A show of diplomatic correctness and conciliation, even pleading, now seemed Guatemala's only hope in dealing with the United States. What made this tactic exceedingly difficult for the Guatemalans was the character of the formidable U.S. ambassador in their country. John Peurifoy, a prickly and heavy-handed diplomat, had been especially chosen to exert pressure on Arbenz and, if that failed, to overthrow him. Peurifoy was an old State Department hand. A West Point dropout, he had worked his way up through the ranks from clerk to service on the Economic Warfare and War Production Boards in World War II to the post of chief American organizer of the United Nations Conference in San Francisco in 1945. Later, in 1949, he was Deputy Undersecretary of State and from 1950 to 1953 U.S. ambassador to Greece.

Within days of his arrival in Guatemala in late 1953, Peurifoy had gone out of his way to lecture President Arbenz on his tolerance of Communists and to warn him that American-Guatemalan relations would remain strained so long as a single Communist remained on the public payroll. After that, Peurifoy and the President seldom spoke, though Peurifoy and Foreign Minister Toriello conferred regularly.

Arbenz now instructed Toriello to meet with Peurifoy about the invasion and appeal to him to defuse the crisis. At one o'clock in the afternoon that June 18, Toriello left the President's office. He told a dozen foreign correspondents and thirty local reporters waiting for him on the first floor of the Palace: "The battle of Guatemala has begun. We stand as one man against this criminal invasion. We will not take one backward step."[12]

So far the United States had given no formal reaction to reports of the rebel invasion. The State Department remained strangely silent in Washington. There was an undisclosed reason for the Department's circumspection. What Arbenz and Toriello might have feared was true: the United States government was in fact the secret creator and sponsor of the "Liberation" movement.

That morning John Peurifoy arrived at his embassy office in an ebullient mood. The night before, he had told his staff: "Well, boys, tomorrow at this time we'll have ourselves a party." He knew that the invasion he had helped plan was underway, and he was eagerly anticipating its outcome. Peurifoy was a blunt, politically ambitious self-described "tough guy" from South Carolina sent to Guatemala with a single mission: to change the direction of the reformist government, no matter how. He had been unable to convince President Arbenz to cooperate, and now Arbenz was about to receive his just deserts. The dawn leafleting and the early radio reports of air attacks and troop movements reassured Peurifoy that the plan, called Operation Success, was working. He sat down and dictated a stream of dispatches to Washington reporting the play-by-play from Guatemala City.[13]

After the unmarked C-47 disappeared from sight, the capital settled into an uneasy calm. By midday, uncertainty was growing about whether the reported invasion was real or not. The "Voice of Liberation" radio was broadcasting repeated bulletins claiming that Castillo Armas was advancing swiftly; the government, on the other hand, asserted it had stopped the enemy. Reporters were confused, not knowing what or whom to believe. Rumors spread everywhere. In the afternoon, President Arbenz

received reassurances of support from the four political parties
that formed his bloc in Congress, including the three center-left
parties and the small Communist party. In a flurry of appeals, he
also sought support from unions, peasant leaders and military
officers.[14]

At midday, Toriello cabled his country's appeal to the UN
Security Council in New York. His two-page plea attacked the
United States for "false" accusations concerning Communism in
Guatemala, reviewed the past days of military incidents and
then implored the Security Council to seek a cease-fire and work
for the withdrawal of "aggressor governments"—Honduras and
Nicaragua—from Guatemalan soil. Castillo Armas and his men
were working "at the instigation of certain foreign monopolies,"
it declared. In private messages, Toriello directed Guatemala's
UN representative to request a special session of the Security
Council and simultaneously ordered his chargé d'affaires in
Washington, Dr. Alfredo Chocano, to ask the OAS Peace Committee to dispatch a fact-finding mission to Guatemala.[15]

Around four that afternoon, Guatemala City's anxious quiet
was shattered by the drone of two planes approaching from the
south. The aircraft, P-47s never seen before in any Latin Air
Force, drew close, dove, fired a few .50-caliber machine-gun
rounds at houses near the Guardia de Honor barracks—one of
five forts in the city—and dropped five-pound fragmentation
bombs, creating a series of loud explosions. Apparently fulfilling
the threat contained in the morning circulars, one plane swerved
about and machine-gunned the National Palace. After scattering
more propaganda broadsides, the two intruders swung away toward the Pacific Ocean, later strafing the port of San José.[16]

The American ambassador, perhaps the only man in town who
knew exactly what was going on, heard the noise of the planes
from his office while he was dictating reports. He ran to his window and watched the aircraft dip and bob above the city. He returned to his desk, jotting down an eyewitness account of the attack for the State Department. A little later he took an urgent
call from Foreign Minister Toriello, who asked for a meeting.
Before Peurifoy left to see Toriello, an aide brought accounts of
"unconfirmed uprisings" in the towns of Zacapa, Quetzaltenango
and Puerto Barrios. Peurifoy recorded this for another dispatch

and, before he departed, transmitted it to Secretary of State Dulles in Washington. He ended the message with a wry aside: "Looks like this is it."[17]

Peurifoy arrived at the Foreign Ministry around 7:30 P.M. Toriello had also called in the French ambassador and the British chargé d'affaires. Most of the talking was between Peurifoy and Toriello. The two men knew each other well; they had conferred frequently during the eight months since Peurifoy's arrival in the country, attempting without success to settle the issue of compensation for the property seized from the United Fruit Company under Guatemala's land reform act. United Fruit wanted about $16 million for the tracts; Guatemala offered United Fruit's own declared valuation for tax purposes—$627,572. The United States ambassador, in an unusual role, had acted as the company's representative in the negotiations with Guatemala.[18]

Toriello began at once with the matter of that afternoon's air strikes. He asked all three envoys to inform their governments that two P-47 planes had attacked Guatemala City. Without looking at Peurifoy, he pointed out that "this type of plane is manufactured in the United States." Peurifoy became indignant —"I interposed," he wired Dulles, "that P-47 planes could be found in many countries, even Czechoslovakia and Russia." He ingenuously suggested to Toriello that the planes might not actually be hostile to Arbenz. When Toriello told him that the planes had hit the National Palace, Peurifoy demurred. "I . . . saw no machine-gunning of the Palace," he told Toriello. The meeting was inconclusive. Peurifoy departed vexed, but undoubtedly bemused at Toriello's diplomatic strategy. He had, in any event, won standard assurances from Toriello that Guatemala would guarantee the safety of U.S. citizens in the country.[19]

That night Arbenz ordered a blackout in the capital. At 11:30 in the evening, the government shut off all the lights in the streets, in official buildings and at the airport. Citizens were required to extinguish lamps in their houses. A half hour later, just as Arbenz had feared, a DC-3 buzzed the city without warning, winging in from the west. It drew .30-caliber machine-gun fire from government gunners on the city's outskirts, and took some shots from larger but older Befors 20-mm. guns at the city's center. Seeing no target in the darkened city, the plane passed overhead, later reportedly dropping a cache of arms by parachute near the Pacific coast.[20]

Near the Honduran border, sporadic fighting continued through the night. The Guatemalan government stayed in close touch with battlefield developments. Around midnight it learned that 150 insurgents had stopped a train running from Guatemala City to Puerto Barrios. The raiders clambered aboard the locomotive and forced the engineer to take them to the small town of Entreríos, where they disembarked. There the band destroyed some tracks, ripped down several telephone and telegraph poles and planted explosives that heavily damaged the bridge at Gualán, just ten miles from the Honduran border. They then departed in the direction of the frontier. Ambassador Peurifoy learned of the train hijacking from his own source, the president of the United Fruit-owned IRCA railroad, who telephoned him with the news.[21]

Guatemala was increasingly jittery the following morning, June 19, the second day of the "invasion." The aerial bombardment, scary but never seriously destructive, continued. At 8 A.M., a P-47 fighter flew over the capital city and strafed the international airport, concentrating on the military section, where it disabled a small Guatemalan bomber. According to a government communiqué issued later in the day, nine persons were wounded by the plane's bullets and a three-year-old girl was killed (she later turned out to be alive but wounded). The plane flew off, and on its way back to its unknown base cruised over the town of Chiquimula, where it dove again and hit a school called the Young Women's Institute, riddling it with machine-gun fire; afterward it strafed the nearby provincial capital of Zacapa.[22]

The aerial assault was intensifying, so far with little response by the Guatemalan Air Force. After one air force plane was shot down, President Arbenz grounded the government's five remaining antiquated planes, all pre-1936 U. S. Army trainers; most, in any case, could not be upgraded to fighter standards in time. In his UN message, Toriello blamed the six-year-old U.S. arms embargo for the nation's ill-prepared air defense. Other observers speculated that the well-publicized defections of several air force pilots might have made Arbenz reluctant to use the few planes he did have available. In any case, the government yielded the skies to rebel planes, which flew in and out of Guatemala at will.[23]

Over the next forty-eight hours, the rebel fliers followed regular patterns. Some planes dropped supplies. Some attacked Guatemalan towns. Others looked for gasoline dumps and military barracks to strafe and bomb. On the first day of the revolt, June 18, a fighter plane had peppered the fuel depots at the port of San José and another had hit a military barracks in Guatemala City with several machine-gun bursts. On the second day, a single-engine Cessna attacked gas storage tanks at Puerto Barrios on the Atlantic while another aircraft spattered the barracks at Jutiapa with gunfire. That night a plane flew over the Flores, Petén, military base with searchlights. The insurgents apparently hoped to inflict psychological as well as physical damage, first by destroying gasoline reserves so the government would be unable to move troops, and then by striking military installations in the hope of turning the Army against President Arbenz. Despite the air strikes, however, the country had not yet suffered any serious military indiscipline or major loss of fuel, and Guatemalan gunners were even occasionally hitting enemy planes.[24]

As the air bombardment continued, the ground "invasion" advanced slowly on the second day. By noon, a dusty collection of "exiles" led by Castillo Armas straggled into the town of Esquipulas, six miles over the Honduran frontier, known as the site of the nation's major Catholic shrine, the Church of the Black Christ. A few hours later, other troops took over the nearby village of Jocotán. By evening, rebel columns occupied two more small border towns further inside Guatemala, Morales and Bananera.[25]

Ambassador Peurifoy remained in his office receiving periodic reports. He learned of an emergency decree by the Guatemalan government banning international air flights and forbidding anyone to leave the country. He tried several times to reach Foreign Minister Toriello to protest the denial of exit permits for U.S. residents, but Toriello was unavailable. He learned also that the

Guatemalan Army had moved "most of [its] military forces" out
of the city during the day (later accounts indicate that 500
troops were sent to Puerto Barrios and to Zacapa). He cabled
the report to Secretary of State Dulles—who was anxiously following the unfolding of the "revolt" he had also helped plan—
but warned Dulles: "[E]normous rumors mostly false . . . are
circulating."[26]

That day the U. S. State Department finally issued a formal
statement on the Guatemalan situation. It said:

> The department has been in touch with Ambassador John E.
> Peurifoy at Guatemala City by telephone and telegraph and the
> Ambassador reports that all Americans there are well and safe.
> Mr. Peurifoy is keeping in constant touch with members of the
> United States community in Guatemala and has made strong rep-
> resentations to local authorities regarding their safety.
>
> The Ambassador also reports that during the past twenty-four
> hours serious uprisings were reported at Quetzaltenango, Zacapa
> and Puerto Barrios. He reports that there have been three over-
> flights at Guatemala City. The first was at 4 P.M. Friday. Another
> at 11:45 last night and the last at 11 A.M. this morning. The Am-
> bassador confirmed that there had been no bombings or strafings
> by planes in the Guatemala City area and that, although the ap-
> pearance of the planes had caused alarm there had been no dis-
> orders. . . . The department has no evidence that indicates
> that this is anything other than a revolt of Guatemalans against
> the government. . . .
>
> The latest outbursts of violence within Guatemala confirm the
> previously expressed view of the United States concerning possi-
> ble action by the OAS (Organization of American States) on
> the problem of Communist intervention in Guatemala. The de-
> partment has been exchanging views and will continue to ex-
> change views with other countries of this hemisphere, who are
> also gravely concerned with the situation in Guatemala regarding
> action needed to protect the hemisphere from further encroach-
> ment by international communism.[27]

By nightfall, President Arbenz, shaken by the two days of air
attacks and by the border crossings, decided to appeal to the nation. At 8 P.M., he went on the air. Some Guatemalans could not
hear him at first because there was a mysterious surge of static

on the airwaves which the government later charged was the result of "foreign jamming." Over the din, Arbenz, angry and emotional, told Guatemalans that "the arch-traitor Castillo Armas" was leading a "heterogeneous Fruit Company expeditionary force" against the country. Then he said:

> [T]his movement cannot be considered as a mere rebellion. It is something more. This is an armed invasion of our territory, carried out by . . . adventurers, mercenaries of various stripes and some Guatemalan exiles. Such is the composition of the expeditionary force equipped, supplied and armed on Honduran and Nicaraguan territory.
> These armed groups displayed themselves publicly in Tegucigalpa before being taken to the Guatemalan-Honduran border. They openly loaded military supplies on planes which took them to Copán [a border outpost in Honduras] from the airport at Toncontin [Tegucigalpa]. They walked in uniforms through the streets of Tegucigalpa. They stated that the Honduran authorities had no authority over them. They were not even silent about the fact that they receive 300 dollars a month in wages and they have ostentatiously exchanged the "greenbacks" in several Honduran towns. They are so well organized that they brought photographers and U.S. war correspondents along on their expedition. . . .
> When the Government of the United States denied all requests to sell U.S. arms to Guatemala, we saw their intentions clearly. That is why we had to turn to other nations to procure the means for our defense. And this has now served the U.S. as a pretext for attempting to destroy the Guatemalan Revolution. . . .
> Ever since we received arms for our defense [from Czechoslovakia], officials in Washington and the U.S. press have redoubled their attacks on Guatemala in a strident campaign meant to bewilder the American people and the continent which probably has not been equalled under similar circumstances before. . . .
> Our only crime consisted of decreeing our own laws and applying them to all without exception. Our crime is having enacted an agrarian reform which affected the interests of the United Fruit Company. Our crime is wanting to have our own route to the Atlantic, our own electric power and our own docks and ports. Our crime is our patriotic wish to advance, to progress, to

win economic independence to match our political independence. We are condemned because we have given our peasant population land and rights.

Unfortunately even the President of the United States of America has made little of his high office, and he too, either through lack of information or other reasons, has lent himself to the campaign of pressure and intimidation against Guatemala. . . .

It it completely untrue that the communists are taking over the Government. On the contrary, it is the anti-communists of the Castillo Armas . . . group and other greedy servants of the foreign companies who are trying to seize power.

We have imposed no terror. It is, on the contrary, Mr. Foster Dulles' Guatemalan friends who wish to spread terror among the people, attacking women and children by surprise with impunity from pirate airplanes, as happened in Chiquimula where they machine-gunned the Young Women's Institute. . . . They are trying to spread terror by machine-gunning buildings, bombing cities and dropping arms and munitions. Morning after morning, afternoon after afternoon and night after night, mercenary pilots are trying to spread panic, but in vain. . . .

And this is so because the people not only do not forget what they were, but because they remember what they can lose. Every worker, every peasant, every employee, every teacher, every member of the Army and every Guatemalan of good heart knows what he stands to lose. One his wages and union rights; one his land; one the opportunity to obtain better living conditions; one his tenure and a woman's right to continue teaching whether or not she is married or pregnant; commanders, officers and soldiers who know that under a dictatorship they are the first to be affected. . . .[28]

On Sunday morning, June 20—the third day of the invasion—the air attacks continued. This time a plane shot up some small southern towns with machine-gun fire and strafed Guatemala's fourth-largest city, Cobán. The aircraft ran out of fuel a short time afterward, the Guatemalan government later reported. Losing altitude, sputtering in flight, the craft steered for Mexico, where it crash-landed just past Guatemala's northwestern border, near the Mexican town of Tapachula. Two crewmen were rescued, one of them wounded. Both were identified by Mexican authorities as Americans. One, William A. Beall, a thirty-year-old pilot from Tyler, Texas, appeared in Mexico City later that day. He revealed that two other American airmen had ditched a disabled plane in the Pacific off Guatemala a few days earlier, but had been rescued by the U. S. Navy.[29]

President Arbenz now declared martial law, requested citizens to loan cars to the Army for transportation and asked unions to provide lists of members in case a civil militia needed to be formed. That morning Foreign Minister Toriello finally returned Peurifoy's call, and around 10 A.M. Peurifoy went to Toriello's office. After an abbreviated exchange of courtesies, the Foreign Minister launched into a long critique of Peurifoy's diplomatic performance, noting bitingly that Peurifoy's exaggerated reports about the war in Guatemala had shown up in the State Department press release the day before.

Toriello read aloud the Department's June 19 statement, in which the ambassador claimed that rebel uprisings were occurring in several Guatemalan hamlets. This was simply untrue, Toriello said; whatever was happening in those villages could not be honestly described as "uprisings." Another Peurifoy assertion, that enemy planes were not strafing or bombing or causing casualties in Guatemala, also was an obvious "misstatement," Toriello said. Peurifoy replied evenly that he had had "no reliable reports" about any bombings, conceding only that there had been strafing at the airport "but eyewitnesses doubted there had been any in the city." The ambassador, playing his role, told Toriello that he was not carrying on any "malicious campaign" against the government. After all, he smiled, he had not yet ordered the evacuation of American citizens, which could create panic in the country. He was now asking only for permits for U.S. citizens to leave the country overland. Toriello accepted the request on the spot, on condition that each individual sign a "waiver of responsibility."

At the end of the conversation, Toriello mentioned that the Mexican government had picked up two American pilots from a P-47 which had flown sorties over Guatemala and crashed across the border. Peurifoy questioned the report's accuracy, and Toriello, apparently realizing that he could not sway his adversary, did not pursue the matter. Finally Toriello broached a key question: whether the U.S. government could help "settle" the "problem" of the invasion because the U.S. had "great influence in this hemisphere." Peurifoy retorted: "Yes, in every country but Guatemala." The meeting ended in a standoff. Both men understood the deep hostility behind their diplomatic niceties. But only Peurifoy knew how carefully the so-called "Liberation" had been planned and what would happen in the days ahead.[30]

No more battles occurred that morning. By afternoon, ground movements also slackened off. None of Castillo Armas' irregulars ventured far beyond their perimeter positions, remaining close enough to the border for hasty retreat if the Army attacked. Castillo Armas himself settled in at the village of Esquipulas, and even rented a residence there. The townspeople couldn't understand why he was standing still; he was not behaving as though he expected to overthrow the government by armed force. What they did not know was that he was awaiting orders from the Americans who had recruited him, trained and paid his men, and were in full control of what was being staged to look like a domestic uprising.[31]

Meantime, gradually realizing that the United States was backing the rebels and that a reckless military response might be suicidal, Arbenz renewed his diplomatic campaign. Toriello dashed off yet another urgent message to Secretary-General Dag Hammarskjöld at the UN, listing the latest incidents but warning that Guatemala would soon be forced to act in "self-defense" under the UN Charter. The Security Council agreed to go into a special session that afternoon, its first Sunday meeting since June 1950, when it debated the invasion of Korea. The U.S. delegate, Ambassador Henry Cabot Lodge, who happened to be president of the Security Council for that month, was apparently caught unprepared; he tried to have the meeting postponed, but to no avail.[32]

The eleven members of the Council began their session at three o'clock and spent five hours debating what to do about the troubles along the Honduran-Guatemalan border. Lodge's strategy was to urge that the whole affair be transferred from the UN to the OAS, which was dominated by the United States. The UN Charter, he argued, gave regional organizations first opportunities to resolve any "civil war," as he described the Guatemalan clash. Though Lodge had the votes of the other nine nations on the Council, the Soviet Union, suspecting that the "civil war" was actually an American-backed plot against an uncooperative regime, vetoed Lodge's resolution. Lodge's response was to tongue-lash the Soviets: "Stay out of this hemisphere! Don't try to start your plans and conspiracies here."[33]

France then introduced a resolution calling for the "immediate termination of any action likely to cause bloodshed" and asking members of the UN to "abstain" from "rendering assistance to any such action." The Council approved the proposal unanimously. It was the first solid relief, albeit symbolic, that the Guatemalans had obtained since the attacks began three days earlier. The country cautiously relaxed for the first time in seventy-two hours. Toriello, perhaps hoping that diplomacy had succeeded in cooling the crisis, canceled his appeal to the OAS Peace Committee for a truce mission.[34]

But the invasion was not over. The UN mandate at best gave Guatemala some diplomatic credibility. It was meaningless on the battlefield, however. Guatemalan democracy was still at stake. Why at the tender age of nine years was it under such sustained attack? A hint could be found between the lines of an enigmatic column by James Reston on that same Sunday in the New York *Times*. Reston suggested that Allen Dulles, Director of Central Intelligence, was the sort of man who could "start a revolution against the Communists in, say, Guatemala." Dulles, he observed subtly, had "been watching the Guatemalan situation for a long time." The article reported nothing else, though the message was not lost on thoughtful readers.[35]

But the more complete answer lay in the events of the past ten years in Guatemala. Though the American public was only dimly aware of it, an audacious social experiment had been underway in Guatemala which seemed so threatening to powerful interests in the United States that they felt obliged to intervene to halt the process.

2

A TEACHER
TAKES POWER

During May and June of 1944, a series of protests shook the foundations of Guatemalan life. In the waning months of World War II, the harsh fourteen-year dictatorship of General Jorge Ubico encountered its first serious opposition. That spring, a growing body of schoolteachers, shopkeepers, skilled workers and students staged public demonstrations demanding freedom to organize. They had emerged almost overnight as a powerful force after over a century of silence following liberation from Spain in 1821. The tiny ruling aristocracy which had long dominated Guatemala was unaware of the rising bourgeoisie, having for so long presided over a large body of passive peasants and indifferent Indians (half of the nation's population was made up of Indians living in rural enclaves isolated from mainstream Guatemala). Ubico's implacable opposition to democracy helped create immense frustrations among this new middle class.

Fifteen hundred days of global warfare also exposed Guatemalans to promises of democracy heard over shortwave radio. President Franklin Roosevelt's "Four Freedoms"—the declaration that all humanity was entitled to freedom of speech, freedom of religion, freedom from want and freedom from fear—stirred a new generation of Guatemalans aware of the inequities in their own society, and made Roosevelt a hero in Guatemala. His advocacy of trade unions also struck a responsive chord in a country where labor was just beginning to think about organizing. Roosevelt's New Deal convinced many Guatemalans, in short, that they deserved a government actively devoted to the public good.

Middle-class Guatemalans were also being influenced by developments in Mexico, their closest northern neighbor. President Lázaro Cárdenas had nationalized his country's oil resources, to the great displeasure, though ultimate acquiescence, of the United States. He had strengthened the country's fledgling labor movement and introduced a major land reform law. These sweeping changes, like those of the New Deal, spurred a growing determination in Guatemala to replace tyranny with democracy.

At the same time, the Ubico dictatorship itself was losing American support. Washington was coming to consider Ubico, a military careerist from an aristocratic family who had attended school in the United States, erratic and unreliable. During the war years, Assistant Secretary of State Nelson Rockefeller had devised a strategy to induce Latin countries to accept loans from the U.S. government and private banks in order to promote economic development and, at the same time, increase financial ties to the United States. An extreme fiscal conservative, Ubico had spurned these loans. In addition, he had expressed pro-Nazi sympathies, until privately upbraided by the Americans. As the war began, the Federal Bureau of Investigation sent agents to Guatemala, with Ubico's nominal permission, to oversee the confiscation of German-owned properties because American officials didn't trust Ubico to do the job himself. The FBI men supervised the internment of German Guatemalans in detention camps, among other tasks. The U.S. military also established an air base near Guatemala City to watch over the Panama Canal—and Ubico.[1]

Ultimately, numerous schoolteachers appealing for higher wages carried out the first overt act of protest against the regime: they announced that they would refuse to march, as tradition demanded, in the annual Teachers' Day parade scheduled for June 30, 1944. In further defiance, the teachers—who soon became the driving force behind the entire anti-Ubico movement—together with students and others, launched a series of nonviolent demonstrations. These protests jolted the regime. Such anti-government activity was without precedent in the nation's history. On June 29, the scattered rallies culminated in the largest protest in the country's modern history. People from nearly every segment of urban Guatemalan life, led by middle-class idealists, converged on the capital's central square to demand that the dictator go. Ubico ordered his cavalry to charge the crowd. Some 200 people were killed or injured. One of those killed was a leader of the schoolteachers, María Chinchilla. She immediately became a national martyr.

Ubico, faced with growing public outrage, declared a state of siege. He was stunned by the turn of events, since his advisers had always assured him he was beloved by all his subjects. He had liked to compare himself with Napoleon, and from the earliest days of his regime had surrounded himself with busts and paintings of the Emperor. He dressed up post office employees, schoolchildren and symphony orchestra members in military uniforms, and—befitting a paternal ruler—even selected the orchestra's music and instruments. Like the exalted personage he conceived himself to be, he traveled around the country on "inspection trips" accompanied not only by cabinet ministers and a military escort, but an official biographer. Landowners greeted him with floral arches and obedient Indian crowds assembled to cheer him.[2]

Ubico's political base was the landed aristocracy, Guatemala's traditional governing elite. His wealthy supporters expected him to suppress dissent and prevent social change. He fulfilled this

expectation with ruthless gusto. In the pattern of his predecessors, he routinely used his army to intimidate poor Guatemalans and solidify his power. He massacred rebellious Indians, killed labor leaders and intellectuals and enriched his
friends. One contemporary commentator suggested that the tradition of despotism in the long-suffering country reached a "sav-
age climax under the megalomaniac General Jorge Ubico." *Time*
magazine accused him of running "one of the world's most
flagrant tyrannies." His contributions were few: a handful of
schools, some inadequate roads and an airport.[3]

Now the autocracy was crumbling. A few days after the massive demonstration in Guatemala City, 311 teachers, lawyers,
doctors, small businessmen and other citizens handed Ubico a
petition of protest. This seminal statement, the "Petition of the
311," expressed the "full solidarity" of the signers with the "legitimate aspirations" of the protesters. The document shocked
Ubico—the more so because it had been presented to him personally by men he knew as friends and prominent citizens. On
July 1, amazed at the passionate opposition to his rule, he
resigned his office and turned over power to one of his military
commanders, General Federico Ponce.

Ponce, equally rigid, misread the drama unfolding around
him. He assumed that people had simply tired of Ubico and
were looking for a new strongman, a role for which he felt well
suited. There had been only brief, isolated violence involved in
Ubico's downfall, and Ponce assumed things would soon return
to normal.

Since independence, Guatemala had been ruled by a proces-
sion of personalistic right-wing leaders who governed for
extended terms and on behalf of the tiny land-based European-
oriented aristocracy. The crude and uneducated Rafael Carrera
was the best known of these *caudillos,* holding power for more
than two decades in the mid-nineteenth century. Manuel Estrada
Cabrera dominated the country from 1898 to 1920.

There had been sporadic resistance to this pattern, beginning
soon after independence in 1821 when progressives, inspired by
the ideals of the French Revolution and the English liberal phi-
losophers, fought for democratic reform. For one brief period
after 1871, there was a great burst of reform. Guatemala's most

formidable leader, Justo Rufino Barrios, an autocratic general with liberal inclinations, became President in that year, and labored for fourteen years to curb the power of the Church, seize land from the wealthy to distribute among the peasants and establish a system of public education. He also tried to revive the concept of a united Central America, which had foundered in the 1820s. But his enlightened—though hardly democratic—rule was only an interlude. When he was killed in battle in 1885 fighting to re-establish the Central American union, his reforms died with him. The nation fell back into the hands of the landowners, who had traditionally considered Guatemala little more than their fiefdom. Ubico's ascension to power in 1931 was only a continuation of the suffocating politics of his predecessors. Ponce now saw himself in the direct line of descent.

But U. S. Ambassador Boaz Long understood that things were different now. He cabled Washington in early July:

> The machinery of government is continuing to function smoothly and the outward life of the country has apparently settled back to normal . . . [but] the next five months will see intensified political activities and a considerable state of political ferment.[4]

Few could have foreseen the extent of that ferment. Ponce raised teachers' salaries and instituted modest reforms in the universities, moves which he supposed would undermine the protest by pacifying its most vigorous leaders. But at the same time he intensified political surveillance, prohibited private meetings and demonstrations and kept the government in the hands of soldiers and *jefes politicos,* local bosses who had helped run the country under Ubico.

As summer turned to autumn in 1944, Guatemala's most prominent journalist, Alejandro Córdova, also a member of the largely powerless National Legislative Assembly, stirred the dissidents with a series of boldly anti-government articles in the newspaper of which he was founder and editor, *El Imparcial.* Córdova followed up his published polemics with a fiery speech in the Assembly in early October. Several days later, he was assassinated, to all appearances on government orders. This was an act new and deeply repellent to most Guatemalans. The convulsion that had already claimed Ubico had evidently not yet reached its climax.

Ponce, attempting a democratic façade, decreed a free election to present himself for popular ratification. The schoolteachers and other opponents of Ponce began searching for a suitable candidate to run against him. Many aspirants came forth, but the teachers were hunting for someone unique, someone not stained by the politics of the past who could unify an awakened Guatemalan people against dictatorship. The revolutionaries found their ideal candidate in Dr. Juan José Arévalo Bermejo, himself a teacher, who had been living in exile for the past fourteen years in Argentina as a professor of philosophy at the University of Tucumán.

Arévalo had a special combination of assets. He had written several patriotic and uplifting textbooks on history, geography and civics that were in use throughout Guatemala, so his name was familiar to the teachers who formed the backbone of the revolutionary movement. He was a visionary, a serious thinker whose heroes included Simón Bolívar, Abraham Lincoln and Franklin Roosevelt. His aspiration was to spread the principles of the New Deal throughout Latin America.

Convinced that they had found the right man, the teachers cabled Arévalo in Argentina proposing the idea of his candidacy. Arévalo responded favorably, but added that he did not even have enough money to pay for his trip home, much less underwrite a national political campaign. No matter, the teachers replied; they wired him funds for a ticket home and gave him a guarantee of financial help upon his arrival. Ponce supporters tried to discredit Arévalo, claiming variously that he was out of touch with the country after such a long absence, that he had lost the right to Guatemalan citizenship and that he had either pro-Nazi or pro-Communist sympathies. But the few objections were lost in the excitement of the moment. Before setting foot back on his native soil, Juan José Arévalo had become the candidate of the revolution.

September 2, 1944, the day Arévalo arrived in Guatemala, saw the most joyous, most tumultuous and most massive demonstration in the nation's history. As the energetic forty-two-year-old schoolteacher stepped off the plane, it seemed that all Guatemala loved him. He was the embodiment of the nation's hopes and dreams, living proof that the long years of dictatorship might finally be ending. Though he had not participated in Ubico's overthrow in any way—and was in fact 2,000 miles away when it happened—Arévalo was welcomed as a conquering hero. But he had to go into hiding almost immediately because General Ponce, threatened by his popularity, had ordered his arrest.

Ponce himself, however, never got to take part in the election he had proclaimed. As he was trying to keep control in mid-October, two young officers who had fled several months earlier to neighboring El Salvador to plan a revolt, slipped back into the country. The two commanders, Major Francisco Arana and Captain Jacobo Arbenz, both at one time stationed at the Guardia de Honor military barracks, made a dramatic move before dawn on October 20. They killed their superior officers at Fort Matamoros and distributed arms stored there to eager students. Joined spontaneously by a number of other army units, they launched quick attacks against police stations and other military installations. Ponce tried to persuade the U. S. Embassy to supply bombs for his air force, but to no avail. After several days of sporadic fighting, on October 22 he finally accepted a settlement with the rebels which the American Embassy had arranged. The U.S. chargé d'affaires signed the pact as a "witness." Ponce then departed for the safety of the Mexican Embassy. (When he left the country soon afterward, $16,000 in cash was confiscated from his luggage.) Ubico, waiting in the wings and hoping for a comeback, entered the sanctuary of the British Legation. Guatemala's "October Revolution" was won in the lightning uprising, which cost less than 100 lives. Major Arana and Captain Arbenz, the victorious heroes, formed an interim junta with a prominent businessman, Jorge Toriello, and announced immediately that free elections—the first in the nation's history under a democratic constitution—would soon be held.[5]

The new ruling junta embraced Arévalo as its candidate. For them, he represented a "clean" civilian, a break with the past. The two military members of the interim junta—Arbenz and Arana—also hoped they would be able to "manage" him after he took office. Other candidates soon saw they must step aside in the face of Arévalo's overwhelming popularity. Almost every one of the political parties which had sprouted in recent months moved to back Arévalo.

The breadth of his support gave Arévalo the luxury of devoting his campaign to speeches extolling the virtues of democracy and social justice. His statements revealed him to be a modern liberal of socialist bent who believed that government could play a vital role in improving the lives of people. But he was quick to distance himself from radical ideologies. He found Communism especially distasteful:

> Communism is contrary to human nature, for it is contrary to the psychology of man, which is composed of great and small things, of noble and ignoble desires, of high and low instincts, of capabilities and weaknesses, of frivolity and heroism. . . . Here we see the superiority of the doctrine of democracy, which does not seek to destroy anything that man has accomplished, but humbly seeks to "straighten out crooked paths." The philosophy of democracy is satisfied with working with human elements, retouching, harmonizing movements as in an unfinished symphony, hoping not for infinity but for infinite beauty.[6]

In the months following his return to Guatemala, Arévalo's impassioned voice and barrel-chested frame became familiar throughout the country. In December 1945, the whirlwind of support swept him into the presidency with more than 85 percent of the (literate male) vote. In the months before he took office, the ruling junta and the constitutional assembly were hard at work preparing the way. Noted one contemporary observer:

> [T]he new government abolished laws, exiled enemies and cleaned house. A clean sweep was made of government employees. The hated secret police was dissolved and replaced by a civil guard. Former President Ubico and his friends were sent packing; not a general was left in the country. In the months between October 20, 1944, and March 15, 1945, fewer *days* were spent in constructing the new system than *years* had been spent building the old. The National Assembly was dissolved; the constitution was repealed; deputies to the [Congress] and the constitutional assembly were elected; a new constitution was drawn up

... and ... approved on March 13, a mere two days before the inauguration.[7]

The liberal constitution, written with the help of the Guatemalan Bar Association, embodied the aspirations of the 1944 revolutionaries, the mass of Guatemalans and the idealistic young President-elect. Though some provisions were based on the enlightened (but largely ignored) constitution that Justo Rufino Barrios had enacted in 1871, the document marked for Guatemala a dramatic break with the past, drawing mainly from the constitutions of revolutionary Mexico and republican Spain. It divided power among executive, legislative and judicial branches. Individual rights were guaranteed in no less than thirty-four separate articles and the Jeffersonian principle of popular sovereignty was dominant.

One remarkable feature was its commitment to a fair, honest political system—a novelty in Central America. Congressmen were limited to two four-year terms; the President could not be re-elected after a single six-year term (except after a twelve-year lapse); and military men were forbidden to run for office. All soldiers were required to pledge loyalty not only to the nation but also to the principle of democracy and the idea of rotation in office. Censorship of the press was forbidden, the right to organize was sanctified and voting rights were expanded (except to illiterate women). Congress was given the right to fire cabinet ministers or Supreme Court justices through a vote of no confidence, and other provisions also limited the power of the President—clearly an effort to prevent the re-emergence of dictatorship. Mayors and local councillors were to be elected for the first time, and all high officials were required to file net-worth statements at the time they took office so the public could later judge whether they had profited from government service.

Just as noble were the constitution's social guarantees. Equal pay for men and women was required in private as well as public employment, and husbands and wives were declared equal before the law. Racial discrimination was made a crime. The constitution banned private monopolies and gave the government the power to expropriate certain private property. The country's main university, San Carlos, was guaranteed complete

autonomy from government control—a cause especially dear to
educator Arévalo. Workers were assured one day off during a
maximum forty-hour workweek and contributory social security
was made mandatory. Employers were to pay workers in legal
currency rather than company scrip, grant paid leaves for child-
birth and permit union organization.[8]

Arévalo's inaugural address, though couched in the generalities that were to become his trademark, made clear his fidelity to
the ideals of the constitution and the October Revolution:

> There has been in the past a fundamental lack of sympathy for
> the working man, and the faintest cry for justice was avoided
> and punished as if one were trying to eradicate the beginnings of
> a frightful epidemic. Now we are going to begin a period of sym-
> pathy for the man who works in the fields, in the shops, on the
> military bases, in small businesses. We are going to make men
> equal to men. We are going to divest ourselves of the guilty fear
> of generous ideas. We are going to add justice and humanity to
> order, because order based on injustice and humiliation is good
> for nothing. We are going to give civic and legal value to all peo-
> ple who live in this Republic.[9]

Arévalo called his progressive political doctrine "spiritual socialism," defining the term as "all of us turning toward everyman
. . . toward the great social entity in which every man is im-
mersed." He proclaimed that "agriculture and popular education
are the two fields that have been the orphans of official interest
in Guatemala" and that they would be among his first priorities.
In closing his inaugural speech, he rededicated himself to the
ideals of Franklin Roosevelt, who as much as any figure had inspired the October Revolution: "He taught us that there is no
need to cancel the concept of freedom in the democratic system
in order to breathe into it a socialist spirit." American diplomat
Spruille Braden, attending the inauguration as Roosevelt's special representative, felt a "chill of emotion" when realizing the
importance of what he was witnessing. It was "not just a Guatemalan ceremony, but an act of great significance for the
Americas," he told a reporter, adding that the United States was
"happy to see that Guatemala now occupies the high place of
one of the hemisphere's democracies." (Braden's chill of emotion

would turn to icy hatred a few years later, when he became a consultant to the United Fruit Company.)[10]

On March 15, 1945, filled like his countrymen with hope and faith in the future, Juan José Arévalo took the oath of office and became the first popularly elected President of Guatemala. Few in the Chamber of Deputies that memorable day could have predicted that there would be only one more in the revolutionary lineage.

3

AN AGE OF REFORM

When Juan José Arévalo took office in March 1945, he set four priorities to guide him during his six-year term: agrarian reform, protection of labor, a better educational system and consolidation of political democracy. The last goal was perhaps the least complicated and most universally demanded. Arévalo liberated the long-suppressed energies of his people by permitting and encouraging the formation of political parties. He guided the nation's first Congress, established on the ashes of the impotent National Legislative Assembly, to full equality with the executive branch. He sought its approval for important measures and scrupulously respected its decisions. For the first time in Guatemalan history, freedom of speech and press flourished. Aré-

valo reveled in the cacophony of democracy and delighted in
the clash of opinions which represents the core of free society.

Arévalo confronted a Guatemala that had changed hardly at
all in the 124 years since independence. Living standards for
most of the population of 3 million were actually in decline. In
the city, an experienced bank clerk took home $90 a month. The
largest labor pools were in foreign-owned enterprises; some
40,000 Guatemalans depended directly or indirectly on the
United Fruit Company and its subsidiaries. The small but growing working and middle classes had no place in the traditional
structure.

In the countryside, population growth forced increasing numbers of people to live off the same amount of available land. The
peasant wage was scaled from five to twenty cents a day. Two
percent of the landowners held 72 percent of the land, and 90
percent of the people together owned just 15 percent of the productive acreage. Indians in the countryside were tied to large
plantations by an age-old system which exacted at least 150 days
each year of debt labor "in lieu of taxes." Though the nation's
first constitution, adopted in 1824, abolished slavery, rural labor
patterns still prevailing in 1945 were only barely distinguishable
from involuntary servitude. The 75 percent illiteracy rate
reached as high as 95 percent among Indians. Life expectancy
was 50 years for *ladinos* (people of mixed Spanish-Indian blood
and westernized culture) and 40 years for Indians.[1]

In October 1946, the Guatemalan Congress approved the nation's first Social Security Law, which revolutionized the
tionship among workers, employers and government. The bill,
largely modeled after the New Deal measure enacted in the
United States, guaranteed workers the right to safe working conditions, compensation for injuries, maternity benefits and basic
education and health care. A newly created Social Security Institute launched a twenty-year program aimed at building sixty-
seven new hospitals to bring medical facilities to peasants and
others living outside the capital.[2]

Even more profound in its impact was the Arévalo administration's 1947 Labor Code, whose framers looked to the American Wagner Act as a model. The new code, later to become a
major factor leading to American intervention, redressed manage-

ment's control over labor. The underlying concept was that government should no longer automatically support large farm owners and other employers. Arévalo's Minister of Labor explained: "A capitalist democracy ought to compensate with the means at its disposal, some of which are legislative, for the economic inequality between those who possess the means of production and those who sell manual labor."

Provisions of the code guaranteed—with some exceptions—the right of urban workers to organize unions, to bargain collectively and to strike. Special labor courts, shaped in such a way as to guarantee a sympathetic hearing for workers, were to adjudicate disputes. Minimum pay scales were fixed and child and female labor were regulated. Later amendments extended protection to some rural workers and required employers to withhold union dues from paychecks. In the context of Guatemalan history, these were truly revolutionary measures.

There were protections in the code for employers as well, and certain loopholes were intentionally included to prevent the destabilization of production. For example, unionization in the countryside was forbidden on all but the largest farms lest strikes interrupt the harvest. Nonetheless, the code had a major impact in a country where until then a peasant could be jailed if his "labor card" did not show that he had contributed the requisite number of days of forced labor to rich landowners.[8]

Arévalo's speeches outlining his views on labor reflected his romantic vision of Guatemala and the potential of its people:

> Our revolution is not explained by the hunger of the masses but by their thirst for dignity. . . . Our socialism does not, therefore, aim at ingenious distribution of material wealth to economically equalize men who are economically different. Our socialism aims at liberating men psychologically and spiritually. We aim to give each and every citizen not only the superficial right to vote, but the fundamental right to live in peace with his own conscience, with his family, with his property and with his destiny.
>
> We call this post-war socialism "spiritual" because in the world, as now in Guatemala, there is a fundamental change in human values. The materialistic concept has become a tool in the hands of totalitarian forces. Communism, fascism and Nazism

have also been socialistic. But that is a socialism which gives food
with the left hand while with the right it mutilates the moral and
civic values of man.[4]

Of all the measures enacted in the Arévalo administration, the
Labor Code drew most attention from the United States. Its passage stirred the Federal Bureau of Investigation—which in
pre-CIA days was responsible for the collection of intelligence in
Latin America—to compile dossiers on Arévalo and important
ministers in his government. Former Ubico supporters piqued
FBI interest by alleging "Communist influence" in Arévalo's
legalization of labor unions.[5]

Arévalo also took the first steps toward rationalizing the nation's land policy. Farm resources had been vastly underutilized,
and much fertile land lay uncultivated. Production beyond the
narrow domestic market centered on bananas—entirely in American hands—and coffee, the major source of wealth for the Guatemalan aristocracy. Plantations larger than 1,100 acres, consti-
tuting just 0.3 percent of all the farms in the country, contained
more than half of the nation's farmland. Despite an abundance of
rich land, its inefficient use forced Guatemala to import some of
its basic foods.[6]

The need to reform the system of ownership was universally
recognized. A Minnesota professor had reported in 1940 that "all
but a very small proportion of the people are landless . . . in
spite of the fact that land is still available to buyers in large
amounts. . . . Large landowners often feel that if a thoroughgo-
ing distribution of land to the Indians were carried through,
cheap labor might no longer be available and the economic basis
of the life of the republic would thus be undermined." Another
American scholar published a Library of Congress study in 1949
emphasizing that "raising the standard of living through diversification and mechanization is greatly dependent upon
changes in the distribution of the profits and/or the land. The
foreign corporations and the native large landowners oppose
diversification and the development of a domestic market. To increase production [without land reform] . . . only benefits the
owners who spend their profits abroad during trips or by the
purchase of foreign luxury items or, as in the case of the United

Fruit Company, the major portion of the profits goes abroad to foreign stockholders. The standard of living under these conditions cannot move strongly upwards without some changes in the distribution of profits or ownership." Modernizing Guatemala thus required an attack on the concentration of land in a few hands—and would naturally be vigorously resisted by those who had benefited from land ownership for so long.[7]

In August 1948, Arévalo formed a National Production Institute to distribute credit, expertise and supplies to small farmers. An effort was also made to register all lands officially according to ownership and use, thereby legalizing the murky "titles" which peasants had held for years but which were never recognized as genuine grants of possession by either the government or wealthy landowners. In December 1949, Congress approved a Law of Forced Rental, which, despite its limited scale, was probably the most important of the modest agrarian measures taken under Arévalo. This law was intended to force fallow land into productive use by allowing any peasant who owned less than one hectare (2.47 acres) to petition for the right to rent unused acreage from nearby plantation owners.[8]

The government also began gradually to distribute land it had confiscated from Germans and Nazi sympathizers, which constituted as much as one third of the nation's total cultivated property and had come under public ownership as "national farms." There were no new confiscations, however, though they were permitted by the constitution. As Arévalo himself explained: "In Guatemala, there is no agrarian problem. Rather, the peasants are psychologically and politically constrained from working the land. The government will create for them the need to work, but not at the expense of the other class."[9]

These reforms, and others such as the creation of a national bank and a national planning office, symbolized the change in Guatemala's social and political direction. They were not, however, so radical as to produce sweeping changes in the daily lives of most people, except perhaps among urban workers and small businessmen. Most of the reform measures promulgated during the 1940s were only partly carried out, and no drastic redistribution of income occurred. Their most important result was simply to accustom ordinary Guatemalans to the fact that the institu-

tions of government did indeed have the ability to function on
their behalf. Arévalo's achievement was less to alter the social
structure in any fundamental way than to consolidate democracy
in Guatemala.

Yet Arévalo was assailed almost from the first day he took
office by pillars of the old order who feared for their place in society. In May 1946, barely a year after he became President, Arévalo was forced to defend himself in this fashion:

> You have heard the accusations of our common enemies. You
> have heard and seen the indefatigable campaign of your enemies,
> my enemies. You know that for those traditional politicians, those
> of the dictatorial ilk, the president of Guatemala is "communist"
> because he loves his people, because he suffers with his people,
> because he is with the poor, because he supports the workers, be-
> cause he refuses to cooperate with the illegitimate interests of the
> potentates, because he refuses to make deals with those who
> would corrupt his public function. You know that they say the
> Congress is "communist" because it passes laws for the good of
> all and especially to defend you [Guatemalan workers].[10]

Arévalo's commanding presence as the symbol of the October
Revolution was enough to maintain a degree of stability for the
first years. But by the middle of his term, in 1948, unrest began
to grow. Despite good intentions, Arévalo had no cohesive program after his first round of reforms and his bickering political
base was eroding. The parties which had united to back him
argued among themselves, and the newspapers used their new-
found freedom to attack the government relentlessly. Labor
unions unsettled the country by a series of strikes, including almost continuous actions against the United Fruit Company
between June 1948 and March 1949. Late in 1948, Arévalo declared a state of national emergency when a large shipment of
arms was found in railroad cars at Puerto Barrios, the Atlantic
terminus of the Fruit Company's rail line. Soon afterward, a
group of disgruntled exiles attempted to depose the government
by invading from Mexico.

Many of the plots, Arévalo suspected, were in some way connected with the conservative Colonel Francisco Arana, the hero
of 1944 who remained a constant threat from his quasi-au-

tonomous post as chief of staff of the armed forces and who had his eye on the presidency. Arana had a following both within and outside the government, and showed it by undercutting official programs with which he disagreed. In 1948, he went so far as to block negotiations for a $50 million loan for highway construction because rivals of his supported the loan in cabinet meetings. By 1949, Arévalo complained about Arana to his colleagues: "In Guatemala there are two presidents, and one of them has a machine gun with which he is always threatening the other." Arana's power grew until he held a virtual veto over presidential decisions. It was even rumored that Arévalo had promised to back Arana's bid for the presidency in 1950 in order to prevent a coup before the election.[11]

The future of the Guatemalan revolution seemed much in doubt. Those opposed to the reforms began to coalesce around Arana. When Congress hinted at an investigation of Arana's refusal to relinquish his army office as required of declared political candidates under the constitution, Arana responded by threatening to call out the armed forces and dissolve Congress.[12]

On the other side, a significant band of liberals were anxious to get on with the next phase of the revolution, the phase in which the basic social transformation promised by the 1945 constitution would actually come to pass. These activists included labor organizers and leftists of various stripes who feared Arana's conservatism and his apparent opposition to the growth of trade unions. They recognized that, given Arana's strength in the Army, they needed a candidate who would not be perceived as anti-military. Their choice was Defense Minister Jacobo Arbenz, who with Arana had led the 1944 military revolt against the Ponce dictatorship and who had the backing of younger, more liberal elements in the Army. Though the political campaign for the 1950 presidential contest was not yet officially underway, the division between the conservative Arana faction and the left-leaning backers of Arbenz emerged in earnest in 1949. Their behind-the-scenes battles contributed to the turmoil that characterized the end of the Arévalo administration.[13]

Though they had collaborated in leading Guatemala's October Revolution, Arbenz and Arana had never been personally close, and saw each other as rivals from the moment the Ubico-Ponce dictatorship fell. Arana had actually tried to seize power while he was chairman of the three-man interim junta that ruled in 1944–45. When Arévalo took office, he named Arbenz Minister of Defense and Arana chief of staff. Temporarily placated, Arana nonetheless continued to plot against the government. In late 1948, the U. S. Embassy reported to Washington that "it is difficult not to attach significance to rumors that he [Arana] is seeking the right opportunity and a reasonable excuse for a military coup d'état."[14]

The tough-talking conservative populist Arana was probably at least as popular with voters as the less assertive Arbenz. Some friends of Arbenz worried that Arana might attempt a coup before election day or that he would at least flex his considerable military muscle to guarantee an electoral victory for himself. A decision was made then that he should be eliminated, either by bringing him before Congress on charges of plotting the government's overthrow or (preferably, considering the likelihood of military revolt in the event of his arrest) by capturing him, putting him on a plane and flying him out of the country, a strategy that had been used recently to dispose of a troublesome general in Mexico.

On July 18, 1949, Arana visited the town of Amatitlán, not far from the capital, to inspect a cache of arms that had been discovered there. As he returned across the narrow Puente de la Gloria bridge, armed men stopped his car. Arana responded by pulling his own pistol and demanding passage. A gun battle ensued. Both the army chief and a companion were killed and his chauffeur wounded. As historian Ronald Schneider described it:

> According to the best available evidence, the group who killed Arana included the chauffeur of Señora de Arbenz, who later became a deputy in the Arbenz congress, and was headed by Alfonso Martínez Estevez, a close friend of Col. Arbenz who later served as private secretary to the president and chief of the National Agrarian Department. The masterminds of the plot reportedly included Augusto Charnaud MacDonald [an Arbenz associate and later Interior Minister] and the communist firebrand Carlos Manuel Pellecer. While we cannot be sure who made the

decision to kill Arana, it was done in the interests of Arbenz, and
Arévalo cannot be considered blameless, since the government
failed to conduct any inquiry into the matter.[15]

Other accounts, some tying Arbenz more directly to the
murder, also began to circulate. Rumors alleged that Arbenz actually watched the deed through binoculars from a nearby hill.
After Castillo Armas' victory in 1954, Arbenz and several associates were officially charged with the crime, though no trial was
ever held. Some Guatemalans, though, continued to defend the
action as a botched effort to arrest a counterrevolutionary. The
full truth will never be known.[16]

The assassination set off a three-day uprising in Guatemala
City by army officers loyal to Arana. Arévalo distributed arms to
several unions to help put down the rebellion. With the assistance of a general strike, his administration managed to survive.
Other efforts to topple Arévalo followed in the next weeks and
months, including a short-lived revolt by Colonel Castillo Armas,
with no success. From that moment on, Jacobo Arbenz was recognized as the likely successor to Arévalo, and no serious challenge to his ascension was mounted.[17]

In the presidential campaign of 1950, Arbenz won the backing
of a broad coalition of younger officers, many of them associated
with the military academy, along with labor and peasant leaders
who saw Arbenz as the instrument by which they could finally
realize their ambition to transform Guatemala. A political coalition, centered on Arévalo's Revolutionary Action Party (PAR),
provided a mass base, and though Arévalo was officially neutral,
his dislike of Arana had been widely known and it was generally
assumed that his heart was with Arbenz. In any event, Arévalo
recognized Arbenz as committed to the principles of the October
Revolution.[18]

But rightists launched a series of demonstrations against the
government during the political campaign. A silent gathering in
front of the National Palace to commemorate the first anniversary of Arana's death with a "minute of silence" just a few
months before the 1950 election frightened the Arévalo administration. Bands of workers from labor unions, some Communist-

controlled, stepped in to break up the protest—and, not inciden-
tally, showed the government once again who its true friends
were.

Arbenz's principal opponent in the campaign was General
Miguel Ydígoras Fuentes, a rather unsavory politician who had
been an ally of Ubico. He now endorsed the "minute of silence"
and other rallies aimed at destroying the Arévalo regime. Supporters of the revolution retaliated by subjecting Ydígoras to
petty harassment, such as killing his dog. The harassment grew
as Ydígoras seemed to gain, and ultimately he was forced to seek
asylum in the Salvadoran Embassy before the results were in.

Arbenz's greatest personal asset during the campaign was his
appearance, which has been compared to that of the late American actor Alan Ladd. His fair complexion, light hair and sharp
profile partially compensated for his lack of personal magnetism
and for the high-pitched monotone in which he addressed campaign crowds. On November 13, 1950, he was chosen to become
Guatemala's second democratically elected President, winning
about 65 percent of the more than 400,000 votes cast. He was
still something of an enigma to many of his countrymen, some of
whom even speculated that he lacked ideology and might bring
a welcome respite from the "radicalism" of his predecessor.[19]

Juan José Arévalo's valedictory on March 15, 1951, at Arbenz's
inauguration, however, was a gloomy assessment of the country's
political state. He somberly observed:

> On the 15th of March 1945, when I ascended to the presi-
> dency of the nation, I was possessed by a romantic fire. I was
> still a believer in the essential nobleness of man, as fervent a
> believer as the most devout in the sincerity of political doc-
> trines, and inspired by the deep aspiration to help people create
> their own happiness. I believed that six years of government of a
> Latin American nation were sufficient to satisfy the crushed pop-
> ular aspirations and to create structures of social service denied
> the people by feudal governments. I still believed, besides, and
> with reason, that the Republic of Guatemala could rule itself,
> without submission to external forces, free from mandates that
> did not emanate from the popular will of the majority. . . . I
> believed then, and I still do, that a nation cannot be free until
> each and every one of its citizens is free. . . . To achieve this

in Guatemala we had to combat the peculiar economic and social
system of the country: of a country in which the culture, politics
and economy were in the hands of three hundred families, heirs
to the privileges of colonial times, or rented to the foreign factors. . . . The banana magnates, co-nationals of Roosevelt,
rebelled against the audacity of a Central American president
who gave to his fellow citizens a legal equality with the honorable families of exporters. . . . It was then that the schoolteacher, ingenuous and romantic, from the presidency of his
country, discovered how perishable, frail and slippery the brilliant international doctrines of democracy and freedom were. It
was then, with the deepest despondency and pain . . . that I
felt, with consequent indignation, the pressure of that anonymous
force that rules, without laws or morals, international relations
and the relationships of men. . . .

The war that began in 1939 ended . . . But in the ideological dialogue between the two worlds and two leaders, Roosevelt
lost the war. The real victor was Hitler. . . . Little carica-
tures of Hitler sprang up and multiplied in Europe and here in
the Americas. . . . It is my personal opinion that the contemporary world is moved by the ideas that served as the foundation
on which Hitler rose to power . . .[20]

The disillusioned Arévalo recognized that his successor would
have to either abandon the ideals of the October Revolution
altogether or press forward to consolidate them. Arévalo himself
had only barely managed to serve out his term, having survived
over two dozen plots, and relied for support on a disparate and
antagonistic coalition bound together only by opposition to the
alliance of large landowners, rightist officers, conservative clergymen and foreign companies. But Arbenz, by upholding the
revolution's ideals, seemed destined, Arévalo feared, to incite
what he had called "that anonymous force" against himself and
against the revolution that he had helped launch with such high
hopes.

4

THE CLOUDS GATHER

Jacobo Arbenz Guzmán assumed the presidency in March 1951. He was a nationalist hoping to transform an oligarchic society. He did not suppose that the change would be accomplished easily but he was determined to carry through the reform program on which he had been elected.

The nation Arbenz took over was unarguably better off than the one which had faced Arévalo six years earlier. At least two giant steps had already been taken: democracy had been introduced, and the country's political leadership had publicly committed itself to altering existing economic structures. The task of carrying out the larger goals of change now fell to Arbenz.

The small but growing urban working class had fared well under Arévalo; wages had increased by 80 percent from the starvation level at which Ubico held them, and an expanding labor movement forcefully fought for the rights of its members. In culture and education, both special interests of Arévalo, the country had made substantial progress; more books were imported and printed and more libraries were established during Arévalo's six-year term than in the previous half-century.[1]

But the central problem of land still remained, and thus the vast majority of the people were still waiting for the tangible benefits of revolution. In 1950, the annual per capita income of agricultural workers was $87. According to the census taken that year, 2.2 percent of the landowners still owned 70 percent of the nation's arable land. Of the roughly four million acres in the hands of these plantation owners, less than one fourth was under cultivation. Agriculture was still responsible for the large bulk of the nation's foreign exchange, industrialization was lagging, and by far the greatest segment of the economy—an investment of nearly $120 million—was in the hands of American corporations, primarily the United Fruit Company. The entire industrial sector employed just 23,000 people—less than United Fruit—and produced only 14 percent of the gross national product.[2]

Arbenz himself was a striking and puzzling figure. He was born in Quetzaltenango, Guatemala's second city, in 1913 of a *ladino* mother and a Swiss father. The father was a pharmacist, alleged to have been a drug addict, who emigrated to Guatemala in 1901 and committed suicide after business reverses while Jacobo was still young. (Howard Hunt, one of the CIA agents involved in overthrowing Arbenz in 1954, claimed that Arbenz's father had filled his mouth with water before shooting himself, thereby assuring that his head would explode "like a bomb.") He spent a lonely adolescence, moving from the home of one relative to another. He enrolled in the Escuela Politécnica, the national military academy, as a young man and went on to compile one of the most brilliant scholastic records in the history of the school. He also excelled as an athlete, starring on the boxing squad and in polo, then very popular among cadets. He graduated with a commission as a sublieutenant in 1935 and returned to the academy in 1937 as a teacher of science and history. None of his associates at that time would have predicted what the future held for the quiet, able, apparently non-ideological soldier.[3]

At a Central American athletic competition in 1939, the blond and handsome young officer met an attractive, lively young woman from El Salvador, María Cristina Vilanova Castro, the daughter of a wealthy Salvadoran coffee-growing family. She became infatuated with him. They kept in touch and the two were soon married. Under her influence, Arbenz gradually acquired new social ideas.

María Vilanova was an even more complex and fascinating character than her husband. She had never accepted her assigned role as a member of Salvadoran high society. She attended exclusive religious schools (including one in California) and was expected to work as a secretary in the office of plantation-owning relatives until she found another member of the local aristocracy to marry. Social inequality troubled her, but after being reprimanded by her parents a few times she learned not to question aloud. Secretly she read books on politics, an unheard-of diversion for a young woman of her position, and while in Mexico bought material about socialism and other ideologies. After her marriage, she expanded her horizons and met leftists and Communists in Guatemala.

In their first years, she and Arbenz argued about her political ideas, since Arbenz still eschewed ideology. She led him to recognize injustice in Guatemalan life, however, and in 1944 urged him into the revolution from which he and Colonel Arana emerged as heroes. She was sometimes compared to Argentina's Eva Perón, skillfully maneuvering on behalf of her husband's career; others thought her more like Eleanor Roosevelt in her compassion and compulsive activism. After Arbenz became Arévalo's Minister of Defense, she grew bitter over the refusal of Guatemalan society to accept her and her husband because of their progressive views.[4]

Two of María's closest associates during this period—each of whom served as her secretary in later years—were the Chilean Communist leader Virginia Bravo Letelier and Matilde Elena López, a Communist exile from El Salvador. Both fortified her developing social conscience, and under her influence, the Arbenz home became something of a leftist salon, attracting many people who would later help Arbenz reach the presidency. María, it sometimes was said, was more ambitious for Arbenz than he was for himself. Certainly she regarded his election to the presidency as a turning point in Guatemalan history.[5]

Many Guatemalans were still uncertain what Arbenz would do in office, and they eagerly awaited his inaugural speech. After Arévalo's gloomy address to the Congress, Arbenz took the podium and spelled out his hopes for the country's future:

> Our government proposes to begin the march toward the economic development of Guatemala, and proposes three fundamental objectives: to convert our country from a dependent nation with a semi-colonial economy to an economically independent country; to convert Guatemala from a backward country with a predominantly feudal economy into a modern capitalist state; and to make this transformation in a way that will raise the standard of living of the great mass of our people to the highest level. . . .
>
> Our economic policy must necessarily be based on strengthening private initiative and developing Guatemalan capital, in whose hands rests the fundamental economic activity of the country. . . . Foreign capital will always be welcome as long as it adjusts to local conditions, remains always subordinate to Guatemalan laws, cooperates with the economic development of the country, and strictly abstains from intervening in the nation's social and political life. . . .
>
> Agrarian reform is a vital part of our program so that we can rid ourselves of the *latifundios* [giant privately owned farms] and introduce fundamental changes in our primitive work methods, that is, to cultivate uncultivated lands and those lands where feudal customs are maintained, incorporating science and agricultural technology.[6]

Just as Arbenz was taking office, the International Bank for Reconstruction and Development (World Bank) issued an exhaustive 300-page analysis of conditions and options in Guatemala written by its president, Eugene R. Black. Even the Bank recognized the obvious inequalities of Guatemalan life and the urgent need for change. Its report called for government regulation of energy companies and establishment of an autonomous

National Power Authority; wages that took into account "the general price level"; regulation of foreign businesses; industrialization to lessen reliance on foreign trade; a capital gains tax; and public spending for projects in transportation, communications, warehousing, education and health care. All these measures were stated goals of the revolutionary government. The report also contained a stinging criticism of the Guatemalan upper classes for holding prices unnecessarily high, seeking exorbitant profits and investing them abroad.

In conclusion, the Bank reminded its subscribers that "the unequal distribution of national income in Guatemala tends to make it easier to divert resources to investment purposes. In more developed countries, where income distribution tends to be more uniform and living standards are appreciably higher, any diversion of resources toward investment by taxation or other means is bound to reduce the real incomes of most consumers with all the difficulties involved in any such downward adjustment. In Guatemala, on the contrary, the measures which have been proposed here, including the tax increases, will hardly affect the traditional way of life of the great majority of Guatemalans." Almost as an afterthought, the Bank warned foreign companies against "any direct or indirect political activity against the government" and counseled them to "accept, perhaps less reservedly than they have thus far done, the need to adapt their legal status and their operations to changed conditions."[7]

The new President set immediately to work. "Arbenz was determined to transform Guatemala into a modern capitalist state," in the words of one American historian, "to free it economically from dependence on world coffee prices and to wrest control of the economy from the U.S. corporations controlling it." To this end, he embraced some of the projects the World Bank had recommended and added several of his own. Among the first were construction of a publicly owned port on the Atlantic coast to compete with the United Fruit Company's Puerto Barrios; a highway to the Atlantic to provide an alternative route to the IRCA railroad monopoly; and a government-run hydroelectric plant to offer cheaper energy than the U.S.-controlled electricity monopoly. His strategy was to limit the power of foreign companies through direct competition rather than nationalization.[8]

In some areas, President Arbenz found change quite difficult; his proposal to institute a mild income tax, the first in Guatemalan history, encountered three years of congressional debate before it was finally passed in weakened form. But in other areas, such as public works and energy, he succeeded more fully. Criticized much as Arévalo had been—especially in newspapers controlled by conservative interests—and often restrained by congressional caution, he nonetheless made progress.[9]

Throughout his first year, Arbenz devoted most of his energy to the passage of his greatest dream, a genuine agrarian reform law. The bill, finally enacted on June 27, 1952, marked a turning point for Guatemala, where some 90 percent of workers were rural. In retrospect, it might be said that the passage of land reform legislation also counted as a fatal moment for Arbenz. Nonetheless the President considered the program his greatest achievement, telling Congress:

> I do not exaggerate when I say that the most important pragmatic point of my government and of the revolutionary movement of October is that one related to a profound change in the backward agricultural production of Guatemala, by way of an agrarian reform which puts an end to the *latifundios* and the semi-feudal practices, giving the land to thousands of peasants, raising their purchasing power and creating a great internal market favorable to the development of domestic industry.[10]

Under the fairly straightforward provisions of Decree 900, the agrarian reform bill, the government was empowered to expropriate only uncultivated portions of large plantations. Farms smaller than 223 acres were not subject to the law under any circumstances, nor were farms of 223–670 acres which were at least two thirds cultivated. Farms of any size that were fully worked were likewise protected against seizure.

All lands taken were to be paid for in twenty-five-year bonds issued by the government bearing a 3 percent interest rate. The valuation of the land was to be determined from its declared taxable worth as of May 1952—a provision that deeply disturbed some targets of the law, especially United Fruit, which had undervalued its land for years in order to reduce its tax liability.

The confiscated lands and the vast "national farms" already in public hands as a result of the nationalization of German property in the previous decade would be distributed to landless peasants in plots not to exceed 42.5 acres each. Most of those receiving the land would hold it for their own lives only, and would not be given legal title to it as a way of preventing speculation and resale of the land. They would pay a rental fee equivalent to 5 percent of the value of the food produced in the case of expropriated private land and 3 percent in the case of "national farms" taken earlier from Germans.

During the eighteen months the program was in operation, some 100,000 families received a total of 1.5 million acres, for which the government paid $8,345,545 in bonds. The property expropriated included 1,700 acres owned by President Arbenz, who had become a landowner after coming into the dowry of his wealthy Salvadoran wife, and another 1,200 acres owned by his friend and later Foreign Minister Guillermo Toriello. In all, 107 "national farms" and 16 percent of the nation's privately owned fallow land were distributed, and another 46 farms were given to groups of peasants organized in cooperatives.[11]

The law was more moderate in almost every respect than the Mexican agrarian reform bill that preceded it by over a decade, and in fact would have been acceptable under the American Alliance for Progress seven years later.[12] As one American lawyer who visited Guatemala during the reform process wrote in a study of its effects:

> The law was the blending of various traditions. One was the American land-grant tradition to open new frontiers. Another was the revalidation of the civil law tradition that all arable lands and national wealth are essentially endowed with the public interest. The third tradition in the new decree was its affirmation of the validity of private property, notwithstanding its socialistic overtones. . . . A fair, impartial and democratic administration of this law would go very far toward destroying the political power of the minority . . . who are vested property-holding interests, both native and foreign.[13]

But implementation of the law proved to be a problem. Peasants anxious for more land, others who had not yet been granted farms for which they had applied, and still others simply hostile toward arrogant or frightened landowners began to invade farms to which they were not legally entitled. Communist leaders, together with other leftists and radicals intent on pushing the revolution along faster, encouraged such takeovers; in particular, Communist Carlos Manuel Pellecer, a fiery orator and fierce advocate of peasants' rights, often traveled the country to goad on the protesters. Between December 1953 and April 1954, about thirty private farms were invaded by peasants without legal sanction. Arbenz tried to halt these abuses, meting out fines and other punishments to local agrarian committees that defied central authority. But he himself was caught in a bind. Since his first days in office, the redistribution of land had defined his friends and enemies. Now he was reluctant to crack down on the Communists with the severity the situation demanded.[14]

Communists, ironically, had never been very successful in Guatemala. They had made several tentative efforts to establish an organization between the two world wars, but political repression wiped them out. The right to organize parties, guaranteed by the 1945 constitution, provided local Communists with their first real opportunity to plant seeds and grow, and in 1945 they opened a small "school" for the discussion and propagation of Marxism. But the Escuela Claridad, as it was called, was soon closed down by President Arévalo under the provisions of Article 32 of the constitution, which prohibited "political organizations of a foreign or international character." A few small informal study groups survived, however, and several Marxist members of Arévalo's political party, the Revolutionary Action Party (PAR), began planning to change the PAR into a peasant- and worker-based Communist party. At the PAR's national convention in November 1946, these radicals were able to wrest important leadership posts from the "moderates," and the skillful Marxist political organizer José Manuel Fortuny became general secretary of the party. Then on September 28, 1947, Fortuny and a group of other Communist-oriented young activists (Fortuny, the oldest, was just thirty) secretly formed a group within the PAR which they called Democratic Vanguard. Fortuny, who was to become the chief Communist organizer in Guatemala, later cited this date as the moment when the Communist party in Guatemala was founded.[15]

A former law student, radio broadcaster and employee of the British Legation in Guatemala City, Fortuny assumed several key positions within the PAR, including secretary of education and propaganda and editor of the party newspaper, *El Libertador*. He was often consulted by Arévalo, who respected his intelligence and energy. He became a confidant of Arbenz and is said to have drafted some of Arbenz's statements, especially replies to periodic questionnaires submitted by army officers about the extent of Communist influence in his administration. Despite his abilities, however, Fortuny never became a widely popular figure in Guatemala. His personal arrogance and brusque manner were offensive to many people, including some of his own followers. He had difficulty convincing people that he was a genuine leader of the working class. When he ran for Congress in 1952, he was, to his extreme embarrassment, soundly defeated, largely because of his personal shortcomings and the view of many voters that he was a "Russia firster"— more concerned with the progress of the world Communist movement than with conditions in his own country.[16]

Just two years after he created Democratic Vanguard within the PAR, Fortuny grew frustrated with its inability to seize control of the party. He decided to lead his followers out of PAR and start his own organization, the Communist Party of Guatemala. Then just as he was beginning to emerge as the undisputed chieftain of Guatemalan radicals, he was challenged by the emergence of a rival Communist body, the Revolutionary Party of Guatemalan Workers, led by the nation's most beloved young labor leader, Víctor Manuel Gutiérrez. Gutiérrez's traits of modesty, discretion and ardent nationalism made him far more popular than the brooding Fortuny.

A former schoolteacher born in 1922, Gutiérrez had advanced rapidly in the ranks of the country's major labor federation, the CGTG (General Confederation of Guatemalan Workers). He refused to wear imported clothing because he preferred to support Guatemalan industry, and was nicknamed "the Franciscan" by Guatemalans because of his spartan life style. In almost every

way except ideology, he was a stark contrast to Fortuny, and
proved it by easily winning election to Congress in 1952. He was
revered by workers around the country, and the good will he
had built up among them was an important factor in attracting
their support for the Communist cause.[17]

At first, the two Communist parties went their separate ways.
Overtures from Communist leaders in other Latin nations failed
to bring the two men and their movements together, and by
1950 it seemed that their rivalry might undermine their common
cause. But in November of that year, Gutiérrez attended the international congress of the Communist World Federation of
Trade Unions, of which his own labor coalition, the CGTG, was
a member. From the Berlin meeting he continued on to Moscow,
and spent two months there and in other Eastern European countries. Upon his return, he announced that he was disbanding his
party, and told its members that they were now "absolutely free
to choose their own political orientation. But the central committee takes the liberty of recommending that comrades join the
Communist Party of Guatemala." In effect, this was a merger of
the two Communist groups; though he remained the key labor
organizer in the country, Gutiérrez from this point on played a
secondary role in political matters to Fortuny, with whom he
had never been personally close. Fortuny soon renamed the new
group the Guatemalan Labor Party (PGT), because he found
that the word "Communist" alienated many poor people.[18]

The extent of Communist influence on Arbenz after his election is the subject of debate. Though the President himself never
joined any political party, he did turn increasingly toward the
Communists—who had helped him in his campaign and formed
the smallest component of his four-party coalition in Congress—
because, with their control of some urban-based unions, they
could mobilize popular support for his programs. In addition, a
small number of Communists entered the bureaucracy and became especially visible in the land reform program, which they
had helped push through Congress. Communists numbered
about 26 in the 350-member staff of the National Agrarian Department, the government agency in which they had the
strongest influence.[19]

Arbenz accepted the PGT as a legitimate part of his ruling coalition representing working people. He consulted its leaders regularly. But in terms of numbers, the party remained marginal. There were only 4 Communist deputies in the 1953–54 Congress. (The rest of the ruling coalition consisted of 24 deputies from the dominant PAR, 16 from the Party of the Guatemalan Revolution and 7 from the National Renovation Party— for the most part moderates and liberals.) No more than seven or eight Communists ever held significant sub-cabinet posts, and neither Arévalo nor Arbenz ever appointed a single Communist to his cabinet. The total membership of the party never exceeded 4,000 in a nation of almost 3 million people.[20]

In a lengthy and detailed analysis of the Communist role in Guatemala during the Arbenz years, historian Cole Blasier came to this conclusion:

> All the . . . evidence leaves no doubt that Guatemalan Communists had made substantial political gains in a half dozen years. They dominated the Guatemalan labor movement and had relatively free access to and influence with the president. Influence is one thing; control is another. It would be difficult to determine by quantitative methods whether the Communists "controlled" or "dominated" the Guatemalan government. As events so dramatically showed later, the Communists most emphatically did *not* control the most powerful organization in the country—the armed forces. And the weight of evidence would seem to show that, lacking a single cabinet post, they could scarcely have controlled Guatemala as a whole. What would, no doubt, be fairer to say is that the groups which controlled Guatemala under Arbenz had interests and policies established independently of the Communists which the Communists supported. As a result of domestic and foreign developments, the government's and the Communists' policies overlapped in many areas. . . . President Arbenz found Communist support useful. As he grew weaker, he needed that support even more.[21]

The government agencies in which the Communists had no influence were far more numerous than those they had successfully penetrated. They had no authority in any part of the National Police, the Ministry of Foreign Affairs and most domestic bureaucracies other than the land reform and communications agencies. Many factions in Guatemala were far more powerful than the party, including the large landowners, the Catholic hierarchy, small businessmen and, of course, the other three parties in Arbenz's coalition. A conservative American journalist visiting Guatemala in 1953 conceded that freedom of the press also thrived under Arbenz; "anti-Communist and pro-American newspapers were still in business. They attacked the government as hotly as Hearst used to attack the New Deal, yet their editors walked the street unharmed." In the labor movement, too, Communist strength was largely limited to urban enclaves; outside the cities, the leftist but non-Communist CNCG (National Confederation of Guatemalan Peasants) had a virtual monopoly on unionized workers.

The support the Communists had in the labor movement, however, remained the key to their influence. Historian Ronald Schneider observed:

> Through the unions the Communists won the confidence of the workers, first on labor and economic matters, then in politics. Through their control of organized labor the Communists were able to exert influence over the government and the revolutionary parties. In short, control of the labor movement gave the Communists a lever in the political process and put them in a position to offer Arbenz readily mobilized popular support.[22]

No evidence has ever been presented to show that Arbenz himself was under foreign control or that he ever had any substantial contact with Communists abroad, though much was made of the fact that Guatemala had become something of a gathering spot for Latin-American leftists. The accusations that Arbenz was a Communist "dupe" appeared so farfetched, in fact, that they actually served to strengthen his position; since each of the much-needed social reforms implemented by Arévalo and Arbenz was attacked as "communistic" despite their relative mildness, many Guatemalans came to dismiss as baseless all charges of Communist influence even when, in later years, those charges had some validity. After an exhaustive study of the matter, Schneider concluded that "[t]he Soviet Union . . . was quite cautious toward Guatemala, making no significant or even

material investment in the Arbenz regime. The emergence of
Communists as the orienting force in the Arbenz government
during its last years in power coincided with the power struggle
ensuing from the death of Stalin. . . . the Soviet leadership was
not inclined towards a major adventure so close to its principal
Cold War adversary."[23]

Arbenz himself, constantly attacked for tolerating Communist
influence, shared the general view of many Guatemalans that if
the Communists were so harshly criticized by all the conservative forces in Guatemala and the United States, they could not
be all bad. In his speech opening Congress on March 1, 1954,
the President took note of the demand from some quarters that
"the Communists be put in quarantine, as well as those who are
alleged to be Communists" and replied:

> The democratic and progressive forces of Guatemala are not
> something isolated from the democratic and patriotic program of
> these same forces, which were grouped around my candidacy
> and now firmly support my government. To attempt to combat
> certain democratic and progressive forces without attacking at
> the same time our program is not only paradoxical but presumes
> an ingenuousness on our part in agreeing to lose the support of
> what has been the basis of the conquests achieved by that pro-
> gram and that regime. This would be the equivalent of suicide
> for the democratic and revolutionary movement of Guatemala.[24]

Thus Arbenz, whose primary ideology was nationalism,
enthusiastically accepted the backing of the Communists. He
never doubted that when the need arose, he could keep them in
line. He challenged those who criticized the Communists,
including the U.S.-based interests, to prove their good faith by
joining to support his reforms. Their failure to do so opened the
way for a reaction against the modest progress he had achieved.
Arbenz emphasized this in an interview after his downfall:

> The political parties which aided the government were of the
> most varied tendencies. Among them were found some moderates
> and some extreme leftists. My government counted also on the
> aid of the Guatemalan Labor Party (Communist). There was a
> great stir over the participation of this party in the activities of

my government, but this was only the external excuse for the aggression. Among the parties, among them all, the Communists had the same opportunities as others. . . . [The Communist party was] always distinguished by the intransigent defense of every action of the government which was in favor of the working class. It never hesitated to criticize firmly all that seemed inconsistent, and its decisive action always maintained without deviations the unity of the workers in favor of the government.

In the rest of the parties the situation was not of the same firmness. . . . [Y]ou could see their party interests come to the forefront. . . . There were, and it ought to be said and denounced firmly, vacillations and fears in moderate parties which retarded the development of our activity.[25]

That substantial social change was made by the Arévalo and Arbenz administrations between 1945 and 1953 is undeniable. Two scholars who observed the progress of the Guatemalan revolution published a study in *Foreign Affairs* magazine in 1956 which viewed the process through the lens of a typical town in the countryside:

San Luis Jilotepeque is a *municipio* in the Department of Jalapa, about 100 miles east of the capital city in a straight line and approximately 170 miles by road. About two-thirds of the population (approximately 10,000) are classified as Indians of Pokomam linguistic stock, and the rest as *ladinos*. Prior to 1944 *ladinos* owned about 70 percent of the agricultural land. . . .

Come the revolution of 1944 and things began to change, even in San Luis, whether for better or worse. By 1955, the following innovations had become established. Roads and bridges had been improved so that regular thrice-weekly bus service connected the town with the outside world both to the east and west. The number of copies of daily newspapers received had risen from five to 35. A diesel electric light plant provided street lighting, home lighting (for some 250 subscribers, mostly *ladinos*) and current for 20 radios, seven electric refrigerators and several corn-grinding mills for making *masa* for tortillas. The number of schools had gone up from four to 12, and school enrollment had increased more than 200 percent, with a proportionately higher augment among Indian children. University-trained principals had been in charge since 1946. All labor for the local government was now paid at a rate officially declared to be 80 cents a day. Movies were shown about once a week. . . . The church was restored by the Arbenz government and a resident priest established for the first time in 50 years. The main street was paved.

These things had provided access for the people of San Luis, Indian and *ladino* alike, to ideas and organizational movements of the nation and the outside world alike.[26]

Not surprisingly, those "ideas" began to take hold among Guatemalans, and as they spread and the nation's poor majority began to stir for the first time in history, leaders of the old order—especially those guiding the destiny of the United Fruit Company—could not help but become alarmed.

5

THE OVERLORD: THE UNITED FRUIT COMPANY

The rise and long reign in Central America of the United Fruit Company reads today like a fable of American capitalism. From the dawn of the twentieth century, the company played the major role in the Guatemalan economy. For even longer, it had sought, through close ties with successive dictators, to control nearly a dozen nations scattered about the Isthmus and the Caribbean.

The saga of United Fruit began in 1870, when Captain Lorenzo Dow Baker of Wellfleet, Massachusetts, landed his schooner *Telegraph* in Jamaica and saw that bananas were among the most popular products at the local markets. Few Americans had ever seen the banana fruit. Baker, with some extra space in his hold, purchased 160 bunches of the still-green crop for one shilling per stalk from Jamaican merchants on the Port Antonio docks. Eleven days later, he brought the *Telegraph* into Jersey City and sold the bunches to curious vendors for two dollars each.

Naturally pleased by this easy profit, Baker continued to carry bananas along with other cargo on his next few trips, usually docking at his home port of Boston. Soon he made an arrangement with a Boston shipping agent named Andrew Preston to sell the bananas on a commission basis. Within a few years, the growing popularity of the fruit convinced Captain Baker that he should concentrate exclusively on the banana trade, leaving more conventional cargoes to other traders. In 1885, together with Preston and nine other men, Baker formed the Boston Fruit Company, capitalized at $15,000. He soon moved permanently to Jamaica to supervise the shipping of the fruit from the island, as well as from Cuba and Santo Domingo, where his company also raised bananas. Preston remained in Boston to oversee distribution and sales. In short order, new ships were purchased and new markets found. The Boston Fruit Company became a remarkably profitable undertaking.

By 1898, the Fruit Company and several smaller American firms were importing 16 million bunches of bananas annually. As demand grew, a new and unforeseen problem presented itself: a banana shortage. The haphazardly tilled fields of Jamaica, Cuba and Santo Domingo were producing all they could. The company needed more bananas and a more efficient harvesting arrangement to accommodate the expanding market in the United States. Its farsighted proprietors now came up with the idea of buying their own land to establish controlled and supervised banana plantations where the fruit could be grown on fixed schedules, freeing buyers from reliance on erratic local harvests.

The ambitious Bostonians cast their eyes on the enterprise of Minor Keith, a Brooklyn-born entrepreneur whose dream had been to monopolize commerce in Central America by building and maintaining rail lines in areas where no other form of transportation was available. With his uncle and brothers, Keith had struck a deal with the President of Costa Rica to construct his first railroad in the country in 1870. He soon duplicated the arrangement in nearby countries. He was constantly in debt, since his business required substantial capital investment and did not pay dividends right away. The human toll of such an unheard-of venture was also heavy: Keith's uncle and three brothers all succumbed to yellow fever.

But Keith kept himself solvent by exporting bananas to New Orleans and other southern ports. He also shrewdly extended his political power in the region where he worked. He married the daughter of a former President of Costa Rica, and by the peak of his career he was powerful enough to be known as "the uncrowned king of Central America." But financial difficulties weakened him, and he eventually decided to accept a partner-ship offered to him by the Boston Fruit Company, the predomi-nant produce firm in the region. The Fruit Company had capital to spare and was looking for new sources of supply. On March 30, 1899, Boston Fruit and Keith merged their enterprises into the United Fruit Company.

The new firm had considerable assets. Keith brought in his 112 miles of railroad in Central America, the skeleton of what he hoped would one day become a network serving the entire re-gion. The newly created firm also owned 212,394 acres of land scattered throughout the Caribbean and Central America, of which 61,263 acres were actually producing bananas. At that time, land in the undeveloped tropical lowlands could be had for almost nothing, since the local rulers had no other use for it and were happy to be paid anything for it. In 1904, one such dictator, Manuel Estrada Cabrera of Guatemala, even granted the Fruit Company a ninety-nine-year concession to operate and finish constructing that country's principal rail line, running from the capital to the Atlantic harbor of Puerto Barrios. (The Fruit Company had already obtained the contract to carry mail from Guatemala on its ships in January, 1901, its first real toehold in the country.) Through such concessions, United Fruit by 1930 had operating capital of $215 million and owned sprawling properties not only on the three Caribbean islands where Captain Baker had laid the foundations, but also in Panama, Honduras, Nicaragua, Colombia—and in its largest domain, Guatemala.[1]

Though Andrew Preston and Minor Keith were both dynamic visionaries, neither could compare with the most flamboyant figure in United Fruit's long history, Samuel Zemurray. He was just a child when his family of poor farmers from Bessarabia in Russia brought him to the United States in 1892. Still bearing his family name of Zmuri, he was working for an aunt and uncle in a country store in Selma, Alabama, when he first saw a banana salesman. Fascinated, he made his way to the port of Mobile, where importers often threw away ripe bananas that would spoil before they could reach markets. Zemurray arranged to buy the ripe fruit and deliver it himself overnight to stores—quickly enough so it could still be sold. This trade won him the nickname "Sam the Banana Man," which stuck with him through his entire career. He soon built up a small importing empire.

In 1905, Zemurray went to Honduras, then as now a major banana producer. His plan was to buy land, build a railroad to the coast and strike a bargain with local authorities that would grant him protection against tax increases and permission to import building materials without paying duty. He was horrified to learn that Honduran President Miguel Dávila, looking for money to bail his country out of its chronic financial morass, was already in negotiation with a New York bank. In exchange for a loan, the New Yorkers insisted on naming their own agent to control Dávila's national treasury—a common arrangement in those days.

Zemurray realized that no New York banker would grant him the one-sided concessions he was seeking, so he made a deal with one of Dávila's enemies, a former Honduran leader named Manuel Bonilla, who was living in exile in the United States. Zemurray bought Bonilla a surplus navy ship, the *Hornet*, a case of rifles, a machine gun and a quantity of ammunition. He personally ferried Bonilla out of New Orleans harbor, slipping past Secret Service boats trying to prevent such expeditions, and sent the adventurers on their way. Within weeks, Honduras had had yet another revolution. When the dust cleared, Manuel Bonilla was President and Sam "the Banana Man" Zemurray was holding an agreement granting him every concession he sought.[2]

Zemurray's own audacity, together with the extremely favorable conditions Bonilla had granted him, were responsible for the rapid growth of his banana production and export business, based around the Honduran town of Cuyamel. According to a study of the early banana trade:

> Zemurray's boundless energy, engaging personality, and many good friends in Honduras pushed him ahead in his new activity as a grower of bananas. He proved to be a good farmer. He risked millions in large-scale irrigation, on selective pruning, on propping trees with bamboo poles to keep the fruit from falling on the ground and bruising. He let the floods overflow in inferior lowlands and when later the water was permitted to drain away, a deep layer of rich alluvial soil was left on which bigger and better bananas grew. Through these practices, Zemurray was shipping to northern markets bananas of equal or better quality than those shipped by United Fruit. He had a further advantage in that he had his headquarters in the tropics and gave banana growing his personal attention. Zemurray had become a very serious competitor; his Cuyamel Company sold more and more bananas and the quotations of his stock rose steadily.[3]

Pressing his advantage, Zemurray expanded his landholdings, and in 1915 he moved into the Motagua Valley along the Honduras-Guatemala border, an area in dispute between the two countries. He was gradually moving closer to properties owned by United Fruit, which had signed a lease with the Guatemalan government in 1906 for a huge tract near the Caribbean. United Fruit responded to his challenge in typical fashion: in 1930, it bought out Zemurray's entire holdings for $31.5 million in United Fruit stock. The sale agreement required Zemurray to retire from the banana business, and he somewhat reluctantly agreed, returning to New Orleans a very wealthy man.

But as the Depression deepened, United Fruit stock began to drop alarmingly in value. The company's profit plummeted from a high of $44.6 million in 1920 to just $6.2 million in 1932, and the value of Zemurray's stock fell by some 85 percent. Convinced that United Fruit's problem was its stuffy management structure based in Boston, thousands of miles from the sweltering plantations, Zemurray, still the largest stockholder in the

company with his 300,000 shares, arrived at a United Fruit
board of directors meeting in 1933 and bluntly declared: "You
people have been botching up this business long enough." With
a combination of threats, promises, characteristic bluster and
charm, he persuaded the owners to name him managing director. Within two weeks, the price of United Fruit stock had more
than doubled, reflecting the reputation Zemurray had built up
among investors during his years in the tropics.[4]

United Fruit had for years been the largest employer in Guatemala as well as the largest landowner and exporter, and during
the 1930s its holdings and power increased even further. In 1936,
the firm signed a ninety-nine-year agreement with General
Ubico to open a second plantation, this time on the Pacific coast
at Tiquisate. Ubico granted the company the kind of concessions
to which it had become accustomed: total exemption from internal taxation, duty-free importation of all necessary goods and a
guarantee of low wages. Ubico, in fact, insisted that laborers be
paid a daily wage of no more than fifty cents in order to keep
other Guatemalan workers from demanding better pay. Around
the same time, the company's relationship with Minor Keith's International Railways of Central America (IRCA) was for-
malized. United Fruit effectively took over IRCA, which owned
two very important properties: the only Atlantic port in the
country, Puerto Barrios, and virtually every mile of railroad in
Guatemala. (The IRCA brought another advantage: it did not
have to pay any taxes to the government until 1954 under
Arbenz.)

Thus United Fruit exercised enormous economic control over
Guatemala. Any business seeking to export goods to the eastern
or southern ports of the United States (or to Europe or Africa)
had to use Puerto Barrios, and since the company owned the
town and all its port facilities, it had nearly complete authority
over the nation's international commerce. In addition, the only
means of moving products to Puerto Barrios was the IRCA rail
line, whose schedule and rate structure were also controlled by
United Fruit. The Fruit Company's "great white fleet" of more
than fifty freighters alone had regular access to Puerto Barrios,
and the company's intimacy with successive Guatemalan strong-

˙men allowed it numerous "side deals" such as running the telegraph service.

Most United Fruit employees lived on the banana plantations and had little if any reason ever to leave. But there was sporadic trouble among workers, who naturally resented the huge profits they could see being extracted from the country through their labor. In the 1920s the company forcibly broke up a spontaneous strike that erupted when management announced it would require a seven-day workweek.[5]

The company's power surfaced occasionally as an issue in American politics. When Louisiana's populist Governor Huey Long ran for the U. S. Senate in 1930, for example, he denounced its most visible figure, Sam Zemurray, as a "banana peddler" engaged in corrupt deals with foreign and American officials to protect United Fruit holdings. "In foreign policy," wrote Long's biographer, "his only issue seemed to be that the United States should not send troops to Latin America to protect the interests of Sam Zemurray."[6]

In some senses, the Fruit Company was benevolent and paternal. Its workers enjoyed better conditions than most farm laborers in Guatemala. The company provided adequate housing and medical facilities and even established a school for employees' children. (Critics liked to charge that the Guatemalan people indirectly paid for this largesse many times over through uncollected taxes on United Fruit property and exports.) Most of the company's American overseers, however, were from the deep South and brought their racial attitudes with them; company policy required "all persons of color to give right of way to whites and remove their hats while talking to them." During the Ubico years, peasants, performing forced labor for plantation owners, were sometimes given small plots for their own use. United Fruit, with more fallow land than any other company or individual in the country, consistently refused to allow the same arrangements. In addition, *la frutera* (as the company was known in Guatemala) had always resolutely opposed the organization of independent labor unions among its employees.

When the government of Juan José Arévalo came to power in 1945, with its outspoken support for the peasantry and its determination to free Guatemala from the domination of foreign interests, United Fruit was a most obvious target. A series of strikes broke out during the late 1940s, with workers demanding better conditions and a wage of $1.50 per day. The company granted some concessions, though its oft-repeated charge that the political deck was stacked against it was partially belied when one major strike at the Tiquisate plantation was declared illegal by the labor court established under the 1947 Labor Code. (The Labor Code was a source of constant anger at United Fruit, which at one point had threatened to "withdraw from Guatemala" because the law promised "to seriously interfere with and possibly make impracticable the further growth of the company.")

A much more serious labor dispute was the two-year struggle in the late 1940s between the company and stevedores at Puerto Barrios over the issue of mechanization and a change in company pay policy from hourly to "piece" wages. As a result of intense lobbying in Washington by United Fruit officials, members of Congress denounced the strife. From that point on, all efforts by workers to confront the Fruit Company were reported in the United States as purely political disputes, the result of deliberate government or "Communist" intrigues to harass the company rather than of genuine worker complaints.

During 1949 and 1950, senators and congressmen of both parties, most prominently Claude Pepper of Florida, Alexander Wiley of Wisconsin and Mike Mansfield of Montana, assailed the Guatemalan government for its failure to safeguard the interests of United Fruit. Democratic Congressman John McCormack of Massachusetts, later Speaker of the House, underlined the concern of his constituents by noting that 90 percent of New Englanders' foreign investments were in Latin America.

The view of Central America as a region to be kept "safe" for American corporations was naturally not shared by all the people who lived there. To many Guatemalans, United Fruit represented with perfect clarity the alliance of American government and business arrayed against their efforts to attain full economic independence. Alfonso Bauer Paiz, Minister of Labor and Economy under Arbenz, expressed the bitterness felt by many of his countrymen toward the giant multinational when he said: "All the achievements of the Company were made at the expense of the impoverishment of the country and by acquisitive practices. To protect its authority it had recourse to every method: political intervention, economic compulsion, contractual imposition, bribery [and] tendentious propaganda, as suited its purposes of domination. The United Fruit Company is the principal enemy of the progress of Guatemala, of its democracy and of every effort directed at its economic liberation."

The history of the company's operations in Guatemala, as one American historian observed in a scholarly study, makes that view plausible:

> For many Guatemalans the United Fruit Company was the United States. . . . In the past, UFCO and its sister companies had bribed politicians, pressured governments and intimidated opponents to gain extremely favorable concessions. To the Guatemalans it appeared that their country was being mercilessly exploited by foreign interests which took huge profits without making any significant contributions to the nation's welfare. In the eyes of many Guatemalans, the foreign corporations had to pay for their past crimes and for the years in which they had operated hand-in-hand with the Estrada Cabrera and Ubico dictatorships to exploit the Guatemalan people. . . . It is not difficult to see how [Guatemalans could believe] that their country was economically a captive of the United States corporations.[7]

Thomas McCann, who spent twenty years working for United Fruit and then wrote a book about the company, summarized its half-century of prosperity in Guatemala succinctly: "Guatemala was chosen as the site for the company's earliest development activities at the turn of the century because a good portion of the country contained prime banana land and because at the time we entered Central America, Guatemala's government was the region's weakest, most corrupt and most pliable. In short, the country offered an 'ideal investment climate,' and United Fruit's profits there flourished for fifty years. Then something went wrong: a man named Jacobo Arbenz became President."[8]

As Arévalo left the presidency and was succeeded by Jacobo Arbenz, the Fruit Company, like the rest of Guatemala, foresaw that idealistic generalities might soon give way to forceful actions. From the outset, Arbenz made clear that he would place a priority on building a highway to the Atlantic in order to end the IRCA/United Fruit stranglehold on the nation's foreign trade; he also announced plans to build an electric power plant which would free the country from reliance on an American-owned facility which was then the only major generating outlet in the country.

In October 1951, just seven months after Arbenz took office, Walter Turnbull, a top executive of the Fruit Company, arrived in Guatemala from Boston to demand that the company's labor contract be extended in its existing form for three more years. He insisted further that Arbenz promise not to increase the very modest taxes being paid by United Fruit and that the company be protected against any possible devaluation of the Guatemalan currency. His tone reflected the long-standing attitude in the Boston office, based on decades of experience under dictators from Estrada Cabrera to Ubico, that the Fruit Company could expect to dictate terms as it pleased to the governments of the countries where it owned property.[9]

Arbenz replied to Turnbull in a manner to which the Boston executive was not at all accustomed. For the contract to be extended, he said, the company would have to pledge respect for the laws and constitution of Guatemala and accept the government as the final arbiter in any disputes between labor and management. In addition, he proposed that the docks at Puerto Barrios be improved, that rail freight rates be reduced, that United Fruit begin paying export duties and that the company consider paying compensation for the "exhaustion" of Guatemalan land. One study of the period described the reaction:

> The Company regarded these propositions as a frontal attack on its privileged position as well as a lack of gratitude on the part of the government for the contribution made by the United Fruit Company to the development of the country. They were all of this, but nobody could dispute the fact that the United Fruit Company had taken out of Guatemala far more in excessive profits than it had ever put into that poverty-stricken nation. The International Development Bank had reported in 1951 that

IRCA, the United Fruit Company railroad monopoly, was charging the highest rates in the world. . . .

The Company's answer to the . . . government proposals was to lay off 4,000 workers. It was then that the Court ruled that a 26,100-acre farm belonging to the United Fruit Company in Tiquisate be confiscated as a guarantee for the back-wage demands of the workers. Finally, in March [1952], the company . . . got what it wanted when Arcadio Chavez, representing the labor union, agreed to end the dispute by signing a renewal of the old three-year contract in exchange for $650,000 in back wages.[10]

The amount of money involved in the settlement was insignificant for United Fruit, but it was a symbol that things were beginning to change. Financially, the company was doing better than ever. Zemurray was in charge of local operations and, though generally unsympathetic to workers' demands, he kept production high and fended off interference from Boston with his slogan "I'm here, you're there." Between 1942 and 1952, the company increased its assets by 133.8 percent and paid stockholders nearly 62 cents for every dollar invested. "It was," recalled the company's public relations consultant, Edward Bernays, "a highly profitable venture," largely because "the company was conducted like a private government." All the more reason, perhaps, for its managers to be worried about the turn of events in Guatemala—especially the adoption of Decree 900, the agrarian reform act, on June 27, 1952. From the beginning, it was understood that though many other landowners were affected, the main target of the law was United Fruit, by far the largest property owner in the country with about 550,000 acres on the Atlantic and Pacific coasts.[11]

In March 1953, the ax of land reform fell on the company, never before the object of such a challenge. In two separate decrees, a total of 209,842 acres of uncultivated land on the Tiquisate plantation in the lush Escuintla area near the Pacific was expropriated. The *frutera* had always left large amounts of its land uncultivated (in 1953, 85 percent of its land was unused); only as many bananas were grown as could be sold abroad. The company claimed it needed the vast fallow lands as insurance against plant diseases that periodically ravaged its ba-

nanas, though critics said its reserves far exceeded its real requirements.

In compensation for the seized property, the government
offered $627,572 in bonds, based on United Fruit's declared tax
value of the land. United Fruit, like other large landowners, had
historically undervalued its property in official declarations in
order to reduce its already insignificant tax liability. But now
that the declared value was being used to determine compensation, the company howled in protest. On April 20, 1954, a formal complaint was delivered to Guatemalan authorities, not by
the Fruit Company but by the U. S. State Department, whose
top officials, beginning with Secretary Dulles himself, had close
ties to the company. The note demanded $15,854,849 in com-
pensation for the Tiquisate land, declaring that the government
offer "bears not the slightest resemblance to just evaluation." It
based its claim on international law, which, it contended, required
fair compensation for lands seized from foreigners despite
domestic laws.

The amount offered by Guatemala averaged about $2.99 per
acre, while the State Department wanted over $75 per acre; the
company had paid $1.48 per acre when it bought the land nearly
twenty years earlier. Foreign Minister Guillermo Toriello refused to accept the State Department note, branding it "another
attempt to meddle in the internal affairs of Guatemala," and bitterly attacked the United Fruit/U.S. government coalition that
had become known in Guatemala as "Senator Lodge and Company."

In October 1953 and February 1954, the government ordered
two more expropriations of uncultivated United Fruit land—this
time on the Atlantic coast—bringing the total of disputed
property to 386,901 acres. Guatemala offered about $500,000 to
the company for its newest takeovers. Throughout this period,
Guatemalan officials were in negotiation with the State Department for an overall solution to the dispute. But at the same time,
a more momentous series of meetings in Washington, called
largely at the urging of United Fruit and its powerful supporters
in the government, considered how to end the process which had
led Guatemala to these unprecedented actions.[12]

Arbenz himself sensed what was going on, as he indicated in his annual message to Congress in March 1954:

> The essential character of the international situation with relation to Guatemala is that, as a consequence of the agrarian reform and the economic and social development of the country, we face a growing threat of foreign intervention in the internal affairs of Guatemala, placing in danger the stability of our constitutional life and the integrity of our national independence. . . . The source of the political controversies and struggles, especially during 1953, was the agrarian question. . . . For some time our measures have conflicted with the policies of great foreign consortiums which form the dominant circles in some countries, principally the United States of America. . . . The explanation is in the progressive measures and in the application of the Labor Code to all companies, including the United Fruit Company. . . . As long as we do not conform to the United Fruit Company and some others affected by the agrarian reform, they will continue to try to recoup the lands which popular sovereignty had legitimately expropriated for the benefit of the nation and the peasants.[13]

Indeed, the Fruit Company was at that moment working quietly but effectively to convince the American government that Arbenz was a threat to freedom and must be deposed. The company hired a corps of influential lobbyists and talented publicists to create a public and private climate in the United States favorable to Arbenz's overthrow. Working behind the scenes beginning in 1950, these men influenced and reshaped the attitudes of the American public toward Guatemala. In their hands the fate of Arbenz and his ambitious social reforms was being determined.

6

ADVERTISEMENTS
FOR MYSELF

"I [have] the feeling that Guatemala might respond to pitiless publicity in this country," Edward Bernays told his worried bosses. The setting was the United Fruit Company's New York headquarters on Pier 3, a ramshackle warehouse on the Hudson River, in 1950. The listeners were Sam Zemurray, president of United Fruit, and the firm's director of advertising and publicity, Edmund S. Whitman, a trim New Englander in his fifties.[1]

Bernays, widely acknowledged as one of the shrewdest public relations experts alive, laid out his plans. A short, dynamic huckster with a vivacious charm and an ego the width of several banana plantations, Bernays warned of a dire future for United

Fruit. Communist-inspired movements were going to "spread in Middle America," he predicted. Only if the Fruit Company alerted Americans now, he continued, might the U.S. government "take steps to improve the situation." The discussion went on for some time, but Bernays' appeal fell on deaf ears. Zemurray, he later wrote in his memoirs, "kept pooh-poohing" his warnings. The Indians, Zemurray told him, were too ignorant for Marxism.[2]

Bernays had been a blazing figure in American public relations for four decades. In 1917, at the age of twenty-five, he had arranged the tour of Italian opera star Enrico Caruso through the United States. A year later, he was a public relations adviser to the U.S. delegation to the Paris peace conference following the end of World War I. Over the years, he had planned marketing strategies for such large American corporations as Procter and Gamble, Crisco and the fledgling network CBS. Bernays campaigns always had a subtle angle; when he promoted cigarettes for the American Tobacco Company, for example, he persuaded prominent socialites to be photographed smoking in public.[3]

Bernays had become the dominant figure in his field. He wrote four books and delivered innumerable lectures on techniques of persuasion. He was bold in his prescription for a successful p.r. campaign. As he wrote in *Propaganda*, published in 1928: "The conscious and intelligent manipulation of the organized habits and opinions of the masses is an important element in democratic society. Those who manipulate this unseen mechanism of society constitute an invisible government which is the true ruling power of our country . . . it is the intelligent minorities which need to make use of propaganda continuously and systematically."[4]

One reason for Bernays' success was his personal acquaintance with the people who ran America's magazines, newspapers and radio networks. He knew most of the powerful editors, publishers and reporters of the time. His friends included the owner of the New York *Times,* the publisher of Scripps-Howard newspapers, the editor of *The New Leader,* editors and reporters with the *Christian Science Monitor* and the San Francisco *Chronicle,* and many other professionals in the news business.

Bernays' method was to bombard these "opinion molders," as he called them, with his mailings, press releases, phone calls, visits and seminar invitations. He boasted that he had a list of 25,000 men and women—journalists, editors, labor leaders, industrialists—who as a group, he believed, shaped the attitudes of the American people.[5]

Bernays had another valuable asset: he was known as a political liberal, notwithstanding his work for large corporations. A nephew of Sigmund Freud, he was close to many leading Democrats in Roosevelt's New Deal, gave time and money to progressive causes and advocated such policies as FDR's non-interventionist Good Neighbor approach to Latin America. He even urged reforms within the companies he worked for. In 1945, for example, he pressed Procter and Gamble to hire more black workers, but with no success.[6]

Around 1940, Bernays had come to the attention of Sam Zemurray. Zemurray had been casting about to improve the public image of his much-criticized company, which was known as *el pulpo*—the octopus—in much of Central America and the Caribbean. It was an awkward moment. President Roosevelt was preaching idealism and the Four Freedoms of democracy, while the American public, like most Latins, still perceived the fruit firm as something of a "colonial exploiter" and Zemurray as a seamy operator.[7]

Zemurray decided to make Bernays his "counsel on public relations," the first time the company had ever hired an outside p.r. expert. Bernays promised to polish up United Fruit's tarnished image. He planned to end the tradition of secrecy, which he believed had hurt the company badly in the past, by flinging the company's doors wide open to journalists and the public. He also intended to make a special effort to reach liberals by describing the "remarkable" things the company was doing in Latin America.[8]

Two strong personalities, Bernays and Zemurray, with their eyes set on clear goals, worked well together from the start. Both had innovative talents, having conceived and virtually invented entirely new industries, one in public relations, one in bananas. Both were Jewish, foreign-born and self-made. Each had battled against social ostracism in America. Bernays, who admired

Zemurray as an "industrial statesman," remarked of his boss
that "he was never accepted in brahmin society." Bernays, like
Zemurray before him, faced anti-Semitism within Fruit Company
ranks. Both men overcame prejudice by native ability.[9]

In the early years of his association with United Fruit, Bernays imaginatively "opened up" the banana firm to public scrutiny. He established a "Middle America Information Bureau" to
supply company "facts and figures" to American and Latin journalists. The company founded newspapers for employees in
Guatemala, Panama, Costa Rica and Honduras. A weekly "Latin
American Report" for journalists and businessmen was spun off,
written by William Gaudet, who was one of several actors in the
unfolding Guatemalan drama said to have had simultaneous
connections with both United Fruit and the Central Intelligence
Agency. But in a period of surging nationalism in Central
America, Bernays' efforts, all under the supervision of sometimes
dubious Fruit Company executives, could do little to stem the
rising hostility toward the company, especially in Guatemala.[10]

Bernays himself was beginning to develop private misgivings.
He was disturbed by the company's feudal practices in Central
America, which he had observed firsthand on a trip to Guatemala in 1947. Upon his return he submitted a report criticizing
the company's lack of basic manuals on banana growing, its failure to provide libraries for workers, its unwillingness to hold
meetings reporting on company activities in the United States
and its lack of interest in offering adequate housing for American
supervisors at its various outposts. In addition, he raised questions about the racism displayed by Fruit Company officials
toward "colored" natives, mainly by Southerners whom the
corporation originally hired because they were accustomed to
living in humid climates. Bernays received a company-wide silent treatment for his memorandum. "I got no reaction to my vo-
luminous report," he later complained.[11]

The company made a major executive change in 1948. Zemurray brought in as the new president a Boston Brahmin, Thomas
Cabot, brother of John Moors Cabot, Assistant Secretary of State
for Inter-American Affairs just before the 1954 coup in Guatemala. Many insiders hoped that Cabot would bring "modern"
ideas to the company. In fact, once in office Cabot proposed

switching United Fruit's banana operations from Central America to Ecuador, where banana diseases were less of a threat. He also decided to cut back on the firm's p.r. operations, sharply reducing Bernays' role. He abruptly abolished the Information Bureau, calling it a waste of money, and cast a cold eye on the four free company newspapers.[12]

Bernays soon grew to abhor Cabot. He perceived the Yankee aristocrat as "narrow in outlook." In fact, Cabot's days were soon numbered at United Fruit. Longtime employees of the company in Central America angrily fought against Cabot's efforts to move banana operations to Ecuador. Cabot even clashed with Zemurray over Zemurray's belief that all the company's problems "could readily be solved by a word from the Department of State." In 1949 Zemurray decided to fire Cabot. Zemurray's decision suddenly to dismiss Cabot precipitously reflected a deep uncertainty about what the company should do about the troubles brewing in Guatemala. The firing also ensured that United Fruit's presence in Guatemala would not diminish, since all schemes for moving to South America were now canceled.[13]

In spite of his disputes with Cabot, Bernays never changed his view of what the company should be doing. He quietly began organizing a counterattack against the Guatemalan government, hoping to persuade United Fruit to take a more aggressive stance. In 1947, the company had become upset over the enactment by the Guatemalan Congress of the Labor Code, which for the first time permitted banana workers to join trade unions. The U.S. government filed a protest over the new law on behalf of the firm, but the protests failed to sway the Guatemalans. Thereafter, the Fruit Company's plantations were targeted by labor organizers. Among the results were strikes, slowdowns, public denunciations and other unaccustomed distractions.

The company enlisted Senator Henry Cabot Lodge of its home state of Massachusetts in a campaign to challenge the Guatemalan government's reforms. Lodge, whose family owned stock in United Fruit, strode onto the Senate floor in 1949 and denounced the Labor Code for discriminating against United Fruit and forcing the corporation into a "serious economic breakdown" through labor unrest. (Lodge repeated his castigation of Guatemala in 1954 as the U.S. ambassador to the United Nations.)[14]

Bernays wanted to broaden the attack. He warned Zemurray in 1950 that "the Caribbean ferment [is] bound to become increasingly important." He added: "Liberals must play a decisive role." Bernays began to prod journalists working for liberal publications to write about the Fruit Company's troubles in Guatemala. He persuaded the New York *Herald Tribune* to send a reporter, Fitzhugh Turner, to Guatemala in February 1950. Turner's series, called "Communism in the Caribbean," was based primarily on conversations with Fruit Company officials in Guatemala; it was splashed across the paper's front page for five consecutive days. New York *Times* publisher Arthur Hays Sulzberger, a close friend of Bernays, had also developed an interest in Guatemala because of a college classmate, U.S. ambassador to Guatemala Richard Patterson. He had recently returned from a visit with Patterson and had observed several political disturbances, which, according to some accounts, were staged for his benefit. Soon after, Sulzberger dispatched a reporter from the city desk, Will Lissner, to Guatemala. Lissner came back convinced that the Communist movement had colonized Guatemala by infiltrating cadres from Chile; his dispatches reflected this novel theory, which was never taken up again.[15]

Bernays' mini-campaign was beginning to pay dividends in U.S. public opinion. One American professor and writer who visited Guatemala in the summer of 1950 and discovered some virtue in the nation's reforms, Samuel Guy Inman, complained upon his return that the United States was paying little attention to the achievements of the Guatemalan revolution. Inman, a teacher of international relations and sometime adviser to the State Department, regarded some of the country's new programs—social security, new schools and hospitals, the establishment of unions, free press and free elections—as important social landmarks, though he had some disagreements with Guatemalan policy. He despaired over Guatemala's poor image in the United States—the image Bernays was assiduously cultivating—and especially the repeated American charges of Communist infiltration in the government. At the very end of his visit to Guatemala, Inman was unexpectedly granted an interview with the nation's proud President, Arévalo, who wanted to tell the American public of his strong anti-Communist sentiments.[16]

On his return to New York City, Inman held a press conference to report on the statement by Arévalo. In it Arévalo had declared the "complete solidarity" of Guatemala with the United States over the Korean War—the United States had charged him with supporting the Communists—and insisted that his government neither had nor contemplated any political ties with the Soviet Union. "Politically speaking," he said, "Guatemala has no connections whatsoever with any extra-continental power, either European or Asiatic." In the event of a worldwide conflict, he added emphatically, Guatemala "has one and only one loyalty geographically, politically and militarily"—to the United States. He said Guatemala was trying to establish a government modeled upon the principles enunciated by Franklin Roosevelt. "The people and the government of the United States," he concluded, "should feel satisfied with the efforts of the Guatemalans." The Associated Press ignored Arévalo's statement entirely. United Press International, *Newsweek* magazine and the Hearst Corporation's International News Service gave only brief accounts of it. The New York *Times* gave some fuller treatment. The New York *Herald Tribune,* which earlier in the year had printed the Fitzhugh Turner "exposé," promised to publish something but ultimately ran nothing.[17]

Though his campaign was beginning to pay off, Bernays still could not rouse the Fruit Company itself to even more drastic action. Zemurray, though he detested the social reforms in Guatemala, had managed to accommodate himself to the new unions. A practical businessman, he had begun working with the Guatemalan government to prevent work stoppages. As his local manager in Guatemala, Almyr Bump, recalled about the Guatamalan President: "Arévalo had a lot of right ideas. He was a very pleasant fellow. We used to conduct labor negotiations in his office."[18]

But then the U.S. ambassador to Guatemala, Richard Patterson, joined the debate on Bernays' side. Patterson, a brash, dim former chairman of RKO Keith Orpheum who couldn't speak Spanish and was given to colorful outbursts on the menace of Soviet Communism in Guatemala, had repeatedly clashed with the Arévalo government. He had taken to insisting that Arévalo fire several of his cabinet ministers for being "Communists"; he even began to meet with conspirators intent on overthrowing President Arévalo. The government finally declared him *persona non grata* and he was recalled in April 1950.[19]

Before Ambassador Patterson departed, he sent a private letter to Sam Zemurray advising "the Banana Man" on how the company could retain its power in Guatemala. Patterson suggested that United Fruit should immediately launch "an all-out barage [*sic*] in the U. S. Senate on the bad treatment of American capital in Guatemala. This takes the onus off the UFCO and puts it on the basis of a demand by our Senators that all American interests be given a fair deal."[20]

Patterson's letter, coming just before Arévalo's departure from office, rekindled Zemurray's concern. Though United Fruit remained ominously quiet in Guatemala during the 1950 presidential election there, not by coincidence the company's spokesmen in the U. S. Congress raised the tempo and frequency of their speeches in Washington, railing against the policies of the Guatemalan government toward American corporations. With Arbenz's election, United Fruit's anxiety deepened. In early 1951, Bernays came to Zemurray again to urge a wider, more aggressive and sophisticated campaign against Guatemala. Iran had just nationalized British properties, he warned Zemurray: "Guatemala might follow suit."[21]

By April 1951, Zemurray had become convinced and he ordered Bernays to kick off a second, larger-scale press campaign against the Guatemalan government. First Bernays visited publisher Arthur Hays Sulzberger at the New York *Times,* who once again called in reporter Lissner. Bernays talked in detail about the growing dangers of Communism in the Guatemalan government and urged the New York *Times* to report on the situation as soon as possible. The following month Sulzberger wrote Bernays that he was sending another journalist, Crede H. Calhoun, to cover the Fruit Company's troubles in Guatemala. Calhoun dutifully wrote a series of alarming reports about "Reds" in the country. Bernays later called Calhoun's articles "masterpieces of objective reporting." They sparked the interest of *Time, Newsweek, U.S. News & World Report, The Atlantic Monthly* and the Latin magazine *Visión,* among others, all of whom dispatched journalists to Guatemala to document what was said to be the advance of Marxism there.[22]

Bernays' next step was to organize a series of press junkets to Guatemala. As the pace of land reform accelerated under Arbenz, the frequency of Bernays' group tours grew. Between early 1952 and the spring of 1954, Bernays put together at least five two-week "fact-finding" trips to Central America, with as many as ten newsmen on each one. The junkets were "months in the planning stage, carefully timed and regulated with no expense spared," according to Thomas McCann, the former United Fruit official who helped arrange them and later wrote a candid history of the corporation. They were designed with the "precision of a space shot," McCann added, "and considering the times, the cost was quite astronomical too—I know because I handled the budgets." They represented, McCann concluded, "a serious attempt to compromise objectivity" of the newsmen.[23]

But the press didn't seem to notice or care. Among the eager participants were editors and reporters from *Time, Newsweek,* Scripps-Howard newspapers, United Press International, the *Christian Science Monitor,* the Miami *Herald* and the San Francisco *Chronicle.* In a friendly mood over a free trip to a lovely country, the visiting journalists were happy to interview whomever the company arranged for them to meet. They were shepherded on elaborately choreographed tours of Fruit Company facilities, and talked to local politicians who were sympathetic to the company's plight (and, not infrequently, were on the company payroll). They listened willingly to Ed Whitman, the in-house p.r. man, who "directed" the jaunts and adeptly depicted the company as a beleaguered progressive institution, uplifting local living standards while being unfairly attacked by Communists who were trying to destroy its good works.[24]

After the first junket in January 1952, the clippings began to flow in. Ludwell Denny, for example, a foreign affairs columnist for the Scripps-Howard News Service, returned to the United States eager to warn Americans about the specter of Communism in Guatemala. He wrote that agitators there were attempting to "engender hatred of Yankee monopoly capital and imperialism,"

and speculated that a Soviet takeover was imminent. "As I anticipated," Bernays noted later with satisfaction, "public interest in
the Caribbean skyrocketed in this country."[25]

Bernays had long been working to convince the U.S. press
that the Arbenz government was irresponsible and recklessly
anti-American. When the land takeovers began in 1953, he
seized on them as final proof that the Arbenz regime was "communistic." Within hours after the expropriations of Fruit Company land in Guatemala, Bernays planned two new expeditions
with many of the same journalists who had been on prior junkets. "An avalanche of publicity favoring the United Fruit Company followed the trips," recalled Thomas McCann. So successful was the company's newest press offensive that Guatemala's
ambassador to the United States, Guillermo Toriello (later Foreign Minister), several times formally protested to the State Department about the "false picture" of his country being painted
in the United States by such publications as the *Christian Science Monitor, U.S. News & World Report, Time* and *Newsweek.* Toriello, an observant diplomat, suspected that this sudden surge of attacks on his government in the American media
was not unrelated to United Fruit's war against Guatemalan
land reform policies.[26]

Bernays continued to cultivate the press with the sophisticated
persistence that had made him so formidable as a public relations strategist. At the New York *Times,* besides Sulzberger and
Lissner, Bernays kept in regular touch with foreign editor
Emanuel Freedman as well as reporters Harry Schwartz, Sydney
Gruson and Herbert Matthews. (Matthews, who soon quit the
Times, later characterized Gruson and Lissner as "God's gift to
the United Fruit Company" for their glowing reports on the corporation and negative descriptions of the Guatemalan government.) At one point later in 1953, Bernays managed to plant a
story with Schwartz about a "school for Red agents" in Prague,
Czechoslovakia, where Latins were supposedly being trained in
subversion. Bernays also knew most of the editors at the *Christian Science Monitor,* which was based in the Fruit Company's
home town of Boston. The *Monitor* ran a series of articles
defending United Fruit's work in Central America. The author

was Ed Whitman himself, of course, the company's public relations director.[27]

Bernays had an especially close relationship with *The New Leader*, a vigorously anti-Communist liberal weekly. He was a friend of the executive editor, Sol Levitas, a Russian émigré who had once been mayor of Vladivostok. Bernays persuaded the Fruit Company to sponsor public service advertisements on behalf of the Red Cross and U. S. Savings Bonds in the magazine at $1,000 a page, far above the going rate. *The New Leader* began to publish stories sympathetic to the Fruit Company's position on Guatemala. It carried numerous articles, both before and after the coup, justifying intervention against Arbenz's regime on the grounds that a Soviet takeover was imminent. The stories made a vivid impression on the U.S. liberal community, which was not well-informed about Guatemala.[28]

The New Leader's managing editor and chief Latin American correspondent, Daniel James, not only wrote some of the early critical pieces on Guatemala but published a book in mid-1954, *Red Design for the Americas*, which offered a well-written, sophisticated rationale for overthrowing the Arbenz government. He alleged that dozens of Guatemalan Communists had sneaked into critical posts in the Arbenz administration and had taken control of the government. The Communists, James asserted, were behind the agrarian reform act, which he compared to the collectivization of land in Mao's China. James's book was so convincing by United Fruit lights that the company, at Bernays' direction, bought up hundreds of copies and distributed them to American correspondents, editors and other "opinion molders."[29] Strangely, the CIA indirectly played a role: James's publisher, John Day, was later unmasked as a conduit of the Central Intelligence Agency. Another contributor to *The New Leader*, Serafino Romualdi, the man sent to Guatemala by the American Federation of Labor just after the coup to reorganize Guatemala's labor unions, also had ties with the CIA and the State Department.[30]

United Fruit used other techniques in creating the climate for American acceptance of a strike against the Guatemalan government. In 1953, it started a "confidential" newsletter on Gua-

temalan political and economic events which was sent to 250
American journalists. The circular soon became highly successful. Much of its information—all written by Fruit Company
publicists—found its way into various American newspapers. In
another project, Bernays and a top executive of the Fruit Company, John McClintock, set out to influence prestigious opinion
institutions such as the Council on Foreign Relations and the
National Planning Association. The two men "educated" the
leaders of these organizations and helped them prepare critical
analyses of Guatemala, which were then sent to members and
journalists. McClintock himself chaired some of the Council on
Foreign Relations meetings on Guatemala.[31]

Bernays' pipeline also extended into congressional offices.
Dozens of legislators, men like Democratic Representative John
McCormack of Massachusetts and Republican Senator Alexander Wiley of Wisconsin, spoke out repeatedly against Guatemala, often at Bernays' urging. McCormack, who faithfully delivered a speech every year on United Fruit and Guatemala,
took to reading into the *Congressional Record* articles by executives of the Fruit Company that lavishly praised the firm's record in Latin America.[32]

By early 1954, Bernays' carefully planned campaign had
created an atmosphere of deep suspicion and fear in the United
States about the nature and intentions of the Guatemalan government. In the publicity battle between the Fruit Company and
the Arbenz government, Bernays outmaneuvered, outplanned and
outspent the Guatemalans. He was far ahead of them in technique, experience and political contacts. In fact, he won the
battle for the hearts and minds of Americans almost by default,
since there was never any organized effort by Guatemala to
present its side of the story in the U.S. press.

All of Bernays' hard work, however, meant nothing without
direct American intervention in Guatemala. The Fruit Company
could no longer in the post war era force a change of government
by itself. As early as 1947, the company had made a decision just
as shrewd—and similarly motivated—as its move to hire the
crafty Bernays several years before. It retained as its "inside"
lobbyist in Washington and "personal counsel" to Sam Zemurray
a savvy, engaging and very well-connected lawyer, Thomas G.

Corcoran, one of Franklin Roosevelt's original brain trusters. Like Bernays, "Tommy the Cork" had a liberal reputation and close ties to Democrats in Washington. He possessed a fine Irish wit and a wonderful flair for song and good times. Corcoran's presence gave Zemurray a "man at court," someone to help translate the growing public concern over Guatemala into concrete action. Zemurray always kept Corcoran's role a closely guarded secret. Bernays himself has claimed that he was not even told of Corcoran's hiring until the early 1950s.[33]

One of Corcoran's attractive assets to employers was his vast network of friends in Washington. "My function in this town," he once said, "is to bring people together." He had worked in the early 1940s to bring Zemurray and Nelson Rockefeller together behind a plan to import Central Americans to work in the labor-starved South. After his retention by Zemurray in the postwar years, Corcoran set as his task "to liberalize the Fruit Company in Central America." In furtherance of that goal, he enlisted a progressive ex-senator, Robert La Follette of Wisconsin, to assist him in his lobbying chores. With his reputation as an enlightened statesman, La Follette was the ideal choice to convince other liberals in Washington that Arbenz was no democrat, but a dangerous radical.[34]

Corcoran also had close friends in the Central Intelligence Agency, including Walter Bedell ("Beetle") Smith, CIA Director in the early 1950s, and the agency's Inspector General, Stewart Hadden. Corcoran had in addition served as counsel to a CIA-front airline, the Civil Air Transport Company (CAT), originally the celebrated Flying Tigers of World War II. The airline was organized by General Claire Chennault and his colleague Whiting Willauer, and later became Air America, and was used extensively in the Vietnam War. Corcoran justly claimed in a 1952 interview that his CIA contacts and other friends in government gave him the finest "intelligence service" in Washington.[35]

Guatemala, however, was a puzzle to Corcoran. The agrarian reform movement perplexed him. Though assigned to stop or moderate it, he did not know how. By 1952, Corcoran was working "overtime," according to a profile in *Fortune* magazine, to find out what American policy had been in Iran as a "guide to what [he] might or might not do to keep his client, United Fruit, from being thrown out of Guatemala." Corcoran had private information in 1951 and 1952 that the U.S. government had already considered intervention to protect the interests of the banana firm in Guatemala. "I knew from Hadden and Beetle," he later explained, "that the CIA was considering a plan. I didn't know the details." Actually, during this period Corcoran was acting as the Fruit Company's secret go-between in a CIA plot called Operation Fortune. The plan was to smuggle arms on United Fruit boats to Arbenz opponents. Nicaraguan dictator Somoza had offered to cooperate. At the last moment, however, the State Department got wind of the operation and blocked it.[36]

While the United States government vacillated, Corcoran stepped up his personal lobbying. In 1953, following Eisenhower's election, he sent La Follette to meet with the new State Department officials, including Thomas Mann, acting Assistant Secretary of State for Inter-American Affairs—the man who a dozen years later, in the same job, presided over the 1965 U.S. intervention in the Dominican Republic. La Follette pressed Mann to persuade the Eisenhower administration to join other Latin nations in "concerted action" against Guatemala's agrarian reform law and against "communist influence" in the country. Mann made no commitment, but took the occasion to ask La Follette's advice on whether the United States should maintain its military presence in Guatemala. La Follette responded that it would be in the U.S. interest to stay.[37]

At the same time, Corcoran approached his friend Walter Bedell Smith, whom Eisenhower had just shifted from the CIA directorship to the State Department as John Foster Dulles' undersecretary. Smith had been involved in the earlier Operation Fortune plot against Guatemala; at Corcoran's urging, he had now pressed Dulles to strike again at Arbenz. While Smith and Corcoran chatted, Smith conceded profound unhappiness about leaving the CIA to work for Dulles, whom he considered dogmatic and uncongenial. Smith wondered about the possibility of a job at the United Fruit Company.

Corcoran recalled: "Right after he became Undersecretary of State, Beetle told me of his desire to assume the presidency of

the United Fruit Company. He told me he always liked to watch
those pretty sailing ships on the Atlantic—the Great White
Fleet. I took the message to the Fruit Company. I told them:
'You have to have people who can tell you what's going on. He's
had a great background with his CIA association.' Their answer
was: 'He doesn't know anything about the banana business.
He'd have to take a subsidiary position.' I told them: 'For Chris-
sakes, your problem is not bananas, but you've got to handle
your political problem.'" Finally, in 1955, the company rewarded Smith for his help in the coup by appointing him to its
board of directors. "The last thing I did for the Fruit Company,"
Corcoran said, "was to get Beetle to go on the board."[38]

Corcoran at this juncture played a crucial role in prodding the
Eisenhower administration into action. "Tommy the Cork," wrote
one participant, began "lobbying in behalf of United Fruit and
against Arbenz. Following this special impetus, our project was
approved by the National Security Council . . ." The commentator was Howard Hunt, one of the key CIA figures in the anti-
Arbenz operation. Corcoran, he claimed, told Bedell Smith that
both Nicaragua and Honduras were prepared to act against Arbenz. Corcoran may also have had a role in arranging the appointment of his friend Whiting Willauer, an associate from
CAT days, to Honduras—Guatemala's southern neighbor—as
U.S. ambassador in 1954. Willauer's skills in directing secret air
strikes, learned under General Chennault in China with the Flying Tigers, were to come in handy when the decision was made
to bomb Guatemala.[39]

Corcoran became the United Fruit liaison with the CIA while
the conspiracy was being planned. "The Fruit Company was in
the middle," he later said. "We always had to be careful. We had
to know what was going on but we couldn't be in on it because
if the plan failed, this could hurt us. We knew what was going
on but we didn't want to get involved. The Fruit Company
didn't refuse to tell the CIA what it thought, but it couldn't
afford to let itself be caught."[40]

After the 1952 American election—when it became possible
that a plot against Arbenz might finally be realized—the banana
firm recognized that, to assure Arbenz's fall, it needed new allies
on the conservative end of the political spectrum, then in

resurgence. Having covered its liberal flank during the Roosevelt and Truman administrations via Bernays and Corcoran, it now sought to cover its right flank so it could reach politicians like Eisenhower and Senator Joseph McCarthy. Retaining Bernays and Corcoran in reserve, the company now enlisted Washington publicists and lobbyists with conservative connections. Zemurray engaged the right-wing John Clements Associates as a new public relations outfit for the company; he instructed it to focus exclusively on the issue of Guatemala. So secret was the work of John Clements Associates and so discreet was its lobbying that not even Bernays or Corcoran knew the firm had been given a contract.[41]

Clements, a stocky ex-Marine with a square Irish face topped by a flat crew cut of stiff white hair, was at the forefront of the McCarthyite "crusade" against Communism. Just as Bernays had been United Fruit's emissary to American liberals, Clements was closely tied to American conservatives. He was a vice-president of the jingoistic Hearst newspaper corporation, but he also headed his own p.r. firm, which represented Hearst interests as well as a select right-wing government and business clientele. He was, in addition, an editor of *The American Mercury*, a McCarthyite organ. He personally knew the whole roster of right-wing luminaries in the McCarthy firmament. He was a friend and sometime business partner of "Tacho" Somoza, the President of Nicaragua. He also was acquainted with other Caribbean strongmen and occasionally took on jobs for them. In producing "in-depth" studies for conservative customers, Clements had use of Hearst's International News Service (INS), a loose collection of correspondents and free-lancers, as a sort of global intelligence service. Like Bernays, Clements had his own list of 800 key "decision-makers" in the country; through Bernays and Clements, in fact, United Fruit reached influential leaders on the political right and left.[42]

The Fruit Company specifically commissioned Clements Associates in 1952 to produce a definitive report on Communist infiltration in the Guatemalan government. The choice of Clements to make the study indicated that United Fruit had now decided to take a hard line against Arbenz, since Clements' hostility to reformers—at home or abroad—was well known. As one observer wrote, "When you retained John Clements as your p.r. man, it was like renting a war machine." Clements' hastily written study predictably came up with a panorama of scheming Guatemalan Communists plotting to take over a corrupt administration run by a crypto-Marxist President, Arbenz. The document's account of supposed Soviet intrusion in the small nation was full of unsubstantiated "facts," exaggerations, scurrilous descriptions and bizarre historical theories. Much of its profuse detail and innuendo apparently came from disgruntled Guatemalan exiles as well as Fruit Company flacks.[43]

United Fruit paid Clements $35,000 for his 235-page study, which was entitled "Report on Guatemala—1952." Authorship was anonymous. Clements had it mimeographed in official-looking binders in June 1952 and then sent it to members of the U. S. Congress as well as his list of 800 "decision-makers." It was passed from hand to hand, and some of the defamatory "research" later found its way into the State Department's White Paper on Guatemala issued in 1954; into the Department's subsequent report "Intervention of International Communism in Guatemala"; into speeches at the United Nations; and into other official releases.[44]

His political and financial interest aroused, Clements was himself soon suggesting ways to oust Arbenz. In late 1953, he put together a second document, a shrill protest against America's refusal so far to overthrow the Guatemalan government. The 94-page study was called "Report on Central America 1954" and argued that Guatemala was ruled by a Communist regime bent on conquering Central America and seizing the Panama Canal. The slim volume soon found its way to the CIA, which, according to one knowledgeable journalist, "took charge of distributing [both] Clements reports to top government officials as the CIA's own."[45]

Clements later claimed to have been the man who discovered Castillo Armas as the "Liberator" of Guatemala. With Clements' links to influential legislators including Senator McCarthy and to the conservative press, he soon gained tacit approval from the Eisenhower administration to assume control of press relations for Castillo Armas' "Liberation Army." On behalf of his client United Fruit, Clements put together what one observer called a "campaign that was almost pure showboating—a paper war." Within months, he was boosting Castillo Armas in the U.S. press, airlifting American correspondents to interview the "Liberator" in his Honduran exile and feeding a steady supply of derogatory nuggets on Arbenz to anti-Guatemalan congressmen in the United States. Through one of the associates of his p.r. outfit—Patrick McMahon, also an editor at *The American Mercury*—Clements persuaded Congressman Patrick J. Hillings, a California Republican who was a protégé of Vice-President Richard Nixon (he succeeded to Nixon's seat), to hold hearings on Communist subversion in Guatemala.[46]

The hearings did not actually convene until after the coup, in August 1954. McMahon then served as a paid consultant to the Hillings subcommittee and helped prepare its report; at the same time, in a direct conflict of interest, he was doing public relations for Castillo Armas. Not surprisingly, John Clements Associates was officially hired by Castillo Armas immediately after the "Liberator" took power to represent his interests in the United States for a fee of $8,000 a month. (When Clements died in July 1975, Hearst Corporation executives seized and burned all his files, concerned that their contents might be controversial or possibly involve the Hearst Corporation in lawsuits.)[47]

Clements was not the last public relations expert placed on retainer by the company. Near the end of the 1940s, Zemurray took on Spruille Braden, who had been Truman's Assistant Secretary of State for Latin America in 1945-47, as a "corporate counsel" and occasional spokesman. Zemurray was apparently desirous that United Fruit have somebody on the payroll who had direct ties with the U.S. foreign service in Central and South America. Braden had served as ambassador to Colombia (1939-41), Cuba (1942) and Argentina (1945), and had been a roving emissary for Truman in Latin America.

Braden did not appear publicly in his new capacity until March 1953, when he made a widely reported address to a Dartmouth College symposium in which he attacked Eisenhower for failing to intervene in Guatemala in order to stop a Communist takeover. Braden declared that the suppression of Communism, "even by force, in an American country, by one or more of the other republics, would not constitute an intervention in the internal affairs of the former." He concluded: "It is necessary to fight fire with fire!" Though many newspapers reported the speech, none identified Braden as an employee of United Fruit. The attack created a stir within the Eisenhower administration, and also occasioned a harsh protest from the Guatemalan ambassador. (Soon afterward, the Guatemalan government stripped Braden of an award it had once bestowed on him.)[48]

With intimidating financial resources and shrewd planning, the United Fruit Company thus deployed a platoon of lobbyists and publicists at a cost of over a half million dollars a year to convince Americans that something evil was afoot in Guatemala. The company worked both the left and the right of the American political leadership and won the backing of both liberals and conservatives for its policies in Guatemala. This campaign, so ably executed by Edward Bernays, Thomas Corcoran, John Clements and Spruille Braden, had a remarkable impact on the U.S. government.

7

OPERATION SUCCESS

When Dwight Eisenhower assumed the presidency in January 1953, the press campaign aimed at Guatemala had not yet caught his interest. His most pressing foreign policy problem—outside of winding down the Korean War and dealing with the Soviet Union—was Iran, where Prime Minister Mohammed Mossadegh had nationalized the British oil companies and was publicly threatening the Shah's rule. A few months after entering the White House, the new President, at the urging of his Secretary of State, John Foster Dulles, gave the signal to launch a CIA coup in Iran. In August, CIA agents under the leadership of Kermit Roosevelt threw Mossadegh out of office and brought the Shah back from exile to the Peacock Throne.

Eisenhower's decision to use the CIA as a blunt instrument of political intervention marked a break from the practices of President Truman, who had used the CIA principally to collect intelligence. Kermit Roosevelt, as he himself later conceded, could not have undertaken such a mission in the previous administration. In his account of the Iranian operation, Roosevelt recalled that when British intelligence approached him in 1952 about overthrowing Mossadegh, he told them: "We had, I felt sure, no chance to win approval from the outgoing administration of Truman and Acheson. The new Republicans, however, might be different."[1]

The newcomers were different indeed. Eisenhower had assailed Truman's foreign policy during the 1952 campaign as "soft on Communism." Republican vice-presidential nominee Richard Nixon accused the Democrats of "twenty years of treason." Dulles, the likely Secretary of State, confidently told audiences that the Republicans would "roll back the Iron Curtain" in Eastern Europe. Privately, his brother Allen—already thought of as the probable Director of the CIA—informed associates that if Communists threatened to take over a country, he wouldn't "wait for an engraved invitation to come in and give aid."[2]

To accomplish their goals, the Republicans once in office acted to liberate the CIA from its Truman-imposed restrictions. The agency's original legislative charter in 1947 contained a phrase authorizing it to "perform such other functions and duties related to intelligence affecting the national security as the National Security Council may from time to time direct." Under this provision in 1948, the NSC had allowed the CIA to set up a covert political and paramilitary unit, which began its work directed by an intense New York lawyer named Frank Wisner, but otherwise the NSC kept the unit under tight control. With Dulles' ascension, however, the CIA embarked on an activist course.[3]

Kermit Roosevelt, on his return from Iran late in the summer of 1953, himself sensed that the agency's free-wheeling policy was already getting out of hand. When Roosevelt made his presentation at the White House about how the coup in Iran succeeded, he noted to his dismay that the Secretary of State's "eyes were gleaming; he seemed to be purring like a giant cat. Clearly he was enjoying what he was hearing, but my instincts told me that he was planning [something else] as well." Roosevelt decided it was important for him, as the acknowledged expert on covert operations, to warn the group—which included President Eisenhower—that future coups wouldn't work unless the people and the army in the country "want what we want." Dulles "did not want to hear what I was saying," Roosevelt remembered. "He was still leaning back in his chair with a catlike grin on his face. Within weeks I was offered command of a Guatemalan undertaking already in preparation. A quick check suggested that my requirements were not likely to be met. I declined the offer."[4]

Secretary of State Dulles was not the sort of person who would have taken much notice of Roosevelt's admonitions in any case. Once set on a course, he was not the type to be budged. He was, Winston Churchill once said, "the only case I know of a bull who carries his china shop with him." His objective was to demonstrate forcefully that the U.S. could "roll back" Communism and reverse "Marxist-Leninist takeovers" anywhere on the globe. Dulles, like religious zealots he often resembled, viewed the world in stark black and white; those countries not for him were against him. No distinctions among variants of neutralism, nationalism, socialism or Communism ever entered his head. Yet Dulles had enough of a survival instinct to realize that he could not, as he had promised during the campaign, simply force the Soviets out of Eastern Europe without provoking a world war. So he set out to do his "rolling back" on safer terrain.

Dulles had also ignored Kermit Roosevelt's warnings for another, more potent reason: he was currying political favor with the crusading right-wing constituency which had helped put Eisenhower into office in 1952. Dulles was determined to placate the recognized leader of American "super-patriots," Senator Joseph McCarthy. Soon after he took office, indeed, he hired a McCarthy associate, Scott McLeod, as Personnel and Security Officer for the State Department and assigned him to check the "loyalty" of all present and incoming department officials, especially new ambassadors. With this gesture to McCarthy, Dulles helped make the Wisconsin senator's view of the bipolar world respectable among State officials.

Among those pleased with the turn of events in Washington

was the United Fruit Company, so long frustrated by Truman's aversion to covert operations. In 1952, it had as noted earlier secured Truman's tentative backing for a plot against the Guatemalan government called Operation Fortune, originally promoted by the dictator of Nicaragua, Anastasio Somoza García. "Just give me the arms and I'll clean up Guatemala for you in no time," Somoza had told State Department officials. They paid little attention, but one of Truman's military aides, a Colonel Marrow, decided the plan had merit and persuaded Truman to endorse it.

Without telling the State Department, Truman gave General Walter Bedell Smith, then chief of the CIA, a go-ahead to proceed with the plot. Smith put Colonel J. C. King, Western Hemisphere director for the agency, in charge. Weapons were gathered and loaded aboard a boat owned by the United Fruit Company, whose chief officers were friendly with King from past operations, as "agricultural machinery" in cases to be shipped to a group of Guatemalan exiles and mercenaries in Nicaragua. Thomas Corcoran, the Fruit Company's counsel, acted as liaison with the CIA during Operation Fortune. Dictators Rafael Trujillo of the Dominican Republic and Marcos Pérez Jiménez of Venezuela, both right-wing anti-Communists, put up cash for the conspirators. But David Bruce, Undersecretary of State, learned of the freighter's sailing and was aghast. He went to his boss, Dean Acheson, who shared his misgivings and quickly persuaded Truman to abort the mission.[5]

After Eisenhower took office, United Fruit sought to resurrect an anti-Guatemalan plot, again using Corcoran as its emissary. The Dulles brothers—Secretary of State John and CIA Director Allen—were responsive to the idea. The Secretary of State had already approved a confidential memorandum stating: Unofficially we can support well-organized counter-revolutionary operations mounted from neighboring countries, if such support would contribute to their success." The brothers gave the job to Colonel J. C. King once again. Bruised by his first venture, King tried a new tack.[6]

The first expropriations of United Fruit land were just occurring in Guatemala. King approached disgruntled right-wing officers in the Guatemalan Army and arranged to send them CIA small arms. The United Fruit Company donated $64,000 in cash. Then just two weeks after Spruille Braden's incendiary speech at Dartmouth College in which he called for American intervention against the Arbenz regime, on March 29, 1953, two hundred raiders seized Salamá, a provincial capital not far from Guatemala City, and held it for seventeen hours. They were soon crushed by government forces, and uprisings planned in other villages fizzled. The government killed four of the captives during an "escape attempt" and jailed the rest. The rebels were quickly put on trial and revealed United Fruit's role in the plot, though not the CIA's.[7]

Following the abortive Salamá revolt, the U.S. government hardened its attitude toward Guatemala. Assistant Secretary of State for Inter-American Affairs John Moors Cabot (brother of Thomas Cabot, one-time president of United Fruit) had already —just a few days before Salamá—sent the Guatemalan government a blistering diplomatic note condemning its seizure of United Fruit land and demanding "just" compensation. He repeated this demand forcefully during a visit to Guatemala in April. On his return he informed the State Department: "The Foreign Minister was a complete jackass who talked endlessly without making any sense. President Arbenz had the pale, cold-lipped look of the ideologue and showed no interest in my suggestions for a change in his government's direction. He had obviously sold out to the Communists and that was that."

Cabot asked the State Department's intelligence unit to assess the impact of U.S. arms sales to countries near Guatemala. The study, in which the CIA also participated, was completed in June and concluded that providing arms to nearby countries hostile to Arbenz would be a clear enough threat to the Guatemalan military to induce it to withdraw support for Arbenz.[8]

Around the same time, Adolf Berle, Roosevelt brain truster and a leader of the New York Liberal Party, sent his own proposal on Guatemala to the White House. Ambassador to Brazil during the Truman administration, Berle had a long-standing interest in Latin America. His New York law firm represented several U.S. corporations operating in Central America, and he had friends at United Fruit—though he was not aware of the Administration's plans to overthrow Arbenz. Berle's memo proposed setting up a network of U.S. ambassadors in the five Central American nations and placing a "theater commander" in the area. Berle argued that the Guatemalan situation represented a "genuine penetration" of Central America by "Kremlin communism" following the "advance planning" of the Russian ambassador to Mexico in 1945, Constantine Oumansky. Berle agreed with President José Figueres of Costa Rica that Arbenz, though "not a communist," was "weak" and "probably a fellow-traveler." Though it is unclear whether Berle's memo ever reached the Dulles brothers, the final plan to depose Arbenz incorporated some of his suggestions.[9]

The Guatemalan ambassador in Washington, Guillermo Toriello, sensed the quickening pace of U.S. activity. He intensified his efforts to reach some sort of accommodation with the Eisenhower administration over the land expropriations. He met repeatedly with State Department officials—at a rate of once a month in the first half of 1953, talking with almost every major figure in the State Department's Latin America bureau— to no avail. In each meeting, Toriello tried to explain the rationale for his nation's agrarian reform act, but each time his explanations were rejected.[10]

Toriello's basic pitch was that the land reform law, having a general character applicable to Guatemalan and foreigner alike, was within the sovereign rights of the republic. He denied it discriminated against the Fruit Company as the firm charged, and asserted that the compensation offered was fair since it was based on the company's own valuation of the land's worth for tax purposes. He noted that the expropriations benefited a large number of landless peasants who lived in terrible poverty and also ended the unfair concessions given to the Fruit Company under Estrada Cabrera and Ubico. While Communists were few in number and generally "discredited" in his country, he added, they nonetheless had the right to exercise their civil liberties under the Guatemalan constitution. He urged the United States to lift its ban on selling arms and airplanes to Guatemala—a ban imposed in 1948 when the United States began to protest some of the social legislation of the revolutionary Guatemalan government—and hinted that a new arms arrangement might be the basis of an overall settlement between the two countries.[11]

American officials replied each time that the disagreements between the United States and Guatemala had nothing to do with the United Fruit Company, but rather concerned the failure of President Arbenz to oust Communists from his government. Until Arbenz did so, they said, relations would remain strained and there would be no American military supplies for Guatemala. As for the United Fruit controversy, the United States made clear its feeling that the seizure of Fruit Company land was "discriminatory" since of the first 337,000 acres taken over under the program, about two thirds belonged to the company. Moreover, the United States argued, the company required generous amounts of extra fallow land as protection in case banana diseases ravaged existing plantations. Without the additional acreage—85 percent of the company's land in Guatemala was uncultivated—the firm said, it might not be able to continue its operations. State Department officers also complained that compensation in bonds did not constitute "prompt or effective" payments under international law and that evaluation of land based on tax assessments was unfair since those assessments were below fair or real value. There was no indication of compromise in the U.S. approach, nor was there any hesitation on the part of the American government to act as an agent for the private corporation.[12]

Some American officials, though, argued for a more temperate course. Major General R. C. Partridge, who visited Guatemala in May 1953 to inspect the U.S. military missions in the country, wrote Cabot afterward that Arbenz's "land and other reforms [are] no basis to quarrel" and we should "approve [them] in principle" while making clear the U.S. desire that the Communists be eliminated from the regime. In a similar vein, a top-secret policy memorandum on Latin America produced by the National Security Council in March 1953 argued for a "hemisphere-wide" approach to problems like Guatemala and warned against unilateral intervention. José Figueres, the influential liberal (and fiercely anti-Communist) President of Costa Rica, also argued repeatedly against armed intervention in favor of collective political pressure.[13]

But such approaches, it was clear, did not appeal to the Dulles brothers. In their view, Arbenz's policy proved his regime

Communist in all but name. The Arbenz government's continuing employment of Communists in low-level posts was taken as a demonstration of bad faith and evil intent. But the takeover of United Fruit land was probably the decisive factor pushing the Americans into action. Without United Fruit's troubles, it seems probable that the Dulles brothers might not have paid such intense attention to the few Communists in Guatemala, since larger numbers had taken part in political activity on a greater scale during the postwar years in Brazil, Chile and Costa Rica without causing excessive concern in the U.S. government.[14]

United Fruit could also count on an especially receptive audience in the Eisenhower administration, particularly among the main players in the Guatemalan drama. John Foster Dulles had been a senior partner of the New York law firm of Sullivan and Cromwell, which did legal work for the international financial house J. Henry Schroder Banking Corporation. Schroder bank was the key financial adviser to the International Railways of Central America (IRCA), which owned most of Guatemala's train lines. In 1936, the United Fruit Company, holding a small interest in IRCA, sought to take over the railroad company to ensure its power to set transportation rates, as well as to block the entry of any rival banana operation into Guatemala. Dulles, as general counsel to Schroder, handled the negotiations, arranging a cozy deal with United Fruit at the expense of his putative client, IRCA, and reaping a tidy profit for the Schroder Banking Corporation.

Allen Dulles also did legal work for Sullivan and Cromwell in the 1920s and 1930s, often helping his brother on Schroder bank matters. Soon he was appointed to the board of directors of the bank. Schroder, meantime, maintained a share of stock in IRCA; indeed, as late as 1954, the president of Schroder was himself on the board of the railroad company, even while it was controlled by United Fruit. The Schroder bank was, coincidentally or not, a depository of secret CIA funds for covert operations.

Among other influential figures sympathetic to the company was John Moors Cabot, Assistant Secretary of State for Inter-American Affairs, whose family owned stock in United Fruit. His brother Thomas had served as president of the corporation in 1948. UN Ambassador Henry Cabot Lodge was a stockholder, too, and had been a vigorous public defender of United Fruit while a senator from Massachusetts. The wife of Edmund Whitman, the Fruit Company's public relations director, was Eisenhower's personal secretary, Anne Whitman. Undersecretary of State Bedell Smith was seeking an executive job with United Fruit while helping to plan the coup against Guatemala (he later was named to its board of directors). Robert Hill, ambassador to Costa Rica during the coup, was close to the Fruit Company hierarchy, having worked for Grace Shipping Lines, which had interests in Guatemala. In 1960, he also became a director of the corporation. Thus many of the significant figures behind the Guatemalan coup were intimately acquainted with high Fruit Company executives and naturally favored their views over those of a Central American government whose "Communism" they publicly abhorred and about which they knew little or nothing else.[15]

American national security considerations were never compelling in the case of Guatemala. State Department analysts in late 1953 treated the influence of Communists as relatively trivial except insofar as they had Arbenz's ear. The much-publicized claim that Guatemala could become a base for a Soviet seizure of the Panama Canal was also difficult to sustain. Guatemala had no diplomatic or military links to Russia or any Eastern European country except for its occasional meetings with officials from Czechoslovakia, from whom Guatemala ultimately purchased a single arms shipment in cash. No serious evidence ever turned up after the coup establishing a secret tie to the Soviets. Furthermore, the country, which sits 800 miles from the Canal, at the time maintained only a tiny, non-functional air force with a range of barely 300 miles. Guatemala had only one airport capable of handling jets, but U.S. observers could watch it at all times.[16]

The principal evidence offered by Americans to justify fears of subversion in Guatemala was the land reform program, particularly as it affected United Fruit. Such writers as Daniel James of *The New Leader* warned that Communists would use the program as a steppingstone to take over Guatemala. Several U.S. congressmen saw a disturbing similarity between the nationalization of oil companies in Iran and the expropriations of Fruit

Company land in Guatemala—though both were accomplished legally under local law. The American public, heavily conditioned by Edward Bernays' press campaigns, had also already located the enemy: Communism.

By the summer of 1953, the U.S. was moving toward a showdown. Pushing arguments for moderation aside, John Foster Dulles and his brother Allen—who in his memoirs referred to Arbenz as a "stooge" of the Russians—decided that the CIA would direct the strike. No further bungled attempts by local operatives would be tolerated. Given the blood ties between the chiefs of the State Department and the CIA, the final authorization for the mission did not take long. As Howard Hunt wrote: "A word from one [brother] to the other substituted for weeks of inter- and intra-agency debate."[17]

The official decision to move against Arbenz was made in early August 1953, at a meeting of the 10/2 committee, charged by the National Security Council with supervision of covert operations. Its members included Allen Dulles; Undersecretary of State Bedell Smith; C. D. Jackson, Eisenhower's psychological warfare adviser; an aide to the Defense Secretary, Charles Wilson; and Robert Cutler, the special presidential assistant for National Security Affairs. Not all were present at the August session; Cutler, for example, did not know about the operation. Nor did one non-member, the Assistant Secretary of State for Inter-American Affairs John Moors Cabot know about the putsch. (He later recalled that he went to Bedell Smith in early fall to insist on a "CIA-organized coup." Bedell Smith "nodded and smiled" and gave him the impression that the plan was already under way.) Eisenhower gave his approval for the plot against Arbenz after Allen Dulles told him that the odds of success were better than 40 percent but less than even. But the President hedged on a final commitment. His *modus operandi* since World War II had been to prepare forces and then decide at the last moment whether to use them or not.[18]

Once the plan received official sanction, the CIA and State Department began to divide up responsibilities for its execution. Having already botched up Operation Fortune and the Salamá revolt, the agency took great pains this time to prepare thoroughly for the coup and not leave its success hostage to unreliable conspirators. Frank Wisner, the CIA's deputy director for "plans" (i.e., operations), was in command. He had served as Mission Chief for the CIA's predecessor, the Office of Strategic Services (OSS), in Istanbul and Bucharest during World War II, and had abandoned a prestigious law firm in Manhattan after the war to return to the dark arts in 1947. He quickly assigned his urbane deputy, Tracy Barnes, a product of Groton, Yale and Harvard Law School, to help hire operatives and work out logistics. The plot was code-named Operation Success, reflecting the optimism of its creators. Wisner and his crew immediately began daily meetings on Guatemala.[19]

Wisner's first major decision was to choose a field commander. Once Kermit Roosevelt had turned Dulles down, Wisner approached Colonel Albert Haney, then CIA station chief in South Korea. Haney was a handsome, rugged six-footer who had left a Chicago business career fourteen years before to enlist in army counterintelligence. He had gained renown within the agency for rounding up alleged Gestapo agents in the Canal Zone during the war.

After the war Haney joined the CIA, to the dismay of his heiress wife, who wanted him to return to business. The Haneys moved to Ecuador and Chile for the CIA, living rather expensively in accordance with Mrs. Haney's tastes. When the agency reassigned Haney to Korea in 1951, his wife refused to accompany him. She soon divorced him. During Haney's term in Seoul, he rapidly built up a crack guerrilla network inside North Korea which won the respect of his superiors. While there, he found as an aide a man named "Rip" Robertson, a CIA paramilitary trainer who once worked on Saipan. Robertson, a tall, husky former college football hero, enjoyed accompanying his Korean guerrillas into Communist territory, in disobedience of orders from Washington.

Allen Dulles summoned Haney to Washington late in October 1953, briefed him about the Guatemalan operation and asked him to direct it. Haney accepted on the spot. Dulles gave Haney carte blanche authority and told him to report directly from that moment on to Deputy Director Wisner. That order—which in effect cut Haney's operation loose from the CIA's Latin America division—was a calculated rebuff to J. C. King, chief of Western

Hemisphere operations, and put Haney on an inevitable collision course with King. King soon called Haney into his office in the CIA building near Washington's reflecting pool and gave him some "friendly" advice. He suggested that Haney meet with Tom Corcoran, United Fruit's Washington lobbyist, to work out arrangements to get hold of the guns from the failed Operation Fortune—then gathering dust in a New York warehouse—and move them back to Nicaragua for use by the Guatemalan exile forces. Haney didn't like the idea and said so. King exploded: "If you think you can run this operation without United Fruit, you're crazy!" From that moment, King was an active bureaucratic foe of Haney's.[20]

Haney lost no time in using the authority he had received from Allen Dulles and Frank Wisner. In November, he submitted a preliminary plan for the Guatemala operation. It proposed an autonomous agency-wide task force to coordinate preparations for the coup, based at the Opa-Locka Marine Air Base in Miami—placing the headquarters far from Washington. The task force chief, Haney proposed, would exercise broad authority over CIA station chiefs in Central America and receive a free tactical hand while leaving strategic decisions to Wisner and Dulles. Haney envisioned a campaign of psychological warfare against Arbenz, rather than direct military action. Richard Bissell, who was brought in to serve as Allen Dulles' special assistant just before the coup, speculated later that Haney's approach was largely dictated by the belief that the CIA would be unable to muster sufficient military force for an invasion or an internal coup without vast outside pressure. There were too few exiles to mount a serious assault over the border, and Arbenz had too much support in Guatemala for the sort of "spontaneous" uprising the CIA had engineered in Iran. As Haney saw it, Arbenz's survival was dependent on the loyalty of the Army, so the objective must be to subvert that loyalty. As for the unions, rural workers and city dwellers who supported Arbenz, the objective was to demoralize them and convince them that Arbenz was finished.[21]

Haney proposed that the operation begin in January 1954 with small-scale psychological harassment and escalate gradually in intensity over six months to larger and more ambitious schemes, culminating in an "invasion" before the rainy season began in July. The idea of assassinating Arbenz with a "silent bullet" was considered and discarded for fear of making him a martyr. Haney's thought, rather, was to bribe Arbenz into resigning. If that didn't work, the CIA would encourage dissension within the Guatemalan Army and help the plotters to launch a bloodless coup. Haney proposed two additional elements: a propaganda campaign by radio and leaflet to frighten the populace and foment violence; and the training of about 300 mercenaries and Guatemalan exiles to infiltrate Guatemala, half to commit acts of sabotage, and the other half to pose as the "spearhead" of a fictitious invasion force. In addition, the CIA would jam Guatemala's radio stations and transmit false messages on its own radio and over army channels—all to disconcert the population.[22]

Haney warned that, as a last resort, the United States might have to send in Marines under the pretext of protecting the safety of American citizens. (The United States had landed troops in Guatemala once before—for eighteen days in 1920 to protect the American Legation during civil violence.) All concerned hoped this final drastic step would be unnecessary. Besides running the risk of turning all of Latin America against the United States and patently violating the Good Neighbor policy of Franklin Roosevelt as well as the OAS and UN charters, an invasion would also force Allen Dulles into a bureaucratic danger—taking the Joint Chiefs of Staff into his confidence. With the Army and Navy involved, the operation might balloon in size to the point that Eisenhower, the ever-cautious chief executive, might turn it down. So Dulles deliberately decided to limit the role of U.S. land and sea forces in the final proposal, permitting only narrow logistical support for U.S. pilots flying for the exile forces during the coup, and allowing for force only if absolutely necessary. Still, almost a dozen U. S. Navy ships and submarines were gathered under the plan and a battalion of airborne Marines were put on standby at Camp Lejeune, North Carolina, during the weeks preceding the coup. Twelve C-47 transports, a unit of National Guard planes from Puerto Rico and fifteen helicopters were also placed on alert.[23]

Haney provided a budget estimate of $4.5 million, though

others later claimed the operation actually cost closer to $20 million. Allen Dulles called the plan "brilliant." Western Hemisphere chief J. C. King was subdued; privately he told associates the plan was too large, too public and too impossible to keep covert. Wisner had similar reservations; he feared that the amount of equipment and personnel that Haney's scheme required would make it difficult to keep the American role secret. He also worried that Haney's autonomy might tempt him to make decisions in the heat of battle that might run counter to the CIA's wishes. Dulles breezily dismissed all objections.[24]

But within a few weeks King, increasingly morose and troubled, began an internal counterattack. When Haney returned from a brief visit to Opa-Locka in early January 1954, King presented new disagreements to Wisner. The Guatemalan plan, he said, was a throwback to Haney's Korean tactics of using guerrillas to overthrow governments. "He'll be starting a civil war in the middle of Central America," King told Wisner. "Do we want another Korean War right at our doorstep?" Instead, why not "kill 'em with kindness," King suggested, by providing the Guatemalan Army with a massive aid program in exchange for its ouster of Arbenz. Wisner replied: "J.C., you've had four years to try that approach. Now the situation is worse than ever."

The question of whether to approve Haney's plan for Operation Success over King's objections was quickly passed up to Allen Dulles. In turn, he decided that only his older brother could make the final determination. He promised to chat with the Secretary of State. He told his CIA subordinates he would transmit the decision at cocktails at his "Highlands" estate in Georgetown. Wisner, King and Haney assembled to await their boss. The Director made a dramatic entrance. He walked directly up to Haney and said with a grim look on his face: "Colonel, there's one question I want to ask you. Do you really think you can succeed?"

"Sir," Haney answered, "with your help, we can win."

Dulles grinned and slapped his hands on Haney's shoulders. "Then go to it, my boy," he laughed. "You've got the green light."

Without a word, J. C. King strode out of the room.[25]

From then on, Haney was in unchallenged control. He made

Guatemala's 1944 revolution brought the downfall of the nation's last old-style military dictator, General Jorge Ubico. (Credit: José Francisco Muñoz)

Until elections could be held, the country was ruled by a triumvirate made up of (left to right) Major Francisco Arana, businessman Jorge Toriello and Captain Jacobo Arbenz. The two young officers led the revolt that toppled the dictatorship but later broke over the course of the new government. (Credit: Rafael Morales)

Juan José Arévalo was forty-two years old when he became Guatemala's first popularly elected President in 1945. He is seen here on the day he took office. Wearing the ceremonial sash, he declared in his inaugural address that his administration would be "a period of sympathy for the man who works in the fields, in the shops, on the military bases, in small businesses." (Credit: Rafael Morales)

Arévalo's successor was one of the heroes of the 1944 uprising, Jacobo Arbenz. He wanted to transform Guatemala "from a backward country with a predominantly feudal economy into a modern capitalist state." (Credit: Rafael Morales)

Sam "the Banana Man" Zemurray of United Fruit standing on one of the two sprawling plantations the company maintained in Guatemala. After President Arbenz took over some of United Fruit's unused land, the Boston-based company asked the CIA to overthrow him. (Credit: Eliot Elisofon, *Life*, © 1951 Time, Inc.)

Charges of Communist influence dogged the Arbenz regime. The two leading Guatemalan Communists in the early 1950's were young organizers Victor Manuel Gutiérrez (left) and José Manuel Fortuny (right). (Credit: Rafael Morales)

Arbenz's wife, Maria Vilanova, skillfully manipulated on behalf of her husband's career and sometimes seemed more ambitious for him than he was for himself. The couple is shown here while Arbenz was President. (Credit: Wide World Photos)

When the United States decided to overthrow Arbenz, the State Department replaced the mild-mannered American ambassador to Guatemala with tough-talking, flamboyant John E. Peurifoy, seen here holding copies of leftist newspapers. (Credit: Wide World Photos)

The most forceful defender of Guatemalan democracy in international forums was Foreign Minister Guillermo Toriello, seen here with President Arbenz. (Credit: Wide World Photos)

Secretary of State John Foster Dulles (seated at right) personally led the American delegation to the Tenth Inter-American Conference at Caracas, Venezuela, in March 1954. He spent two weeks there lobbying for passage of a resolution condemning Communism in the Americas—a proclamation Dulles thought he might need to justify the Guatemalan coup he was planning. Among those present in Caracas was Guatemalan Foreign Minister Guillermo Toriello (left). (Credit: Wide World Photos)

CIA Director Allen Dulles was the godfather of Operation Success, the plot to overthrow Arbenz. (Credit: UPI Photo)

American pilots paid by the CIA flew air raids for the rebel forces. One struck a gasoline storage depot (top) and another bombed Fort Matamoros, a key military installation in the capital (bottom). (Credit: Top—Wide World Photos; bottom—Leonard McCombe, *Life,* ©Time, Inc.)

The military government of Honduras, which strongly supported the U.S.-backed rebels, complained at the height of the battle that it had been bombed by Guatemalan planes. But photographers who visited the site of the "attack," the small Honduran town of San Pedro de Cobán, found only this unexploded bomb and no damage. (Credit: Wide World Photos)

frequent visits to Opa-Locka to supervise the construction of his headquarters. He carefully arranged to conceal a complex of offices just above a children's nursery. He installed more than a hundred security personnel, project officers in military reserve uniforms and female secretaries, as well as telexes, heavy cables and communications equipment. He lined the walls of the operations room with a forty-foot chart, on which the phases of the plan were laid out in detail, as if they were part of a factory production schedule. He subdivided each chronological phase into categories: defection efforts, logistic preparations, exile organizations, propaganda and paramilitary readiness. Though the Opa-Locka base was semi-deserted, the whirlwind of activity around the two-story barracks soon attracted the curiosity of other military men in the area. No word leaked out about the nature of the operation, however.[26]

Meantime in Guatemala, Haney's operatives began their efforts to bribe Arbenz. Haney had a large sum of money deposited in a Swiss bank for Arbenz. But the Guatemalan President—or his subordinates—rejected the offer. Haney's early attempts to induce Guatemalan Army officers to turn on Arbenz also failed. His staff at Opa-Locka had closely studied the records of every member of the Guatemalan officer corps. Haney's emissary to them, a former CIA station chief in Berlin with a German accent named Henry Heckscher, went to Guatemala to see the army officers disguised as a coffee buyer with a straw hat and dark glasses, but was unable to foment a revolt. Arbenz had wisely packed the Army with loyalists and cautious career men; they were unwilling to move against him at this stage.[27]

In Florida, Haney now began to recruit men and equipment for paramilitary raids, propaganda attacks and the token "invasion." Hoping to use Nicaragua as a supply and training base, he needed the full cooperation of Nicaraguan dictator Anastasio Somoza García. Over King's objections, Haney brought in his commando sidekick from Korea, Rip Robertson, to handle the Nicaraguan negotiations. Pretending to be an American businessman organizing opposition to Arbenz, Robertson secretly flew to Nicaragua to confer with Somoza. Somoza enthusiastically agreed to the CIA plans and assigned his son Tachito to be his daily liaison with Robertson.[28]

With Somoza's blessing, Haney set up training camps in Nicaragua in February. One was on Somoza's plantation, El Tamarindo, and was used to instruct about 150 men in sabotage and demolition. Another 150 exiles and mercenaries went to the volcanic island of Momotombito in Lake Managua for weapons training. Finally Haney assigned a small group of about a dozens pilots to an airstrip at Puerto Cabezas on the Atlantic coast (the same airstrip used for the Bay of Pigs invasion of Cuba seven years later). He also established a radio camp near the Nicaraguan capital, Managua, to acquaint a few of the men with broadcasting techniques.[29] He began to place hidden communications stations around the perimeters of Guatemala: one in Managua; one in the Dominican Republic; one in Honduras (where the newly appointed U.S. ambassador, former Flying Tiger Whiting Willauer, helped pressure a reluctant government into cooperation with the CIA); and two in Guatemala itself, one actually inside the U. S. Embassy. Some of the stations were equipped with jamming devices and others were programmed to broadcast on the same wavelengths as Guatemala's regular radio stations. Haney also kept one transmitter in reserve on Swan Island off Honduras' Atlantic coast in case the others were discovered.[30]

Wisner's top assistant, Tracy Barnes, had selected as the operation's political and propaganda chief a CIA veteran, later notorious in the Watergate scandal, E. Howard Hunt. Equipped with an alias, authentic but non-functional credit cards, bank references and a sheaf of other phony documents, the bilingual Hunt joined Haney at Opa-Locka. He soon began periodic forays to countries bordering Guatemala, including Mexico, where he had served in the CIA station in the early 1950s. He recruited David Atlee Phillips, an ex-actor who had worked with the CIA on several previous projects, as his deputy for the duration of Operation Success. Returning to Florida, Hunt settled in with Phillips to prepare a vast quantity of prerecorded radio "terror broadcasts," articles, pamphlets and leaflets, all in Spanish, for dissemination throughout Guatemala. Hunt also brought in three Guatemalan exiles to be trained by Phillips for eight weeks in the art of waging "psychological warfare" by radio. He even flew in girlfriends for them from Central America when they grew restless.[31]

Through a former CIA employee, Samuel Cummings, the CIA set up a dummy arms company, called the International Armament Corporation (InterArmco), and endowed the company with over $100,000 in capital. InterArmco began to supply the CIA-organized "Liberation Army" with rifles, submachine guns and 50-mm. mortars. The CIA stashed many of the arms in the Panama Canal Zone and from there gradually distributed them to the rebels. Other CIA units gathered Soviet-marked weapons to plant inside Guatemala just before the invasion to reinforce American charges that the Russians were trying to establish a foothold in the country.[32]

The agency also provided the exiles more than thirty planes for use in the "Liberation." In order to disguise U.S. ownership, Allen Dulles persuaded a secretive American entrepreneur of right-wing views to set up a "charitable foundation" in December 1953 in Miami in the form of a Medical Institute. The financier's aircraft company then bought a number of war-surplus fighter planes, and donated them to the Institute as tax-deductible charitable contributions. The Medical Institute then sold the planes to "private firms," taking the proceeds of the sales as non-taxable income under the Institute's tax-free status. The purchasers of the planes were actually CIA "front" corporations in the Caribbean ostensibly engaged in aerial photography, crop dusting and recreational aviation. The Institute's income from the sales later went as awards to "medical research" organizations who used the cash to pay the salaries of the CIA's mercenary pilots and air mechanics. In addition, selected National Guard units in the deep South loaned planes to the CIA, which in turn "rented" them to the government of Nicaragua for $1 apiece.[33]

The U.S. managed gradually to sneak many of its planes into Honduras and Nicaragua and the Canal Zone under the cover of "arms assistance" to the two nations. The U.S. sent down at least six aging Thunderbolt P-47s (also called F-47s) and three P-51 fighter-bombers (also called F-51s), none of which had ever been seen in Latin air forces. They also held a dozen C-47 trans-

ports in readiness in the Panama Canal Zone. In addition, the
CIA came up with a Cessna 180, a PBY-5 naval patrol bomber
and a P-38 fighter. It also had access to chartered DC-3s. Despite its makeshift nature and appearance, this air force was actually overwhelming by Guatemalan standards, designed to
scare, if not bomb, the Arbenz government into submission.[34]

Since there were few exile airmen available, Haney had to recruit American pilots for the "Liberation Air Force." For the
most part, the pilots were men who lived in the area, some of
whom held Guatemalan citizenship. Others were employees of
the CIA's Civil Air Transport Company (CAT, formerly the Flying Tigers), whose ex-director, Whiting Willauer, was conveniently stationed in Honduras. Lawrence Houston, general counsel of the CIA, later admitted: "We brought over CAT pilots to
do the training and maintenance of the Liberation Air Force before the coup." Indeed, in early June, a self-styled State Department "covert operation," run by William Pawley, a right-wing
businessman on temporary assignment to the government, helped
sneak ten American airmen into Nicaragua via Havana—despite
at one time an embarrassing discovery of the band by FBI agents
in Cuba. Among the pilots Haney and Willauer found were William Beall, a thirty-year-old American flier from Tyler, Texas;
Jerry Fred DeLarm, a former U.S. naval pilot, a native of San
Francisco who gave flying lessons and had an auto dealership in
Guatemala; Fred Sherwood, onetime U.S. air attaché in Guatemala; Ferdinand F. Schoup, a former deputy chief of the U. S.
Air Force Mission in Guatemala then employed as a pilot by the
United Fruit Company; Carlos Cheeseman, who served as a U.S.
naval pilot in World War II but had become a Guatemalan citizen; Joseph Silverthorne, an American bush pilot under CIA contract; a native of Delaware, "T-Bone" Williams, and his friend
Bob Wade, two ex-Marine fliers; Leo Crutcher, a U.S. citizen
living in Colombia; and Douglas McLean, Crutcher's son-in-law.
The pilots earned $500 a month during the planning and training
stage; once they began bombing, their wages increased to $1,000
a month. The leaflet and supply runs were flown by C-47s based
in Honduras; the strafing and bombing was handled by P-47s
and P-51s stationed in Nicaragua.[35]

As operations in Florida were taking shape, J. C. King once

again raised objections. He had sent one of his deputies, an intelligence officer newly returned from Rome who was also a relative of Allen Dulles, to visit Opa-Locka in early 1954. The deputy was upset by Haney's paramilitary plans, including the air raids. "What Teddy Roosevelt did in Panama," he warned Haney, "will pale by comparison with what you're planning to do in Guatemala. You'll start a civil war and have the blood of thousands on your hands!" Wisner was beginning to share some of King's doubts. Haney had a habit of asking for more men and more weapons at regular intervals—often unnecessarily, in Wisner's view. And several of King's own people had dropped out of Operation Success rather than participate in a plan which their boss so vigorously opposed.[36]

Finally both Dulles and Wisner visited Haney's headquarters in Florida to see for themselves. The trip eased their fears. Wisner, as a gesture of confidence—and as a way of keeping King at bay in the future—named his own assistant, Tracy Barnes, as Haney's permanent contact at CIA headquarters. Barnes began to spend more and more of his time in Florida. Operation Success, the CIA plot to overthrow the Guatemalan government, had won a final go-ahead.[37]

8

THE LIBERATOR

Before the CIA could progress into its final planning, it had to recruit one more key actor: a Guatemalan exile to lead the "Liberation" forces. The United Fruit Company was especially preoccupied with the choice because its future in the country lay in the hands of the new leader. The man chosen for this role did not need great military skills, since his army was not expected to do much fighting. But the Fruit Company would have to deal with him once he took power, and it wanted someone suitably pliable. The company's ubiquitous lobbyist, Thomas Corcoran, who had prodded Washington into action, now sought assurances that United Fruit's interests would be "looked after" following Arbenz's removal.

Very troubling to the Fruit Company was the exclusion of

J. C. King from the pre-coup deliberations. King had been the company's top contact at the CIA. He had worked with United Fruit in planning and carrying out the abortive Operation Fortune and the short-lived Salamá uprising. As a former representative of Johnson & Johnson Pharmaceutical interests in Latin America for twenty years, he was a strong supporter of American companies abroad and would guarantee that any post-coup government returned all of the Fruit Company's land forthwith. There would be no need to seek "assurances" if King were masterminding things. But, despite King's exclusion, the company had other intimate friends at the top. At some point during the preparations for the invasion, a United Fruit official—possibly Corcoran—met privately with Allen Dulles to discuss the status of United Fruit properties following Arbenz's downfall. Dulles promised that whoever was selected by the CIA as the next Guatemalan leader would not be allowed to nationalize or in any way disrupt the company's operations. He even urged the company to take a role in the search for the expedition's commander.[1]

The first exile approached by the CIA, together with the Fruit Company, was General Miguel Ydígoras Fuentes, a former official of the Ubico dictatorship who had gained some renown as a prickly and corrupt right-wing politician with a modest conservative following and some leadership ability. He had contested the presidential election of 1950, finishing a poor second behind Arbenz in an election he always grumbled was fraudulent. Since then, he had been living in El Salvador, dreaming of another chance.

Ydígoras, however, had a reputation for opportunism and a bent toward military repression. He had spent most of his life in the Guatemalan Army, where he displayed dishonesty and cruelty. Critics charged that he was especially hostile toward Indians, and he was accused of ordering several massacres while an officer under Ubico. He had also zealously enforced harsh "vagrancy" laws requiring Indians to work at least 150 days per year for local landowners and even executed peasants who slipped over from Mexico to sell homemade baskets. In 1944, he had tried to act as an intermediary between Ubico and the Guatemalan revolutionaries in order to grab power for himself.[2]

"A former executive of the United Fruit Company, now retired, Mr. Walter Turnbull, came to see me," Ydígoras later wrote in his autobiography, *My War with Communism*, accompanied by "two gentlemen whom he introduced as agents of the CIA." This was in late 1953. "They said I was a popular figure in Guatemala and that they wanted to lend assistance to overthrow Arbenz." Ydígoras was interested, but he wanted to know what their conditions would be. "Among other things," he recalled, "I was to promise to favor the United Fruit Company and the International Railways of Central America; to destroy the railroad workers labor union; to suspend claims against Great Britain for the Belize territory; to establish a strong-arm government, on the style of Ubico . . . Further, I was to pay back every cent that was invested in the undertaking on the basis of accounts that would be presented to me afterwards." Even Ydígoras' flexible scruples were offended. He called the conditions "abusive and inequitable" and asked for time to prepare a counter-offer. The three strangers agreed, but, apparently sensing that Ydígoras was not their man, never returned. Turnbull was the United Fruit official who had earlier handled sensitive wage negotiations with the Guatemalan government.[3]

Howard Hunt later maintained that the State Department vetoed Ydígoras as leader of the "Liberation" forces because he was too "authoritarian" in temperament and a "right-wing reactionary." Hunt also offered another interesting rationale, suggesting that Ydígoras was objectionable because he looked too much like a Spanish nobleman. He remarked of Ydígoras: "You don't rally a country made up of *mestizos* with a Spanish don." But Ydígoras himself was probably more accurate when he surmised that his own "unmanageability" decided the case against him.[4]

United Fruit next proposed its own candidate to the U.S. government, calling him vastly preferable to Ydígoras: a Guatemalan lawyer and coffee grower named Juan Córdova Cerna. Corcoran curiously called Córdova Cerna "the liberal" among the exiles. He expected that, since Córdova Cerna had long served the Fruit Company as a paid legal adviser, he would, if he achieved power, certainly be disposed to return all of the company's land to its "rightful" owner. Córdova Cerna's name had cropped up as a possible Guatemalan leader in connection with Operation Fortune and the Salamá rebellion, both conspiracies sponsored by the banana company. He had served briefly as Minister of Justice under the interim junta that ruled in 1944–45 following the overthrow of the Ubico-Ponce dictatorship. After his son's death in a short-lived revolt against the government in late 1950, however, Córdova Cerna became an active conspirator against Arbenz.[5]

Howard Hunt also cast his vote for Córdova Cerna because he considered the sophisticated Guatemalan "a distinguished and respected jurist" and because he favored a civilian exile as opposed to a military type like Ydígoras. Hunt went so far as to meet secretly with Córdova Cerna in a room at the Mexico City YMCA. But Córdova Cerna ultimately lost out because he was hospitalized with throat cancer in New Orleans at a crucial moment in the pre-invasion maneuvering. As a third choice, Córdova Cerna suggested his friend Colonel Carlos Castillo Armas.[6]

Castillo Armas seemed a natural, if less than ideal, choice after Ydígoras and Córdova Cerna were eliminated. He had no strong ideology beyond simple nationalism and anti-Communism. But he "had that good Indian look about him. He looked like an Indian, which was great for the people," Howard Hunt recalled. He had also a vaguely heroic reputation among the exiles and was considered malleable as far as the CIA and United Fruit were concerned. "They picked Castillo Armas," a former *Time* magazine correspondent remarked flatly, "because he was younger than Ydígoras, but also because he was a stupid man." One of the CIA agents agreed. "He was a small, humble, thin guy," said Fred Sherwood, who led Castillo Armas' air force. "He didn't know what he was doing. He was in way over his head." Other CIA officials had a more pragmatic reason. The "paramilitary people" liked Castillo Armas because he was a military commander. Since the invasion was going to be billed as a military operation, they reasoned, a known military leader would add credibility to the fiction that Operation Success was simply a domestic uprising.[7]

Castillo Armas was born in 1914, the illegitimate child of a landowner who abandoned him to the care of his poor mother. He attended Guatemala's "West Point," the Escuela Politécnica, with Jacobo Arbenz and was then trained at Fort Leavenworth in the United States, where he made many friends within the American military. President Arévalo appointed him director of the Politécnica, but he quit after the 1949 assassination of Colonel Arana, whom he revered.[8]

On November 5, 1950, Castillo Armas led seventy men in rebellion against the Guatemalan government and tried to capture the Aurora military base. The uprising failed, sixteen of his followers were killed and ten, including Castillo Armas himself, were wounded. His captors were dragging him to a cemetery when he emitted a moan. They rushed him to a hospital. He recovered from a bad foot wound and was condemned to death and imprisoned in Guatemala City. Six months later he pulled off a surprise escape, apparently through an IRCA railroad tunnel. The story had it that Castillo Armas had made friends in prison with an architect who provided him with the floor plan of the jail. He supposedly discovered the tunnel just two days before he was to face the firing squad. True or not, the dramatic escape "put him high on the list," according to one historian, "of macho heroes for many Guatemalans." Some observers, however, wondered if Arbenz had not allowed Castillo Armas to flee just to be rid of him. And Ydígoras came to believe Castillo Armas got out not through any tunnel, but by a more traditional route: bribery.[9]

Castillo Armas soon became a familiar figure in anti-Arbenz circles outside Guatemala. One commentator described him as "short, slender, almost petite. Always immaculate, he looked as though he had been packaged by Bloomingdale's. But he was personally brave. He had a dreamy air about him, almost mystical, or perhaps just plain dopey." He was certainly willing and anxious to play a role in any uprising against Arbenz. At times he made overtures toward the peasants, promising that he would repeal Arbenz's agrarian reform measure and replace it with a "real" law granting laborers full ownership of the land. He also held his fellow exile leaders in contempt. He came to picture himself as his country's only possible liberator. After his escape from prison, Colombian authorities following Latin tradition granted him political asylum. In 1952, he moved to Honduras, where he soon supported himself with various jobs, including a stint as a furniture salesman.[10]

Well before the CIA's involvement, Castillo Armas had been casting about for someone to sponsor a military strike against Guatemala. In 1952, he received funds, estimated at around $60,000, from the dictator of the Dominican Republic, Rafael Trujillo, who held a long-standing grudge against the Guatemalan regime. President Arévalo had permitted members of the so-called Caribbean Legion—a loose-knit band of liberals, reformers and revolutionaries seeking to bring down tyrants in the region—to take refuge in his country. At one point (June 19, 1949), the Legion carried out a military foray from Guatemala in a vain effort to topple Trujillo. Thereafter Trujillo sought revenge, repeatedly supporting counterrevolutions, first through a right-wing Ubico functionary named Roberto Barrios y Peña, for a time Ydígoras and finally Castillo Armas.

Trujillo's cash inadvertently precipitated a fight within Castillo Armas' ranks between a pro-Trujillo wing and a more nationalist faction. The two groups have been portrayed as the reactionary and the more moderate sides of the "liberation" movement, but the battle was really over the division of spoils. The struggle later poisoned Trujillo's relations with Castillo Armas. At the time, however, it was an internal contest with no apparent victor. In any event, Trujillo gained some repayment after the coup: Castillo Armas adopted his motto "God, Fatherland and Liberty" and hired some of the dictator's Dominican agents for his security forces.[11]

Castillo Armas also acted at this time to forge an alliance with Ydígoras, his only serious rival. On March 31, 1952, he left his home in Honduras to meet with Ydígoras in the capital of neighboring El Salvador. There he informed Ydígoras that he was receiving "substantial economic assistance and large quantities of arms" from Trujillo and had the "promise of assistance from official U.S. agencies"—although nothing concrete yet—as well as "offers" of help from Honduras and Nicaragua. After some negotiations, the colonel and the general initialed a "gentleman's agreement" under which Castillo Armas assumed supreme command of the counterrevolutionary troops and then arranged to serve as provisional President. Ydígoras agreed to abstain from a role in the invasion to preserve his "civil status" and thus be eligible to run for President after Arbenz's fall. Whether Castillo

Armas really had any tangible support other than Trujillo's money is unclear, but by the agreement he shrewdly neutralized Ydígoras and, by doing so, made himself the logical choice to lead the CIA "invasion" force.[12]

The two men met again on August 13 and 14, 1953, at Castillo Armas' headquarters in Tegucigalpa, Honduras, just after the CIA had anointed Castillo Armas as the "Liberator" of Guatemala. There they reaffirmed their "gentleman's agreement." Castillo Armas by now had gained the backing of Nicaragua, the United States and the Dominican Republic, as well as El Salvador and Venezuela. Ydígoras was reduced to the position of President-in-waiting. Privately Castillo Armas treated him with contempt.[13]

On November 3, 1953, for example, Castillo Armas attended the Panamanian Independence Day reception at that nation's embassy in Honduras. There his friend Córdova Cerna introduced him to a U. S. Embassy official, who took the trouble of jotting down Castillo Armas' remarks that evening. Castillo Armas, the diplomat reported, scorned Ydígoras, who he said wanted the Guatemalan presidency on a "silver platter" but "does not want to fight for it." Castillo Armas dismissed Ydígoras' various schemes against Arbenz as "reckless adventures" doomed to failure because they were not "military actions carefully planned and carefully considered."[14]

Castillo Armas remained in frequent touch with Córdova Cerna, who had escaped to Honduras after the Salamá uprising. The two men met and worked out preliminary plans for Castillo Armas' post-coup government. The first three years, Córdova Cerna proposed, would be a period of "de facto" rule to consolidate power. Castillo Armas was to be chief executive and Córdova Cerna would preside over a Council of State, a post in his blueprint more powerful than the national executive itself. The three years would be used vaguely for "organizing for governing" by an "outfit of men." Elections would follow in which both Córdova Cerna and Ydígoras could freely compete. The plan was designed to attract the various exile factions into a united anti-Arbenz front. Two events doomed it from the start: Córdova Cerna's incapacitating illness and Castillo Armas' thirst for power.[15]

By this point Nicaraguan dictator Somoza was aggressively supporting Castillo Armas. In July 1953, when the CIA was considering the designation of Castillo Armas but had not finally approved him, Somoza's son Tachito slipped Castillo Armas copies of written offers for the sale of arms, ammunition and other military equipment from an arms dealer in Hamburg, Germany. (Castillo Armas apparently never made use of this channel.) A few months later, on September 20, 1953, Castillo Armas wrote the elder Somoza a note, reflecting their close relationship: "I have been informed by our friends here that the government of the North . . . has taken the decision to permit us to develop our plans," but then added somewhat ambiguously that he had no further word "confirming the foregoing." Finally, on October 15, he wrote Somoza's son an exultant letter: "Our work with our friends from the North has ended in complete triumph in our favor and . . . shortly we will enter into very active plans which will inevitably end with the victorious result we all desire."[16]

In the twenty-five-day period between the two letters, the CIA had taken Castillo Armas to Florida "in black"—without normal immigration clearances—to meet with J. C. King, the CIA's Western Hemisphere chief. King laid out the agency's plan, an elaborate scheme which Haney had developed to elevate Castillo Armas to the leadership of a "political party" created by the CIA and to provide him with ten paramilitary groups of twelve soldiers apiece. The CIA also promised Castillo Armas $3 million to finance an invasion of Guatemala. The United Fruit Company agreed to supply arms to Castillo Armas and smuggle other weapons into Guatemala via the company's railroad, the IRCA, to equip a "subversive fifth column." (In return, it was understood, United Fruit would get its land and its privileges back after Arbenz was deposed.) Castillo Armas accepted King's offer with no conditions or objections. It was not dissimilar to the deal Ydígoras had considered but rejected.[17]

Castillo Armas made public his new "National Liberation Movement" on December 23, 1953, when he released his "Tegucigalpa Plan" in Honduras, signed by a number of other exile leaders. It outlined the general aims of his crusade and declared: "The organized opposition against the Sovietization of

Guatemala, aware that the government of Col. Jacobo Arbenz and Dr. Juan Arévalo is acting along lines dictated by international communism, hereby raises the banner of struggle for national liberation." Announcements of this kind were hardly new, and the "Tegucigalpa Plan" attracted only moderate attention in Guatemala. However, as one observer later wrote, in a war fought mainly through the media, this "was to be the first torrent of publicity."[18]

The declaration stirred anger and jealousy among Guatemalan exiles who had not been the beneficiaries of CIA largesse. Some visited the American embassies in Honduras and Nicaragua (as well as in Guatemala itself) to argue for their own crusades, and several flew directly to Washington, D.C., to present their cases before friendly senators or government officials. The scores of Guatemalan exiles panting after Arbenz's job exasperated even chronic conspirators like Trujillo. "Every time something started, there were twenty people who wanted to be President after the uprising and none would cooperate with the other nineteen," Trujillo complained.[19]

A good example of these would-be conspirators was one José Luis Arenas, who dropped into the U. S. Embassy in Guatemala City on November 18, 1953. The CIA had already chosen Castillo Armas as its "Liberator," but for security reasons it had not yet informed lower-level U. S. Embassy officials of the decision. Thus, as part of their duties, U.S. officers in Central America spent untold hours politely talking to hustlers and exiles who wanted to offer themselves as the ideal leaders to oust Arbenz. José Luis Arenas assured American diplomats that of all the exile figures, including Castillo Armas and Ydígoras, only he was fit to lead a revolt. He offered his own party, the Party of Anti-Communist Unification, as the only entity capable of overthrowing Arbenz. Arenas asserted that his organization had backing throughout the country and could easily topple Arbenz through "civic pressure"—if only the Americans would give him $200,000. The embassy turned down the solicitation *pro forma*, as it had so many others. Arenas threatened to fly to Washington to touch his "friend" Vice-President Richard Nixon for the funds, but soon faded from view.[20]

In early January 1954, the first President of Guatemala after

Ubico's downfall, General Federico Ponce, also stopped by the U. S. Embassy in Nicaragua to let officials there know about his plot to depose Arbenz. After brushing aside all other Guatemalan exiles as "selfish opportunists," Ponce asserted he had an organization numbering 10,000 in Guatemala City alone, but was in need of several bombers, air crews, explosives and weapons. The diplomats listened patiently to the general's scheme, but they had orders not to encourage conspirators and would not help Ponce.[21]

There were a few other free-lancers at work. One colorful American official, Fred Sherwood—described as an "air attaché" at the U. S. Embassy in Guatemala during the Arbenz era—recalled for a 1965 American television documentary that "several of us" considered "vigilantes or night raiders" as a solution to the nation's "Communist" problem. One man in his group, he said, approached some Puerto Rican and Cuban gangsters and offered to pay them $50,000 to murder any twelve Communists in the country. Sherwood's friends, however, never raised the money to finance the project.[22]

Assured of CIA backing and therefore secure in his position, Castillo Armas disregarded his competitors and began to assemble a modest expeditionary force in Honduras and Nicaragua. Following his Tegucigalpa declaration in December, he began to establish the invasion and propaganda schedule with his CIA handlers. In late January 1954, however, a hitch developed. As General Ydígoras explained: "By some act of treachery" the Liberation plan "fell into the hands of Arbenz . . ." One of Castillo Armas' couriers to Somoza, Jorge Isaac Delgado, a Panamanian diplomat serving in Managua, flew his private plane to Guatemala City and betrayed the plot to Arbenz, some say for $100,000, turning over to the government a full photostatic file of Liberation documents. A few days later, on January 29, 1954, Guatemala's newspapers published copies of correspondence signed by Castillo Armas, Ydígoras and the Somozas under banner headlines.

The reports revealed that President Somoza was providing staging and training bases for Castillo Armas' troops and organizing an invasion of Guatemala with the assistance of El Salvador, the Dominican Republic, Venezuela and the "government of the

North." The documents suggested that Castillo Armas' invasion would come by sea on the nation's Pacific coast and overland through Honduras. However, the CIA did not get upset over the betrayal. Reflecting its confidence, the CIA simply continued with its preparations as if nothing had happened.[23]

In the United States, indeed, the operation's exposure caused scarcely a ripple of comment. The State Department labeled the charges of a U.S. role "ridiculous and untrue" and said it would not comment further on Guatemala's accusations because it did not wish to give them a dignity they did not deserve. A spokesman added ingenuously: "It is the policy of the United States not to intervene in the internal affairs of other nations. This policy has repeatedly been reaffirmed under the present administration."[24]

Time magazine typified the U.S. media response to the revelations, conceding that conspiracies did exist against Arbenz but calling this particular one "fantastic" and "completely fanciful. . . . The real plot in the situation was less of a plot than a scenario—a sort of Reichstag fire in reverse, masterminded in Moscow and designed to divert the attention from Guatemala as the Western Hemisphere's Red problem child."[25]

Castillo Armas redoubled his work. The CIA brought in its mercenaries and assembled arms, and Haney readied the radio and leaflet offensive. The next step was to prepare the populace in Guatemala for the Liberator's imminent homecoming.

9

THE PROCONSUL

While Allen Dulles and his subordinates were recruiting and briefing Castillo Armas for his role, Foster Dulles, the Secretary of State, was still searching for a "theater commander" who could represent official American interests in Guatemala City during Operation Success. The State Department's role in the plot was designed to complement the agency's; State would push publicly while the CIA pushed covertly to depose Arbenz. The problem at the front had arisen because the current American ambassador to Guatemala, Rudolf Schoenfeld, a gentlemanly, taciturn, soft-spoken man, had tried to maintain correct relations with the government and actually got along rather well with President Arbenz. Schoenfeld scarcely knew the first thing about directing a coup.[1]

In the late summer of 1953, Frank Wisner, the CIA's operations chief on Guatemala, and Bedell Smith, the Undersecretary of State, began a serious hunt for a new ambassador to Guatemala, someone who would not flinch from the role of executioner. Wisner finally tracked down a free-wheeling diplomat from South Carolina named John Peurifoy, then ambassador to Greece. Peurifoy had drawn considerable attention in Washington for his aggressive behavior in Greece from 1950 to 1953, when he jumped into the Greek political fray and rammed together a right-wing coalition government acceptable to the United States and the royal family in the aftermath of the country's bloody civil war. (He always kept a picture of himself with the royal family in his office.) Leftist Greek guerrillas had nicknamed him the "Butcher of Greece," though the fighting had long since ended. In Athens, he collaborated directly and enthusiastically with the CIA. According to one account, CIA agents "functioned more or less undercover in and out of the embassy."[2]

With the advent of the new Republican administration in 1953, Peurifoy's future had initially been in doubt. He owed his livelihood to political connections in the Democratic Party, and Dulles was in no mood to retain members of the opposition. But Wisner saved him. "I picked him off the beach," Wisner later joked. There may have been a more Machiavellian reason for Wisner's choice: Peurifoy, as a Democrat, was a perfect fall guy for the Republican administration if the coup went awry. But Peurifoy may have gotten the job simply because he sought it more actively than anybody else. "He heard he was going to Honduras after Greece, not Guatemala," one of his aides recalled. "He got angry and asked someone to leak a story to Drew Pearson, an old friend, that his reward for brilliant service in Greece was a secondline job in Honduras. That's how he got Guatemala."[3]

The flamboyant, tough-talking Peurifoy, forty-six, was just what both Dulles brothers wanted. He was a brassy anti-Communist in diplomat's clothing who loved action and never entertained doubts about his mission. A husky man of medium height with forceful brown eyes, he had a loud voice, a swaggering manner, a blunt style and a flair for intrigue. The press was dazzled by his colorful personality, reflected in his choice of outfits. He habitually wore a green Borsalino with a feather stuck in the band, a gaudy necktie, a loud sports jacket and bright slacks, and was known to carry a pistol on occasion. Some of Wisner's colleagues worried that he'd do something rash and get himself shot. But his image was actually more form than substance. He was sort of a "cowboy, a naive man," one correspondent concluded.[4]

Peurifoy was no deep thinker. He was not a reader. Drew Pearson wrote that he "did not seem to have much imagination." Like the Dulles brothers, he did not seem to recognize any shadings of belief. He spoke no Spanish and knew nothing about Guatemala, but he expressed himself with certitude on the issue of "Reds" in the Arbenz government. As in Greece, he also understood how to scare a small country. He skillfully used the press to convey threats. He displayed an elemental shrewdness and a bullheaded determination to get his way, though he was sometimes unpredictable because he couldn't always keep his mouth shut. Even so, as an instrument of destruction, Peurifoy was a crude but potent gun aimed at the head of the Arbenz administration.[5]

In some ways, though, it was puzzling that John Peurifoy had risen so far so fast. Born in 1907, he was a small-town boy from Walterboro, South Carolina, a sleepy southern village of 1,800 people with frame houses, dusty streets and oak trees draped in Spanish moss. He was from an established family, but he had lost his parents when he was young—his mother when he was six, his father, an attorney, to tuberculosis before he was eighteen. He grew up in the households of various relatives and friends (as had President Arbenz himself). From an early age he nursed an ambition to become a lawyer and run for Congress, but he lacked the money for law school. Instead he wangled an appointment to West Point in 1926, but had to quit after two years because of a long bout with pneumonia. After recovering, he took one odd job after another, from stock clerk in Kansas City to assistant cashier in a New York restaurant to a spot in the American Surety Company in Manhattan.

He moved to Washington in 1935, a few years after Franklin Roosevelt was elected President. The best job he could get was as an elevator operator in one of the Senate office buildings, supplemented by stints shoveling snow off the sidewalks in Georgetown. He attended night school at American University, and for a time worked in the Treasury Department. He married another government employee, Betty Jane Cox, in 1938. The couple worked in a Washington department store to make ends meet for a while until Peurifoy, in late 1938, finally found a slot as a $2,000-a-year clerk in the State Department, probably with the help of a fellow South Carolinian, Senator James Byrnes, who was a friend of his family. He rose rapidly through the ranks over the next eight years, taking time out to serve on the Economic Warfare and War Production Boards during World War II. In 1945, Peurifoy was given the task of setting up the San Francisco Conference that created the United Nations, and he acquitted himself admirably. He attracted the eye of then Assistant Secretary Dean Acheson, who made him a special assistant on his return in 1946. He earned an appointment in 1947 as Assistant Secretary of State for Security Affairs.[6]

Soon his career entered a rocky period. There is some evidence from FBI wiretaps that he won his job as the Department's security chief through the influence of a fellow worker, Alger Hiss. But in August 1948, Peurifoy, acting on his own, slipped secret security files on Hiss's past to the House Un-American Activities Committee, then probing Hiss. He delivered the material to Congressman Karl Mundt, Republican from South Dakota, in the middle of the night. A few months later, he advised committee members not to publish excerpts from Wittaker Chambers' "pumpkin papers," for reasons of national security. He reminded them that any person in the State Department who passed such documents elsewhere or copied them for an individual outside the Department would be breaking the law.[7]

He had another brush with public notoriety in 1950 when he was Deputy Undersecretary of State for Administration, in charge of personnel. Senator Joseph McCarthy, then a little-known Republican from Wisconsin, made his famous charge in Wheeling, West Virginia, that dozens of Communists were working for the State Department. Peurifoy telegraphed him immediately asking for the names. McCarthy never answered the wire, but accused the State Department, including Peurifoy, of covering up. Peurifoy was deeply offended by the allegation; he told one reporter, "I'm a Star-Spangled Banner guy." His career was relatively undamaged. Thereafter, though, he showed a certain impatience to prove his staunch anti-Communism.[8]

Wisner told Peurifoy, when he first approached him in the summer of 1953, that he would be a sort of referee declaring Castillo Armas the winner at the coup's end, and he hinted that the assignment would revitalize his diplomatic career. The eager Peurifoy needed little persuasion. He accepted the job on the spot. Ambassador Schoenfeld was reassigned to Colombia. Shortly afterward, in one of his first acts as Chief Justice of the Supreme Court, Earl Warren, an old friend, swore Peurifoy in as the American ambassador to Guatemala. Peurifoy prepared to depart for his new post in late October 1953. At this delicate moment, John Moors Cabot, Assistant Secretary of State for Inter-American Affairs, uttered an ominous warning to the Guatemalan government. He attacked Arbenz for "openly playing the communist game" and said he could expect no "positive cooperation" from the United States. That pronouncement set Peurifoy's appointment in the desired context.[9]

Before Peurifoy left Washington, the CIA made certain that it would have a direct line to him at all times. The agency worked out a clandestine means to pass instructions to Peurifoy through "back channels." Once received by the CIA Guatemala station, the messages would be hand-carried or conveyed verbally to the ambassador by Birch O'Neil, the CIA station chief (an ex-FBI man, as were most agents in Latin America). This procedure guaranteed that no one in the embassy would know Peurifoy had any contact with the CIA or any knowledge of Operation Success.[10]

Peurifoy's arrival in Guatemala on October 29, 1953, was accorded unusual attention by the government. Foreign Minister Dr. Raúl Osegueda (soon to be replaced by Guillermo Toriello) met him within an hour after his plane landed. The two men talked at length about the situation in Guatemala. Osegueda enumerated in detail the virtues of the Guatemalan revolution. Peurifoy did not speak until the closing minutes, but then went straight to the point, chastising Osegueda's government for taking over United Fruit Company land. Was the Foreign Minister aware, he inquired, that "agrarian reform had been instituted in China and that China today was a Communist country"? Osegueda replied by denying that he himself was a Communist.

Peurifoy responded that he had seen Osegueda in a photograph in a magazine with the Guatemalan Communist leader Fortuny. Osegueda let the remark pass. He told Peurifoy that here "the people really wanted" land reform and advised him to "go into the country and see." Peurifoy agreed to do so, and the meeting ended. Later Raymond Leddy, the State Department officer in charge of Central American and Panamanian Affairs, saw Peurifoy's memo on his talks with Osegueda and dropped him a note complimenting him on his "straight response" to Osegueda. It "may well serve to jar him out of the haze about agrarian reform," Leddy told him. In his first confrontation with the Guatemalan government, the new ambassador had shown the combative qualities his superiors had hoped for.[11]

Over the next month, Peurifoy began to sketch out expansive propaganda goals. He held discussions with the United States Information Agency in which he suggested an "information program" for Guatemala. The USIA agreed, and began sending Peurifoy and other U.S. envoys in Central America "anti-Communist" materials. USIA also began to place unattributed articles in foreign newspapers labeling particular Guatemalan officials as Communist and also calling certain actions of the Guatemalan government "Communist-inspired." In one instance, the agency surreptitiously inserted a piece in a Chilean newspaper calling a Guatemalan personality a Marxist. The story was reprinted all over Latin America with a Chilean dateline. Peurifoy's publicity offensive was initially aimed at gradually creating a hemispheric consensus against Guatemala.[12]

Peurifoy's most dramatic initiative was to arrange a direct meeting with Arbenz himself. On the night of December 16, 1953, Peurifoy and his wife went to dinner at Arbenz's residence at the President's invitation; their discussion lasted six hours, until two o'clock in the morning. It was Peurifoy's only face-to-face meeting with Arbenz during his entire tour of duty. The encounter produced repeated clashes through the evening over the issues of Communism and the United Fruit Company.

Peurifoy wrote a five-page memorandum to Secretary Dulles

on the talks. Among the observations Peurifoy cabled Washington:

> The President stated that the problem in this country is one between the Fruit Company and the Government. He went into a long dissertation giving the history of the Fruit Company from 1904; and since then, he complains, they have paid no taxes to the Government. He said that today when the Government has a budget of $70 million to meet, the Fruit Company contributes approximately $150,000. This is derived solely from the one-cent tax applied to each stem of bananas which is exported.
>
> I interrupted the President at this point to tell him that I thought we should consider first things first and that it seemed to me that as long as the Communists exercised the influence which they presently do with the Government, I did not see any real hope of bringing about better relations. . . . The President then said there were some Communists in the Government and that they had a certain amount of influence. He launched on the usual line that these Communists are "local." He went into the past history of his friendship with Gutiérrez and Fortuny, both of whom he claimed were honest men. I told him that many countries had thought they were dealing with honest men in the past but awakened too late to the fact that the Communists were in control. . . . He said this could not happen here. The Communists were no threat to the country. . . .
>
> The President said that my predecessor had told him that the manager of the Guatemala Institute of Social Security, Alfonso Solorzano, was a member of the Communist Party but he, the President, knew better. I informed him that my information agreed with Mr. Schoenfeld's and that we did consider Solorzano a Communist, perhaps not a member of Fortuny's PGT. . . .
>
> I asked the President why it was that this Congress had during the current year held memorial services for Stalin when he died. Mrs. Arbenz interjected to state that the reason for this was that the people of Guatemala had regarded Roosevelt, Churchill and Stalin as saviors of the world and that perhaps when Mr. Churchill passes on, Congress will hold memorial services for him, that all during the war the Guatemalan people had been led to believe that these three men were the saviors of the world. . . .
>
> [Arbenz] then reverted to the Fruit Company and said this was the biggest stumbling block; that this was a large American

organization which dominated the press of the United States. I told him the Fruit Company was relatively a small corporation by American standards and that, in so far as I knew, no corporation dominated any press in the United States. After all, I pointed out, there have been many newspapermen who have come to Guatemala and have determined on the spot the facts. They have talked with all types of people here in the city and have reached their conclusions independently. . . .

The President reverted to the subject of agrarian reform. He commented on how there had been opposition from American circles and others in the country. I told him that we had worked and were working with countries who had introduced land reforms. I cited my experience in Greece. . . . I told him the difference seemed to lie in the administration and not in the principle of assisting poor people to obtain land which they could work. I pointed out that perhaps the explanation was in the fact that the National Agrarian Department was dominated by Communists. . . .

I told the President that not only were we concerned but that his neighbors were concerned. He said most of his neighbors were permitting the Fruit Company to finance counter-espionage and counter-revolutions within their countries against his Government. I asked him whether he had any proof of the activities in this field. I told him as far back as 1945 my Government had declared that U.S. business should not intervene in the internal affairs of nations in the Hemisphere if they expected U.S. support. Therefore, I would be very interested in knowing of any proof which he might have. The President said that the next time we met he would give me some photostats which, while not naming the Fruit Company, would certainly indicate that Castillo Armas was receiving money.

Peurifoy wound up his after-dinner comments by observing ruefully that Americans find "it hard to understand why this country tolerates the great Commie influence from so few people." The meeting broke up uncomfortably, but Arbenz provided Peurifoy with an unlisted phone number should the envoy wish to reach him.

Peurifoy's cable rang the death knell on Arbenz's presidency. His long memorandum to Dulles concluded that if Arbenz "is not a Communist, he will certainly do until one comes along," and expressed the view, already accepted in Washington, that "normal approaches will probably not work in Guatemala." Peurifoy summed up with a dramatic flourish: "The candle is burning slowly and surely, and it is only a matter of time before the large American interests will be forced out completely." Though President Eisenhower had given the initial go-ahead for a coup four months earlier, the chief executive later claimed that it was this cable from Peurifoy which finally convinced him that Arbenz must be brought down.[13]

A few days later, Peurifoy dispatched an even tougher telegram to Dulles: "[T]here appears no alternative to our taking steps which would tend to make more difficult continuation of [the Arbenz] regime in Guatemala." He spelled out a series of retaliatory economic measures: cutting off agricultural missions, trade treaties (83.2 percent of all Guatemalan exports went to the United States), U.S. exports to Guatemala (representing 62.9 percent of all Guatemalan imports) and all foreign gasoline shipments to the country. He also suggested stepping up overt and covert anti-Communist propaganda and withdrawing the U. S. Army and Air Force missions. Peurifoy's recommendations for the most part went unheeded because the CIA's own military operation was already on track.[14]

Meantime Peurifoy's embassy took on the aspect of a busy headquarters. The CIA staff on the guarded fourth floor grew rapidly in size, and began to undertake a variety of destabilization programs. The station arranged to provide support for agents casing the country, like Henry Heckscher, the former German operative who was trying to bribe army officers into defecting, and David Atlee Phillips, who was in search of local color to authenticate his radio broadcasts. The agency also installed in the embassy secret communications equipment which could later be turned into a radio station and a jamming device to obstruct official radio broadcasts and an amplifier to scare the populace with bombing sounds during the coming coup. In addition, Peurifoy had a cash fund to encourage military defections, leaks of information and government intrigues. One observer wrote: "The cafes in Guatemala in those days were alive with rumors and American CIA agents, many of whom operated openly. There was no mystery about their headquarters and hangouts or where and how some interesting bits of information could be sold to them for U.S. dollars."

Peurifoy also permitted overt acts of interference in Guatemalan affairs, including regular meetings by his staff aides with anti-Arbenz plotters. Peurifoy even dropped public hints of what was to come. In early January 1954, he told *Time* magazine: "Public opinion in the U.S. might force us to take some measures to prevent Guatemala from falling into the lap of international Communism. We cannot permit a Soviet Republic to be established between Texas and the Panama Canal." So provocative was this observation that Peurifoy later had to deny he said it in order to save himself from expulsion.[15]

Peurifoy also kept in touch with other U.S. envoys in Central America. Whiting Willauer, the ambassador to Honduras, years later confirmed at a congressional hearing that the State Department and the CIA had placed Peurifoy, himself, Robert Hill in Costa Rica and Thomas Whelan in Nicaragua as a "team" in Central America to assure the ouster of Arbenz. (Actually Hill and Whelan had already served in their posts for a few years, but both helped out.) Willauer boasted that he had kept the Honduran government "in line so they would allow this revolutionary activity to continue . . ." Willauer's duties, based on his experience as a director of the CIA's Civil Air Transport Company, were to arrange air training sites and obtain air instructors and fliers for the rebels. "I am literally working day and night on the problem [of Guatemala]," he wrote his former boss, the one-time head of the Flying Tigers, General Claire Chennault. One participant wryly suggested that several of Castillo Armas' pilots could probably speak Chinese because they arrived fresh from fighting the Chinese revolution. Willauer's involvement in the coup was so well known that the Guatemalan envoy in Honduras actually pleaded with him to hold back the invasion a few days and let the Guatemalans deal with their own problems themselves.[16]

Peurifoy communicated daily with the State Department, primarily with Undersecretary Bedell Smith, who presided over the Guatemalan operation as John Foster Dulles' liaison with the CIA. Smith was a hard-driving taskmaster whose anti-Communism was so zealous that he once reportedly called Nelson Rockefeller a "Red" for a lukewarm statement in favor of trade unions. His opposition to Arbenz was implacable. Perhaps his private maneuvering with United Fruit to obtain a job for himself lent a certain emotional edge to his dislike of the Guatemalan President.[17]

Guatemala's ambassador to the United States, Guillermo Toriello, called on him in Washington in mid-January 1954. Smith called Toriello a "persuasive apologist for his fellow-travelling government." In a memo for President Eisenhower—who was due to meet Toriello a few days hence—he reminded Eisenhower that Guatemala was involved in "merciless hounding of American companies," including the United Fruit corporation. This was apparently to assure that Eisenhower would not be taken in by the urbane Toriello. Oddly, Toriello later said he thought he had persuaded Smith that "a change in the condition of operations of the United Fruit was necessary" in Guatemala to resolve problems between the two countries.[18]

Toriello then met with President Eisenhower. It was a bizarre encounter. Toriello's principal impression was of Eisenhower's abysmal ignorance of Guatemala. Eisenhower "could hardly believe the exaggerated privileges which [foreign] firms have enjoyed [in Guatemala]," Toriello wrote in his memoirs. "With frightening ingenuousness, he suggested to me that on my return to Guatemala I discuss possible solutions with Ambassador Peurifoy." Eisenhower even showed sympathy for a proposal, according to Toriello, that "an impartial mixed commission of Guatemalans and U.S. citizens" iron out the knotty differences between the nations.[19]

Eisenhower was certainly feigning that "ingenuousness" with Toriello, since he had given the order for Arbenz's overthrow six months earlier. Three months after this meeting, Eisenhower told Senate and House leaders that he had once given Toriello "unshirted hell" while he was ambassador because "he's playing along with the communists." The President's memory hardly squares with Toriello's more astringent recollections of his talks with the former general.[20]

Ten days after Eisenhower saw Toriello, Guatemalan police arrested some labor leaders following the capture of Castillo

Armas' "Liberation file." Smith then wired the U. S. Embassy in
Costa Rica requesting that Serafino Romualdi, head of the AFL's
Latin America committee, persuade the AFL-sponsored Inter-
American Organization of Workers (known by its Spanish
initials as ORIT) to denounce the arrests. Romualdi replied that
ORIT was reluctant to issue a rebuke for fear it would further
inflame nationalists in Guatemala. The State Department and the
CIA, however, did persuade the American Federation of Labor
under George Meany to send a public letter to Arbenz asking
him to purge the country's unions of Communists. The following
month, after a private conference with Allen Dulles, Meany also
attacked Latin-American governments for opposing intervention
in Guatemala.[21]

The most important public denunciation of Guatemala by the
United States came at the Tenth Inter-American Conference of
the Organization of American States (OAS) in Caracas, Venezuela, in March 1954. The conference was originally called to
deal with economic matters, but Dulles used the occasion to push
through a broad anti-Communist resolution for use against
Guatemala. Dulles was seeking multilateral blessing for unilateral intervention by the United States. The Monroe Doctrine,
under which the United States had traditionally acted freely in
the hemisphere, no longer was popular; it was, in fact, a red flag
to Latins, who considered it the epitome of "Yankee Imperialism."[22]

Personally leading the American delegation at Caracas, Secretary Dulles proposed the resolution declaring that "the domination or control of the political institutions of any American state
by the international communist movement . . . would constitute
a threat" to the entire hemisphere and require "appropriate action in accordance with existing treaties." The treaty Dulles had
particularly in mind was the Rio Treaty of 1947, specifically Article 6, which gave OAS foreign ministers authority to take action if two thirds of the member nations of the OAS agreed that
the political independence of an American state was affected by
"an aggression which was not an armed attack." The countries
could then decide to impose economic sanctions or jointly intervene.[23]

Dulles' Caracas Resolution was a sort of warmed-over Monroe

Doctrine. Its purpose was to condemn Guatemala without actually mentioning its name, as well as put in place the juridical authority with which to defend Operation Success in the face of anticipated protests. As President Eisenhower later put it in his memoirs: "This resolution formed a charter for the anti-communist counterattack that followed." Though this strategy was no secret, Dulles went to great lengths to present his action as a protective curtain for weak countries. In a private State Department memorandum, though, policy planners openly conceded the resolution was a way of saving the United States from "appearing as leading a movement against any one of its small neighbors." At best, it could persuade the nations at the conference to approve "multilateral measures against Guatemala" immediately, the memo suggested; at a minimum, the Caracas Resolution might lay the groundwork for "positive action" by the OAS at a later date against Guatemala.[24]

Guillermo Toriello, Guatemala's new Foreign Minister (Osegueda had resigned because he refused to attend any meeting in Venezuela while dictator Pérez Jiménez was in power), fully realized that the American resolution was aimed squarely at Guatemala. "What is the reason for this campaign of defamation?" he asked delegates on March 5.

> What is the real and effective reason for describing our government as communist? From what source comes the accusation that we threaten continental solidarity and security? Why do they wish to intervene in Guatemala?
>
> The answers are simple and evident. The plan of national liberation being carried out with firmness by my government has necessarily affected the privileges of the foreign enterprises that are impeding the progress and the economic development of the country. . . . With construction of publicly owned ports and docks, we are putting an end to the monopoly of the United Fruit Company. . . .
>
> We feel this proposal was merely a pretext for intervention in our internal affairs. . . . They wanted to find a ready expedient to maintain the economic dependence of the American Republics and suppress the legitimate desires of their peoples, cataloguing as "communism" every manifestation of nationalism or economic independence, any desire for social progress, any in-

tellectual curiosity, and any interest in progressive and liberal reforms. . . .

President Franklin Roosevelt put an end to this policy [of interventionism] and with him there flourished a new Pan Americanism filled with promise. But it appears that certain United States officials wish to restore that policy that did so much damage. . . .

There was widespread applause. One Latin-American diplomat observed: "He said many of the things some of the rest of us would like to say if we dared." Even *Time* conceded Toriello made the "biggest oratorical hit" of the conference, though it also suggested he was playing "his role of underdog to the hilt."[25]

Toriello's words went for naught. Dulles, accompanied by an impressive array of U.S. officials, spent two full weeks in Caracas twisting arms, threatening to withhold aid from non-cooperative nations and repeating his sermons on the Communist peril. He finally secured 16 votes for the resolution, and it passed on March 26. Only Mexico and Argentina abstained, and Guatemala alone voted in opposition. (Costa Rica boycotted the conference to protest the Pérez Jiménez dictatorship.) Dulles accepted a few cosmetic changes in his declaration to placate Latin nations, including one which required a "meeting of consultation" before countries could consider taking action under its provisions. This and other minor modifications somewhat allayed anxiety about possible unilateral U.S. intervention, though the Secretary of State provoked some skepticism when he assured the delegates: "I believe that there is not a single American state which would practice intervention against another American state."[26]

The price of Dulles' victory came high. Press reports of the conference, even in the United States, concluded that America's heavy-handed tactics had decreased its prestige in Latin America. Indeed, the United States had never before encountered so much opposition to one of its proposals at the OAS. The nations most enthusiastically backing the Dulles pronouncement included the ugliest dictatorships in Latin America. The common motive among the few democracies supporting Dulles was reluctant recognition of America's power in the hemisphere. Uruguay's chief delegate, Dr. Justino Jiménez de Arechaga, confessed he had voted for the resolution "without enthusiasm, without optimism, without joy, and without the feeling that we are contributing to the adoption of a constructive measure." The United States tried manfully to counteract this widespread view with a flow of news briefings, as well as tape recordings and photos of the Caracas Conference put together by a special USIA team, but it was to little avail.[27]

After the conference, Dulles flew off to other world trouble spots, but he continued adding new people to the State Department's Guatemala team. With Eisenhower's approval, he sought a "civilian adviser" to help expedite Operation Success. Milton Eisenhower, the President's brother, originally turned the job down. The next choice was William Pawley, a Miami-based millionaire with a long history of consorting with reactionary Latin leaders. Pawley had gained renown for setting up the Flying Tigers in the early 1940s and then helping to transform it into the CIA's airline, Civil Air Transport (CAT). He was a friend of both Thomas Corcoran, the Fruit Company lobbyist and attorney for CAT, and Whiting Willauer, U.S. ambassador to Honduras and ex-director of CAT. As the "outside" adviser, Pawley spent his time in semi-weekly sessions at the State Department on the Guatemalan matter. He soon became the Department's liaison with the Pentagon and one of the key officials handling plans for Guatemala following Castillo Armas' victory.[28]

Dulles also fired John Moors Cabot as Assistant Secretary of State for Inter-American Affairs following policy disagreements on various matters and sent him off to be the U.S. ambassador to Sweden. Dulles replaced him with a Texas lawyer named Henry Holland. After the Caracas conference, at which Holland was a member of the American delegation, Bedell Smith took him aside and briefed him on the CIA plan to overthrow Arbenz. A man of independent views, Holland told Smith that he strongly opposed the adventure because of its high cost, its reliance on military rather than political tactics and its ostentatious scale, which Holland feared could lead to a bloody civil war. Holland was the first highly placed official in the Administration to raise a voice against the coup, though admittedly he directed his argument against the means, not the end. "You don't know what you're talking about," Smith snapped. "Forget those stupid ideas and let us get on with our work." It was the end of Holland's dissent—temporarily. One other State Department official, Deputy Assistant Secretary Robert Woodward, also challenged the operation within the Department, but he had no more success than Holland.[29]

In late April 1954, Dulles and Smith suddenly called Ambassador Peurifoy back for consultations. The American ambassador to El Salvador, Michael J. McDermott, had coincidentally returned home a few days earlier for "personal reasons." The New York *Times* surmised that "the primary purpose of Peurifoy's Washington visit will be to exchange ideas at the State Department about the United States' next move on the anti-Communist resolution adopted at the Tenth Inter-American Conference last month at Caracas." The *Times* also reported that Peurifoy had secretly submitted to the State Department a series of recommendations for new steps to punish Arbenz for allowing Communists into his government. The leak to the *Times* apparently came from Peurifoy himself, arising probably from his growing impatience with Secretary Dulles for not acting immediately against Arbenz. But it also served as a further warning to Guatemala about U.S. impatience.[30]

Peurifoy need not have worried. Eisenhower was beginning to move hard and fast against Guatemala. He warned congressional leaders on April 26 that Guatemala was spreading "Marxist tentacles" into El Salvador. "The Reds are in control [in Guatemala]," he informed the congressmen and senators, "and they are trying to spread their influence to San Salvador as a first step to breaking out of Guatemala to other South American countries."[31]

The die was about to be cast. The United States only had to trap Arbenz into making a false move. Within a few weeks, Arbenz obliged.

10

THE SECRET VOYAGE
OF THE *ALFHEM*

On the steamy tropical morning of May 15, 1954, a group of high Guatemalan officials led by the Minister of Defense waited near the docks of Puerto Barrios, the nation's Atlantic seaport. The town had been closed to visitors and the taking of photographs was temporarily forbidden. Few Guatemalans knew what cargo would be brought into port that day, though dock workers sensed that something unusual was happening.

Before 9 A.M., the lumbering 4,900-foot Swedish freighter *Alfhem* was sighted on the horizon. She soon nudged into a dockside berth and was immediately placed off-limits to all but the stevedores who had to unload her. Even the local agent of the shipping company operating the *Alfhem* was prevented from boarding. Within hours, railroad boxcars were being packed with heavy wooden crates labeled "Optical and Laboratory Equipment." Over the next several days, more than a hundred boxcars left Puerto Barrios for Guatemala City. Each train was under military escort.[1]

The ship's cargo was a closely held secret. It was a shipment of weapons—rifles, ammunition, antitank mines and artillery pieces—which Guatemala had bought from Czechoslovakia for well over one million dollars. The United States had refused to sell any weapons to Guatemala since 1948. Other Allied nations, under American pressure, had also declined approaches from Guatemala. The U. S. State Department said it imposed the embargo because of Guatemala's refusal to sign the Rio Security Pact of 1947, but Guatemala responded that it could not sign due to technicalities relating to its unrecognized claim on the neighboring Belize territory. Guatemalans noted that the embargo coincided with the passage in their Congress—over vehement U.S. protests—of reform legislation threatening the power of foreign corporations.[2]

President Arévalo thereafter tried to buy arms from Denmark, but the transaction was upset, according to Arévalo in his memoirs, by "North American espionage agents." Acting in concert with Great Britain, the Americans also used diplomatic pressure to stop arms deals with Mexico, Cuba, Argentina and Switzerland during the Arbenz administration. In 1952, the famed "Black Eagle of Harlem," aviator Hubert Fauntleroy Julian, slipped twelve 20-mm. antiaircraft weapons of Swiss manufacture into Guatemala. After learning of the incident, U.S. officials intensified their surveillance with a special eye toward preventing Guatemalan arms purchasers from obtaining antiaircraft shells (a month before the invasion, U.S. authorities blocked delivery of six tons of shells from Europe). By 1954, the Guatemalans were complaining that the American embargo had become so effective that not only were they unable to equip their army, but they could not even buy low-caliber ammo for the Hunting and Fishing Club, a favorite gathering place for well-to-do sportsmen.[3]

Arbenz seems to have turned to Czechoslovakia as a "kind of

last resort" when Guatemala's normal suppliers refused his requests to purchase military hardware, concluded historian Cole Blasier. It was a gamble taken with an inadequate appraisal of the political repercussions, but it was apparently prompted by a clear recognition that Castillo Armas' invasion was impending and Guatemala's own armed forces needed reinforcement.[4]

If Arbenz hoped he could buy guns from Czechoslovakia undetected by the CIA, he was mistaken. The Americans, in fact, had first learned of Arbenz's interest in Czech weapons as early as April 4, 1953, more than a year before the *Alfhem* steamed into Puerto Barrios. On that date, Frank Wisner sent a memo to J. C. King, asking him to verify a rumor that "arms from Czechoslovakia were being clandestinely introduced into Guatemala (with or without the assistance of the Russians)." Neither King nor Wisner found evidence of the traffic, but from then on they were on the lookout for it. Their vigilance was rewarded a year later when a CIA agent in Szczecin—a Polish port called Stettin before World War II when it was German territory—reported the sailing of a suspicious ship, the *Alfhem,* on April 17, 1954.[5]

At first the CIA was uncertain of the precise cargo aboard the *Alfhem,* but analysts strongly suspected it was from the Czech munitions plant at Skoda. The agent who made the sighting noted only that the vessel was loaded at top speed, with over 2,000 tons of cargo packed in the hold within twenty-four hours; he could not provide her destination or even her name (though the spy learned it contained six letters). Through the use of Navy and CIA electronic listening devices, the United States tracked the ship intermittently as it plowed the seas toward its "official" destination, Dakar, in French West Africa. Six days after sailing, the *Alfhem* suddenly altered course, and the agency briefly lost its quarry. The vessel meanwhile headed toward Curaçao, Dutch West Indies. On May 7, she switched course again and made for Honduras. On May 13, the ship—now in the Caribbean—received orders to steer for Puerto Barrios, Guatemala, where she finally docked. Only as she arrived off the Guatemalan coast did the CIA rediscover the boat. Eisenhower's press secretary, James Hagerty, complained privately: "Someone pulled a fast one and we were watching the wrong ship." The Navy had hoped to intercept the boat before it entered Guatemala waters, Hagerty revealed. (But some Guatemalans, including Foreign Minister Toriello, felt that the United States might have deliberately allowed this ship to dock just in order to create an "incident" to justify the invasion.)[6]

Once the freighter was berthed, the CIA easily learned her name and traced her registry. The ship was originally Swedish, owned by the firm of Angbats, Bohuslanska and Kusten, Inc., and operated out of the Swedish port of Uddevalla. She was chartered to a shipping agent in London, E. E. Dean, known as one of the London agents of Čechofracht, the Czech shipping monopoly. Dean had in turn rechartered the vessel to a Swedish businessman named Christianson, who had a history of acting as an intermediary for the Czechs. Czech funds paid for the "straw charter" by Christianson. The cargo—15,424 cases of military weapons with a gross weight of 4,112,145 pounds—was handled in Szczecin by Metrans, the Czech international freight forwarding agency, and by Spedrapid, the Czech agency that represented Metrans in Poland.[7]

News of the ship's arrival in Guatemala sent shock waves through several Washington bureaucracies, especially the CIA and the State Department. Within the CIA, the dominant reaction was one of relief. The agency had long been searching for a credible pretext under which to "unleash" Castillo Armas, who was then languishing in Nicaragua awaiting orders. Just a week earlier, the CIA had even started to plant boxes of rifles with conspicuous Soviet markings near Nicaragua's Pacific coast, and to arrange for their "discovery" by Nicaraguan police who could claim they came from a "non-American submarine" sighted offshore. Nicaragua's dictator Somoza cooperated with the ruse. He called in the Managua diplomatic corps in early May and told them, in a voice shaking with anger, that his police had located a secret Soviet shipment, including forty rifles, two machine guns, twenty hand grenades and four pistols "bearing the hammer and sickle," and suggested that the Communists wanted to convert Nicaragua into "a new Korean situation." The world press was skeptical and paid little heed to the fabricated Nicaraguan "incident."[8]

On May 16, the day after the CIA formally confirmed the *Alfhem's* cargo, Director Allen Dulles chaired a meeting of the Intelligence Advisory Committee, which counted as members top intelligence officers from the Army, Navy, Air Force, Joint Chiefs of Staff, State Department and Atomic Energy Commission. The men made a "quick crash estimate of the Guatemalan situation" and—apparently without evidence—concluded that the Czech shipment provided enough arms for Arbenz to crush his neighbors and sweep into the Panama Canal Zone. The next day, Allen Dulles went to the National Security Council and urged Eisenhower's top strategists to increase "U.S. assistance" to Castillo Armas and the rebels; the Council agreed. With the official backing of the NSC, Dulles set the invasion date for the following month.[9]

Dulles also won authority to dispatch a secret commando mission by Colonel Haney's sidekick, Rip Robertson, then based in Nicaragua, to blow up the trains carrying the *Alfhem* weapons from Puerto Barrios to Guatemala City. Robertson had wanted to send a frogman team to sink the *Alfhem* when she was first observed off the coast, but Washington then turned him down. Dulles liked the commando idea better, and told Haney to sneak a band of saboteurs into Guatemala through Honduras. On the morning of May 20, five days after the ship's arrival, Robertson led a small paramilitary squad to a hilly area overlooking the tracks near Puerto Barrios and planted explosives on the rail line leading to Guatemala City. After the charges were laid, however, a torrential downpour drenched the ground, soaking the detonators. Only one explosive went off, slightly cracking a track. Robertson and his men then opened fire on one train as it passed by, killing one Guatemalan soldier and wounding three others. Robertson lost one of his guerrillas in the exchange. The military convoy of ten freight trains sped safely to its destination.[10]

With the CIA just a few weeks away from ordering Castillo Armas across the border, the Department of State and the White House seized on the *Alfhem* incident as new evidence of Communist subversion in Guatemala. On May 17, the State Department issued a statement deploring the Czech arms shipment as a "development of gravity." Two days later, at a White House press conference, President Eisenhower warned that the arrival of Czech weapons in Guatemala might lead to the establishment of a "Communist dictatorship . . . on this continent to the detriment of all American nations . . ." Within days after this alarming prediction, Secretary of State John Foster Dulles told reporters that one purpose of the arms sale might be to create a Communist "bastion" near the Panama Canal 800 miles away. Both the President and Secretary Dulles made further statements of this nature over the next days, always adding the charge that the Czech weaponry "exceeded" the "legitimate" needs of the Guatemalan Army compared to neighboring countries—though they did not note that Guatemala, with the largest population in Central America, required equipment for a military force triple the size of its neighbors'.[11]

A year afterward, journalist Keith Monroe wrote in *Harper's Magazine* that the U.S. government suspected the "real" reason Guatemala wanted the armament was to form a "people's militia" under the Communists, start a revolution against Somoza in Nicaragua and convert a general strike in Honduras into an armed workers' revolution. Like Dulles and Eisenhower, Monroe offered no evidence for his theories and gave no weight to the needs of Arbenz's forces. Even the CIA's Richard Bissell—at the time Allen Dulles' logistical aide for the Guatemalan operation—conceded years later that Washington's public indignation over the arms "blew the shipment up in an important way, beyond what was merited."[12]

Ironically, the *Alfhem* cargo was no bargain for Arbenz. It turned out to consist largely of obsolete, impractical and nonfunctional weapons. The antitank guns were worthless since no Central American country owned tanks. The German artillery pieces were built to move on modern highways which did not exist in Guatemala, and many of the World War II-vintage British, Czech and German rifles and machine guns did not work. The New York *Times* later concluded that Arbenz had been sold a shipload of "white elephants."[13]

Still, in a cable to Dulles on June 1, Ambassador Peurifoy reported that "Guatemalan Army morale [is] generally enhanced by *Alfhem* arms shipment, but it is not certain this will redound to Arbenz's benefit." He suggested that some army officers now believed they could even employ the Czech weapons to over-throw Arbenz. In any event, he added, the "arms shipment has not made Army officers more friendly to communists, and any open move by the government to arm civilians might have serious repercussions."[14]

As the cable revealed, Peurifoy was aware, contrary to his own government's public charges, that the Czech weaponry was intended solely for the Guatemalan Army. The Army showed no intention of sharing it with trade unions or employing it for a march to the Panama Canal or using it for a strike against neighboring dictators or for any other covert purpose. But the Americans were determined to dominate the front pages of the world press with alarms about Soviet subversion in order to foster a climate in which the invasion of Guatemala would be "understood." The Dulles brothers used the occasion of the Czech arms arrival to accelerate their efforts to encourage heads of major American news organizations to support the U.S. thesis about the Arbenz regime. Their success became swiftly evident in the coverage of an agricultural strike just then occurring in Honduras.

On May 5, Honduran workers at a United Fruit Company plantation had walked off their jobs in a wage dispute. The President of Honduras, Manuel Gálvez, was a former counsel to the Fruit Company. On the day of the strike, he expelled two Guatemalan consuls in the area, charging they had encouraged the walkout (though they were probably spying on Castillo Armas). The strike soon began to spread throughout Honduras. On May 9, Ambassador Willauer cabled Dulles his conclusion that the strike was "inspired" by Guatemalan Communists and warned that Guatemala might invade Honduras—speculation that had no basis in fact. On May 13, Dulles publicly announced plans to supply "military assistance" to Honduras in the event of a Guatemalan invasion.[15]

Time magazine dispatched two reporters to take a look at the work stoppage and to evaluate its impact on Honduras. The two journalists wired home reports generally sympathetic to the workers' plight. However, "*Time* rewrote our accounts," one later said, "as an anti-strike diatribe" favorable to the United Fruit Company, hinting at a Guatemalan role in the shutdown. The changes in the story were apparently due to a personal con-

tact between a U.S. government official and *Time* chairman
Henry Luce, the journalist suggested. The CIA had apparently
planned to use the Honduran strike as public justification for the
Castillo Armas invasion. But the *Alfhem's* docking gave it a
more plausible excuse and the Honduran strike was forgotten.[16]

If the CIA's tactic was to rewrite stories filed from the scene
in weekly magazines like *Time*, it used another technique to
affect reports in the New York *Times*. This time the CIA focused
on Sydney Gruson, an experienced *Times* correspondent based
in Mexico City with a beat including Guatemala. He had been
briefly expelled from Guatemala by the Arbenz regime for writing a piece on November 6, 1953, depicting the President as a
captive of Communists in his government. Gruson was readmit-
ted following vigorous protests by Ambassador Peurifoy. Soon
Peurifoy himself, however, began to complain about Gruson's
stories. His anger grew when Gruson filed reports after the
Alfhem incident suggesting that Guatemalans and other Latins
were rallying around Arbenz in face of American attacks. "The
reaction has served to remind observers," Gruson wrote at one
point, "that the dominant feeling among articulate Guatemalans
is not pro- or anti-communism or pro- or anti-Yankeeism but fer-
vent nationalism." This was precisely the angle which the CIA
wanted to keep out of the American press.[17]

Frank Wisner, the director of Operation Success, shared
Peurifoy's concern about Gruson's reporting. After the *Alfhem*
articles appeared in print, Wisner asked his boss, Allen Dulles,
to do something to silence Gruson. Dulles obliged by tele-
phoning General Julius Adler, business manager of the *Times*
and an old friend. The two men dined in Washington during the
first week of June, and Dulles quietly told Adler that he and his
brother, the Secretary of State, had confidential information
which caused them to be concerned about the political reliability of Gruson and his then wife, reporter Flora Lewis. Dulles
backed up his charge only by noting that Gruson traveled on a
British passport issued in Warsaw; that his wife also made trips
on that passport; and that Gruson was suspected of "liberal lean-
ings." Therefore, the CIA Director suggested, Gruson should not
be assigned such a delicate story as the developing conflict in
Guatemala.[18]

Adler passed the tip up to *Times* publisher Arthur Hays Sulzberger. Believing he was performing a patriotic act, Sulzberger ordered Gruson to stay put at his Mexico City bureau on the spurious ground that there might be an unspecified "Mexican angle" to the impending coup in Guatemala. Gruson was about to launch an investigation of the Castillo Armas invasion force when he was grounded. He did not return to Guatemala until after the coup. (Curiously, his wife, Flora Lewis, was later to write an admiring account of Peurifoy's role during the coup for *The New York Times Magazine*.)[19]

The campaign by the Dulles brothers to influence the U.S. press had its counterpart in an effort to enlist the American Catholic hierarchy. A CIA official asked Francis Cardinal Spellman of New York to arrange "clandestine contact" between Guatemalan Archbishop Mariano Rossell Arellano and a CIA agent "so that we could coordinate our parallel efforts." Spellman eagerly agreed, and a CIA emissary soon called on the Guatemalan Archbishop. Then on April 9, 1954, a pastoral letter read in all Guatemalan churches called the attention of citizens to the presence of Communism in the country and demanded that "the people of Guatemala . . . rise as a single man against this enemy of God and country." The CIA, Howard Hunt wrote later, "air-dropped many thousands of leaflets carrying the pastoral message into remote areas of Guatemala."[20]

In the final days before the coup, the Dulles brothers worked systematically to smooth over last-minute problems and complete fine-tuning on the operation. Allen Dulles made a few abrupt switches in his Guatemalan team. He yanked Birch O'Neil, the CIA station chief in Guatemala, out of the country several weeks before the invasion because O'Neil reportedly objected to some aspects of the operation. He was replaced by his deputy, John Doherty, a local figure with ties to Guatemalan businessmen, who himself left the job a few months later to open a cement company. In March, Dulles also appointed Richard Bissell as his special assistant to handle technical chores on the coup.[21]

Allen Dulles also refereed another dispute between Haney and his bureaucratic foe, J. C. King. Late in 1953, Wisner had placed a former *Time* correspondent named Enno Hobbing, a towering six-footer, on Haney's staff, partly to watch over Haney and partly to help Haney write reports to his Washington superiors justifying plans for Operation Success. Hobbing had dashed off a flurry of farfetched memos setting forth various rationalizations for the CIA conspiracy. One suggested that the agency push Arbenz into increasing acts of repression, thereby estranging him from his people and setting off an internal revolt. But CIA officers loyal to J. C. King, who still favored the original plan of relying heavily on United Fruit, did not care for Hobbing's approach. Hobbing was called in and accused of being "subversive" and an opponent of the United Fruit Company. Haney was able to protect his underling during the grilling. Later, however, during his annual CIA physical, Hobbing was once again ambushed by J. C. King's allies. One of them gave a CIA psychiatrist records of Hobbing's extraordinary political ideas. The dutiful doctor detected in Hobbing symptoms of emotional imbalance. A seething Haney finally persuaded Dulles to recruit another psychiatrist to overrule the doctor's observation. Hobbing stayed on the job.[22]

Allen Dulles confronted another problem just before the invasion. President Gálvez of Honduras had acceded to Ambassador Willauer's request to provide the jumping-off base for Castillo Armas and his troops. But as the deadline neared, Gálvez began to worry that, if Operation Success failed, the United States might abandon him to Arbenz's wrath. He insisted on proof of the U.S. commitment: the dispatch of a planeload of weapons. Haney hastily arranged for a C-47 transport based at the Canal Zone to fly to a Honduran military airstrip laden with bazookas, .50-caliber machine guns and grenade launchers for Castillo Armas' band. At the moment the plane was set to take off, however, a cable arrived in the Canal Zone ordering the transport to remain on the ground; it was signed by J. C. King.

Colonel Haney, controlling the flight from Opa-Locka, ignored the telegram by going to bed. One of his men wired another cable to the Canal Zone reversing King's edict. The plane finally took off for Honduras. Haney's unilateral action outraged State Department and CIA officials. Wisner, thoroughly exasperated with the colonel by now, summoned him to Washington. Haney played the role of the innocent bystander, and Allen Dulles offhandedly forgave him, saying: "Admiral Nimitz was once ordered not to attack the Japanese fleet. He attacked anyway and won. And Washington forgot about his disobeying orders." Dulles, however, sent Tracy Barnes to Opa-Locka to stay with Haney permanently from then on.[23]

One last complication was a sudden attack on the CIA launched by an unlikely foe, Senator Joseph McCarthy. McCarthy had dominated American television screens during May with his investigation of alleged Communist infiltration of the U. S. Army, but by the end of that month he sensed that his probe was no longer reaping political benefits. He cast about for a new target, and on June 2 held a press conference to denounce the CIA for harboring Communists. He indicated that a round of hearings on the CIA would follow the Army hearings. Dulles flatly rejected the charges, though he never informed McCarthy of his plans for Operation Success, which would probably have pleased the demagogic senator. Eisenhower responded to McCarthy by promising to establish a blue-ribbon commission to look into the CIA, a body he later created but stacked with friends of the agency. McCarthy's threatened probe of the CIA never materialized, and Operation Success continued on schedule.[24]

11

THE FINAL
COUNTDOWN

The arrival of Czech arms gave the Secretary of State the evidence he had been seeking of a Soviet conspiracy to seize Guatemala, subvert Central America and take over the Panama Canal. Without some concrete "proof" like this, he would have been hard-pressed to deny accusations that he was acting solely on behalf of United Fruit. Dulles now intensified his pattern of public attacks against Guatemala. He issued threats of military intervention, hints of blockades, and proposals for punishment under the anti-Communist resolution the Americans had forced through at Caracas two months before. Castillo Armas, still waiting in Honduras and not yet even acquainted with his troops, watched Dulles' fusillade with delight.

Only five days after the *Alfhem's* visit to Puerto Barrios, Dulles ostentatiously signed a mutual security treaty with Honduras. (He had reached a similar agreement with another Central American dictatorship, Nicaragua, three weeks earlier.) On May 24, the U.S. government announced that it was sending several Air Force Globemaster cargo planes to Honduras and Nicaragua carrying arms provided under the new security treaties. Eisenhower recalled in his memoirs that this "initial shipment comprised only 50 tons of rifles, pistols, machine guns and ammunition, hardly enough to create apprehension in neighboring states." In fact, the shipments were calculated to do exactly that: "create apprehension" in the one state the United States wished to destabilize, Guatemala.[1]

Most of the weapons never went to the Nicaraguan or Honduran armies, however; they were quickly delivered to Castillo Armas' soldiers, equipping each of them with a burp gun, a pistol and a machete. Using the same cover of aiding the two "besieged" nations of Honduras and Nicaragua, the United States also sent Castillo Armas loads of weapons by sea. In addition, to underline the point of Dulles' actions, the U. S. Navy dispatched two submarines from Key West on May 23, saying only that they were going "south"; four days later, amid considerable fanfare, the Air Force sent three B-36 intercontinental bombers on a "courtesy call" to Nicaragua. The New York *Times* pointedly noted that the planes were capable of delivering atomic bombs. As the vise tightened on Guatemala, the capital had become a "tense, nervous city" by May's end, the New York *Times* reported.[2]

President Eisenhower called in congressional leaders on May 24 to announce yet another step against Guatemala. He informed them he was ordering the U. S. Navy to stop "suspicious foreign-flag vessels on the high seas off Guatemala to examine cargo." The politicans offered no objections; but as Eisenhower's interception order gradually leaked out, it created an international stir. Assistant Secretary of State Henry Holland even received a private opinion from the State Department's own legal adviser disputing the right of the United States to intercept peacetime commercial shipping. The brief warned:

In the absence of an armed attack, measures such as interception (involving the use of force) could not be justified either
under the Rio Treaty or under the United Nations Charter. On
the facts now known to this office, there appears to be no basis
for concluding that any nation is committing an armed attack
against any American state. Guatemala apparently is not committing armed attack against any of its neighbors. . . . In these
circumstances, if the United States were to intercept and escort
by force any ship in Guatemalan territorial waters or on the high
seas to an American port, there would be no legal justification for
such action either under the Rio Treaty or under the United Nations Charter. Such action would constitute a violation of international law . . .

Consequently the State Department's initial orders to the
Navy limited the operation to "surveillance" of shipping near
Guatemala beginning May 23. Two days later, however, Dulles
informed the British, the major seafaring power in the area besides the United States, that the American naval watch might go
further than surveillance in the case of a "suspicious vessel," but
he hoped for British cooperation.[3]

On that day, one of Dulles' own senior advisers tried to pull
the Secretary back. Robert Murphy, a highly experienced diplomat who had served as Franklin Roosevelt's confidential agent in
North Africa before the Allied landings in 1942 and later as
General Eisenhower's political adviser, was now Deputy Undersecretary of State. Murphy, who had not known about the interception order until he chanced upon a copy of the cable to navy
commanders, dashed off an angry, unsolicited memorandum to
Dulles on May 25 condemning the idea as "wrong" and "very ex-
pensive over the longer term." He cautioned: "My instinct, and
perhaps my ignorance of Guatemalan problems, tells me that to
resort to this action confesses the bankruptcy of our political
policy vis-à-vis that country." Murphy, citing the Department's
own legal brief, was particularly concerned over the forcible detention of foreign shipping on the high seas. "Our present action
should give stir to the bones of [WWI] Admiral von Tirpitz," he
wrote, "and no doubt the conversation of some German naval
officers will relate to our 'good neighbor' policy as *spurlos ver-
senkt* [sunk without a trace]."[4]

The next day, May 26, the Navy went ahead anyway and searched the French merchant ship *Wyoming* at the Canal Zone —with French cooperation—and discovered some twenty-two unregistered hunting rifles on board, but nothing else objectionable. On May 27, overruling the doubters, Eisenhower signed a secret National Security Council directive authorizing full interception of shipping in the Caribbean. Dulles admonished him to say publicly only that we were "checking up very closely on papers and cargoes of ships going into Guatemala but we had not established a blockade." On May 28, as the *Alfhem* was passing by Florida on its return voyage to Europe, the U. S. Coast Guard "escorted" her to Key West for a search that turned up nothing. On June 4, the Navy stopped and searched the Dutch freighter *Wulfbrook* at San Juan, Puerto Rico, occasioning a protest from the Dutch government. Other ships were allowed to pass without incident, though they were photographed. As late as June 7, it was still not exactly clear what the American "stop and search" policy was. A confused State Department finally informed the Chief of Naval Operations not to stop any more ships "without the (direct) O.K. of State."[5]

The new American maritime policy provoked an especially sharp response from Britain. Anthony Eden, the Foreign Secretary, thought Dulles overreacted to the Czech shipment since the weapons were mainly "small arms." His government, he warned, "could not possibly acquiesce in forcible action against British ships on the high seas." Eden sought assurances that the United States would not intercept a British ship without at least first seeking "permission." But Dulles rebuffed Eden, telling him that the Cold War meant "rules applicable in the past no longer . . . meet the situation and [are] required to be revised or flexibly applied." On June 18, Eden finally said the British government would reject a U.S. request to search its boats but would itself detain suspected United Kingdom ships "where practicable." Eden complained privately that free transit on the seas "was a proud right which the British had never before given up even in wartime and the Americans never said thank you." At least one Eisenhower aide thought the British had a point. Presidential press secretary James Hagerty wrote in his diary that the

State Department had "made a very bad mistake." The United States, he recalled, had fought the War of 1812 over the right of neutral boats not to be searched on the open waters. "I don't see how, with our traditional opposition to such search and seizure, we could possibly have proposed it, and I don't blame the British for one minute getting pretty rough in their answers."[6]

In the same May 24 meeting with congressional leaders at which he disclosed the policy on shipping in the Caribbean, Eisenhower also announced another step. He said he would call for a special meeting of the Organization of American States—the regional body then largely dominated by the United States—to "consider" what to do about developments in Guatemala. Secretary of State Dulles had already assigned Assistant Secretary Henry Holland to the task of lining up support among other Latin nations and, after the *Alfhem* docked at Puerto Barrios, he enlisted a former diplomat, Walter Donnelly, then working for the United States Steel Corporation, to coordinate preparations for an OAS session. He also recalled John Hill, an officer at the U. S. Embassy in Guatemala, to Washington to write an indictment of Arbenz that could be used as a diplomatic weapon (Hill produced a 50-page tome entitled "Soviet Communism in Guatemala"). In addition, he asked the Hondurans to appeal for OAS intervention in Guatemala on the grounds that Guatemalan Communists were fomenting labor unrest in Honduras. And he briefed executives of the United Fruit Company on the accelerating progress of Operation Success.[7]

At the same time, Dulles revved up a congressional offensive. An inquiry by the House Select Committee on Communist Aggression, chaired by Charles Kersten, was readied; the Senate Subcommittee on Internal Security, chaired by William Tenner, also prepared to hold hearings. Senator Margaret Chase Smith introduced a resolution to investigate the "extent to which Guatemalans imposed unjustified increases in the price of coffee." The State Department drafted speeches for Senator Alexander Wiley (R.-Wisconsin), Senator George Smathers (D.-Florida) and others on such subjects as comparing the "communist problem in Indo-China and the communist problem in Latin America."

A preliminary agreement also took shape to hold the OAS

meeting in Montevideo, Uruguay, in early July. At the urging of several Latin diplomats, Dulles agreed to delete from his draft resolution a clause demanding that Arbenz resolve his differences with United Fruit. He narrowed the resolution to a few stern punitive measures: detention and inspection of all Guatemala-bound ships by the U. S. Navy and a ban on the travel of Communists to and from Guatemala.[8]

Since the OAS conference was set for July and the Castillo Armas invasion for June, it seems likely that Dulles was using the threat of OAS sanctions as another psychological weapon against Arbenz. It certainly sent a new wave of concern through Guatemala, where it was accurately interpreted as a sign that the Americans would never compromise with Arbenz. And it was widely assumed—rightly, as it turned out—that the State Department had other, stronger weapons waiting to be used. In fact, American strategists were just then making contingency plans to cut off Guatemalan credit abroad, disrupt its petroleum supplies and persuade local businessmen to weaken the economy by sending their money to foreign banks.[9]

Arbenz decided to make one more effort to negotiate with the United States. Foreign Minister Toriello met with Peurifoy on May 24 to see if any settlement could be reached. Three days later, Toriello surprised both the Americans and the Hondurans by offering to sign a non-aggression treaty with Honduras. On June 1, the Foreign Minister tried a new tack with Peurifoy. He recalled that President Eisenhower had favored in January the creation of a neutral non-governmental commission to review all problems between the two nations, and told the ambassador that Guatemala was now ready to accept the proposal. He also said that President Arbenz would like to meet personally with Eisenhower in Washington. He even promised that Arbenz would be willing to negotiate with United Fruit over the issue of compensation for its expropriated land. But it was too late; Operation Success was irrevocably on course.[10]

In Guatemala, Dulles' attacks were having their desired effect. A plot against the government was uncovered on June 2, and police rounded up a dozen suspects. The Army also responded to the growing campaign against Arbenz. On June 3, a group of high-ranking officers, at Peurifoy's urging, called on the President to ask that he dismiss all Communists who held posts in his administration. Arbenz reassured them that the Communists were not dangerous. He himself was a property owner, he said, and he was not afraid of them. He told the officers that it was better to have the Communists working in the open than forcing them underground. He quoted Juan Perón to the effect that "communism is like strychnine, beneficial in small doses but highly dangerous in large quantities." The army men left dissatisfied.

The next day, rumors floated through Guatemala City that one of the large labor confederations, the rural union CNCG, had sent telegrams to its provincial affiliates instructing them to be alert to "reactionary elements" and prepare to "fight enemies." Peurifoy cabled Dulles that there was no "credible information" to indicate that the Army was about to turn weapons over to the labor unions. But the specter of the "peasant army" still frightened military officers. A few days after their first confrontation with Arbenz, the same commanders urged him again to remove Communists in his government and also demanded that he reject the creation of paramilitary "people's militias." Arbenz again replied that Marxists did not run his government and that it would be undemocratic to oust them.[11]

The country was growing increasingly agitated. On June 5, a retired chief of staff of the Guatemalan Air Force (1944–47), Rodolfo Mendoza Azurdia, mysteriously fled in a small plane. With him was Ferdinand Schoup, a onetime U. S. Air Force major who served until 1952 as deputy chief of the U. S. Air Force Mission to Guatemala. (Both men surfaced soon afterward as strategists for the Liberation air force.) On June 8, Arbenz won congressional permission to suspend constitutional guarantees for thirty days, citing the threat of invasion.

Over the next days, Peurifoy sent urgent cables to Dulles recommending that he turn up the diplomatic heat by abrogating existing U.S. trade agreements with Guatemala and by publicly urging resident Americans to leave the country. Taken together, Peurifoy believed, these two acts might cause panic and push the Army to act on its own. Alarm was already growing, he added dramatically: "As behind the Iron Curtain, husbands and sons are disappearing daily and families have no recourse to courts. Situation now a combination of gangsterism and Communism."[12]

Actually the situation was scarcely that grim. As even *Time* pointed out, suspending constitutional rights was hardly a novel act in Guatemala; it was specifically permitted by the constitution, and Arévalo had done it thirteen times during his six-year term. Arbenz himself had done it twice before. Moreover, by now the rural labor federation, CNCG, had backed off from its statement that it might arm its members, perhaps out of fear of the Army's reaction. There was no real evidence of widespread torture or murders. But restrictions on the press and the arrest of over a hundred anti-Arbenz activists, coupled with some unexplained deaths, gave an aroused Peurifoy cause to cable Dulles melodramatically in mid-June that "a reign of terror" had begun. Dulles borrowed the words for use in a statement he made to the international press on June 15, three days before the CIA invasion. In Guatemala, he told reporters, "there is going on somewhat of a reign of terror." He added ominously: "There is no doubt, in my opinion, but what the great majority of the Guatemalan people have both the desire and the capability of cleaning their own house."[13]

The Americans left nothing to chance in this final push. By late May, the CIA had covertly sponsored a "Congress Against Soviet Intervention in Latin America" in Mexico City, funneling funds for it through Mexican trade unions. Howard Hunt, the ubiquitous "propaganda chief" of Operation Success, was the conference's organizer. His task was to bring together "anti-Communist leaders" from all over the hemisphere to condemn Arbenz. With an ineptness that later became his trademark, Hunt stacked the conference with notorious political reactionaries and reportedly some Latin gangsters, along with a handful of liberals. Costa Rican and Ecuadoran delegates soon walked out to protest wild charges leveled against them by some of the ultra-rightists Hunt had invited. The congress ended as a press and public relations fiasco.[14]

The United States Information Agency cranked up a more sophisticated crusade. In June alone, USIA propagandists wrote more than 200 articles about Guatemala based on information from CIA sources, and distributed them for anonymous placement in scores of Latin newspapers. The agency shipped more than 100,000 copies of a pamphlet called "Chronology of Communism in Guatemala" throughout Latin America. Twenty-seven thousand copies of anti-Communist cartoons and posters were also distributed. The USIA also produced three special movies on Guatemala, including one on the Caracas OAS meeting, as well as reels of news footage favorable to the United States for showing free in movie houses in Latin America. The agency persuaded radio stations in friendly countries like Cuba to run "hard-hitting commentaries" on Guatemala at peak listening hours as the Castillo Armas invasion neared. An experienced USIA press officer was sent to the American Embassy in Honduras to brief "selected correspondents" on "inside" accounts of events once the coup began as a way of offsetting anticipated hostile foreign news reports about the invasion. One internal State Department memo reported that "the program of smearing Guatemalan maneuvers in advance was proceeding satisfactorily."[15]

The most successful covert enterprise of all was the CIA's clandestine radio campaign launched against Guatemala seven weeks before the invasion. The American actor-turned-agent David Atlee Phillips directed the radio effort. Tracy Barnes, Wisner's assistant, had hired Phillips on a contract basis to take on the assignment at Opa-Locka starting in March 1954. Phillips, something of an independent spirit, bluntly asked Barnes at that time what right the United States had to overthrow an elected foreign President. Barnes replied only with a restatement of the American position that the Soviets were creating an "easily expandable beachhead" in Guatemala. Phillips pressed him again, beseeching him for evidence of Soviet involvement, but Barnes replied firmly: "Our marching orders on this operation come from President Eisenhower." Phillips suppressed his objections and took off on a brief spin around Guatemala with CIA agent Henry Heckscher—both men wore disguises. Then, after a visit to CIA headquarters in Washington, he flew to Opa-Locka to begin work with three young Guatemalans who had been recruited for the radio broadcasts.[16]

Phillips and the crew concocted a classic "disinformation" campaign to spread fear and panic inside Guatemala. One of the three Guatemalans, José Torón Barrios, known as Pepe, assessed the Guatemalan radio audience for Phillips: 2 percent hard-core Marxists; 13 percent Arbenz supporters; 60 percent neutrals; 23 percent opposed to the "Communist drift" within Guatemala; and 2 percent militant anti-Communists. "Our job," Pepe proposed to Phillips, "is to intimidate listeners in the first two groups, and then to influence the mass of neutral types in the third group . . . and induce them to join the fourth and fifth categories." The foursome christened their clandestine station the "Voice of Liberation" and gave it a slogan: *"Trabajo, Pan y Patria"*—"Work, Bread and Country." They put it on the overseas band since many Guatemalans owned shortwave sets. Their first radio transmitter was installed in Nicaragua; it could beam its strong signal into the same channels as the Guatemalan government's station TGW, as well as other major radio airwaves. The clandestine outfit even took out advertisements in Guatemalan newspapers the day before the station went on the air, promising a galaxy of Latin stars, including Cantinflas, the popular Mexican comic, and many famous singers. Listeners tuned in the next day, May 1, and heard all of the headliners—on records.[17]

The announcer explained the deception by saying that it was the only way the rebel station could attract an immediate audience. From then on, the station broadcast regular propaganda to four groups—women, soldiers, workers and young people—urging them to join the Castillo Armas Liberation movement. After the *Alfhem's* arrival, the radio team aimed new messages at army officers in an attempt to split the military from Arbenz. The theme of these broadcasts was that Arbenz was secretly planning to disband the armed forces and replace them with a people's militia. The CIA began its leafleting flights carrying the same message: Arbenz is about to disarm the military and create a peasant army.

After the defection of the retired Air Force Colonel Mendoza Azurdia on June 4, Phillips' team sought him out to make propaganda broadcasts. Phillips recalled:

> Pepe . . . asked him to tape a special broadcast, an appeal to his former colleagues urging them to defect with their aircraft

and instructing them how to do it safely. "Not a chance," was his reply. "My family is still in Guatemala City." . . . That evening the three of them relaxed over a bottle of scotch. The pilot was a good aviator and a poor drinker. He became expansive, verbose. Pepe refilled his glass frequently. The pilot was sitting on the floor of the [radio] shack, his back against an old sofa. "If you did broadcast a plea to your air force friends," Pepe asked, "what would you say?" The pilot was eloquent and fiery in the best Latin tradition as he delivered a hypothetical speech to his friends persuading them to defect with their planes and to join Castillo Armas and his rebels. . . . The aviator had had a long day; soon his eyes closed and he was dozing. Pepe removed the tape recorder they had hidden in the sofa cushions. It was only an hour's work to cut up the tape, then splice it together again so that only the voice of the pilot—in what appeared to be a voluntary exhortation—remained in an impassioned request to his flying friends to join the winners. The tape was broadcast the next morning.

Phillips speculated later that Mendoza's exhortations were the motivation behind Arbenz's decision to ground his entire Air Force permanently. But, in fact, Arbenz had no functioning Air Force, except for six training planes built before 1936. Even Mendoza Azurdia had escaped in a small Cessna, not a fighter plane.[18]

The radio team also worked to create the impression that rebels were everywhere in Guatemala. Pretending to be part of a major insurgent force, announcers appealed to citizens to assist Liberation planes by locating drop sites for the "partisans." Some planes did drop supplies to Castillo Armas near the Honduran border, but they also made dummy parachute drops in rural areas to convince Guatemalan peasants that the rebels were nearby. To prevent Arbenz from calming public fear of a fifth column in the hills, members of the CIA radio team jammed the President's address to the nation on the second day of the invasion.[19]

Phillips' radio crew played a clever game of cat-and-mouse with the Guatemalan police. Though most of the broadcasts emanated from a ramshackle barn on a Somoza-owned plantation in Nicaragua and others were beamed from Honduras and the Dominican Republic, the announcers repeatedly proclaimed that their facilities were hidden "somewhere in Guatemala" (actually some transmissions did come from the U. S. Embassy in Guatemala City) and that they had successfully outwitted the Guatemalan constabulary. The New York *Times* and *Life*, among other publications, faithfully reported that the "Voice of Liberation" was based deep in the Guatemalan jungle.[20]

As the invasion date neared, President Eisenhower held a final meeting on Operation Success at the White House. He convened a breakfast session on June 15 with the Dulles brothers, Secretary of Defense Charles Wilson, the Joint Chiefs of Staff and several White House aides. Assistant Secretary of State for Congressional Affairs Thurston Morton was also there, at Dulles' bidding, so he would be prepared to brief Congress "in case the invasion doesn't succeed." Eisenhower said to the people around the table: "I want all of you to be damn good and sure you succeed. . . . When you commit the flag, you commit it to win." Assured that they would, Eisenhower declared his unequivocal endorsement: "I'm prepared to take any steps that are necessary to see that it succeeds, for if it succeeds, it's the people of Guatemala throwing off the yoke of Communism. If it fails, the flag of the United States has failed."[21]

Two days before that meeting, the CIA's handpicked Liberator, Colonel Carlos Castillo Armas, had finally gone to Tegucigalpa, Honduras, to meet his troops for the first time. The CIA transported about 170 of its mercenaries to Honduras for the encounter with their "commander." These were the men—Guatemalan exiles, American soldiers of fortune and a mixed crew of Central Americans—whom the CIA had trained at its hidden bases in Nicaragua. Afterward it moved them into positions close to the Guatemalan border.

The original plan had been to send the troops into Guatemala from El Salvador, but at the last moment Salvadoran officials got cold feet and reneged on their agreement with the Americans. Castillo Armas' rebels were therefore dispatched instead to several small frontier villages in Honduras, including a plantation town owned by United Fruit's Honduras division. (The fruit company also surreptitiously was providing to the CIA its Guatemalan railroad system to smuggle in arms; its Atlantic port to land equipment; its telegraph, telephone and radio to relay messages; its Guatemalan properties to give cover to the rebels; and its p.r. men to disseminate photos and bulletins about the advance of Castillo Armas' forces.) With the men in place, CIA trucks brought them bazookas, machine guns, grenade launchers and rations (later found to be spoiled) from Tegucigalpa. The invasion was now just forty-eight hours away.[22]

Castillo Armas' strategy was to seize the Guatemalan town of Zacapa, a key military prize because it was located at an important railroad junction, with tracks leading to El Salvador, Guatemala City and Puerto Barrios. At the same time, he planned to take Puerto Barrios itself, Guatemala's sea link to the outside world and the only significant Atlantic harbor in the country. (Though the plan eventually was followed—Zacapa was later bombed and several schooners did unload men and arms at Puerto Barrios—the rebels never captured either town.) Castillo Armas also assigned "hit and run" raiders to enter Guatemala, fan out and disrupt the country with sabotage, assaults and attacks on military patrols.[23]

The day before the invasion, the CIA chartered several DC-3s (at $400 per planeload) to airlift the remaining Liberation troops to the Honduran border towns of Copán, Macuelizo and Nueva Octotepeque. Then on the morning of June 18, Carlos Castillo Armas, dapper in his customary checkered shirt and leather jacket, climbed into his command car, a battered station wagon, and led a string of trucks across the frontier and into Guatemala. The Liberation was now officially underway. However, once it became clear that no spontaneous revolt was occurring, the CIA ordered Castillo Armas and his men to stay put six miles inside the frontier, avoid battles and await further instructions.[24]

The CIA now sent its pilots to work. A few days earlier Jerry DeLarm, a slim, sharp-featured ex-U. S. Navy pilot, armed with the .45 pistol he habitually carried, had arrived in Honduras on a regular Pan American flight from Guatemala City, leaving behind a flying school and an auto dealership, both covers for his secret role as a CIA agent code-named "Rosebinda." DeLarm, who once did skywriting and aerial broadcasts for Arbenz's election campaign in 1950 and claimed he'd never been paid, had made one of the first air forays, the dramatic trip to drop leaflets on Guatemala City from a C-47 on the morning of the invasion. The day after that expedition, DeLarm raided Puerto Barrios, flying a Cessna with Carlos Cheeseman, also an ex-U. S. Navy pilot. Cheeseman dropped a hand grenade and a dynamite stick from the plane's window onto the port's fuel tanks, causing a loud explosion and damaging several of them.

DeLarm and Cheeseman, however, only managed to inflict minor damage; other pilots in the ragtag air force had even worse luck. William Beall, an American from Tyler, Texas, was sent to strafe the city of Cobán. He completed his mission, but neglected to keep track of his fuel supply and ran out of gas while still airborne. He was forced to crash-land his plane just over the Guatemalan border in Mexico, and was briefly detained by the Mexican authorities before the CIA had him released. Two other planes were hit by small-arms fire from the ground and rendered useless.[25]

These few minor setbacks suddenly left the carefully planned invasion on the edge of failure. The plan to intimidate Arbenz into submission by sustained aerial harassment was now endangered. Arbenz had a few crucial days to regroup his forces and expose the fact that there was no real rebel army in the hills. On June 20, Allen Dulles bluntly told President Eisenhower that the battle could now go either way. That same day, James Reston's New York *Times* column suggested that the anti-Arbenz operation was Dulles' handiwork, thus putting him and the United States publicly on the spot.[26]

12

ARBENZ
FIGHTS BACK

On the afternoon of June 20, 1954, CIA Director Allen Dulles received a telephone briefing on the faltering air operation from the day-to-day chief of Operation Success, Colonel Albert Haney. The situation in Guatemala was getting worse, Haney reported from his command post at Opa-Locka, Florida, passing along the news about the loss of the three planes. In normal circumstances, the losses might not have seriously hurt such an expedition. But because the CIA, in order to preserve some measure of secrecy and deniability, had limited Haney to a dozen transports and a dozen front-line aircraft—of which only three were bombers—the sudden problem was potentially disastrous. The mercenary airmen were forced to improvise, Haney said, some tossing grenades out of cargo doors as Cheeseman had over Puerto Barrios, others carrying aloft hand-held machine guns to strafe targets.[1]

Things were not going well for Castillo Armas and his ragtag Liberation army on the ground, either. The plan to seize the rail center at Zacapa and the Atlantic harbor town of Puerto Barrios was going nowhere. The Guatemalan Army had turned back the tentative thrusts Castillo Armas' rebels had made toward the two towns; it had even seized a Honduran schooner, *Siesta de Trujillo*, at Puerto Barrios as it was trying to unload machine guns, rifles, grenades and radio equipment for the Liberator's troops. The CIA had not really expected Castillo Armas to take any great territory anyway, given the size of Arbenz's army. But it did want to create the impression that military defenses were crumbling. Combined with air raids on Guatemalan cities, that strategy was designed to provoke dissension in the Guatemalan Army and cause it to turn on Arbenz.[2]

In an effort to increase his stature, Castillo Armas now held a heavily publicized "Mass of Thanksgiving" on June 21 at the religious shrine in Esquipulas, the famed Church of the Black Christ. He wanted to add to the sense of impending triumph he hoped to project inside Guatemala by identifying himself with the Catholic Church. But his religious mentor, Archbishop Mariano Rossell Arellano, then waiting expectantly in Guatemala City, was no longer completely confident about Castillo Armas' mission, despite the Mass. That day he told Ambassador Peurifoy that direct U.S. intervention might be the only way to protect "anti-Communists and Christians" in Guatemala.[3]

To prevent the invasion's collapse, Haney urgently appealed to Allen Dulles to send replacement fighter-bombers for his makeshift air force. The plot against Arbenz, he argued, would succeed or fail according to the number of air strikes the CIA could launch. On June 21, Dulles and his top staff debated Haney's request. One of the military men present, General C. P. Cabell, reminded the Director that he had a full squadron of National Guard fighter planes standing by in Puerto Rico for just such an eventuality. But Dulles decided against dispatching the modern American fighters on the grounds that such a move would make American involvement too obvious.

Instead, he agreed to send just two World War II-vintage planes, subject to the approval of the State Department. Later in the day Dulles, with Richard Bissell and Frank Wisner, went to the State Department to seek clearance for this decision. At the meeting, Bedell Smith had no qualms, but Henry Holland expressed grave doubts about sending the replacement aircraft. He worried aloud about possible international repercussions if the U.S. role became known. Indeed, he had become convinced that Castillo Armas had already lost the "war." When Smith overruled his protests, Holland insisted on a direct appeal to Eisenhower. A meeting was arranged for the next afternoon at the White House.[4]

Events were moving quickly in Guatemala, reinforcing Dulles' determination to press his case for the additional planes. As the air attacks had faltered, Haney had activated a contingency plan to fabricate an "incident" that could be used to justify open military intervention. He sent one of his pilots, an American named Joseph Silverthorne, to drop several bombs around a Honduran airstrip near the border so the Hondurans could claim they had been attacked by Arbenz. Honduras, according to the scenario, would then call for help from the Organization of American States or even the United States itself.

Unfortunately, the attack was ill-conceived and poorly executed. The Honduran military leaders, naturally ready to cooperate with any plot against the liberal Arbenz, could not even agree on which town had been bombed. One leader denounced an air strike against Santa Rosa, but another said bombs had hit San Pedro de Cobán. The confusion did nothing to convince neutral observers. Credibility further declined when a New York *Times* correspondent visited San Pedro to inspect the damage. After some searching, he could find only two unexploded and obsolete 250-pound bombs lying on the runway and a few small craters made by test bombs filled with water instead of explosives. It was hardly compelling evidence of a serious raid.[5]

Also that day, the Liberation air force demonstrated its amateurishness in another way. An ex-Marine pilot was given the assignment of knocking out the government's radio station in Guatemala City. The station's destruction, Haney hoped, would make it more difficult for Arbenz to rally his forces in the climactic hours, and would also free another radio frequency for the "Voice of Liberation." "But be careful," Wade was warned. "Just down the road is the transmitter of an evangelical station, and there are two American missionary ladies there. You can tell the difference because the Arbenz station is all concrete and the mission has a red tile roof."

The pilot returned from his mission, claiming success. "Are you sure you hit the right place?" he was asked.

"Absolutely," he replied. "You should have seen them red tiles flying!"

The station the pilot had hit was TGNA, operated by Harold Von Broekhoven, an evangelist from Passaic, New Jersey. By good fortune, the Americans who worked there were out of the building when the bombs hit.[6]

As part of the same botched mission, the pilot tried to destroy the Shell Oil storage tanks at the La Aurora Airport near Guatemala City. His explosives missed the mark, however, and he returned to his base after only managing to spray one tank with about thirty bullets. The local Shell manager reported that the container had lost half of its 140,000 gallons of gasoline, but that the important backup tanks were undamaged.[7]

In Managua, President Somoza grew more agitated by the hour. He had never liked or trusted Castillo Armas very much, and now that the invasion was bogging down, he began to fume aloud. "He's a little prick!" Somoza exploded. "He doesn't know his business. He's poor timber." Somoza made a show of inviting Castillo Armas' rival, General Ydígoras, to lunch at his official quarters. Ydígoras arrived accompanied by Rip Robertson, Haney's deputy in Operation Success. Somoza stood in front of a map with pins showing the location of Castillo Armas' troops. He bitterly denounced the Liberator for his lack of forward progress. "What kind of crummy military school did Castillo go to?" he shouted at one point.

"The same one I did," Ydígoras answered mildly.[8]

President Arbenz was guardedly hopeful as he learned of the

setbacks that were befalling the Liberation forces. He began to think that the Castillo Armas assault, like others before it, might soon be repelled. The Chief of the General Staff visited the front and declared upon returning to the capital: "Victory is near." Though some army officers, including many who had been loyal to the assassinated Colonel Arana, privately opposed Arbenz, there was no sign of military rebellion or mass defections. In an interview a year later, Arbenz recalled that at this point "it was clear to everybody that the military situation had been dominated, the aggression defeated . . ." Guatemala City was coming back to normal, and Arbenz even lifted the night blackout.[9]

But he was not aware of the meeting taking place in President Eisenhower's office. Allen Dulles made his appeal once more for permission to send two more planes to the Liberation forces, and Assistant Secretary of State Henry Holland once more opposed the request. Dulles, speaking first, flatly told Eisenhower that without the replacement planes, Operation Success would be seriously endangered. Holland countered that, while it might have been defensible to supply aircraft before the invasion, to do so while the eyes of the world were focused on Guatemala would expose the United States to charges of unilateral intervention in the affairs of a sovereign state. The President briefly considered the arguments, and then asked Dulles directly what chance the Liberation would have without the planes.

"About zero," replied Dulles.

"Suppose we supply the aircraft," Eisenhower wondered. "What would be the chances then?"

"About twenty percent," said the CIA Director.

Eisenhower later wrote that he considered the answer "realistic" and "honest." He decided to approve the planes, and said that, if the decision was discovered and questioned, he would claim to be acting under the resolution the OAS had approved in Caracas the previous March. (The resolution condemned Communist subversion in the Americas, it is true, but Eisenhower conveniently overlooked the fact that it specifically barred unilateral action by nations without prior consultation among OAS members.) As the meeting broke up, the President told Dulles: "If you'd said ninety percent, I'd have said no."

Dulles grinned. "Mr. President," he said, "when I saw Henry walking into your office with three large law books under his arm, I knew he had lost his case already."

Soon afterward, in fact, Eisenhower privately confessed great irritation over Holland's complaints. He told General Andrew Goodpaster, an aide, "If you at any time take the route of violence or support of violence . . . then you commit yourself to carry it through, and it's too late to have second thoughts, not having faced up to the possible consequences, when you're midway in an operation."[10]

Richard Bissell, Dulles' aide at the CIA, quickly arranged for delivery of the two replacement planes to the rebel forces. A "cover" transaction was made in which the planes were sold to Nicaragua after the CIA had provided President Somoza with the $150,000 purchase price. The intermediary was Somoza's son-in-law and ambassador to Washington, Guillermo Sevilla Sacasa. The planes were flown to Managua and then to the clandestine airstrips from which they began to launch their raids against Guatemala.

At this time, Bissell also prepared a contingency plan in case the new planes were unsuccessful in turning the tide of battle. He enlisted the cooperation of a New York shipping firm, the Metropolitan Shipping Company, for a possible sea lift. The scheme was to use several freighters to transport Castillo Armas' mercenaries secretly from a point in Honduras to Puerto Barrios, the United Fruit port in Guatemala, from which they would move southward to link up with their comrades around Zacapa and Esquipulas. (As it happened, this backup plan was not needed.)[11]

Unaware of Eisenhower's reaffirmed commitment to his overthrow, Arbenz continued to press for a diplomatic resolution. He felt secure enough to reject advice he was receiving to call a mass rally of supporters in the capital, a move some historians later speculated might have saved his presidency. Instead, he asked President Oscar Osorio of El Salvador—a military dictator who was most anxious for his demise—to help bring an end to the fighting by mediating between him and Honduran officials. Arbenz did not grasp the extent to which the Americans and the Hondurans (and other neighbors) had become allies pledged to his destruction. He hoped that he could induce the Hondurans to crack down on the Liberation forces operating from their territory. At the same time, Arbenz sent Foreign Minister Toriello to see Ambassador Peurifoy again to urge the Americans once more to call a halt to the hostilities. Guatemala's military, Toriello told Peurifoy, could handle Castillo Armas and his men on the ground, but he added prophetically that it could not "cope with air attacks."[12]

On June 21 and 22, Toriello also sent two impassioned appeals to the United Nations for help in resolving the crisis. Arbenz still wanted the UN to play a mediating role; the United States remained determined to prevent it from doing so. The Americans preferred the forum to be the Organization of American States, where the result was more predictable than at the UN. Toriello's first appeal was a methodic recounting of the events of recent days:

> . . . acts of aggression against this Republic continued last night and today, from bases in states, members of the United Nations, in open contravention of the [June 20 resolution] of the Council, as follows: between midnight on June 20 and 2 P.M. on June 21, the following incidents occurred . . . (c) At 7:16 A.M. unidentified aircraft machine-gunned the town of Zacapa. (d) At 7:30 A.M. the same aircraft damaged the railway station of the same town. (e) At 8:35 A.M. unidentified aircraft machine-gunned the towns of York and Cristina, and bombed the northern railway line, causing considerable damage at Kilometer 68. (f) At 8:50 piratical aircraft again flew over the town of Zacapa, and the Zacapa railway bridge was bombed and severely damaged; repairs will require at least a week. . . . I consider it necessary to repeat the important fact that all the flights mentioned were without exception made from airfields situated outside the national territory of Guatemala.[13]

The challenge Toriello presented to the UN was whether it could stop a battle in which a major power had a direct interest. UN Secretary-General Dag Hammarskjöld believed that the world body had been created precisely to deal with this sort of crisis. Hammarskjöld and his supporters—some of whom, the New York *Times* observed at this point, wore "pink-tinted glasses"— also pointed out that Guatemala was not even a member of the OAS (because of the Belize dispute), to which the Americans wanted to send the matter, though it was a member of the UN.

In addition, Article 103 of the UN Charter stipulated that in any conflict between the Charter obligations and other regional obligations of a member state, the Charter obligations should prevail. This interpretation, Hammarskjöld argued, had further support in Articles 34 and 35 of the Charter, which allowed any nation to bring any situation to the attention of the Security Council at any time. He noted that the American delegation to the original San Francisco Conference that established the UN in 1945 had supported the adoption of those articles. Hammarskjöld also cited Article 24 of the Charter, which conferred on the Security Council "primary responsibility for the maintenance of international peace and security."[14]

America's UN ambassador, Henry Cabot Lodge, a strong backer of United Fruit during his Senate years, who opposed a UN role, had a somewhat weaker legal case. He pointed to Article 52, which directed UN members who were part of regional treaty organizations to "make every effort to achieve pacific settlement of local disputes, through such regional arrangements or by such regional agencies, before referring them to the Security Council." Lodge also cited Article 20 of the OAS Charter, which provides: "All international disputes that may arise between American states shall be submitted to the peaceful procedures set forth in this Chapter, before being referred to the Security Council of the United Nations."[15]

In fact, of course, the issue was not one of legalisms, but of power. The United States had the votes to control any proceeding of the OAS. At the Security Council the outcome would be less certain. Dulles was also afraid that, if the UN were allowed to consider Guatemala's complaint, the debate would be peppered with anti-American speeches and might cause a wave of foreign condemnation of the Eisenhower administration. When Hammarskjöld telephoned Lodge to discuss Guatemala's request for a Security Council session, the American delegate was unfriendly, characterizing Toriello's appeals as Communist maneuvers. He also told the Secretary-General that he would resist calling a meeting of the Security Council—a prerogative that was his as president of the Council for June. (It has been suggested by some historians that the invasion may have been planned to coincide with his term as president.) For twenty-four hours, Hammarskjöld lobbied to pressure Lodge into calling a meeting; Lodge finally agreed that the Security Council would meet at three o'clock on the afternoon of June 25—fully eight days after Castillo Armas had crossed into Guatemala and the Liberation air force had begun its bombing.[16]

While Lodge worked on the smaller nations represented on the Security Council to support the United States and send the issue to the OAS, Eisenhower and John Foster Dulles concentrated on two essential votes: France and Great Britain, the pillars of the Atlantic alliance. Lodge had tipped Dulles off that both countries were preparing to back a proposal that the Council send a team of observers to Central America. When Eisenhower heard this, he angrily instructed Dulles at a White House meeting on Thursday, June 24, to veto the proposal if the British insisted on offering it. This would have marked the first time the United States had used the weapon against an ally at the United Nations. The British, Eisenhower said, had no right to stick their noses into matters which concern this hemisphere. "The British expect us to give them a free ride and side with them on Cyprus," Eisenhower exclaimed. "And yet they won't even support us on Guatemala! Let's give them a lesson."[17]

It happened that British Prime Minister Winston Churchill and Foreign Secretary Anthony Eden were visiting the White House the next morning—the very day of the Security Council session—on an unrelated mission. Eisenhower and Dulles used the occasion to talk "cold turkey" to Churchill and Eden, suggesting that, if they did not withdraw their backing for a UN inquiry, the United States would not support Great Britain and France on issues of importance to them such as the Suez Canal, Cyprus or Indochina. The British leaders finally agreed to abstain on the vote, and the French followed suit.[18]

Later that day, the Security Council voted 5 to 4—with Britain and France abstaining—to defeat the resolution for a UN investigation. (Actually the abstentions made no difference since seven votes were required for passage.) An understanding was reached that the OAS would now look into the Guatemala crisis and report back to the Security Council. Hammarskjöld was so upset with the American machinations, which he believed undercut the strength of the UN, that he even considered resigning his post as Secretary-General. Five days later, after Arbenz had fallen, Hammarskjöld wrote Lodge a restatement of his views that the UN had initial jurisdiction over the matter of Guatemala. U.S. officials reacted sharply, calling the letter a "warped presentation" and asking that it not be circulated among the delegates.[19]

The goal of American strategy at the United Nations was to prevent any new factors from disrupting the already endangered Operation Success. With the OAS now handling the matter, the United States had fulfilled that objective. As it turned out, however, the OAS never got to prepare a report on Guatemala. As Assistant Secretary of State Henry Holland began arrangements for the OAS's dormant Inter-American Peace Committee to dispatch a stacked investigating mission to Guatemala, he was overtaken by events. The planned Montevideo OAS summit also had to go. Just as the Americans had hoped, events in the field were moving faster than diplomacy.[20]

In the midst of this maneuvering, Haney finally got his two new planes. As soon as they arrived on June 23, they were launched on a seventy-two-hour rampage over the Guatemalan countryside; this time CIA pilots picked their targets carefully and committed few errors. On the first day, they bombed the military barracks in Zacapa and later strafed nearby Chiquimula, about twenty-five miles from the Honduran border. The next day, four of the planes dropped incendiary explosives on Chiquimula, setting houses afire as Castillo Armas' troops surrounded and seized the town. In the battle to take Chiquimula, seventeen soldiers on both sides were killed and dozens of others were wounded. Castillo Armas proclaimed the village the headquarters of his "provisional government." It was the most costly battle of the Liberation, and represented the deepest penetration by the rebels into Guatemala.[21]

On June 25, the day the Security Council voted not to discuss Guatemala, three rebel planes strafed Zacapa a second time, striking an ammunition dump. Around five-thirty in the afternoon, the same three planes assaulted Guatemala City, bombing, among other targets, the oil reserves at the Guatemala City airport. Later, one flier dropped a large smoke bomb in the middle of the parade grounds of the Matamoros military fort, creating an ominous black cloud and delivering an implicit threat, but causing no real damage. During a nighttime raid, the Americans played a tape recording of a bombing attack over large loudspeakers set up on the embassy roof that heightened the anxiety of the capital's residents.[22]

By now the effectiveness of the planes had earned them the nickname of "*sulfatos*" (laxatives) for the effect they supposedly had on Arbenz and other government leaders. On the morning of June 25, an obviously tense and weary Foreign Minister Toriello addressed a last-minute cable to Secretary of State John Foster Dulles asking for U.S. understanding.

> I regret to inform your Excellency that a savage attack with TNT bombs took place yesterday on the civilian population of Chiquimula as well as strafing of that city and the cities of Gualán and Zacapa in this Republic by invading planes coming from the neighboring Republic of Honduras. . . . We also know that other planes are based in Nicaragua using civil and military airports. We have information that from today until Sunday such pirate planes will massively bomb the capital of this Republic, Guatemala lacking modern aircraft to repel them owing to United States boycott on sale of planes to us for several years; that circumstance makes it impossible for us to defend ourselves from modern bombers and fighters which the mercenary invading forces possess. Guatemala appeals urgently to your Excellency to communicate to you this painful situation and asks that your enlightened government, always respectful of the human rights of which it has been the standard bearer, be good enough to intercede with the Security Council of the United Nations so that its resolution of the 20th of this month regarding an immediate cessation of all activity provoking bloodshed not be flouted, and that the member states who lend overt assistance to the invaders comply with the abstention ordered in that resolution. Confident that your Excellency's enlightened government and the people of your cultured nation will condemn the inhuman and criminal aggression of which the unarmed civilian population of Guatemala is the victim and that your valued moral

support will contribute to prompt reestablishment of the peace and security disturbed by the aforementioned mercenary invasion, I express to your Excellency the assurance of my highest and most distinguished consideration.

It was an eloquent statement, but did not speak to the concerns of the Dulles brothers. It represented an old-fashioned but futile plea to the United States to return to the Good Neighbor policy of another administration.[23]

Many Arbenz loyalists in Guatemala refused to back down in the face of the air onslaught. One was a twenty-five-year-old Argentine doctor named Ernesto "Che" Guevara. Guevara had originally come to Guatemala in January 1954, attracted by its climate of social reform, and was earning a living selling books and magazines. His ostensible purpose was to study the role of medical care under Arbenz's regime. When the air raids began, he volunteered to go to the front, but the Guatemalan Army was using only full-time soldiers, not civilians. He then tried unsuccessfully to organize units to guard the capital. In the final hours, he helped move a cache of arms to a putative resistance brigade. After Arbenz's fall, he thought the former President should retreat to the mountains with a band of armed workers and peasants and fight on indefinitely. Guevara himself sought refuge at the Argentine Embassy. Ultimately he was granted safe passage to Mexico City, where he met Fidel Castro and soon joined him in his guerrilla war against Cuban dictator Fulgencio Batista. "It was Guatemala," wrote Guevara's first wife, Hilda Gadea, "which finally convinced him of the necessity for armed struggle and for taking the initiative against imperialism. By the time he left, he was sure of this." Guevara also learned another lesson—from the conduct of the Guatemalan armed forces, which he felt had betrayed Arbenz. He later advised Castro: "We cannot guarantee the Revolution before cleansing the armed forces. It is necessary to remove everyone who might be a danger. But it is necessary to do it rapidly, right now."[24]

Despite isolated acts of resistance by Arbenz supporters like Guevara, rumors of Castillo Armas' proximity to Guatemala City demoralized most residents of the capital. The CIA's "Voice of Liberation" radio operators, whose transmissions cleverly "snuggled up" to the frequencies of Guatemalan radio stations and "spoofed" Guatemalan military signals, skillfully painted a picture of war and upheaval. Fabricated reports of large troop movements, fearsome battles, major Guatemalan defeats and growing rebel strength frightened an already confused and disheartened populace. Just at this time, trains were bringing home the first wounded soldiers from one of the few real battle fronts, Chiquimula. Colonel Carlos Enrique Díaz, the Army Chief of Staff, visited the men in the city hospital on June 25; pictures of the bandaged troops the next day in Guatemalan newspapers gave credence to the CIA broadcasts.[25]

The CIA now intensified its psychological warfare over the airwaves. Bulletins over the "Voice of Liberation" announcing major losses for Arbenz in clashes (later rebroadcast on military channels) finally convinced some of Arbenz's officers that the reports were genuine. The CIA also answered real military messages from Arbenz commanders with fake responses. The agency frequently sent meaningless "orders" to fictitious rebel encampments over its radio band. "Disinformation" over the Liberation network fomented other rumors. A typical broadcast assured listeners: "It is not true that the waters of Lake Atitlán have been poisoned." (So convincing were the psychological tricks that some U.S. congressmen later wanted to use the "Voice of Liberation" techniques to "improve" the Voice of America.)[26]

The one rumor that most disturbed Guatemalan authorities was that Castillo Armas was garnering volunteers as he marched. As early as June 20, the New York *Times* reported that Castillo Armas was "doing his best to spread the impression that his movement involved thousands of men . . ." "Voice of Liberation" announcers incited further speculation by pretending ignorance: "At our command post here in the jungle we are unable to confirm or deny the report that Castillo Armas has an army of five thousand men." Repeated frequently enough, the rumor soon took on a momentum of its own. On June 25, even Arbenz's Minister of Communication, Colonel Carlos Aldana Sandoval, told friends he was convinced that Arbenz was sinking because the rebel forces "were being swelled by thousands of volunteers." Actually Castillo Armas never had more than 400 men under his command.[27]

The fiction of a massive rebel army was believed partly because the international press corps reported it. In Guatemala
City, under virtual house arrest by Arbenz, who was fearful that
unfriendly reporters might send out dispatches harmful to the
regime, foreign journalists knew little more of what was really
taking place than residents. Twenty-nine-year-old Clay Felker,
then a reporter for *Life* magazine, spent most of his time in the
Pan American Hotel with other foreign correspondents, playing
cards and exchanging stories. He once snapped photos of a rebel
air attack on Fort Matamoros. Barred from the action, the press
corps regarded the whole affair as something of a lark.[28]

The main source of "inside" news was the U.S. ambassador,
John Peurifoy. In the midst of the fighting, Peurifoy cut a
dashing figure. Dressed in natty clothes, with a confident smile
and a free-wheeling command style, he charmed the press corps.
He dropped tidbits of information, confided private thoughts to
correspondents and drank with reporters at the American Club
downtown in the midst of the aerial bombardment. All were
struck by his courage; none realized that he knew precisely
when the raids were coming and where the bombs or bullets
were expected to hit. During one attack, his air attaché even reassured journalists indiscreetly that they need not worry about
the pilots: "They're well trained and they're doing their jobs."
Peurifoy openly coveted the press coverage; it was no secret that
he had ambitions to enter politics and perhaps run for the gover-
norship or the U. S. Senate in his home state of South Carolina.[29]

The foreign correspondents in Tegucigalpa, Honduras, were
even worse off than those in Guatemala City. Castillo Armas, on
wise advice from the Fruit Company's New York p.r. firm, Clements Associates, barred newsmen from the "war zone," even cutting phone lines leading to the area. The CIA naturally did not
want the small size of Castillo Armas' army or any of its other
shortcomings to become known to Arbenz. Clements publicists
doled out "war bulletins" which generally shaded the truth but
did not openly lie. For example, one communiqué reported:
"Liberationist land, sea and air forces are striking at Puerto Barrios and San José . . ." This was technically true but considerably exaggerated, since only two boats had appeared at Puerto

Barrios with a few soldiers and two planes had briefly strafed San José. At the same time, Clements released photos of the Liberation troops being joined by "volunteers" in small border towns like Esquipulas and La Florida. Actually Castillo Armas' men had merely thrust empty rifles into the hands of bewildered villagers, lined them up and photographed them at Clements' request. To convey an impression of violence and unrest, Liberation forces left the ground littered with dead mules.[30]

One or two resourceful journalists broke through the security ring around Castillo Armas. Evelyn Irons, a correspondent for the London *Evening Standard,* rented one of the few live mules left in the area and somehow slipped past Castillo's guards and into Esquipulas. She located Castillo Armas and got a brief but noncommittal interview with the surprised leader. She went on to the "front lines" at Chiquimula, but by the time she arrived the battle was over. (Following her exclusive, the New York *Times* wired its stringer in Guatemala City: "Get off ass—get on burro.") Other journalists, like Homer Bigart of the New York *Herald Tribune,* who was in Esquipulas when Castillo Armas marched in, had been summarily expelled.[31]

Kept at arm's length by Castillo Armas, the journalists sought out the best-known "reliable source" for news about Central America: the United Fruit Company. Foreign correspondent Tad Szulc recalled later that the company's Boston headquarters was an "excellent source for newsmen in following almost on an hourly basis the progress of the invasion." Thomas McCann of the Fruit Company's press office circulated photographs of mutilated human bodies about to be buried in a mass grave as examples of the atrocities committed by the Arbenz regime uncovered by Castillo Armas. McCann later admitted that the bodies in the pictures could have been almost anything from earthquake victims to executed foes of Castillo Armas himself.[32]

Most reporters, whether in Guatemala, Honduras or Boston, had no idea of what was really going on. All portrayed the affair as a romantic crusade pitting Castillo Armas and his plucky irregulars against a Goliath-like Red Army. The principal anti-Arbenz figures, Peurifoy and Castillo Armas, were depicted as heroes. All newsmen accepted on faith the diet of war reports supplied by the U.S. embassies in Guatemala and Honduras, by

Castillo Armas' American press agents, by the United Fruit
Company and by the governments of Honduras and Nicaragua
as well as the one in Washington. Practically no one questioned
the contents of the press handouts, communiqués, photos or
briefings. Nor did any raise the questions of how Castillo Armas
obtained the money for his planes and weapons and trucks;
where his soldiers and pilots came from; who had arranged the
broadcasts of the "Voice of Liberation"; and why Honduras
and Nicaragua had agreed to let Castillo Armas' forces camp
and train on their territory. A few reporters suspected CIA
involvement, but none pursued it. No correspondents reported
Arbenz's side of the story. Clay Felker's coverage in *Life*
summed up the prevailing mood among American journalists
and editors: "If the Arbenz forces are successful," he wrote, "the
Kremlin will gain a *de facto* foothold in the Western Hemisphere."[33]

Largely because so many reporters and editors shared this common conviction, the dozens of anti-American protests and demonstrations that exploded all over Latin America in late June were
given scant coverage and regarded as scarcely credible. *Life*
noted the hemispheric show of support for Arbenz only by observing that "world communism was efficiently using the Guatemalan show to strike a blow at the U.S. . . . in the form of
Red-run anti-U.S. demonstrations which loudly supported Guatemala and waved the bloody shirt of Yankee imperialism from
Mexico City to Santiago." Yet most neutral observers could not
recall such a widespread continental outpouring of anti-
American feeling over a single incident. In Mexico, students and
workers marched against the United States in marketplaces and
at the university. In Honduras, where the government supported
the Liberation invasion, students held a rally in the capital
against U.S. policy and "Wall Street interests." Panamanian students called a twenty-four-hour strike to protest U.S. intervention. Demonstrators stoned the offices of United Press International and the North American Electric Company in Cuba
and called a twenty-four-hour strike to express their outrage.
Hundreds of young Cubans also began converging on the Guatemalan Embassy in Havana to enlist in the Guatemalan
Army. In Ecuador, students rallied to the Arbenz cause and

the government characterized the U.S. role in Guatemala as "intervention." Large labor unions in Bolivia held mass meetings and issued statements of protest. The prominent anti-Communist Brazilian newspaper editor Carlos Lacerda strongly criticized the United States. Argentina's Congress passed a resolution backing Arbenz and Uruguay's Congress enacted a resolution condemning U.S. "aggression" in Guatemala. Chile's Chamber of Deputies voted 34 to 15 to assail the United States for its actions in Guatemala.[34]

Privately top State Department officials recognized the seriousness of the Latin reaction. On June 23, the Department took its own secret survey of protests south of the border. It found "significant indications of public reactions" in eleven countries during June 18–22: Argentina, Brazil, Chile, Colombia, Cuba, Honduras, Mexico, Panama, Peru, Uruguay and Venezuela. Contrary to what was being reported in the press, the State Department privately acknowledged that much of the reaction against the United States in these countries was emanating from non-Communist and even pro-American moderates.[35]

The new wave of attacks by the Liberation air force was meantime having an effect on the Guatemalan military, just as the planners of Operation Success had hoped. On June 25, Arbenz received what he later called an "ultimatum from the front: I should resign or [the Army] would come to an agreement with the invaders." The CIA had authorized its paramilitary teams at the front lines to promise cash payments to any officer thinking of defecting, and one army commander reportedly accepted $60,000 to surrender his troops. Arbenz himself noted that several top field officers had also received an "excellent offer" of money from Ambassador Peurifoy. There was still no sign, however, that ordinary Guatemalans were flocking to Castillo Armas' banner. In the midst of the fighting, Castillo Armas still had to hire Guatemalans off the street as truck drivers, since he could not muster enough volunteers to transport his supplies.[36]

But the masses also seemed to be growing apathetic toward Arbenz. In a few isolated areas, peasants and workers gathered in small groups awaiting orders to help defend the government. Víctor Manuel Gutiérrez, the Communist leader, made radio appeals calling for the formation of "brigades" of "commandos"

to fight for Arbenz. A peasant brigade actually assembled near
Cobán. But there was no organized plan for resistance. Many
Guatemalans, accepting the fabrications of the CIA's "Voice of
Liberation" over Arbenz's deteriorating position, resigned them-
selves to defeat.[37]

On June 25, President Arbenz finally made a last desperate
effort to distribute army weapons to the "people's organizations
and the political parties." If the Army would not fight for him,
the President had finally decided, he would arm those who
would. He ordered Colonel Díaz to open the Army's weapons
caches to civilians. The same tactic had been used by President
Arévalo when his government was threatened with overthrow
after the Arana assassination in 1949. But Arbenz was too late.
The next day, Colonel Díaz reported to his leader that he had
tried to turn the weapons over to civilians, but "I did not have
the obedience of the chiefs of the troops."[38]

That stark statement shook Arbenz deeply. Without the loyalty of his Army and without any other armed force to defend
him, the end was near.

13

THE LONGEST DAY

As usual during the summer rainy season in Central America, Sunday, June 27, dawned cool and cloudy over Guatemala City. President Arbenz was exhausted; like his tormentor, Ambassador Peurifoy, whose residence was on the opposite side of town from the National Palace, the President had slept very little during the last two weeks. He was drinking heavily, a problem he had at one time conquered in the past. All the adjectives that friends and enemies alike had used over the years to describe him— firm, decisive, strong-willed, commanding—now seemed quite mistaken. Arbenz was thoroughly shaken, just as a man who has been victim of a successful psychological warfare campaign might be expected to be. He was an emotional wreck, and his political condition was not much better.

Given the collapsing state of affairs, David Phillips, the CIA propaganda chief of Operation Success, had decided before the weekend that "now was the time for the final big lie." A series of broadcasts through Saturday night and Sunday now proclaimed that two large and heavily armed columns of rebels were making their way toward Guatemala City. As the hours ticked by, the progress of the mythical "columns" was followed closely by the broadcasters.

Castillo Armas and his tiny band were still sitting in Chiquimula just a few miles inside the border, awaiting orders from their American superiors while staying close enough to the foreign sanctuary of Honduras for quick retreat at the first sign of sustained attack. Castillo Armas' caution was unnecessary, though he remained unaware of it at the time—he knew little more than the average Guatemalan radio listener—but the CIA's more sophisticated techniques, including the Phillips transmissions and the maddening air assaults, were thoroughly demoralizing the Arbenz forces, diminishing the possibility of a military counter-attack against the Liberationists by the hour.

Frightened Guatemalans listening to the CIA radio broadcasts began fleeing from the city, not wanting to be caught in the tremendous battle believed imminent for control of the capital. "Voice of Liberation" announcers actually appealed to fleeing refugees to make way for the nonexistent rebel columns. Few of the panicked citizens stopped to wonder why, in their flight along the major highways, they never encountered any advancing soldiers. But of course the broadcasts were intended primarily to scare Arbenz and his aides in the palace. Interspersed with the "news" reports were simulated military messages: "To Commander X, to Commander X. Sorry, we cannot provide the five hundred additional soldiers you want. No more than three hundred are available; they will be joining you at noon tomorrow." With no one he could trust to give him accurate information, Arbenz could no longer be certain that there wasn't at least some truth to the radio bulletins.[1]

A well-organized rumor mill also was put into effect by the planners of Operation Success. Americans in contact with the U. S. Embassy, as well as embassy employees, benignly asked Guatemalan friends if it was true that cruisers and aircraft car-

Colonel Carlos Castillo Armas, hand-picked by the CIA to be the "Liberator" of Guatemala, greets townspeople in Esquipulas, Guatemala (left). A few of his band are seen in front of the town's religious shrine, the Church of the Black Christ (bottom). (Credit: Wide World Photos)

After Arbenz's defeat he was searched at the airport before departing for Mexico. (Credit: Francisco Rivera/*Time* magazine)

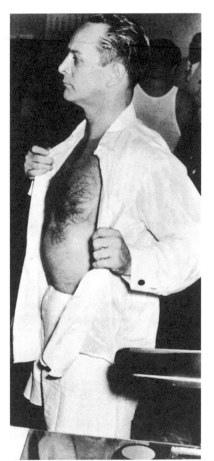

At the height of the CIA's Operation Success, the plot to overthrow Arbenz, Ambassador Peurifoy was visibly in command. He is seen here with one of the principal CIA agents working on the coup, Enno Hobbing (left). (Credit; Leonard McCombe, *Life*, © 1954 Time, Inc.)

With Arbenz dethroned, Castillo Armas and other presidential aspirants met in El Salvador to work out a peace treaty and the composition of the next government. Three anti-Arbenz activists, Papal Nuncio Monsignor Gennaro Verrolino, Salvadoran Ambassador Funes and Colonel Elfego Monzón, flew to El Salvador on June 30, 1954, on Ambassador Peurifoy's plane (note seal on door). (Credit; Rafael Morales)

Castillo Armas arrived the same day (left, carrying jacket). (Credit: Wide World Photos)

The El Salvador negotiations broke down amid squabbling and political disputes, and Ambassador Peurifoy—the director of the drama—felt compelled to make a personal appearance. He is shown arriving in San Salvador on July 1, 1954 (left, with sunglasses). (Credit: Wide World Photos)

Peurifoy confers with Castillo Armas. (Credit: Leonard McCombe, Life, ©Time, Inc.)

The El Salvador agreement was confirmed with an awkward embrace for the benefit of photographers. Castillo Armas (foreground) with Colonel Monzón. Three months later, Monzón was out of the government and Castillo Armas was President of Guatemala. (Credit: Wide World Photos)

Four of the five members of the original Armas junta pose with Papal Nuncio Monsignor Gennaro Verrolino, a bitter Arbenz opponent. Left to right: Lieutenant Colonel Mauricio Dubois, Colonel Elfego Monzón, Castillo Armas, Major Enrique Trinidad Oliva and Monsignor Verrolino. Absent from the photo is Lieutenant Colonel José Luis Cruz Salazar. (Credit: Wide World Photos)

Castillo Armas, the CIA's handpicked "Liberator" (at microphone) addresses supporters in front of the National Palace soon after taking power. (Credit: Wide World Photos)

Not all Latin Americans, however, were so pleased by the overthrow of Arbenz in a U.S.-backed coup. A wave of protest demonstrations, this one in Santiago, condemned the United States. (Credit: Wide World Photos)

A year after he took office, President Castillo Armas visited the United States. Here he reviews an honor guard after being received by Vice-President Richard Nixon. (Credit: Wide World Photos)

riers had anchored off the coast or that paratroopers had landed in the north. Rumors came back within hours to the people who started them, nearly always expanded to ludicrous proportions.[2]

Arbenz began that Sunday morning with a conference of military commanders, led by his confidant, Army Chief of Staff Colonel Carlos Enrique Díaz. As the President listened to their gloomy summations, word arrived of yet another blow: a commercial British freighter taking cargo out of the Pacific port of San José had just been bombed and sunk off the dock. Oddly this attack had in fact been a freelance job, conceived by General Somoza in Nicaragua, not by the CIA. Convinced over the weekend that it was carrying gasoline for Arbenz's planes and trucks, Somoza had told Rip Robertson: "You've got to stop that ship!"

Robertson tried to obtain CIA permission to bomb the boat, a Norwegian-built craft called the *Springfjord* that a British shipping firm had chartered for routine cargo carrying. Haney and Tracy Barnes, overseeing the operation from Opa-Locka, received Robertson's plea at two o'clock Sunday morning. Bleary-eyed from lack of sleep, the two men considered the idea briefly. They concluded that an air attack would be too risky since it might cause an international furor; the decision to search neutral ships had caused enough trouble. They told Robertson not to bomb the *Springfjord*, but encouraged him to destroy it by some less obvious means, using commandos or frogmen.

Somoza was enraged. "If you use my airfields, you take my orders!" he shouted at Robertson, who was also disappointed by Haney's response. Making an impulsive move, Robertson decided to ignore the orders from Florida. He dispatched one of his American pilots, Ferdinand Schoup, from Nicaragua at seven o'clock Sunday morning. At seven-fifteen Schoup made a pass over the *Springfjord* and dropped leaflets warning of his imminent attack while the British captain stood on the deck waving a friendly greeting. On his second pass, he opened his hatch and sent a single 500-pound bomb straight down the smokestack of the ship. The bomb tore an enormous hole in the *Springfjord's* hull, and she rapidly listed to starboard but only partly sank; warned in advance, all of the crew had fled before the explosion. The freighter turned out to be carrying no gasoline, but only what was listed in the official manifest: 8,500 bags of coffee and 1,500 bales of cotton from Guatemalan farms.[3]

When word reached CIA officials of Robertson's disobedience, there was general dismay. Richard Bissell agreed the attack "went beyond the established limits of policy," but tempered his criticism: "You can't take an operation of this scope, draw narrow boundaries of policy around them, and be absolutely sure that those boundaries will never be overstepped." Lawrence Houston, general counsel to the CIA, called the raid "a stupid thing." Frank Wisner immediately went to the British Embassy that morning to apologize personally. Allen Dulles, sorely vexed, soon dropped Robertson from the CIA payroll, though officials later reinstated him for the 1961 Bay of Pigs invasion, where, once again in defiance of orders, he landed on the beachhead. Following quiet negotiations, the CIA later agreed to pay Lloyd's of London, the *Springfjord's* insurer, $1.5 million to compensate for her destruction.[4]

The attack cast a deeper pall over Arbenz and his colleagues in the National Palace. A ship which had nothing to do with the unfolding events inside Guatemala was now lying at the bottom of San José harbor; would the Americans continue to attack commercial freighters until the nation was completely choked off from foreign markets? Colonel Díaz took Arbenz aside and told him that a group of important officers were preparing a "final ultimatum" demanding his resignation. The President was at the Americans' mercy. He had lost only a total of fifteen soldiers, with another twenty-five wounded. But the populace was quiescent, and his Army restive. Arbenz could no longer doubt the U.S. determination to see him go. He directed Foreign Minister Guillermo Toriello to find out from Peurifoy what terms could be arranged for his surrender.[5]

The meeting was quickly set, and Toriello began, according to Peurifoy's subsequent cable, by saying:

> . . . he knew I could stop [the] fighting in 15 minutes if I wished. He asked if I would do so if military junta took over the government. He asked specifically whether Arbenz would have to leave office and whether Toriello's own resignation would do any good. He said he was willing to do anything in [his] power to

prevent bloodshed and further bombing by planes which he said had damaged vessel *Springfjord* at San José this morning. He said he personally and his brother Jorge had always been very anti-communist and that as far as he was concerned the junta could take all the communists in Guatemala and send them to Moscow. Toriello stated that if the government were turned over to a junta, Castillo Armas must not come to power as this would cause great bloodshed in the country. He stated that I could cause the end of fighting through pressure, if not on Castillo Armas, then on Honduras.

I replied that I had no control over situation but would do anything I could to bring about peace. Re Arbenz remaining in power, I said I could not speak for insurgent forces but would think the situation demanded a clean sweep.[6]

Peurifoy was pleased. "Situation appears to be breaking," he concluded in his cable to Dulles. A few hours later, just after noon, Colonel Díaz called Peurifoy to a second meeting. Peurifoy brought along an embassy counselor and sped across town through what were described by one American magazine as "deserted, shuttered streets" to Díaz's residence. His cable describing the meeting conveys both the tension of the moment and his own self-confidence.[7]

After my arrival Colonel Díaz entered room accompanied by Colonel Sánchez, Minister of Defense Colonel Parinello, Chief of [Air Force] Staff Colonel Girón, and Colonel Sarti, president of the Superior Defense Council. Díaz began by describing horrible situation created by aerial bombardment of Chiquimula and Zacapa. He said towns were virtually wiped out; that in Zacapa dead lay unburied in the streets and buzzards were having feast on them; civil population had fled. Army could cope with Castillo Armas' ground forces, but not with his aviation. He said Castillo could not have obtained these arms without U.S. acquiescence. I replied sharply that if he had brought me to his house to make accusations against my government, I would leave immediately. He hastily said he was not accusing U.S. He therefore asked what U.S. would wish in return if it used its good offices to put end to fighting. Constantly emphasizing that I could speak only as an individual and not for the U.S. government, I said there was only one important problem between our governments: that of communism. Colonel Díaz said he knew that and was prepared to guarantee in the name of army that Communist Party would be outlawed and its leaders exiled.

I said this was fine, but that government had long known this and neither government nor army had ever acted; how could I be sure army would be able to carry out its decision? After some hesitation Díaz agreed this was crucial question. Solution designed by army officers was that he should assume presidency. . . . I asked whether he had attempted any direct arrangement with Castillo Armas. He replied in strongest terms (and was strongly seconded by others) that direct negotiations with Castillo Armas were out of the question; they would rather die than talk to him. Díaz said Castillo Armas could never govern Guatemala after massacres his air forces caused; he might have had some supporters in the army before, but no longer.

I stressed again that I could neither speak for Castillo nor commit my government, but that if Díaz assumed power and ousted communists, I would strongly recommend that U.S. attempt to bring about cease-fire until arrangement could be made. Once again Díaz and his colleagues insisted that truce, at least cessation of air raids, would be essential before they could act against Arbenz. . . . I simply replied that when I knew Díaz was in control I would recommend cease-fire.

After further discussion and several private conferences with colleagues, Díaz said they had decided to act at once, relying on my promise to urge a cease-fire. He then said, "[N]ow comes the tough problem. Who is going to bell the cat? Who is going to tell Jacobo?" But with moment's hesitation, he made decision: "Colonel Sánchez will visit all garrisons and announce I have assumed presidency. Colonel Girón will inform Air Force. I will go to the Palace with Parinello and Sarti and we will tell Jacobo." After some other talk, Díaz said, "Arbenz may answer in two ways. He will either say 'yes' or he will say 'This is insubordination' and call the guard. In the latter case, we will not emerge from the Palace. If we are not out in reasonable period, Sánchez will bring up artillery . . ."

At one point Díaz asked whether any members of present Cabinet were unacceptable to U.S. I said I could not attempt to dictate his Cabinet and that if he appointed reasonable men I was sure all of our secondary problems could be worked out, such as difficulties of American companies . . .[8]

As Peurifoy was leaving, he turned and offered another suggestion: "I emphasized [the] necessity of acting quickly to round up leading Communists before they could mobilize forces." Díaz appointed Colonel Sánchez to give the "necessary orders," and within hours, Communist leaders were being picked up by military police.[9]

Díaz, accompanied by Colonel Sarti and Defense Minister Parinello, drove directly to the National Palace. The men were ushered into Arbenz's office at about three-thirty. As the President later recounted the confrontation, his Chief of Staff "told me it was decided to present me with a final ultimatum: I had until 4 P.M. to leave the National Palace; I must turn over command to a military junta. . . . Immediately thereafter the presidential palace was occupied by officers armed with machine guns . . . and we were completely disarmed." Díaz recalled that he found Arbenz "very tired" but fully aware that "he could not continue without Army support." Arbenz said he would leave office "gracefully" by making a national radio address that evening in which he would turn power over to Díaz. He stipulated only that Díaz give his "word of honor" never to negotiate with Castillo Armas, and Díaz—who despised the Liberator as much as Arbenz did—readily agreed.[10]

Díaz returned to his home and immediately called Peurifoy and his aides to another meeting. At five o'clock that afternoon, the same group reassembled in the same room at Colonel Díaz's house in which they had met less than six hours earlier. The mood was subdued, not jubilant; all participants undoubtedly sensed that they were engaged in a distasteful piece of work. Díaz curtly told Ambassador Peurifoy that President Arbenz had assented to the military ultimatum and would read his farewell speech over the government radio network within a few hours. He stressed that he had obtained the presidential resignation only by giving his solemn pledge not to enter into any talks with Castillo Armas. Peurifoy nodded his approval; he did not say, however, that U.S. plans did not allow for Díaz or any other Arbenz ally to hold power for long. Díaz then pressed Peurifoy on the cease-fire. The ambassador was evasive, saying only that he would do what he could, but that all that was really in his power was providing "good offices" to both sides. He emphatically rejected Díaz's plea that he instruct Nicaragua and Honduras to close their airfields to the rebel fliers.[11]

At the end, Arbenz acted realistically: he had no support from any quarter except from those, like his Communist backers, who knew that his departure would doom them and their hopes for Guatemala. He realized that the pressure would never let up until he was gone. All that could be accomplished by his refusal to leave, he had concluded, would be an escalation of fighting, the loss of many lives, and his ultimate downfall.

A broad analysis would also have to conclude that his country had deserted him. The upper classes had no use for him and would not come to his defense, though for all the fuss stirred up by agrarian reform, in fact his measures never seriously affected their holdings. His actions in recent months, including tough measures against the opposition by his police, had cost him much of his middle-class backing. Attacks by the Catholic Church had caused further loss of support. Many in the military, too, had never forgiven him for what they believed was his role in the 1949 killing of Colonel Arana. The lack of substantial economic progress and the constant turmoil of recent months had begun to convince even neutrals that it might be best for Arbenz to go. Only the lower classes, many of whom were beneficiaries of his policies, still felt affection for the aloof President. But among the poor, the tradition of political passivity always dictated that they sit back and await events rather than attempt to influence them.

The deviousness attributed to Arbenz turned out, as this crisis proved, to be greatly exaggerated. If he were truly as Machiavellian as critics asserted, Arbenz might have surreptitiously prepared himself for the confrontation, stockpiling weapons in the countryside, mobilizing a popular defense force or even arranging new arms shipments from Iron Curtain countries. But because he was never more than he seemed to be—a bourgeois reformer whose ideology did not extend beyond basic precepts of nationalism and the stimulation of domestic industry and agriculture—he had been doomed from the moment eleven months earlier when the Dulles brothers told President Eisenhower he had to go.

At 9:15 Sunday evening, President Jacobo Arbenz addressed his countrymen by radio. How many actually heard his words is uncertain, because the transmission was partially jammed by the CIA and many Guatemalans were in any case tuned to the news broadcasts by the "Voice of Liberation." Arbenz's text was not allowed to be published in the newspapers for over a month. He read the speech over government radio into a microphone brought to the presidential office especially for the occasion.

Workers, peasants, patriots, my friends: people of Guatemala: Guatemala is enduring a most difficult trial. For fifteen days a cruel war against Guatemala has been underway. The United Fruit Company, in collaboration with the governing circles of the United States, is responsible for what is happening to us. . . .

In whose name have they carried out these barbaric acts? What is their banner? We know very well. They have used the pretext of anti-communism. The truth is very different. The truth is to be found in the financial interests of the fruit company and the other U.S. monopolies which have invested great amounts of money in Latin America and fear that the example of Guatemala would be followed by other Latin countries. . . .

I have made a sad and cruel judgment. After reflecting with a clear revolutionary conscience, I have made a decision that is of great importance for our country in the hope of containing this aggression and bringing peace back to Guatemala. I have decided to step down and place the nation's executive power in the hands of my friend Colonel Carlos Enrique Díaz, chief of the armed forces of the republic.

I have placed my confidence in Colonel Díaz because I am certain he will guarantee democracy in Guatemala and that all the social conquests of our people will be maintained. I hope all popular organizations will give him their backing and support.

I was elected by a majority of the people of Guatemala, but I have had to fight under difficult conditions. The truth is that the sovereignty of a people cannot be maintained without the material elements to defend it. . . .

The military situation in the country is far from difficult. The enemy who commands the bands of foreign mercenaries recruited by Castillo Armas is not only weak, but completely cowardly. We have seen this in the few combat encounters we have had. The enemy was able to advance and take the area of Chiquimula only because of the attacks of mercenary aircraft. I believe that our armed forces would not have great difficulty in defeating him and expelling him from the country.

I took over the presidency with great faith in the democratic system, in liberty and in the possibility of achieving economic independence for Guatemala. I continue to believe that this program is just. I have not violated my faith in democratic liberties, in the independence of Guatemala and in all the good which is the future of humanity.

One day the obscured forces which today oppress the backward and colonial world will be defeated. I will continue to be, despite everything, a fighter for the liberty and progress of my country.

I say goodbye to you, my friends, with bitterness and pain, but remaining firm in my convictions. Remember how much it has cost. Ten years of struggle, of tears, of sacrifices and of democratic victories. . . .

I have always said to you that we would fight regardless of the cost, but the cost should not include the destruction of our country and the sending of our riches abroad. And this could happen if we do not eliminate the pretext which our powerful enemy has raised.

A government different from mine, but always inspired by our October revolution, is preferable to twenty years of fascist bloody tyranny under the rule of the bands which Castillo Armas has brought into the country. . . .

Perhaps many people will believe I am making a mistake. From the bottom of my heart, I do not believe this. Only history will decide.

I want the popular conquests of the October revolution to be maintained and I want peace to be re-established after the invaders have been expelled from the country, and I have faith in the success of the government being organized by Colonel Carlos Enrique Díaz.

With the satisfaction of one who believes he has done his duty, with faith in the future, I say to you: Long live the October revolution! Long live Guatemala![12]

A few minutes later, Colonel Díaz took the microphone to accept the reins of power.

It was not yet midnight when President Jacobo Arbenz, forty-one years old, walked slowly down the steps of the opulent National Palace facing Guatemala's Central Park. As he left he passed a member of his presidential guard, who asked where he was going. *"Me voy al frente,"* replied Arbenz. Thinking Arbenz meant literally, "I'm going to the front," the young guard protested immediately, fearing the pressure had caused his leader to break. "You can't do that," the guard protested. "You can't go to the front. Which troops will you lead?" Arbenz couldn't manage a smile, but repeated *"Me voy al frente"* and pointed through the side door of the Palace. Then the guard understood. Arbenz had used the phrase in its colloquial sense, meaning "I'm going across the street." The guard fell silent and watched the President slowly cross Sixth Avenue and open the door of the Mexican Embassy.[13]

Historians and participants in the events of 1954 argue to this day about the causes of Arbenz's failure and the wisdom of his resignation. Arbenz himself said a month later that his decision "was forced on me by the military cliques that had been under terrific pressure from Peurifoy. . . . [T]he truth is that most of the officers had betrayed me and if it is true that the helpless masses were loyal to their government, they had lost their attributes."[14]

The Guatemalan Communists, in a booklet written some time later, claimed that their party had urged Arbenz not to submit his resignation because "as soon as it was announced it would dishearten the popular forces and break the spirit of the resistance, this in view of the enormous prestige and authority Arbenz enjoyed among the popular masses. It would have been better to bring the crisis out into the open, to denounce to the people the vile treason committed by the army chiefs, but President Arbenz underestimated the role that the masses could play." The Communists were especially bitter at Arbenz's final call to support Díaz, "whose treacherous commitments to Peurifoy were well known to Arbenz, thus creating the illusion and leading the people to believe that with the change in government, the democratic and revolutionary conquests could be salvaged, alleging the totally false and demoralizing argument that it was impossible to defend the national independence of Guatemala without having all the material means needed to do so."[15]

A leading leftist intellectual of the period, Luis Cardoza y
Aragón, condemned Arbenz for not moving into the countryside
and leading a peasant army against the invaders, thereby maintaining the legitimacy of his presidency both at home and in the
eyes of the world. His decision not to do so, says Cardoza, was
"a crude error of grave historical consequences." But it must be
borne in mind that such a solution, while quite plausible today,
had not been attempted by anyone anywhere at the time of Arbenz's fall. Arbenz was not the sort of man who could strike out
on an entirely new historical path. Cardoza, indeed, places much
of the blame on the person of Arbenz himself:

> What kind of man is President Arbenz? A professional soldier
> who rose from the petit bourgeoisie to become a large landowner
> . . . a sour man who has not yet ripened, filled with good in-
> tentions, but in politics it is acts that count. . . . Jacobo Ar-
> benz allowed the opportunity of fulfilling a great historical obli-
> gation to slip through his fingers. . . . Arbenz [had] half a
> lifetime before him.[16]

Years later, a leading Guatemalan politician and social commentator, onetime Guatemala City mayor Manuel Colom Argueta, interpreted Arbenz's demise in the broader context of
American politics and the Cold War. Colom Argueta, later assassinated for his outspoken liberal views, saw the 1954 coup as a
turning point in Guatemala's modern history from which the
country hadn't recovered. Speaking at a ceremony in 1977 com-
memorating the 1944 revolution, he observed:

> The polarization of power between the United States and the
> Soviet Union after the Second World War placed in crisis the
> principles which had inspired the creation of the United Na-
> tions. . . . The liberal policies toward Latin America initi-
> ated by Franklin Delano Roosevelt changed with the ascension to
> power of the Republican Party. McCarthyism unleashed an inter-
> nal inquisition and a changed foreign policy: support for political
> democracy and economic development for the majority of the
> countries of Western Europe [but] the strengthening of fascist
> and conservative dictatorships in Latin America and other re-

gions of the world under the pretext of continental security against communism.

If the economic and social reforms made in Guatemala generated sympathy among the peoples of Central and Latin America, many dictatorial governments frightened by the Guatemalan experiment and favored by the Cold War unfurled the banner of anti-communism to use all means to combat the Guatemalan regime.[17]

Some American journalists who covered the events of 1954 in Guatemala later concluded that the motivation of the United States was just what Arbenz had claimed: to protect the corporate interests of the United Fruit Company. "If the United Fruit Company had not existed," an experienced *Time* correspondent said years later, "there would have been no U.S. pressure or intervention. The U.S. wouldn't have cared. With no threats to U.S. property, there would have been no problems." The overthrow of Arbenz, he added, in addition had an incalculable effect on other Central American nations, for whom Guatemala had always been and remains something of a regional leader. "If Arbenz had survived his term in office, it would have influenced and strengthened democrats in Honduras and El Salvador and isolated Somoza in Nicaragua." His downfall, on the other hand, fortified reactionary forces in the area and guaranteed that future movements for social change would be more extreme and more anti-American than Arbenz's had been.[18]

Arbenz also never established a strong popular following to rally to his program. He allowed the opposition to plot and allowed himself to be subjected to unjustified accusations of brutality and repression by conservatives. He permitted the Army to develop on its own rather than reconstructing it, as Bolivia had done after its revolution two years earlier, under new leadership drawn from the classes he was trying to help. His measures against American corporate control of the country were strong in the context of his time, but ultimately of no great depth. His most vociferous supporters were young Communists without experience or genuine ties to the people; and for his association with them, he paid a heavy price without gaining much in return. He was surrounded by hostile governments and

antagonistic forces in the world—such as the Catholic Church—
dedicated to his destruction out of fear of what he might take
from them.

His overthrow was, in a narrow sense, a victory for his enemies. Yet years later, both his government and the manner of its
defeat provided lessons which even today help influence the
policies of governments and insurgent movements throughout
Latin America. Whether his demise was inevitable can be
debated endlessly. Of all people, David Phillips, mastermind of
the "Voice of Liberation" radio network, was desolate as he tuned
in to Arbenz's final speech that Sunday evening. "We expected
him to tell his people he had won," Phillips recalled afterward.
"We thought we'd lost. . . . We were so surprised by his departure."[19]

If some of the American operatives were surprised, all were
pleased. Mrs. John Peurifoy, wife of the victorious American ambassador, typified the lighthearted jubilation of the moment with
a piece of doggerel published in July in *Time* magazine:

> Sing a song of quetzals,* pockets full of peace!
> The junta's in the Palace, they've taken out a lease.
> The commies are in hiding, just across the street;
> To the embassy of Mexico they beat a quick retreat.
> And pistol-packing Peurifoy looks might optimistic
> For the land of Guatemala is no longer Communistic![20]

* Guatemala's national bird and symbol.

14

THE LIBERATION

As the door of the Mexican Embassy closed behind a forlorn Jacobo Arbenz, Guatemala's new President, Colonel Carlos Enrique Díaz, turned his attention to the most urgent problem facing the nation: the presence of Castillo Armas' ragtag Liberation army on Guatemalan soil. Díaz began at once to consider various plans to expel the invaders, in keeping with his promise to Arbenz. In his brief radio speech earlier, he had restated that vow. He then told Guatemalans that his regime "would be inspired by the October [1944] revolution" and promised that "the struggle against the mercenary invaders of Guatemala will not abate. Colonel Arbenz has done what he thought was his duty. I shall carry on."[1]

The two top CIA operatives in Guatemala reacted angrily to

Díaz's radio remarks. Both independently concluded that the colonel was unreliable and would have to go. At around 10:10 that Sunday evening, an irate John Doherty, the CIA station chief, and an exasperated Enno Hobbing—the former *Time* Paris bureau chief who had just arrived in Guatemala to help shape a new "constitution" for the incoming regime—met and decided they would overthrow Díaz themselves. In his place, they planned to install Colonel Elfegio Monzón, an officer who had worked with them in the past as a secret leader of anti-Arbenz forces within the military.[2]

At his residence, Ambassador Peurifoy also listened incredulously to the radio speeches by the outgoing Arbenz and incoming Díaz. A reporter watched the envoy's jaw tighten when Díaz referred to Arbenz as "my friend" and pledged to follow Arbenz's policies. Finally Peurifoy pounded his desk and snapped: "O.K., now I'll have to crack down on that s.o.b." When Doherty and Hobbing soon consulted Peurifoy, the tired ambassador approved their mission gladly. "Washington is happy enough that you've gotten rid of Arbenz," he told the CIA men. "From now on I don't care what the hell you do. Just leave me out of it."[3]

Doherty and Hobbing sped a short distance through the darkness and picked up Colonel Monzón. At midnight the three men arrived at the headquarters of the new Guatemalan President, Colonel Díaz. Outside Díaz's office, guards disarmed the two intelligence agents and then permitted them to enter the room.

After a stiff exchange of civilities, Monzón, under a withering glare from Díaz, sat down nervously in a corner. Doherty abruptly launched into an impassioned diatribe on the evils of Arbenz's "Communist" policies. Díaz objected, and the two men began to argue about the merits of Arbenz's social reforms.

"Wait a minute, Colonel," Hobbing suddenly interjected. "Let me explain something to you," he said sternly, pointing a finger at Colonel Díaz. "You made a big mistake when you took over the government."

Hobbing paused to let his words sink in. Then he continued: "Colonel, you're just not convenient for the requirements of American foreign policy."

Díaz was taken aback. "But," he stammered, "I talked to your ambassador. He gave me his approval."

"Well, Colonel," Hobbing said, "there is diplomacy and then there is reality. Our ambassador represents diplomacy. I represent reality. And the reality is that we don't want you."

"You mean I can't stay in office?" Díaz meekly asked.

Hobbing shook his head.

Emboldened for a single moment, Díaz inquired: "Can I hear it from the ambassador?"

With a groan, the CIA men left Monzón at Army headquarters and returned to the ambassador's house. It was 3 A.M. Peurifoy, roused from his bed, was not happy to see them again.

"You sons of bitches," he shouted. "I just want to sleep!"

But the CIA agents convinced Peurifoy that he alone could put the finishing touches on their mini-revolution. So the ambassador hurriedly dressed in a wartime zipper suit, loaded up his shoulder holster and went into the night to confront Díaz.[4]

At 4 A.M., Peurifoy arrived at Díaz's suite with Hobbing and Doherty. There are varying accounts of what happened next. Peurifoy later cabled Dulles a mild account of his two-hour meeting:

> I told Colonel Díaz that I was annoyed and astounded at [the] fact that he had permitted Arbenz in delivering his valedictory to charge that U.S. was responsible for supplying aviators to forces attacking Guatemala. . . . I told him that, this being his first act, I did not see how we could work together toward bringing about a peace. I suggested that perhaps he might wish to designate Colonel Monzón, well-known for his anti-Communist feelings, as President. He said that he agreed with me in principle and would give me his answer today at noon. . . .[5]

According to Díaz, however, Peurifoy was not so delicate. Foreign Minister Guillermo Toriello recounted the scene as Díaz recalled it:

> Peurifoy waved a long list of names of some leaders. He was going to require Díaz to shoot those who were on that list within twenty-four hours. "That's all, but why?" Díaz asked. "Because they're communists," replied Peurifoy. Díaz refused absolutely to soil his hands and soul with this repugnant crime and rejected the pretensions of Peurifoy to come and give him orders. "It

would be better, in that case," he went so far as to tell him, "that
you actually sit on the presidential chair and that the stars and
stripes fly over the Palace." Saying too bad for you, Peurifoy
left.[6]

(Peurifoy and Dulles were, in fact, at that time cabling names of
Guatemalan "Communists" back and forth to each other to
prepare a list for Díaz or Monzón or whoever was in power to
round up, making Díaz's version seem somewhat plausible.) In
any case, at 11:45 that morning, Díaz went ahead with his own
plan to announce the creation of a three-man junta with himself
at the head of it. He named Colonel Monzón and Colonel José
Angel Sánchez to join him. He hoped that Monzón's presence
would placate the Americans. But Peurifoy was angry as he
arrived for his noon meeting with Díaz.

"I expressed surprise at this development," Peurifoy later
cabled Dulles. Peurifoy thought he had an understanding with
Díaz that Monzón would take over the presidency and Díaz
would quit. But now Monzón informed the ambassador of his
own anxiety. He told Peurifoy that "he did not feel himself
strong enough [to] assume [the] presidency alone." Díaz's
resignation or dismissal, Monzón said, would undoubtedly cause
"dissension within the Army" and lead to internal disorder.
Monzón instead wanted Díaz to stay on as head of the junta, and
said that Díaz and Sánchez had promised not to take any action
without his approval. Peurifoy did not argue with Monzón, whom
he regarded as a pliable U.S. loyalist. He accepted the arrangement as a *fait accompli*. But he had other plans in mind.

Díaz spoke next. He repeated his plea to Peurifoy to order
Castillo Armas to "lay down his arms." Castillo Armas, Díaz
said, had been fighting "under [the] banner of anti-communism
[but this] new junta was thoroughly anti-communist; if Castillo Armas were [a] sincere anti-communist, he would stop
fighting at once." Díaz said he would give the "Liberator" and
his followers "every guarantee," and permission to contest the
next presidential election. Peurifoy asked whether Díaz was now
prepared to negotiate directly with Castillo Armas—now putting
Díaz in the position of breaking the promise he had made to Ar-

benz and to the nation only hours earlier. Díaz said he needed time to consider his reply.[7]

As the meeting broke up, Díaz casually mentioned that he was about to proclaim a general amnesty and release all political prisoners. Since this included Communist organizers rounded up the previous day, Peurifoy was livid at the idea; it was the last straw. After he left, with Doherty and Hobbing, he composed a brief cable and sent it off to the Operation Success nerve center at Opa-Locka. The message said simply: "We have been double-crossed. BOMB!" At three o'clock in the afternoon, the always-available Jerry DeLarm took off from a clandestine airstrip in Honduras in a P-47 Thunderbolt. Accompanied by a fighter escort, he made for Guatemala City. There he dipped low over the principal military installation, Fort Matamoros, and dropped two bombs directly onto the parade grounds, causing a tremen-dous racket but no injuries. Before heading back, he swooped down and destroyed the government radio station, which his fellow pilot Bob Wade had missed during a previous raid.[8]

Peurifoy tarried a few hours to let the meaning of the bomb-ing sink in before finally returning to Díaz's office. At about 5 P.M., he arrived there and found all three junta members—Díaz, Monzón and Sánchez—waiting for him. In a despair following the latest air strike, Díaz grudgingly agreed to talk directly to Castillo Armas, whom he detested. He asked for two conditions: that Peurifoy call a cease-fire while the talks were underway; and that a neutral observer, preferably the Papal Nuncio, be present at the negotiations. The ambassador had no trouble with either condition, especially the latter. The Nuncio was strongly anti-Ar-benz and had privately told Peurifoy earlier that day that "over 90 percent of [the] people favored Castillo Armas."[9]

Díaz was clearly weakening in the face of the American on-slaught. Nicknamed "Sad Chicken" by his military friends, he was a professional officer with little background or interest in politics. He naïvely believed, as had his one-time commander Arbenz, that once the elected President was removed from the scene the Americans would be disposed to compromise with the new leader. He was learning otherwise.

Late that night—about 2 A.M.—Peurifoy and Díaz spoke again by telephone. They agreed to meet right away to discuss the arrangements for Díaz's meeting with Castillo Armas. Peurifoy sped through the empty streets to the armed forces headquarters, where Díaz was staying. He proposed to Díaz that the meeting take place in El Salvador; before replying, Díaz said he needed to consult with his colleagues on the junta, Monzón and Sánchez. Peurifoy drove off to confer with Ambassador Funes of El Salvador, a Castillo Armas sympathizer who was helping to set up the negotiations.[10]

When Peurifoy returned to Díaz's suite at 4 A.M., he found Colonel Sánchez, who gave his approval for the meeting with Castillo Armas, but he did not find Monzón, who could not be located. At that moment—by coincidence or not—Guatemalan military officers decided to move against Díaz. The details of the "coup" are in dispute. Picturing himself as an innocent observer, Ambassador Peurifoy described the events this way in a cable to Secretary Dulles:

> Just as I was about to leave, Díaz received [a] telephone call from [the] Palace and he and Sánchez left to confer with several officers. While they were out, Colonel Martin, our Air Attaché, arrived and informed me [a] plot was afoot to assassinate Díaz and Sánchez and urged me to leave [the] building at once. I spent a difficult moment wondering if I would be caught in cross-fire, but finally decided [to] remain.
>
> Shortly thereafter Díaz returned and wearily informed me that things had changed: He and Sánchez had decided to retire from [the] Junta since it appeared they were unacceptable to Castillo Armas. . . .[11]

In her own diary, Peurifoy's wife recalled the scene more starkly. The "plot" to kill Díaz and Sánchez was actually hatched by Monzón who was on his way to the conference room with a group of armed soldiers to murder the two junta members. "Hardly had my husband returned to the room," wrote the ambassador's wife, "then Díaz and Sánchez announced their resignation. They, too, had been warned by someone! At that moment the Monzón party invaded the house, and it's more than likely that the unexpected presence of the American ambassador saved the lives of Colonels Díaz and Sánchez."

News accounts by American correspondents told a somewhat similar, if even more dramatic, story than Mrs. Peurifoy's. One report said that Díaz left the room to "stall" some officers just next door who were "grumbling" about his leadership. Peurifoy "thoughtfully checked his pistol." Waiting for Díaz to return, another journalist wrote, "Mr. Peurifoy leaned back and crossed his arms over his chest—where he had a shoulder holster. A United States Marine aide in civilian clothes edged nearer the envoy, fearing bullets might fly." At that moment, according to *Time* magazine (which had excellent sources in the American Embassy), "an outside door burst open, and Colonel Monzón entered with two other colonels. They said nothing as they strode through the room to join Díaz and the others, but one of the men slapped his holster significantly. Díaz, with a Tommy gun in his ribs, was unceremoniously escorted to a side door. Monzón reappeared. 'My colleague Díaz has decided to resign,' he explained suavely. 'I am replacing him.' "[12]

After Díaz's "resignation," Peurifoy chatted with Monzón as dawn neared. Díaz abruptly reappeared to pledge his support to Monzón. The ambassador cabled Dulles that Díaz "helped explain" the U.S. negotiating plan to the victorious but exhausted Monzón. To nobody's surprise, Monzón "eagerly" embraced it. Díaz then departed for good. A little later, Peurifoy briefed reporters on the change in command. He gave an impressive performance. Foreign journalists portrayed him as a tough, battle-hardened pro who hadn't flinched under pressure. Peurifoy told one reporter after the event: "As it turned out, what I might have had to do wasn't necessary."

At 4:45 that morning, Monzón announced that his partners on the new junta would be two trusted comrades, Lieutenant Colonel Mauricio Dubois, who commanded the only reliable force left in the capital, and Lieutenant Colonel José Luis Cruz Salazar, a thirty-four-year-old officer who had been trained in the United States. Their first move was to agree unanimously to meet with Castillo Armas in El Salvador to negotiate a peace treaty, but also first to seek a cease-fire through Peurifoy.

Ironically, some of the men involved in Operation Success immediately began expressing doubts about the reliability of the new leader, Monzón. Somoza, for one, thought Monzón was tainted with the ideals of the 1944 revolution. Hearing of these misgivings, Peurifoy cabled the State Department to assure his superiors that Monzón was "sincerely anti-communist."[13]

Another minor problem arose when Castillo Armas, acting without orders from his CIA handlers, issued an "ultimat⸱ım" to Monzón to capitulate or face the consequences. Castillo Armas' airmen also continued to bomb the border area of Zacapa in violation of an informal "cease-fire" that Peurifoy was now seeking to put in place. The ambassador called Assistant Secretary of State Henry Holland in Washington and asked him to halt the bombings, saying they were weakening Monzón's willingness to negotiate with Castillo Armas. Holland also communicated with the "Liberator," and by that evening, all was finally calm in Guatemala.[14]

The summit Peurifoy had organized began the following day, June 30, in San Salvador. Secretary Dulles had worried that Peurifoy's presence at the negotiations "would be subject to serious misinterpretation" because it "would inflate propaganda against the U.S. for alleged complicity in movement against Arbenz's government." The ambassador agreed to remain in Guatemala; Monzón made the short flight to San Salvador in a plane piloted by a military attaché of the American Embassy. Under the auspices of Salvadoran President Oscar Osorio, Monzón and Castillo Armas met in the Casa Presidencial.[15]

The meeting did not go well. The two officers had never been allies. Each perceived the other as trying to steal what was rightfully his. Monzón considered himself the legitimate President of Guatemala, as had the ill-fated Díaz only a day earlier. Castillo Armas was equally convinced that, as chief of the Liberation forces, the presidency belonged to him. Supported by his adviser, United Fruit Company attorney Juan Córdova Cerna, Castillo Armas insisted that he be given both the presidency and control over the armed forces; Monzón refused to yield. By four o'clock in the morning of July 1, the two colonels were ready to give up talking and return to the battlefield. Monzón announced he was going back to Guatemala. A planeload of journalists covering the negotiations flew out of the airport first, expecting Monzón's plane to be right behind. But when they landed in Guatemala City, they suddenly learned that Monzón, fearing Peurifoy's wrath, had decided at the last moment to remain in El Salvador.[16]

A breakdown in the negotiations was the last thing the United States could afford. It was unthinkable that an American-created government would now fight against an American-created rebel army. Secretary of State Dulles telephoned Peurifoy as soon as he learned of developments in San Salvador and ordered the ambassador to go there immediately to "crack some heads together." Around noon on July 1, eschewing his bright-colored jacket and jaunty hat for a funereal dark suit, Peurifoy flew to San Salvador and drove straight to the Casa, where the two adversaries were dozing. "In all due modesty," he told Henry Holland later, "within an hour—after talking for about 30 minutes with each man—[I] had a basic agreement."[17]

Peurifoy's quick success was not surprising, since he held the high cards in the game. Neither Monzón nor Castillo Armas could take power without his blessing. Peurifoy at first reacted harshly when Córdova Cerna urged Castillo Armas to take a hard line and he reported: "[I] asked Castillo who was the boss and asked him to bring the boss in so [I] could talk with him." Peurifoy recalled: "This took Castillo aback." For emphasis, the ambassador also brought in the Papal Nuncio, Monsignor Gennaro Verrolino, a symbol of Catholic opposition to Arbenz, and Ambassador Funes, the Salvadoran diplomat who had done so much to aid successive plots against Arbenz.[18]

Under this intense pressure, Castillo Armas and Monzón came to term. The agreement, by all accounts, was Peurifoy's work. It provided for a "definitive and total halt to hostilities" and pledged that a new constitution would be written to replace the liberal 1945 document, considered by all present to be at the root of the nation's problems. All members of the Communist PGT and of the Arbenz administration were to be arrested and tried. The country would be governed by a five-man junta consisting of Monzón and his two chosen comrades, Dubois and Cruz Salazar, together with Castillo Armas and an officer of his choosing (he selected his most trusted lieutenant in the Libera-

tion force, Enrique Trinidad Oliva). Monzón would head the
junta for fifteen days, at which time the junta would select a
Provisional President from its ranks. Peurifoy privately assured
Castillo Armas he would have the presidency, and also "guaranteed" Castillo Armas' personal safety in Guatemala. Most
difficult of all for Monzón to accept, the agreement stipulated
that all members of the ragged Liberation force who wished to
join the regular Guatemalan military would be accepted.[19]

Peurifoy stood silently as his document was signed by Monzón
and Castillo Armas. The two soldiers offered an awkward embrace for the benefit of photographers. Though the principals to
the armistice were still deeply suspicious of each other, the signing triggered an outburst of euphoria among others present. It
signified the final destruction of ten years of reformist government in Guatemala and the return to power of the Army and
upper classes. President Osorio immediately proclaimed Castillo
Armas "the man of destiny" for Guatemala. Guatemalan Archbishop Rossell Arellano sent Castillo Armas a telegram which
was read to the gathering:

> I send you warm greetings and fervent congratulations in the
> name of the nation which awaits you with open arms, recog-
> nizing and admiring your sincere patriotism. May our Lord God
> guide you and your heroic companions in your liberating cam-
> paign against atheistic communism. You all have my pastoral
> benediction.[20]

Never one to miss a chance for symbolism, Peurifoy asked
Castillo Armas to accompany him to Guatemala City aboard the
ambassador's private plane rather than at the head of his troops.
But then the "Liberator" suddenly disappeared from San Salva-
dor to return to Chiquimula to calm fears among his men that he
had capitulated to Monzón. This delay caused Peurifoy to post-
pone the return to Guatemala until the following day, July 3.
Then, shortly after noon that day, Peurifoy's plane left San Salva-
dor carrying the five members of the new junta, Monsignor
Verrolino, Ambassador Funes and a handful of aides as well as
Peurifoy himself. It touched down less than an hour later at La
Aurora Airport, where a huge crowd had gathered to greet
Castillo Armas.[21]

The throng cheered expectantly as the plane's door opened and onto the top step strode—none other than Peurifoy. He surveyed the scene and signaled to his charges that they could debark. As they gathered before microphones on the runway, the Papal Nuncio blessed the multitude. The Salvadoran envoy, Funes, a key intermediary in the talks, proclaimed himself "full of legitimate pride to have made a small contribution to the happiness of Guatemala." Castillo Armas spoke briefly, saying only that he was "happy to be in my country once again" and assuring the audience, which needed no assurances from its hero, that he had fought on behalf of "all good Guatemalans." Peurifoy was pushed to the front and asked to speak, but modestly chose not to. His job now largely over, the ambassador contented himself with waving to the crowd and saying, "Many thanks and Viva Guatemala!" Downtown about 150,000 people turned out to welcome Castillo Armas. The celebration was highlighted by the explosion of hundreds of firecrackers distributed by the CIA.[22]

Only a month earlier, Peurifoy had told a reporter that he and his wife were "making out our Fourth of July reception invitations, and we are not inviting any of the present [Arbenz] administration." As the Fourth arrived, Peurifoy held to his promise and gave a lavish celebration for a new administration at the U. S. Embassy residence. Some 500 guests, mostly conservative Guatemalans, packed Peurifoy's home, "Las Conchas," in the fashionable Santa Clara neighborhood. Peurifoy was misty-eyed over the behavior of some of the partygoers, recalling later a "most touching" scene when 400 Guatemalans assembled, lifting their voices in the words and music of "The Star-Spangled Banner."[23]

During the festivities, Peurifoy conferred with the new leaders about further changes. Three days later, his maneuvers led to the resignations of Monzón's two allies on the junta, Colonels Dubois and Cruz Salazar. The two apparently agreed to step down after receiving a sum of money (reportedly $100,000 apiece) and diplomatic posts abroad, leaving Castillo Armas in firm control; the three-man junta formally elected him Provisional President on July 8. His longtime friend and aide, Colonel Trinidad Oliva, cast the decisive vote.[24]

On July 5, Castillo Armas and Colonel Monzón held a joint

press conference. The two men devoted their remarks to denunciations of Communism and assurances that the advances of recent years would not be wiped out. "It is false that we intend to do away with the social conquests won by the workers of Guatemala," Castillo Armas promised. On the contrary, he said, "we have shown that we will consolidate these conquests, which have only been a farce and a source of political propaganda." Colonel Monzón told reporters that his biggest problem was finding enough jail cells to hold the thousands of prisoners then being rounded up.[25]

A week later, Castillo Armas made his first speech to a huge crowd in front of the National Palace to celebrate the junta's declaration of "Anti-Communism Day." To the cheers of thousands, many of them poor people, the nation's new *caudillo* sounded the same themes he had expressed at his press conference:

> Communism . . . has been completely destroyed by the force of arms. But communism still remains in the consciences of some bad sons of our Guatemala. . . . The battle has begun, the hard battle that requires us to demand each citizen to be a soldier of anti-communism. . . . To eradicate communism does not signify to persecute the worker and honest peasant who in every case merits the protection of the government. . . . Workers and peasants have in me their best friend. . . . My unshakable spirit of justice will be their greatest guarantee.[26]

The next day, July 13, the United States granted official recognition to the Castillo Armas government.

The exultation over Castillo Armas' triumph was undisguised in Washington. Within days of Arbenz's defeat, Secretary of State John Foster Dulles went on national radio to tell the American people that the events in Guatemala added "a new and glorious chapter" to hemispheric traditions. He explained why the United States was so heartened to see Arbenz deposed:

> Communist agitators . . . dominated the social security organization and ran the agrarian reform program. . . . Throughout the period I have outlined, the Guatemalan government and Communist agents throughout the world have persistently

attempted to obscure the real issue—that of Communist imperialism—by claiming that the U.S. is only interested in protecting
American business. We regret that there have been disputes
between the Guatemalan government and the United Fruit Company. . . . But this issue is relatively unimportant. . . . Led
by Colonel Castillo Armas, patriots arose in Guatemala to challenge the Communist leadership and to change it. Thus the situation is being cured by the Guatemalans themselves.[27]

Dulles also sent telegrams of congratulations to Ambassadors
Peurifoy and Willauer.

Not all of America's allies took such pleasure in the overthrow
of Arbenz. In Britain, Labour Party leader Clement Attlee said
he was shocked at "the joy and approval of the American Secretary of State on the success of this putsch." Attlee added: "[T]his
was a plain act of aggression, and one cannot take one line on
aggression in Asia and another line in Central America." The
protests, however, were dismissed in the euphoria that followed
the triumph of Operation Success. President Eisenhower was ec-
static about the outcome, and in mid-July summoned CIA
officials to the White House.[28]

The CIA prepared carefully for the presidential briefing. First
the key CIA agents in Operation Success gathered at Allen
Dulles' Georgetown home on a warm summer evening. Drinking
iced tea in Dulles' garden, they rehearsed their speeches for the
President. Tracy Barnes, J. C. King, Henry Heckscher, Rip
Robertson, David Atlee Phillips and Albert Haney all gave prac-
tice talks. When it came to Haney's turn, Allen Dulles' face
turned dour. Haney rambled on about his experiences in Korea.
Dulles abruptly cut him off: "Al, I've never heard such crap!"
He ordered Phillips to rewrite Haney's report.

The next day, the operatives arrived at the East Wing of the
White House. They brought movies, charts and slides. Waiting
for them were President Eisenhower, his wife Mamie, and their
son John; the Joint Chiefs of Staff; the Dulles brothers; most of
Eisenhower's cabinet; and a late arrival, Vice-President Richard
Nixon.[29]

Haney used slides to illustrate his ghost-written narrative, and
the others followed with equally elaborate presentations. The
session was a complete success. According to Phillips, the official

who asked the most incisive questions was Nixon; Phillips called his performance "impressive," noting that Nixon "demonstrated thorough knowledge of the Guatemalan political situation." Eisenhower then asked Rip Robertson how many men Castillo Armas had lost. Only one, Robertson replied. Eisenhower shook his head, perhaps thinking of the mass slaughter he had seen in World War II, and muttered "Incredible!"[30]

He then asked half seriously: "Why the hell didn't you catch Arbenz?"

"Mr. President," laughed one member of the cabinet, "that would have set a very dangerous precedent for you."

Finally Eisenhower shook Allen Dulles' hand and turned to the CIA contingent, saying: "Thanks to all of you. You've averted a Soviet beachhead in our hemisphere."[31]

In Guatemala, the United Fruit Company was already looking for the spoils of victory. Secretary Dulles told Peurifoy to be sure Castillo Armas offered the company a generous contract. On July 17, he directed Peurifoy:

> United Fruit Company has instructed [Almyr] Bump [the local United Fruit manager] to confer with you and make his recommendation re timing of overture by company to government. Cable your views after discussion with Bump.

Dulles closed his telegram with a report on the company's attitude toward the new junta:

> UFCo official states company disposed [to] initiate talks [with] Guatemala [in] near future as means [to] demonstrate confidence [and] cordiality [in] new government but would not consider contract revisions finalized until ratified by elected Congress under new constitution as company [is] opposed [to] making new arrangements with military de facto regime.[32]

Peurifoy cabled Dulles a few days later saying that United Fruit should not worry about constitutional "technicalities" like "ratification by Congress," but instead should make its own deal with Castillo Armas as soon as possible. Within two months, the Fruit Company concluded a pact directly with Castillo Armas. It included the return of all expropriated land and a modest new income tax.[33]

The banana firm also benefited from several other developments in Guatemala during the weeks following Arbenz's overthrow. On July 1, seven employees who had been active labor organizers on its farms during the past years were mysteriously murdered in Guatemala City. Later in the month, Castillo Armas canceled the legal registration of some 533 union locals, in one stroke wiping out the banana workers' federation. His other revisions of the Labor Code virtually outlawed new labor organizing. Around this time, the State Department wired Peurifoy to inquire "when the time was propitious for [the AFL's] Romualdi to come down" to help reorganize Guatemala's labor movement. A week later, Serafino Romualdi reached Guatemala and set up a "National Committee for Union Reorganization" to eliminate "Communists" from the unions.[34]

But even Romualdi was upset by what he saw. Though fiercely anti-Communist, he was upset over Castillo Armas' fundamentally anti-labor views. He later reported in the AFL's newspaper, *The American Federationist*, that "it is generally accepted that the decree dissolving the banana workers' and the railway workers' union . . . was issued at the insistent request of the American companies," United Fruit and its subsidiary, the International Railways of Central America (IRCA). Romualdi offered some hope though; he said he had received "definite assurances" from Castillo Armas that trade union rights would be restored. But, in fact, during the first year of the Liberation government union membership dropped from 100,000 to 27,000.[35]

Though it had won the victory, Washington was disturbed by attacks on the new Guatemalan regime appearing in the world press. Many commentators and political figures in Latin America and elsewhere were wondering aloud whether Arbenz had really been a Communist and what role the U.S. had actually played in his overthrow. CIA agents working with Castillo Armas decided to counter this concern with a new mini-campaign of their own. One of their first ploys was to take foreign newsmen on a tour of Arbenz's residence behind the Presidential Palace. Paul Kennedy, the New York *Times* correspondent, recalled: "We discov-

ered rooms filled with school textbooks" with imprints indicating
they were published in the Soviet Union. Even Kennedy, generally considered strongly anti-Arbenz, concluded that the "books
had been planted" and filed no story. *Time* also reported the discovery of "four bags of earth, one from Russia, China, Siberia
and Mongolia," at Arbenz's home. It made a colorful sidebar,
but was no more accurate than the story of the "Red" textbooks.[36]

In another effort to demonstrate Arbenz's links with the Soviets, the CIA dispatched counterintelligence officers to scoop up
all the "Communist documents" they could find in Guatemala.
Its agents gathered over 50,000 files from the offices of the Communist PGT. They later formed the basis of historian Ronald
Schneider's book *Communism in Guatemala,* published in 1959
as an "official" history of the Guatemalan overthrow. In addition,
the Department of State's Intelligence and Research Division
sent two researchers to Guatemala at Peurifoy's request. One of
these was a scholar named Stokes Newbold, whose real name
was Richard Adams, later a professor of anthropology at the
University of Texas. Adams worked under a pseudonym because
his employer, the UN-affiliated World Health Organization, had
asked him to do so out of fear of being "implicated" in his project. Adams interviewed some 250 inmates in three Guatemalan
prisons who had been arrested after the coup. He concluded
that few if any of the prisoners knew anything about Communism, though many had participated actively in Arbenz's land
reform program. Adams' conclusion did not endear him to the
CIA or the State Department. Later the United States Information Agency sent two cameramen to Guatemala to film evidence
of "Communist atrocities" allegedly committed by Arbenz. Two
shorts were produced and distributed in Latin America and
elsewhere.[37]

Stung by international criticism, the Eisenhower administration tried to distance itself from the United Fruit Company.
The Department of Justice had for some time been examining
the company's operations and had reached the conclusion that
its monopoly on banana exports from countries like Guatemala
was a violation of American antitrust laws. Dulles did nothing to
stop the probe, and in fact hoped it would show that the Ameri-

can government had no special interest in protecting United
Fruit. However United Fruit's lawyer Thomas Corcoran bluntly
observed that "Dulles began the antitrust suit against UFCo just
to prove he wasn't involved with the company." Five days after
Arbenz resigned, the Justice Department sued the company in
federal court. The litigation dragged out until 1958. The company tried to defuse the issue by donating 100,000 acres of its
Guatemalan holdings to peasants. The land turned out to be
mainly jungle. Ultimately, despite repeated efforts by United
Fruit lobbyists to have it dropped, the suit had a major impact
on breaking up the firm's banana business and ending its role in
Guatemala.[38]

The next goal of the CIA and State Department was the apprehension of suspected Communists and "sympathizers" remaining at large in Guatemala. At the CIA's behest, Castillo
Armas announced on July 19 the creation of a "National Committee of Defense Against Communism." A few weeks later, he
followed that action by decreeing the Preventive Penal Law
Against Communism. The Penal Law established the death pen-
alty for a series of "crimes" that could be construed as "sabotage," including many labor union activities. Meantime, the National Committee was given the power to meet in secret and
declare anyone a Communist with no right of defense or appeal.
Those named by the Committee could be arbitrarily arrested
and held for periods of up to six months; they could not own radios or hold public office. By November 21, 1954, the Committee
had some 72,000 persons on file and was aiming to list 200,000 in
all.[39]

The "Liberator" took other actions. Almost immediately upon
taking power, he disenfranchised three quarters of Guatemala's
voting population by banning illiterates from the electoral rolls.
At the end of July, he officially canceled the controversial
Decree 900, Arbenz's agrarian reform legislation. On August 10,
he outlawed all political parties, labor confederations and peasant organizations. A week later, he restored Ubico's secret police
chief, José Bernabé Linares, to his former post. Soon Castillo
Armas subordinates began burning "subversive" books, including
Victor Hugo's *Les Misérables*, Dostoyevsky novels, the writings
of Arévalo and other revolutionaries and novels by Guatemala's

Nobel Prize-winning writer, Miguel Angel Asturias, a biting critic of United Fruit.[40]

Secretary Dulles expressed no displeasure at these actions. The only thing that disturbed him was Castillo Armas' unwillingness or inability to seize the 700 or so Arbenz followers who had taken refuge in foreign embassies following the coup. Dulles feared that they might "recirculate" throughout the hemisphere if they were allowed to leave Guatemala. His fear soon became an obsession. All through the summer he bombarded Peurifoy with telegrams insisting that Castillo Armas be ordered to arrest the "asylees." Early in July, he told Peurifoy to instruct the new regime to bring "criminal charges" against "Communist" refugees as a way of preventing them from leaving the country. Next Dulles concocted an elaborate legal scenario to trap those "Communists" who had no criminal records. He suggested they be "convicted of having been covert Moscow agents." As an alternative, he suggested that Castillo Armas grant safe-conduct passages to Communists only if they would agree to be sent directly to Russia, where almost none had ever been before.[41]

As Peurifoy pressed Castillo Armas' government on these matters, he met with increasing resistance. One of Castillo Armas' cabinet ministers even surprised Peurifoy by suggesting that simply being a Communist did "not provide legal basis for prosecution." An exasperated Dulles finally directed Peurifoy to be sure that safe-conduct passes were withheld from Guatemalan Communists not agreeing to go to Russia "whether or not legal basis exists." Dulles offered a new twist on his various legal doctrines: Communists should be automatically denied the right of asylum because they were connected with an international conspiracy. He restated with a fresh variation his earlier recommendation—now "Communists" in the Mexican Embassy, where over half the refugees were huddled, should be sent at Guatemala's expense to the Iron Curtain countries.[42]

In the end, Castillo Armas disregarded Dulles' suggestions. He himself was a product of the widespread belief in Latin America that embassy asylum and safe-conduct passes were a fair resolution to political conflicts. Virtually every politically active Guatemalan, including Castillo Armas, had sought political asylum

in an embassy at one time or another and had obtained safe conduct from the government. Dulles' suggestion for a "modifica-
tion" of the asylum doctrine was not even popular within the
American Embassy. Castillo Armas settled the matter later in
the summer by quietly granting safe-conduct visas to several
hundred refugees. Peurifoy later admitted that "it looked like
[Castillo Armas] double-crossed us." The "Liberator's" only overt
act of vengeance was to have Arbenz stripped and searched at
the airport in front of hundreds of jeering Castillo Armas followers before he flew to exile in Mexico.[43]

Castillo Armas still faced turbulence at home. On August 2,
something happened to which Guatemalans had become accustomed and almost inured: a military uprising. In the early morning hours, a group of 125 cadets at the Politécnica, embittered
and humiliated at being forced to admit the unschooled peasants
of the Liberation army into their ranks, seized their own academy
and called on Colonel Monzón, still a member of the ruling
junta, to support them. At this point, Ambassador Peurifoy intervened, telling Monzón that he did not have the backing of the
Americans. Monzón passed the news along to the cadets, declining their appeal, and the Guatemalan press praised him as "military loyalty personified." The brief revolt ended with a whimper,
the cadets laying down their arms on the assurance they would
not be punished. Most were later dismissed from the military
academy.[44]

But even that show of loyalty did not heal the breach between
Monzón, the always-correct military leader, and the unpolished
Castillo Armas. At the end of August, Castillo Armas called a
meeting of the junta to decide the future of the presidency
which he clearly wanted for himself. The key vote, as always, lay
with the third member of the junta, Trinidad Oliva. Trinidad
Oliva not unexpectedly sided with his mentor, Castillo Armas,
with whom he had participated in a major pro-Arana uprising
against Arévalo in 1949 and in the Aurora revolt of 1950. Thus
on August 31, Castillo Armas got his way and Trinidad Oliva and
Monzón gave up their posts and announced their "resignations"
from the junta. They explained that "it is essential for the development of normal life in Guatemala to offer the citizenry a guar-

antee of peace, tranquillity and work based on national progress, and we are certain that the only manner of obtaining it is through an individual leader."[45]

On September 1, 1954, Carlos Castillo Armas took over full-fledged the presidency of Guatemala, a job which had been for him only an impossible dream until the Americans rescued him from obscurity. Feeling the need to legitimize his power, however, he called a plebiscite for October 10. The ballot was an oral one with a single question: "Are you in favor of Lieutenant Colonel Carlos Castillo Armas continuing in the presidency of the republic for a term to be fixed by the constituent assembly?" The right of illiterates to vote, which had been abolished immediately after Castillo Armas swept into the capital, was re-established especially for the plebiscite. The results were predictable: 485,531 in favor, 393 opposed and 655 giving no answer, according to official figures.[46]

Now Castillo Armas could get down to the hard work of putting his own imprimatur on the country. He quickly re-established ties with the conservative Catholic Church, which Guatemalan governments had kept at arm's length since the nineteenth century. He restored the right of the Church to own property, to give religious instruction in public schools and to bring in foreign clergy. In addition, he lifted a prohibition on foreign oil concessions imposed under Arévalo and Arbenz and encouraged foreign companies to purchase drilling rights. He brought Guatemala back into the Organization of Central American States, a regional pact from which Arbenz had resigned after it became clear other members were plotting against him. He even sought and was granted aid from the United States to finish Arbenz's pet public works project, the highway to Puerto Barrios. Both Castillo Armas and the United States had once denigrated the road because it competed with the Fruit Company's railroad, the IRCA.[47]

All in all, despite the rather messy footnote of the asylum question, the Guatemalan operation was considered a complete success by the Americans. The U.S. "cover story" held. Eisenhower and Dulles dutifully maintained that the coup was executed "by the Guatemalans themselves." Peurifoy even told a congressional committee later in the autumn that his role had been "strictly that of a diplomatic observer." Richard Bissell, reflecting years later on the coup, observed: "Our job was simply to get rid of Arbenz. We did that successfully. It was a success at one point in history, but this does not assure a happy ultimate outcome."[48]

15

THE AFTERMATH

From the perspective of history, no one could judge the outcome of the 1954 coup as happy. Even the "official" historian of the coup, Ronald Schneider, conceded a decade after the invasion: "While the short-run outcome of the intervention in 1954 was viewed at the time as a success for the United States in the Cold War, in a larger perspective it is increasingly difficult to see it as such. Indeed, in light of subsequent events it might reasonably be considered little short of disaster." Or as William Krieg, Peurifoy's counselor at the U. S. Embassy in 1954, later put it: "Having a revolution is a little like releasing a wheel at the top of a hill. You don't know where it's going to bounce or where it's going to go."[1]

The wheel of intervention took many different bounces in

Guatemala and in the subsequent careers of Operation Success
participants. John Peurifoy was one of the first to find his life
changed. Before 1954 was out, Dulles gave the flamboyant envoy a new ambassadorial assignment in Thailand. Diplomats in
Bangkok familiar with his record in Greece and Guatemala immediately wanted to know: "Is a coup about to occur?" On August 18, 1955, Peurifoy was driving one of his sons in his pow-
der-blue Thunderbird across a narrow bridge outside the capital
when a truck entered at the other end. The ambassador tried to
squeeze past the vehicle, but he was testing his skill at high-
speed driving once too often. There was a crash, and Peurifoy
and his son were killed instantly.[2]

The State Department also reassigned other important embassy officers to posts around the globe. ("They didn't want anybody left around to tell the story," one of them explained.) In
later years, it staffed the American Embassy in Guatemala with
counter-insurgency specialists from South Vietnam; twenty-five
foreign service officers with experience in Saigon were posted to
the Central American nation between the years 1964 and 1974.

The Central Intelligence Agency's covert operatives also scattered. John Doherty, the ex-CIA station chief, went into the
cement business in Guatemala City, dismaying the CIA, which
ordered an ineffectual ban thereafter on agents benefiting financially from operations. The CIA's other principal field agent,
Enno Hobbing, returned to New York and joined *Life* magazine.
(Later he came back to Guatemala to do a flattering piece on
Castillo Armas.) Jerry DeLarm stayed in aviation in Central
America. Carlos Cheeseman, DeLarm's flying partner, took a job
in Guatemala. (Fate soon caught up with him; in the 1960s leftist
guerrillas gunned him down.)

The CIA as an institution got a renewed lease on life. The
ease with which it had deposed Arbenz (and Prime Minister
Mossadegh in Iran a year before) encouraged the agency to try
similar operations against Sukarno in Indonesia and Castro in
Cuba. Lawrence Houston, the CIA's counsel, later observed: "As
a result of Guatemala, I thought there was a great deal of over-
confidence in the agency in the preparations to invade Cuba."
The abject failure of the Bay of Pigs invasion indeed resulted in

the downfall of two of the men who originally plotted the Guatemalan government's overthrow, CIA Director Allen Dulles and his aide, later Deputy Director, Richard Bissell. (Some years later one of the other central figures in Operation Success, Frank Wisner, committed suicide.) Over the longer term the coup gravely damaged American interests in Latin America. The gusto with which the United States had ended the Guatemalan revolution embittered many Latins, and strengthened deep-seated anti-Americanism throughout the continent.[3]

Nor did United Fruit prosper. Despite heavy lobbying (by lawyer Thomas Corcoran, among others), the company failed to persuade the Justice Department to withdraw the antitrust suit that threatened its operations in Guatemala. At one point, United Fruit even produced a film entitled *Why The Kremlin Hates Bananas* to discredit the justice department action. However, in 1958, the company accepted a consent decree forcing it to curtail its business in Guatemala by surrendering some of its trade to local companies and some of its land to local businessmen. Due to another suit, it also had to give up its ownership interest in the IRCA Railroad Company. In 1972, it finally sold all of its remaining Guatemalan land holdings to the Del Monte corporation, gaining the consent of the Guatemalan government to the deal, according to Thomas McCann, through "the promise of a bribe." It retained only a few small subsidiaries.

In the late 1960s, United Fruit became caught up in the corporate merger craze. "It had survived nearly every form of upheaval possible to imagine," wrote Thomas McCann in his book about the company, "but it was not to survive much longer." Under the presidency of a financial wheeler-dealer, Eli Black, the company merged with a conglomerate called United Brands. As the financial climate darkened in the 1970s, Black saw his two-billion-dollar empire gradually disintegrate before his eyes. He broke under the pressure. On the morning of February 3, 1975, he walked to his corner office on the forty-fourth floor of the Pan Am Building in New York, smashed a hole in the quarter-inch-thick window and jumped to his death.[4]

Most of the Guatemalans who played important roles in the drama also suffered extraordinary ends. One of the strangest stories concerns Communist firebrand Carlos Manuel Pellecer, who during Arbenz's land reform had often urged peasants to seize land illegally. Pellecer had always seemed an unlikely Marxist. He was a member of an old Guatemalan family, a descendant of Manuel José Arce, a nineteenth-century independence hero. His father was a judge and four-time mayor of Antigua. As a young cadet, Pellecer had plotted against the Ubico dictatorship, and in the Arévalo era he joined the Communist PGT. After the Castillo Armas coup, however, he fled to Mexico, where he soon renounced his long-held beliefs and began writing anti-Communist booklets under CIA sponsorship. ("Best deal I ever had," said a Mexican printer who published some of them. "The CIA pays for the printing, and then they buy all the copies!") Some in the intelligence agency toyed with the idea of sending Pellecer back to Guatemala, hoping that he would spread his new gospel and perhaps ascend to political leadership, but Pellecer did not have the kind of support to make it possible.[5]

Of the other principals, Foreign Minister Toriello fled to Mexico City, but was able to hold on to his lands in Guatemala for a while. Communist leader José Manuel Fortuny escaped to Mexico City too. Colonel Díaz, the short-lived successor to Arbenz, soon left Guatemala but later returned to reside quietly. Colonel Monzón, Castillo Armas' uneasy partner, retired from the Army after the junta collapsed. Former President Arévalo was allowed to re-enter Guatemala only in the 1970s; he later served as a roving diplomat for several Guatemalan governments.

The most torturous case of all was that of Jacobo Arbenz himself. The defeated President first fled to Mexico. Then, with his wife and three children, he went to Switzerland, hoping to make a home in the country of his father's birth. But the Swiss government said he would be permitted to stay only if he renounced his Guatemalan citizenship; he indignantly refused to do so. The family proceeded to Paris, where they lived under the watchful eye of French police. Given U.S. hostility, like France no other Western country promised to be any more congenial. After a month in Paris, Arbenz received word that he would be welcome to live freely in any Soviet-bloc country. He chose Czechoslovakia, then considered the most cosmopolitan of the Eastern European nations. He said at the time: "Politically I am a man without a party, but I believe that every person who is concerned

with the destiny of humanity ought to be interested in familiar-
izing himself with the socialist countries." But he was not warmly
received; Czech officials feared that he would demand some kind
of refund for the mostly useless arms they had sent him aboard
the *Alfhem* (he never did). After three months in a villa outside
Prague, he and his wife, María Cristina, moved to Moscow, placing their children in a school for foreigners 400 miles from the
Soviet capital.

The couple traveled a bit, including a month-long trip through
China, but Arbenz was depressed by conditions in Eastern
Europe and Russia and anxious to return to Latin America.
Uruguay was the only country that would accept him, and only
if he promised not to take a job, not to become involved in politics, and to report to the police once a week. In 1957, the former
President accepted the stipulations and thereafter lived in Montevideo until 1960. In that year, the newly triumphant Fidel Castro invited him to live in Cuba.

Arbenz jumped at the chance. He had become morose and de-
spondent in Uruguay, and was drinking more heavily than ever
before. Revolutionary Cuba, he thought, might be just the place
for him to regain health and self-respect. When he arrived at
José Martí Airport in Havana, a huge crowd was waiting, and
he was deeply moved. It turned out, however, that the joyous
Cubans were there to welcome a youth delegation, not Jacobo
Arbenz.

Still plagued by family and personal problems and soon upset
by the direction Castro was taking in Cuba, Arbenz remained
troubled and unhappy. He was occasionally invited to sit on the
official platform when Castro spoke, but became irritated when
the Cuban leader, warning the United States against trying to
topple his regime, took to declaring: "Cuba is not Guatemala!"
Arbenz had especially painful problems with his eldest daughter, Arabella, his favorite. She had refused to follow him to
Cuba, and instead stayed in Paris studying to be an actress. A
rebel in the family, she had years earlier quarreled bitterly with
her father over his insistence on educating his children in exclusive private schools despite his egalitarian views. She also in time
irritated her teachers in the Soviet Union by refusing to join the

Communist youth group. "She was essentially non-political," recalled one of her friends, "but became something of a rightist because of her parents' leftism."

After Paris, Arabella accompanied her boyfriend, a bullfighter, around Latin America. In September 1965, during an evening out in Bogotá, Colombia, she argued loudly with him at a restaurant. She abruptly stormed out of the place, dashed back to her hotel, then quickly returned. Marching straight to her boyfriend's table, she pulled a revolver out of her purse, held it to her head and killed herself. She was twenty-five years old.[6]

Arbenz was devastated by her death. The Mexican government gave him special permission to hold his daughter's funeral there and to stay in the country for a time on his own. Old friends who saw him commented on his physical deterioration, and his few political observations also raised eyebrows. Leaning over Arabella's coffin, he was heard to whisper: "*Hasta pronto, mi hijita*"—"I will be with you soon, my little daughter." One of his former associates reported that "his disillusionment was palpable." He told one friend, "I have failed as a politician, as a husband and as a father." He said he had no alternative except returning to Cuba "to vegetate, to do nothing, to ruminate."[7]

Arbenz had been trying for years to move to a more friendly country, and in 1970, Mexican authorities finally gave him permission to live there permanently. On January 27, 1971, Arbenz died at the age of fifty-eight, drowning in his bathtub at his Mexican home. According to one account, he had been "abandoned by his family and Communist friends, who had lately taken to insulting him." His death was attributed to natural causes, though there are still those who doubt that explanation. María Cristina, his wife, returned to El Salvador and made peace with her family. Her political views moderated considerably. As political violence spread through her country during the late 1970s, she moved to Paris.[8]

A final casualty of the U.S. intervention was Castillo Armas himself. He benefited initially from a substantial infusion of foreign aid from the United States, which had refused any important help during the Arévalo and Arbenz administrations. The United States gave his regime some $80 million in the first three years after the "Liberation." It was nearly all in the form of direct grants; none of it, except an $18.2 million World Bank loan, had to be repaid. To gauge the magnitude of this assistance, when the United States gave Castillo Armas $36 million in 1956–57 alone, it amounted to a fourth of the U.S. aid sent to India that same year. American assistance, which had totaled only $600,000 during the entire revolutionary era of 1944–54, soon reached a level of $45 million annually.[9]

But though these funds revitalized certain areas of the private sector, they did little for the nation's poor. Indeed, in abruptly reversing the industrialization and land reform policies of Arévalo and Arbenz, Castillo Armas shocked and destabilized the Guatemalan economy. His economic plan, which consisted largely of returning the country's economy to its traditional reliance on the coffee and banana crop, helped only a tiny aristocracy. By the time Castillo Armas had governed for eighteen months, he had managed to drive all but one half of one percent of the peasants who had won plots under the Arbenz agrarian reform off their new land. Most Guatemalans who had improved their lives in the 1940s and early 1950s found their hard-won progress had slipped away.[10]

Castillo Armas also proved to be no democrat. It soon became apparent that he intended to extend the "emergency" security and anti-union measures he had decreed after taking power, including press censorship. Not surprisingly, he sought to manipulate the electoral process for his own ends. In late 1955, he decided to postpone the next year's scheduled presidential election. Instead he held congressional elections, permitting only his own party, the National Liberation Movement (MLN), to offer candidates. Moderates and conservatives who had disliked Arbenz and welcomed the Liberation now began to wonder whether they had not traded a lesser evil for a greater one. They urged the "opening" of the political system, but Castillo Armas was unmoved. "My historic promise to the Guatemalan people was to exterminate Communism," he told an interviewer, "and I would rather have criticism than betray this trust."[11]

Castillo Armas retained the unswerving support of the American government. The Eisenhower administration continued to regard his survival as a centerpiece of its policy in the region. Some Americans envisioned making Guatemala "a showcase for democracy." Vice-President Nixon, after visiting Guatemala in 1955, declared that "President Castillo Armas' objective, 'to do more for the people in two years than the Communists were able to do in ten years,' is important. This is the first instance in history where a Communist government has been replaced by a free one. The whole world is watching to see which does the better job." A prominent former U.S. ambassador to Mexico, William O'Dwyer, pointed out that "the foreign policy of the U.S. is . . . on trial in Guatemala. Every nation in Latin America is watching to see how far the U.S. intends to go in helping Guatemala . . ."[12]

But despite American aid, the situation within Guatemala deteriorated. Many leading officials of the new regime considered Castillo Armas' victory a license to steal money. They did not share even the modest nationalism of the Liberator; they were ambitious and greedy officers anxious for the fruits of victory. A number became involved, some apparently in collaboration with American gangsters, in casino gambling, which was forbidden by the straitlaced Liberator. The officers opened several lightly disguised gambling halls, which were enthusiastically patronized by the capital's social elite. Archbishop Rossell Arellano appealed to his old friend Castillo Armas on moral grounds to close the casinos. Castillo Armas authorized several raids, but either through lethargy or indifference or possibly complicity, never completely stamped them out. In this area as in others, the Liberator did not appear in full control of his administration.[13]

A variety of scandals further besmirched his regime. One of the most personally embarrassing to Castillo Armas was the "corn caper" of 1955. The government had been seeking a license from Mexico to import badly needed fodder. Suddenly a company organized by several former Liberation officials sprang up and announced that it had secured a difficult-to-obtain Mexican permit. The new firm was given a lucrative government contract to import corn. Soon afterward, United Nations health technicians took test samples from some of the shipments and found them unfit for consumption. Then the weekly student newspaper *El Estudiante*—the only publication free to criticize the government since it was protected by university autonomy— implicated Castillo Armas himself. The paper discovered and printed a photo of a check for $25,000 from the head of the new importing firm, payable to the Liberator. This evidence, *El Estudiante* concluded, "could only have one interpretation." Castillo Armas indignantly denied any bribery accusation, saying that he had received the check as repayment of a personal loan. The daily *El Imparcial* leaped to his defense, running the "Liberator's" denial under a headline stating: "The Honor of the President Is Resplendent." Few Guatemalans were convinced, especially after the President ordered a crackdown on critics of the deal.[14]

An atmosphere of spreading disarray gradually paralyzed Castillo Armas' government. Plots against the administration began to crop up almost weekly. At the annual May Day rally in 1956, workers angered by anti-union laws booed government speakers off the platform. A frightened Castillo Armas responded by declaring a state of siege and authorizing his soldiers to "impede, suppress or suspend strikes of any nature" because, he explained, "Communist agitators have prepared a conspiracy and it has become indispensable to adopt severe and drastic means of repressing it." The President's tough actions inflamed university students already upset by the repeal of social legislation. They launched a series of demonstrations that shook several cities. Castillo Armas responded by expelling thirty student leaders from the country.[15]

Castillo Armas had held on for three years. Then on the evening of July 27, 1957, walking with his wife to dinner down the main hallway of his official residence behind the National Palace, the President approached his dining room precisely at nine o'clock. Several shots rang out. Castillo Armas collapsed and died almost immediately. Police found the assassin, an army guard named Romeo Vásquez Sánchez, dead on the floor nearby, apparently a suicide. President Eisenhower dispatched his son John to Castillo Armas' funeral. The police portrayed Vásquez Sánchez as a lone Communist fanatic embittered by the Liberator's "patriotic" policies. They even produced some leftist propaganda that had supposedly been found in his pockets and a suspicious "diary," but few if any Guatemalans believed the official explanation. Corridor gossip first indicted one ambitious officer, then another. There were whispers that mobsters from the United States, angered by the Liberator's harassment of their incipient casino business, were responsible. There were even rumors that the killing had a foreign link, specifically to Dominican Republic dictator Rafael Trujillo, who had backed Castillo Armas during his exile but later fell out with him. "The affair of Castillo Armas is one of those mysteries that Trujillo took with him to the grave," concluded a close Trujillo associate years later.[16]

The dead President's military clique, by then grouped into the National Liberation Movement (MLN), sought to keep the chief executive's office in its own hands. Interim MLN leaders hastily called elections and designated as their candidate an obscure government functionary, Miguel Ortiz Passarelli, who had served as Interior Minister under Castillo Armas. But the MLN did not reckon on the opposition of the former exile leader General Miguel Ydígoras Fuentes, then ambassador to Colombia, who had been biding his time abroad waiting for a chance to take power. Ydígoras never stopped believing that he had been twice cheated out of the presidency, once by Arbenz, whom he accused of rigging the 1950 voting, and then by Castillo Armas in 1956, when the Liberator broke his "gentleman's agreement" to call an election. With Castillo Armas now off the scene, the wily Ydígoras determined to take power. On the very day the MLN announced that an election would be held for October 20, 1957—the anniversary of the 1944 revolution—Ydígoras proclaimed he would return home and offer himself as a candidate. He was still a popular figure among many Guatemalans who recalled his days as an anti-Arbenz plotter and an early ally of Castillo Armas. Many hoped his reappearance would signal a rebirth of normal political life. But the frightened interim government became determined to prevent the unpredictable "Old Fox" from contesting the presidency.

Despite the turbulent atmosphere at home, the sixty-one-year-old Ydígoras boarded a plane for Guatemala City early in September. While the plane was airborne, a flight attendant brought him a radio message saying a mob was waiting at the Guatemala airport to lynch him. The pilot would have to make an unscheduled stop in San Salvador to let Ydígoras off there. Ydígoras walked into the cockpit and closed the door behind him. With a flourish, he reached under his jacket, pulled out his .45 revolver and held it against the astonished pilot's forehead.

"You son of a bitch!" he shouted at the American pilot in heavily accented English. "We go to Guatemala or we all die."[17]

Ydígoras rightly suspected that the message was a ruse. A crowd had indeed gathered at the airport, but it contained as many supporters as opponents of the veteran general. He disembarked to a tumultuous reception, and right away began campaigning across the country. Many who remembered his rightist predilections and shady past cautioned against his election. The centrist daily *La Prensa Libre* warned that he represented "a system which is the perfect antithesis of democracy, in which all the rights of man [are] denied" and predicted he "would give the country no life but that which is found under the Prussian boot."[18]

The MLN was not prepared to let Ydígoras take power. Five days after the voting—in which Ydígoras polled a plurality—the official electoral tribunal curtly announced that Ortiz Passarelli was the winner. Ydígoras was enraged, believing he had lost the presidency by trickery for a third time in less than a decade. Within hours, his followers poured onto the streets, newspapers denounced the fraud and the general himself threatened to stage a coup. The interim junta members were shaken by Ydígoras' show of strength. The next day they called him to a meeting at the National Palace. Military attaché Donald Cubbison and air attaché Robert Hertzel of the American Embassy attended to guarantee U.S. approval for a settlement. In short order, a pact was worked out under which a new election would be called for January 19, 1958. It was understood that should Ydígoras gain a victory, it would be recognized.

The second election went smoothly. This time the ruling group named José Luis Cruz Salazar—the colonel who had joined Monzón on his short-lived junta in 1954—to oppose Ydígoras. The CIA, which mistrusted Ydígoras, surreptitiously provided Cruz Salazar $97,000 in "campaign funds." The contribution made little difference. Ydígoras again won a plurality of the popular vote—though not enough to be elected outright—and Congress confirmed him by a vote of 40 to 18. He took office for a six-year term on March 15, 1958.[19]

Ydígoras at first entertained his countrymen. Early in his term, a newspaperman alleged that Ydígoras was a *viejo enclenque*, or an enfeebled old man. Ydígoras became indignant. He quickly arranged for a television appearance. Once before the cameras, he repeated the charge and said: "I will show him." Then he proceeded to skip rope and juggle Indian clubs before the incredulous Guatemalan audience.

But the interest in Ydígoras among Guatemalans soon waned. The Ydígoras star started to fade when the United States approached the President for a favor. Ydígoras had owed the U.S. a debt when American military men showed up at the National Palace meeting in late 1957 to ensure recognition of Ydígoras' presidential candidacy. The Americans were secretly planning an invasion of Cuba to overthrow Fidel Castro and needed a base of operations on foreign soil. President Ydígoras agreed to cooperate, provided the U.S. back him fully inside Guatemala. He persuaded conservative businessman Roberto Alejos, an old friend and associate, to turn over his plantation in the province of Retalhuleu to the Americans for use as an air base and training site. Alejos was a former employee of both the CIA and United Fruit and had been a confidant of Castillo Armas. He acted officially as President Ydígoras' link to foreign aid programs, a lucrative position for graft. His brother Carlos, Guatemala's ambassador to Washington, was Ydígoras' intermediary with the CIA in setting up the deal.

The presence of CIA instructors in Guatemala training Cuban exiles to overthrow Castro soon became an open secret. The Guatemalan Army in particular was painfully aware that Ydígoras was permitting the CIA to construct several airstrips, haul in huge amounts of cargo through La Aurora Airport in the capital and establish large bases in Retalhuleu, without its involvement or consent. Many officers, schooled in Guatemala's strong nationalist tradition, felt humiliated and angry at the alacrity with which Ydígoras was cooperating with the Americans. Many flatly opposed the use of Guatemalan soil to train foreign invaders, especially for purposes of attacking Castro, whom some officers admired as a nationalist.[20]

On the night of November 13, 1960, a large group of angry Guatemalan Army troops, including 120 disgruntled officers,

representing as much as half of the entire Army, staged an uprising at Fort Matamoros in Guatemala City and seized it. Another
dissident group took control of Puerto Barrios on the Atlantic
and the barracks of Zacapa. At one point, 800 peasants converged on the Zacapa garrison after it was taken to ask "for arms
with which to fight against the government . . . [but] the rebels
. . . could not make up their minds to arm the peasants," according to one historian. The Americans immediately feared a
coup that might upset the Bay of Pigs operation. They moved to
help Ydígoras crush the revolt. The United States provided several CIA B-26 bombers, piloted by Cuban exiles, to attack rebel
positions. President Eisenhower sent five U. S. Navy vessels, including the aircraft carrier *Shangri-La,* to patrol off Guatemala's
coast.[21]

Faced with such a strong military response from the United
States, the ill-planned revolt fizzled. But the strength of the plotters did not go unnoticed. As a *Christian Science Monitor* dispatch noted:

> [T]he fact that the rebels could take over two garrisons before
> the government learned of the revolt and that it took huge gov-
> ernment forces to put down ill-equipped men is cause for much
> comment here. This indicates a greater degree of discontent than
> most people imagine. It is believed by many here that the pres-
> ence of the United States Navy on the coast did discourage any
> intentions that local communists might have had of taking advan-
> tage of the rebellion . . .[22]

Some of the officers who led the revolt refused to accept the
traditional punishment for such insurrections: demotion, a return to the barracks and stern reprimands from the President.
Encouraged by the peasant support they saw for their cause, several groups of idealistic soldiers fled to the hills. The most out-
standing of the rebels was a young lieutenant, twenty-two-year-
old Marco Aurelio Yon Sosa, who had been trained by the
United States in the Panama Canal Zone. He crossed the border
into Honduras. Nineteen-year-old Luis Turcios Lima was another
leading rebel. He had received U. S. Ranger training at Fort
Benning, Georgia, in 1959 and 1960. After the November 13 up-

rising, he escaped to El Salvador. Both men soon re-entered Guatemala, determined to wage guerrilla warfare against the regime.
Turcios said he was taking his fateful step "because the government is a puppet" for foreign interests. Yon Sosa gave a somewhat more detailed explanation of his own goals:

> The aim was to clean up the government, not to destroy capi-
> talism. The Ydígoras administration, which had risen to power as
> a result of the electoral fraud of 1958, not only devoted itself to
> the defense of imperialism and the large landowners, but also
> lined its pockets with national treasury funds. . . . It was the
> movement's intention to prevent Guatemala's utilization as the
> base for aggression against Cuba, as planned by the U.S.[23]

During 1961, the two young officers lived underground and
made contact with a number of exiles. Turcios soon became associated with several leaders of the banned Partido Guatemalteco de Trabajo (PGT), Guatemala's Communist party. Both
men were encouraged by the support they received from Guatemalan peasants as they moved through the countryside. They
went about transforming their group, essentially made up of the
army officers who had staged the 1960 revolt, into a guerrilla
force. Their strategy was to topple the government by seizing
military installations. "The first guerrillas were formed with a
view to swiftly overthrowing the government, not for a long war
of attrition," according to one study of their tactics.

In February 1962, Turcios and Yon Sosa issued a call for national rebellion against "tyranny and humiliation":

> Democracy vanished from our country long ago. No people
> can live in a country where there is no democracy. That is why
> the demand for change is mounting in our country. We can no
> longer carry on in this way. We must overthrow the Ydígoras
> government and set up a government which represents human
> rights, seeks ways . . . to save our country from its hardships,
> and pursues a serious self-respecting foreign policy.[24]

The political climate seemed ripe. Protests over electoral fraud
in the congressional elections two months earlier were going on

in the capital. The chief of the Ydígoras secret police, Ranulfo González, had been slain January 24. Ydígoras blamed the killing on "Marxism directed from Cuba." Finally on February 6, the small and ill-prepared guerrilla band led by Turcios and Yon Sosa launched its first offensive. The rebels now called themselves the "Alejandro de León November 13 Guerrilla Movement"—a tribute to both a fallen comrade and the date of their abortive army uprising. In their first actions, they raided army outposts in Bananera and Morales, near Puerto Barrios, but soldiers soon appeared and chased them back into the hills.

During March, a second guerrilla group sprang up, presided over by a former Arbenz Minister of Defense, Carlos Paz Tejada. This band took the name "October 20 Front" to commemorate the 1944 revolution. In its call to arms it condemned the newly elected Congress as "government stooges" and declared: "We are indignant over the foreign military bases in our country and the military treaties with foreign powers." The statement asserted: "The only road left is the road of uprising. The only way to end the calamities torturing our country is to overthrow the despotic rule of Ydígoras and set up a government which proves by deeds that it is worthy of the people's trust."[25]

In mid-March, the three major opposition political parties—the Christian Democrats, the Revolutionary Party (successor to Arévalo's PAR) and the MLN, which Castillo Armas had founded—jointly demanded the resignation of Ydígoras. On March 16, student demonstrators took to the streets, and 20 or so died and 200 were injured in two days of confrontations. Ydígoras called thousands of soldiers to active alert. In a gesture to the Army, he named a new cabinet composed almost entirely of military officers.

Always sensitive about threats to Central America, the United States grew alarmed at the growing public support in Guatemala for movements seeking Ydígoras' overthrow. With the cooperation of a grateful Ydígoras, President John F. Kennedy approved a pacification program aimed at the most rebellious provinces—Zacapa and Izabal—including both "civic action" projects such as digging wells and building clinics and a sharp increase in military assistance. Starting that spring, the Americans equipped the Guatemalan Air Force with U.S.-made T-33 jets and C-47 transport planes. In May, two officers and five enlisted men of the U. S. Special Forces, all trained in Laos, established a counter-insurgency base at Mariscos in Izabal; the instructors were mostly of Mexican or Puerto Rican descent who would blend in better with the natives. With them came fifteen Guatemalan soldiers who had taken American guerrilla warfare courses in the Canal Zone. The U.S. military advisers soon concluded that the Guatemalan Army was "weak, disorganized and unprepared to meet the guerrilla threat."[26]

With the help of the Americans, however, Ydígoras finally crushed the revolt before summer. His forces killed or jailed hundreds of students, labor leaders, peasants and professionals as well as ex-soldiers. They also decimated the fledgling rebel bands of Turcios and Yon Sosa and Carlos Paz Tejada. In January 1963, two American generals attached to the Caribbean Command, Andrew O'Meara and Theodore Bogart, made a three-day tour through the country and pronounced the counter-insurgency program a success.[27]

Ydígoras was still in deep domestic trouble despite his military victories. Even the Catholic Church started to criticize him. A pastoral letter signed by a number of Guatemalan bishops in August 1962 attacked the government for allowing peasants to receive "salaries that hardly permit [them] to avoid death by starvation" and permitting plantation workers to live "in situations closely resembling concentration camps. . . . It is here that infant mortality triumphs, reaching astonishing ratios, as well as sickness and social disintegration." Archbishop Rossell Arellano, who had proclaimed Castillo Armas a "legitimate saint," thundered against Ydígoras' followers: "These are not anti-communists who have sealed with their blood the conviction that Guatemala had to be freed from the atheistic ideology of Marxism. These are not the anti-communists faithful to the ideals of the *caudillo* of the Liberation . . ."[28]

Ydígoras' relationship with the Americans, never close, was also deteriorating. The CIA had not forgotten that he had turned down the leadership of Operation Success in 1953. When he visited Washington in 1958, Ydígoras claimed angry CIA operatives even came to him and insisted he repay a debt of $1.8 million incurred by Castillo Armas to mount the invasion of 1954. On that same trip, Secretary of State Dulles also greeted him very coldly, apparently doubting the durability of his anti-Communism. Though President Kennedy later approved counter-insurgency help to Ydígoras, he was dissatisfied with the general's corruption and his failure to cooperate with the Alliance for Progress.[29]

Ydígoras had promised he would leave the presidency when his term expired in 1964. With increasing civil strife, worsening economic mismanagement, growing poverty and estrangement from the United States, the principal question was whether Ydígoras could even survive until the scheduled election. Then from Mexico came startling news. Juan José Arévalo, the schoolteacher who had led Guatemala from dictatorship to democracy in the 1940s, declared on November 26, 1962, that he was ready to "assume the leadership of all revolutionary forces in the country" in another bid for the presidency. Ydígoras, like most Guatemalans, was taken by surprise. He first demanded that Arévalo be "extradited" for trial in the 1949 murder of Colonel Arana, but then changed his mind and said he would let Arévalo return to run for President.[30]

The Americans were not pleased by this development. Arévalo had published a book called *The Shark and the Sardines* in which he pictured the United States as trying to dominate Latin America. Then in late 1963, when conspirators close to then Defense Minister Peralta Azurdia approached the U. S. Embassy about a "preventive coup" against Ydígoras to stop Arévalo's election, they found a sympathetic audience. On top of existing American doubts about Ydígoras, his apparent readiness to permit Arévalo's re-entry tipped the balance against him.[31]

Citing "top sources within the Kennedy administration," one American journalist disclosed that President Kennedy chaired a secret meeting in early January 1963 which authorized a coup against Ydígoras. However two of the five participants alleged to be present at the session denied the meeting ever took place. One, Assistant Secretary of State for Inter-American Affairs Edwin Martin, insisted that the United States never approved an overthrow. "It is my impression," he stated, "that no initiative was required for the military to oust Ydígoras." But he did concede: "I would guess that we may have decided not to try to stop the military if they moved to overthrow Ydígoras, a quite different thing than initiating a coup."

Another reputed participant at the secret conference who also denied its taking place was the then U.S. ambassador in Guatemala, John O. Bell. Bell also denied that the United States was involved in the coup against Ydígoras. "This coup was not suggested by the U.S., it was not arranged, managed or supported by the U.S.," he said. He did concede that the American Embassy had advance word of a "preventive" action: "the possibility of it was known and was reported to Washington." He was not entirely upset by Defense Minister Peralta Azurdia's coup: "While from a philosophical standpoint I would have preferred that the electoral process be followed, I did not find the military's attitude surprising or illogical." On March 29, Arévalo sneaked back into Guatemala. The reaction in the country was swift and immediate. Ydígoras awoke the next day to find an American-made tank parked on his front lawn, its main gun only inches from his door. Time had finally run out for the "Old Fox." Ydígoras agreeably surrendered power to his U.S.-approved successor, Minister of Defense Enrique Peralta Azurdia, an officer decidedly more reactionary than Ydígoras.[32]

Under General Peralta Azurdia, the Guatemalan dictatorship took on a new zeal. Peralta Azurdia abandoned most efforts to improve the lot of the masses of poor people. Instead he heavily militarized the country. He specially trained army squads to track guerrillas, keeping the rebels on the run and inflicting many casualties. Peralta Azurdia, however, turned down insistent U.S. offers of Special Forces, "Green Beret" troops trained in guerrilla warfare, to fight the rebels, preferring to rely on his own men. His forces murdered hundreds of anti-government activists, but never completely wiped out the insurgent movement. At one point, on March 6, 1966, Peralta Azurdia's police raided a secret meeting of the banned Communist party PGT and arrested twenty-eight people, including Víctor Manuel Gutiérrez, the former pro-Arbenz congressman. None of those apprehended was ever seen again; Gutiérrez's body was reportedly dropped from an airplane 20,000 feet over the Pacific Ocean.[33]

Peralta Azurdia kept his promise to bring the nation to the polls in 1966, however. Liberals and anti-military activists rallied around the candidacy of Mario Méndez Montenegro, a centrist politician who had managed to survive by cooperating with the dictatorship. But four months before the election, Méndez Montenegro was found dead in his home, a bullet in his head. Authorities called it suicide, but his family strongly rejected that conclusion. The truth, as one study concluded, "remains in doubt to this day, and is listed with the murders of Col. Francisco J. Arana and Col. Carlos Castillo Armas as murky political events of primary magnitude in a murky political environment."[34]

As a substitute candidate, civilians settled on the dead man's brother, Julio César Méndez Montenegro. He won the election, held March 6, 1966. Moderate Guatemalans hoped that, as a civilian, Méndez Montenegro would be able to institute the social reforms the guerrillas were demanding. But the military abruptly tried to oust Méndez Montenegro, only backing down under intense American pressure. The Army nonetheless forced a frightened Méndez Montenegro to give its commanders a free hand. The President's capitulation now made it possible for American defense officials to place U. S. Green Beret soldiers in Guatemala.[35]

The anti-guerrilla campaign soon took on a fresh intensity. Pressured by his military commanders, Méndez Montenegro named a tough colonel, Carlos Arana Osorio, as military commander of Zacapa province, the center of guerrilla activity. Arana Osorio set aside July to October 1966 for special training of his men in counter-insurgency warfare. U. S. Green Berets conducted much of the instruction. The United States gave nearly $6 million in aid to Guatemala's armed forces under the Military Assistance Program (MAP) and $11 million in American military equipment. The U.S. involvement put the rebels on a spot. Their years-old habit of operating casually in the open no longer could work because they were particularly vulnerable to Green Beret detection and killing. The insurgents had also lost their original commanders. Yon Sosa had retreated to a fringe Trotskyite group, and Turcios, who had gained Fidel Castro's endorsement, lost his life in a car crash in Guatemala City in October 1966.[36]

Under Arana Osorio's leadership, the Zacapa-Izabal campaign reached an unprecedented intensity. Familiar anti-guerrilla tactics were used, but a new weapon was also introduced: political assassination on a mass scale. Forces in the military had decided that if Guatemala was ever to return to its ideal time—the "quiet" days before the 1944 revolution—they would have to destroy anybody tinged with liberalism. Thousands of people suddenly met death at the hands of unseen gunmen under the presidency of Méndez Montenegro. Few of the victims were actual guerrillas; many were middle-class professionals who had supported Arévalo and Arbenz. As one scholar has written of the period following Arana Osorio's appointment in Zacapa:

> Shortly thereafter, anti-communist civilians drawn from among participants in the 1954 coup were integrated into the military's security apparatus. The first in a series of right-wing paramilitary groups commenced operations. In the beginning, such groups as the National Organized Anti-Communist Movement (MANO), the New Anti-Communist Organization (NOA), and the "Eye for Eye" (OJO) chose their victims from individuals who could be associated with the Arévalo-Arbenz years or with the more recent guerrilla insurgency. However, under the cover of anti-guerrilla activity, non-communist leftists were sought out by right-wing terrorist groups and eliminated. Leaflets appeared threatening not only prominent members within the PGT and rebel groups, but also students, intellectuals, trade unionists, and professional people who sought to organize or protest against what they considered social injustice. Between October 1966 and March 1968 an estimated 3,000 to 8,000 Guatemalans were reportedly killed in the Zacapa-Izabal campaign. The use of "counter-terror" methods by civilian paramilitary groups is credited for much of the success against rural guerrillas and their suspected supporters.[37]

A Guatemalan government had finally unleashed unrestrained power against the guerrillas, much to the satisfaction of the Americans. Four months after the Méndez Montenegro regime took office, the New York *Times* reported that the United States

had now finally found a "willing partner" in Guatemala. The
United States "can talk with and accomplish things with" the
new Guatemalan government, the *Times* quoted U.S. officials as
observing. The year 1966 truly marked the beginning of ferocious
warfare in Guatemala. Amnesty International, the London-based
human rights organization, concluded that in the decade and a
half following 1966, more than 30,000 people were "abducted,
tortured and assassinated" in the country.[38]

The extent of American involvement in the carnage is difficult
to quantify, but it was substantial. In September 1967, a reporter
interviewed Clemente Marroquín Rojas, who was vice-president
under Méndez Montenegro:

> Marroquín Rojas stated that in recent months a squadron of
> United States aircraft piloted by U.S. personnel had flown from
> bases in Panama, delivered loads of napalm on targets suspected
> of being guerrilla haunts, and flown back to their bases without
> landing on Guatemalan soil. . . . United States Special Forces
> are carrying out intensive training of local personnel in anti-
> guerrilla warfare, interrogation of prisoners, and jungle survival.
> The United States advisers are also currently accompanying
> Guatemalan patrols on anti-guerrilla duty.[39]

During this period, the United States also provided assistance
for the Guatemalan national police force. The United States
allocated more than $2.6 million from 1966 to 1970 for police in-
struction and equipment under the U. S. Office of Public Safety
(OPS) Program. Over the same period, the United States
helped increase the size of the national police force from 3,000
to 11,000 men. According to official U.S. figures, by 1970 over
30,000 Guatemalan police had benefited from OPS training. At
the end of the 1960s, Guatemala had the second-largest American police assistance program in the hemisphere—after Brazil,
which had twenty times the population.[40]

By late 1967, the new phenomenon of right-wing terror
squads had spread deep into every area of Guatemalan life. In
December, one of the rightist gangs maimed and killed beauty
queen Rogelia Cruz Martínez, a former Miss Guatemala known

for her anti-government views. In response, leftist guerrillas decided to attack the United States military, which they now held responsible for the surge of savagery in their country. Their targets were Colonel John Webber, head of the United States Military Mission, and an aide, Lieutenant Commander Ernest Munro. (Another U.S. military adviser, Colonel Harold Hauser, had been slain in 1965.) Webber was thought to have conceived the "counter-terror" strategy used against guerrillas in the Zacapa-Izabal area. On January 6, 1968, rebels gunned the two men down. In a communiqué following the killings, they accused the United States of "creating" the new death squads which were "sowing terror and death" through Guatemala. "The genocidal work of such bands of assassins has resulted in the death of nearly 4,000 Guatemalans," they charged.[41]

The guerrillas next decided to kidnap the American ambassador, John Gordon Mein, to prevent the execution of a partisan leader then held by the government. But, as one historian told the story, "the plan misfired. The guerrillas forced his car to stop as it was driving along the Avenida Reforma in the middle of the city. The ambassador got out of his car and attempted to resist capture. He was promptly shot." Mein was the first American ambassador to be killed in the line of duty.[42]

But Colonel Arana Osorio so distinguished himself in the counter-guerrilla campaign that his fellow officers—the real power in the country—decided he should be the next President. He was elected as a "law and order" candidate. By this point, the Army and ultra-rightists had completed a climb back to power in Guatemala. This ruling elite now began to turn its ex-defense ministers into the new presidents. It controlled all subsequent elections. The officers did not forbid contests, but instead limited participation and rigged results to prevent undesired outcomes. Moderate and leftist parties had great difficulty gaining places on the ballot; political terror cowed other politicians into silence or withdrawal. The chief party of the extreme right, Castillo Armas' old National Liberation Movement, began to play the role of electoral muscleman. In a radio broadcast in 1980, one official spokesman for the MLN bluntly admitted: "The MLN is the party of organized violence . . . there is nothing wrong with organized violence; it is vigor and the MLN is a vigorous movement." Elections had in effect become little more than rough "jockeying" between rightist factions.

In his role as the new President, Arana Osorio institutionalized his Zacapa strategy in the Presidential Palace. He was determined to exterminate all opposition, especially the leftist guerrillas who had by now moved on to urban warfare. "During the first three years of his presidency," according to one academic study, "the incidence of murders and disappearances reached unprecedented levels. Depending on the source, the estimates of victims, many of whose mutilated corpses made identification impossible, range from 3,500 to 15,000."[43]

In 1974, despairing Guatemalans of moderate political views proposed a centrist military officer, General Efraín Ríos Montt, for the presidency. Ríos Montt won that year's contest, but his fellow military officers barred his assumption of power. Instead, with Arana Osorio's backing, they installed the "official" candidate, a bland and agreeable conservative general named Kjell Eugenio Laugerud García. Ríos Montt went into exile as Guatemala's attaché in Madrid. Unrest in the country increased markedly after an earthquake struck Guatemala in February 1976, killing over 25,000 people. The government provided scant relief to survivors and it persecuted foreign missions bringing in outside aid. Around that time a new round of guerrilla activity began. The newest insurgency, collecting remnants of earlier rebellions, came together as the Guerrilla Army of the Poor (EGP). Among its first victims was Jorge Bernal Hernández Castellón, an MLN congressman who, as one American professor noted, "had been one of Arana Osorio's principal security advisers and [was] thought to have been responsible for the disappearance of many leftists in the early 1970s." Other guerrilla movements meantime sprang up too, including the FAR (Rebel Armed Forces), the PGT (a militant wing of the Communist party) and ORPA (Revolutionary Organization of the People in Arms), mainly an Indian group.[44]

In 1978, a new general and wealthy landowner, Fernando Romeo Lucas García, took over as President after a fraudulent election. He promised "a harsh campaign against guerrilla groups," but faced continuing opposition. In October 1978, thousands of Guatemalans took part in mass protests in the capital against bus-fare increases. During the first twelve days of that month, at least 30 people lost their lives, 350 were injured and 600 arrested. In response, labor leaders called for a national strike and set October 20—the anniversary of the 1944 revolution—as the date for a huge rally in Guatemala City "to protest against institutionalized repression." The demonstration took place. As it broke up, one of the principal speakers, Oliverio Castaneda de León, head of the Association of University Students, was machine-gunned to death just across the plaza from the National Palace. His assailants calmly drove away while police looked on.

The scale and breadth of the terror that now enveloped Guatemala became difficult to grasp. One who tried to explain it was René de León Schlotter, leader of Guatemala's center-left Christian Democrats. At the time he made his statement, in 1976 before a committee of the United States Congress, de León was secretary-general of the worldwide Christian Democratic movement. He said:

> Guatemala has suffered a spectacular form of violence: spectacular not only for having lasted through the past two decades, but also for its intensity—the high number of victims and the cruelty of the methods used.
>
> One of the characteristics of violence in my country is that it comes basically from political groups. Quite apart from the violence that comes from normal, ever-present social and economic factors, this phenomenon of violence is political, carried out for political reasons: the establishment of terror for the general purpose of eliminating an adversary.
>
> Another feature of this phenomenon is that it is mainly from the right. . . . [G]roups of the extreme right have used violence as their only tool. . . .
>
> The violence organized by these groups has a double purpose: first to sow terror and bring people to their knees in fear of their lives . . . [a]nd second to eliminate opponents. . . . In Guatemala, in order to avoid responsibility for unjust and arbitrary sentences, they don't bother with detention: the opponent is killed or "kidnapped" in the streets and just disappears. . . .
>
> Allow me to reaffirm that the responsibility of the United States, although indirect, is very real and serious. With its policy of supporting dictatorships, the United States has collaborated in the strengthening of these regimes and burdened our people with

debts, often for the most superfluous programs. With its policy of
military and police assistance, the United States has collaborated
in the acts of repression, and consequently in the violation of
human rights. . . . [T]hese types of assistance weigh heavily
on a developing people, whose efforts should all be concentrated
on promoting production and achieving greater social justice.[45]

As the 1980s began, the position of Guatemala's ruling generals and their civilian backers remained unchanged. By now,
the 14,000-member Guatemalan armed forces had become a
wealthy caste unto itself. It claimed its own bank, ran an investment fund for its members, and launched industrial projects. Its
leaders owned vast ranch acreage and regularly sold protection
to large landowners. The discovery of huge oil reserves in Guatemala in the late 1970s, estimated to provide 10 percent of the
annual needs of the U.S., opened up fresh possibilities for profit
by the careerists.

Meantime, death squads linked to the Army reached into
every sector of national life. Street-corner murders of lawyers,
schoolteachers, journalists, peasant leaders, priests and religious
workers, politicians, trade union organizers, students, professors
and others continued on a daily basis. "If you look back," observed former Guatemala City mayor Manuel Colom Argueta,
one of the leading liberal politicians in Guatemala in the 1970s,
"you will see that every single murder is of a key person. They
are not all of the same ideological orientation. They are simply
the people in each sector or movement who have the capacity to
organize the population around a cause." (A few days after
making that statement, Colom Argueta himself was assassinated.)[46]

The intention of the military leaders was essentially to destroy
the political center. Anyone not supporting the regime was almost by definition a leftist, and therefore an enemy. The military apparently believed that eliminating the center precluded
the possibility of a moderate government, therefore leaving the
citizenry a sterile choice between a revolutionary Communist
regime and the existing military dictatorship. In mid-1980, this
reasoning drove out the last moderate in the Lucas García administration, Vice-President Francisco Villagran Kramer, who
resigned to protest the government's role in terrorism. "Death

or exile is the fate of those who fight for justice in Guatemala," he said.[47]

In January 1980, a group of impoverished Indians from Quiche province, an EGP stronghold, traveled to the capital to protest the army tactics being used against civilians in their area. The peasants and their campus supporters marched into the Spanish Embassy to dramatize their demand that the government name a commission to investigate the grievances. Over the anguished protests of the Spanish ambassador, who urged negotiations, Guatemalan police stormed the embassy, in violation of international law. In the chaos, one of the occupiers apparently knocked over a Molotov cocktail he had brought in. The ensuing blaze killed all but one of the thirty-five peasants, several embassy employees and two former Guatemalan government officials. Spain immediately broke diplomatic relations with Guatemala, but the Guatemalan generals did not seem to care. One American correspondent on the scene wrote:

> It would be an overstatement to call the conflagration at the embassy a turning point in the violent modern history of Guatemala. But it does reflect the basic currents now running through both the government of this land and its increasingly militant opposition. . . .
>
> [T]he Guatemalan generals are fully willing to pay [the price of international condemnation] to maintain the hard-line policies that they consider essential to their survival. These policies take forms other than mass assaults on those who challenge the regime. Most common is the deadly efficiency of the so-called "death squads," which have come to dominate Guatemalan life. . . .
>
> Unlike the [guerrilla] groups active in the 1960s, the EGP has attracted some support from the rural Indians who, according to most theories, are fundamentally apolitical and prefer not to become involved in opposition movements, much less armed guerrilla groups. . . .
>
> During recent months, the rebels have carried out some spectacular actions. They have assassinated the army chief of staff, who was reputed to be a leading organizer of "death squads." They have bombed two office buildings in the capital, including the modern headquarters of the National Tourism Agency. And

they have kidnapped the son of one of the nation's most prominent families, holding him for 103 days until a ransom estimated
at $5 million was paid and laundered abroad. It was the first kid-
napping on that scale to be seen yet in Guatemala, and the ransom money will presumably be used to buy weapons.[48]

Guerrillas fighting against the Guatemalan government trace
their lineage directly to Operation Success, as this 1981 statement by the EGP makes clear:

> The Guatemalan revolution is entering its third decade. Ever
> since the government of Jacobo Arbenz was overthrown in 1954,
> the majority of the Guatemalan people have been seeking a way
> to move the country towards solving the same problems which
> were present then and have only worsened over time.
> The counterrevolution, put in motion by the U. S. Government
> and those domestic sectors committed to retaining every single
> one of their privileges, dispersed and disorganized the popu-
> lar and democratic forces. However, it did not resolve any of
> the problems which had first given rise to demands for economic,
> social and political change. These demands have been raised
> again and again in the last quarter century, by any means that
> seemed appropriate at the time, and have received each time the
> same repressive response as in 1954.
> The revolutionary guerrilla movement of the 1960s . . . was
> defeated militarily by an army trained by the United States in
> the counter-insurgency techniques learned in Vietnam. . . . The
> temporary defeat of the armed movement by the end of the
> 1960s did not demonstrate the impossibility of armed struggle.
> . . . Today, the expansion of the guerrilla war and the qualitative
> growth of guerrilla units are occurring faster than ever before.[49]

The economic conditions the EGP speaks of are far worse than
those of the Arbenz period. The quality of life for the average
Guatemalan has not even returned to the level of the Arbenz-
Arévalo years. The World Bank, which in 1950 had recommended
reform in Guatemala, issued another report in 1978. According
to its data, 10 percent of Guatemalan landowners still owned
more than 80 percent of the land, much of which had been con-
verted to the cultivation of exotic spices and other export crops

that have produced consequent shortages of basic foodstuffs like corn and beans. In rural areas, only 15 percent of the population have access to piped water and just 4 percent have electricity. Without land of their own, many peasants are still forced to spend months every year working for low wages on big plantations, just as in the Ubico era. About one third of the rural population is said to be undernourished.[50]

Over the same decade, too, an increasing number of Guatemalans have died not just from bullets, but from the scarcity of medical care and from malnutrition. The death rate in the country from all causes (11 per 1,000 inhabitants) trailed only Nicaragua and Haiti in the Western Hemisphere in the 1970s. Infant mortality was extremely high; the government's own figures indicated that 83 of every 1,000 children born alive did not survive their first two years. Four out of every five children were reported to be undernourished. Life expectancy was 60.5 years for *ladinos* and only 44.5 for Indians. The illiteracy rate had risen to 70 percent, second only to Haiti in the hemisphere. The reasons for a growing popular frustration, then, were not hard to find.[51]

The forcible interruption of the Guatemalan political process with a violent coup in 1954 has remained the central episode in the modern history of that country. The fragile political institutions created by the 1944 constitution did not have a chance to mature. The evolutionary process of social growth leading toward nationhood was prematurely stunted. The age-old alliance of the rich and the military regained its hold on Guatemala, ruling through a series of corrupt regimes, uninterested in national development or improving the lives of its poor majority. A cycle of violence grew up, traceable to the bitter hostilities engendered by Operation Success. And in a regional context, the 1954 coup showed other countries in Central America that the United States was more interested in unquestioning allies than democratic ones. As a result, movements toward peaceful reform in the region were set back, dictators were strengthened and encouraged, and activists of today look to guerrilla warfare rather than elections as the only way to produce change.

Guatemala has now become a test of John Kennedy's favorite

axiom, "Those who make peaceful change impossible make violent change inevitable." In almost uninterrupted control since 1954, the military has shown no inclination to give up power. "The country is presently engaged in a politics of attrition, intimidation and terror," wrote an American political scientist in 1980.[52] The guerrillas have won growing support from Guatemalans terrorized by unceasing violence. Moderate leaders, most of them in exile, attack the government more urgently than ever before. International trade union federations and human rights groups beginning in the 1980s launched a worldwide campaign including a tourist boycott, to isolate Guatemala from the civilized global community. Guatemala, impervious to outside pressures, however, has gone on practicing its form of politics in which there are no victors, only victims.

AFTERWORD
TO THE 2005 HARVARD EDITION

For more than 30 years, outsiders who share Guatemala's anguish were unable to point to any true improvement in the conditions of life there. Armed conflict ravaged the country and took a staggering human toll. Many of the victims were unarmed peasants slaughtered by an army blinded by ignorance, hatred and fear. Among the survivors are hundreds of thousands of widows, orphans and refugees.

As the war raged, cruel economic injustices put prosperity and even decent survival beyond the reach of the indigenous peoples who form the majority of the population. In a country where owning even a tiny plot of land can mean the difference between dignity and misery, huge amounts of land have remained in the hands of a small elite while the masses go hungry. Added to these gross imbalances are a host of social ills that combine to make this potentially rich country a wretched place for most of its people.

In addition to these problems, a deep-seated culture of violence has taken root in Guatemala. Military regimes, army units and police squads have set an awful example, teaching entire generations that terror and murder are appropriate ways to achieve both political and personal ends. For their crimes they have enjoyed nearly complete immunity, as the police and judicial systems exist to serve the unjust ruling order.

This has been a deadening litany for Guatemalans and their friends around the world. The last years of the twentieth century, however, brought a series of breakthroughs that could provide the foundation for a new Guatemala. Enormous challenges remain, but a true springtime may finally have dawned in the country where the tourist slogan "Land of Eternal Spring" has for years sounded like a cruel joke.

The early 1980s marked a new high point for violence in Guatemala. Terrified by the triumph of leftist guerrillas in nearby Nicaragua and the subsequent unification of Guatemalan insurgents into a single coalition called the Unidad Revolucionaria Nacional Guatemalteca (URNG), and encouraged by the Reagan administration to fight insurgents with every means at their disposal, military leaders launched a series of devastating military sweeps in large areas of the countryside deemed to be pro-guerrilla. An estimated one million people who lived in these areas fled their homes to escape military rampages, among them 150,000 who sought refuge across the northern border in Mexico. Many who did not move quickly enough were killed. Survivors were concentrated in areas euphemistically called "model villages" or "development poles" where they could be watched by soldiers and their civilian allies. At the same time, a new round of assassinations decimated the ranks of intellectuals and civilian organizers.

Having effectively destroyed the guerrilla movement, in the process devastating their country and making it a pariah in much of the world, military commanders began looking for a new strategy. In 1985, following nearly fifteen years of uninterrupted military rule, they launched a process that led to the adoption of a new constitution and the election of a civilian president. The process had a shaky start. Its first hero, Marco Vinicio Cerezo Arévalo, a dynamic young politician who had escaped assassination more than once and who assumed the presidency in 1986 with more than seventy percent of the popular vote, unaccountably lost much of his anti-military zeal upon taking office. But although his four-year presidency was a disappointment to those who had hoped he would begin a decisive break with the past, it marked the beginning of a process of democratization that was painstakingly slow, but ultimately produced profoundly important results.

President Vinicio Cerezo and some of the members of Congress elected with him began to speak about human rights and the need to work toward resolving Guatemala's age-old problems. Guerrillas of the URNG were scornful, rejecting "reformist plans of the so-called democratic opening" and calling for "acceleration of the development of revolutionary war." In reality, however, the guerrilla force had been crippled by army sweeps, which had resulted in the death of many militants and shattering of their civilian support networks. They were also unable to count on as much support from Nicaragua's Sandinista regime as they had hoped. In a gesture of pragmatism but also remarkable courage, Vinicio Cerezo refused to collaborate with the Reagan administration's anti-Sandinista campaign and resisted pressure to allow Nicaraguan "contras" to open training and supply bases in Guatemala. As a result, the Sandinistas were reluctant to alienate him by openly backing Guatemalan guerrillas.

In May 1986, Vinicio Cerezo hosted a meeting of Central American presidents at the Guatemalan town of Esquipulas. The presidents issued a statement favoring peaceful solutions to regional conflicts, which in Guatemala suggested the possibility of negotiations between the government and the guerrilla leadership. At first the guerrillas said they would participate only after Vincio Cerezo completed sweeping reforms, among them purging the army, abolishing paramilitary groups and punishing those responsible for past political crimes. This was far beyond what any civilian leader could accomplish, and the government replied with demands that the guerrillas disarm unilaterally before any talks could be held.

Slowly, however, the tone of this public debate began to soften. In a series of statements, Vinicio Cerezo and several of his senior aides signaled that they were open to the ideal of dialogue with guerrilla leaders. Army commanders were unhappy with the prospect of their government sitting down with what one general called "a group of ruffians," but the process had been set in motion.

It was given further momentum by a second meeting of Central American presidents in August 1987 and the subsequent establishment of a National Reconciliation Commission made up of representatives from political parties, the government and, most significantly, the Roman Catholic church. Catholic priests and bishops had watched the conflict from close range over many years, and many had emerged as clarion voices defending the rights of indigenous people and condemning military abuses. The day after the reconciliation commission was officially constituted, low-level representatives of the guerrilla movement and the Guatemalan government met in Madrid. Nothing of substance was achieved, but that such a meeting could take place at all would have been unthinkable even a few years earlier.

Under the auspices of the reconciliation commission, a "grand national dialogue" was inaugurated in February 1989. This dialogue, whose eighty-four invited participants included journalists, university professors and government officials as well as representatives of trade unions, business groups and farm cooperatives, spent a year drawing up a series of recommendations for social and political change. Perhaps even more important than the recommendations themselves was the fact that such a diverse group of Guatemalans had come together to talk seriously about their country's future.

Naturally, not everyone applauded this development. Obscure groups with names like "Officers of the Mountains" and "Fighters for Peace" emerged to warn against the dangers of reconciliation and what one of them, in a newspaper advertisement, described as "the democratic fiction." But for the first time, defenders of the old repressive mentality seemed unsure of themselves. Leaders of civilian groups were emboldened and began to speak their minds more freely. Momentum toward a peace settlement began to gather force.

In March 1990, members of the reconciliation commission met with guerrilla leaders in Oslo, Norway to prepare the way for direct talks. The first round of meetings between government and guerrilla negotiators was held a year later in Mexico City. It produced an eleven-point agenda for ending the long war and beginning the process of bringing democracy to Guatemala.

Both sides had good reasons to pursue dialogue. The army could not ignore the fact that a new political dynamic was taking hold within the country. In the wider world, the Cold War was coming to an end and the era of military dominance in Latin America was drawing to a close. The end of the Reagan presidency also meant that the generals could no longer count on Washington to support a policy of endless repression based on anti-Communist rhetoric.

For the guerrillas, incentives to make peace were at least as great. They had been all but defeated on the ground. Like army commanders, they saw that Latin America's future did not lie with guerrilla warfare. Undoubtedly they were also influenced by the examples of two other Central American guerrilla movements with whom they had long identified.

The first example, that of the Sandinistas in Nicaragua, was a negative one. With their confrontational policies and contempt for dissent, the Sandinistas botched their chance to build a consensus for reform in Nicaragua and were thrown out of office in a national election in 1990. They grabbed huge amounts of property for themselves as they left office, and in opposition clung to the divisive policies that had alienated them from broad segments of the population. Their Guatemalan counterparts saw the error of these ways and decided to pursue the opposite path, that of reconciliation.

A far more hopeful example emerged from El Salvador. Guerrilla leaders there evidently matured far more than their Nicaraguan counterparts during the late 1980s. Although they faced a military-backed power structure based on repression and anti-democratic ideals, Salvadoran rebels ultimately accepted the fact that they could not win on the battlefield and would have to compromise in order to achieve peace. Some rebel leaders may even have come to the conclusion that a government arising out of such a compromise would, in the long run, prove more stable and more able to forge a national consensus that one composed exclusively of guerrilla commanders. In any case, they began an extraordinary process of negotiation that ultimately led not only to an end to the Salvadoran war, but the emergence of the former guerrilla movement as a strong and democratic political party.

Propelled by these diverse influences, the peace process in Guatemala proceeded with fits and starts through the troubled presidencies of Jorge Serrano Elías and Ramiro de León Carpio. Representatives of the warring sides met in Sweden, Mexico, Panama and elsewhere. Slowly they hammered out agreements over what sorts of human rights practices could realistically be implemented in Guatemala; how refugees could be resettled; what sorts of tax and economic codes could set the country on the path to prosperity; how the role of civilians could be strengthened and that of the army weakened; what steps could be taken to safeguard the cultural as well as political rights of indigenous peoples; and which kinds of land reform were both desirable and practical.

Finally they tackled the crucial questions of how a cease-fire would work and how guerrillas could be demobilized and integrated into a newly democratized political structure.

The peace process, which despite this progress could still have been derailed, was given a vital boost when Alvaro Arzú Irigoyen was elected president in a runoff election in January 1996, taking just 51 percent of the vote. Although Arzú had talked about peace and reform during his campaign, such rhetoric had long since become obligatory for members of the political elite. Sad experience had taught Guatemalans and their foreign friends to judge politicians only by their acts in office. To the surprise and delight of many of his compatriots, President Arzú proved as good as his words. In his first month in office, he cashiered eight of the country's sixteen active-duty army generals and dismissed more than one hundred notorious police commanders. Even more astonishing, he met personally with senior guerrilla leaders, the first Guatemalan president ever to do so.

The moment many Guatemalans had despaired of ever seeing unfolded before their eyes on December 29, 1996. At a solemn ceremony in Guatemala City, leaders of the government and the guerrilla movement put their signatures to an accord grandly titled "Global Agreement for a Firm and Lasting Peace." One of the longest wars in Latin American history had come to an end.

The peace agreement did not, of course, resolve all of Guatemala's problems. Guatemala remains a country in which the judiciary is weak, the police are accustomed to threatening public security rather than defending it, and the army—though committed to reducing its size and power under terms of the agreement—is shackled by a history of unspeakable brutality. Criminal gangs, some of them made up of former soldiers and police officers, have emerged to make illicit livings from kidnapping, car theft and narcotics smuggling. Perhaps even more important, Guatemala's great economic potential is matched by equally great poverty, environmental destruction and social inequalities. Less than five percent of the landowners own more than two-thirds of the land. Rates of infant mortality, malnutrition and illiteracy are appalling. The peace agreement stopped a long and cruel war, but difficult as it was to reach that agreement, it pales beside the difficulty of establishing true peace.

One vital question hanging over Guatemala, as over many countries that have emerged from periods of repression and dictatorship, is how to confront the evils of the past. This exceedingly painful and difficult challenge came to American attention several times because of the involvement of American citizens. In one case, an American woman named Carol Ann DeVine told Congress in 1995 that her husband Michael had been murdered in Guatemala and that she suspected the killers were tied to the Central Intelligence Agency. In another, an American lawyer, Jennifer Harbury, who had been married to a Guatemalan guerrilla, made similar allegations about the soldiers who abducted and killed her husband. These charges turned out to have strong basis in fact, leading the CIA to fire two high-level officials and discipline ten others. Successive CIA directors, however, resisted repeated calls to release historical documents about the agency's involvement in the 1954 coup and its support for subsequent repression.

Guatemalans, however, are interested not simply in the role of foreign agencies in their country's tragedy, but in the role of their own rulers. Establishing a "truth commission" modeled after the one in Argentina became a key goal of guerrilla negotiators during the peace process. Agreement was finally reached to create a "Commission of Historical Clarification," but the commission was given a limited life span and no powers of search, seizure or subpoena. According to its charter, it could not assign responsibility to individuals "nor have any legal implications." Many Guatemalans were naturally dissatisfied by these restrictions. In response to their unhappiness, the Roman Catholic church, which had already launched a "historical memory project," announced its intention to publish a report of its own.

Church leaders assigned one of the country's wisest and most experienced clergymen, seventy-five-year-old Auxiliary Bishop Juan José Gerardi Condera, to direct the effort. It was a logical choice. Gerardi had been a leading figure in the church's human rights office during the 1980s, and at one point had been threatened so vividly that he was forced to close his diocese in the northern part of the country and flee for his life. He was also a driving force behind the 1988 pastoral letter called "The Clamor for Land," which documented the injustices of Guatemala's land tenure system and asserted that there could be no true peace until poor people were allowed access to plots of their own. As the peace process took shape, he emerged as a key figure in the National Reconciliation Commission.

Bishop Gerardi and his aides conducted more than six thousand interviews with survivors of the war, and in April 1998 presented the grim results of their study in a 1,440-page report entitled "Guatemala: Never Again." The report estimated that during thirty years of fighting, 150,000 people had been killed and another fifty thousand had disappeared. Eighty percent of the casualties, it asserted, were inflicted by government forces.

"As a church, we collectively and responsibly assumed the task of breaking the silence that thousands of victims have maintained for years," the Bishop said in releasing his report. "We have made it possible for them to speak, to find their voices, to tell their stories of suffering and pain so they might feel liberated from the burden that has been weighing down on them for so long."

It was a cathartic moment, but two days later it was followed by an act of tragic violence that bore uncanny resemblance to those documented in the thick report. An assailant surprised Bishop Gerardi in the garage of his home and beat him to death with a concrete block, smashing his skull, jaw and cheekbones. The nation was shaken, and the news magazine *Crónica* wondered if the attack meant "the return of the demons." A suspect was arrested, but the case was never fully clarified.

In the eighteen months preceding Bishop Gerardi's murder, there had been virtually no political killings or disappearances. Dissidents who had lived abroad for years and decades returned, and many have plunged into the great work of reforming their country. Signs of economic revival are beginning to glimmer. The murder may have been a last gasp of a dying order. It may even have been a random criminal act without political motivation. But it forced Guatemalans to remember that they have been plagued for decades not only by a culture of violence, but a culture of impunity.

An even more shattering reminder came in early 1999 when the Historical Clarification Commission, established under the peace agreement, issued a report that was, if anything, more horrific than Bishop Gerardi's. The commission, which was headed by a German lawyer, Christian Tomuschat, estimated that the conflict had caused more than two hundred thousand deaths, and blamed the military for ninety-three percent of them. In a speech presenting the report, Mr. Tomuschat said that while he and his fellow commissioners knew when they began their work more or less what had happened during the conflict, "no one of us could have imagined the dimensions of this tragedy, not even the Guatemalan commissioners who had lived through the experience directly."

"It is with profound sadness that the commission learned of the extreme cruelty with which many of the violations were committed, of the large number of girls and boys who were victims of violent cruelty and murder, and of the special brutality directed against women, especially against Mayan women, who were tortured, raped and murdered," Mr. Tomuschat said. "State security forces blindly pursued the anti-Communist struggle without respect for any legal principles or the most elemental ethical and religious values."

Mr. Tomuschat also asserted: "Until the mid-1980s, the United States government and U. S. private companies exercised pressure to maintain the country's archaic and unjust socioeconomic structure." The American ambassador in Guatemala, Donald J. Planty, quickly rejected that conclusion by repeating the old line that "this was an internal conflict." But a few days later, something quite extraordinary happened. President Bill Clinton, paying a visit to Guatemala, gave a very different and far more candid response. "For the United States," he said, "it is important that I state clearly that support for military forces and intelligence units which engaged in violence and widespread repression was wrong, and the United States must not repeat that mistake." Coming as it did after decades of denial and mendacity from American leaders, Clinton's statement was a sign that change had come not only to Guatemala, but perhaps also to the way Washington perceives and deals with Guatemala.

The path back to normality in Guatemala continues to be strewn with obstacles. Just two months after President Clinton's visit, voters were called to the polls for a national referendum on amending the Guatemalan Constitution. The proposed changes would have added checks and balances to the president's office, strengthened protections for indigenous peoples, and reformed the army. Only eighteen percent of the nation's registered voters turned out. Bewildered by a scare campaign conducted by the old elite, they overwhelmingly rejected the changes. Then, in the election of

2000, Alfonso Portillo, the favored candidate of former dictator Efraín Rios Montt, won the presidency.

Portillo sought to undermine the reform process by refusing to demobilize the notorious Presidential Guard that had directed assassinations of government opponents, and by doubling the military's budget in violation of limits established in the peace treaty. During his term, prominent Indian leaders were murdered in ways that recalled the bad old days; the United States placed Guatemala on a list of countries that was refusing to help combat the drug trade; and the United Nations "human development index" ranked Guatemala 120th of 173 countries—the lowest ranking for any North, Central or South American state. After leaving office in 2004, Portillo was indicted on a variety of charges related to corruption and repression. His administration did, however, complete the reduction of the army from fifty thousand to fifteen thousand soldiers, a considerable achievement that was a key goal of the United Nations and others working to stabilize the country.

The next presidential election offered Guatemalans a modicum of renewed hope. Oscar Berger, a former mayor of Guatemala City, backed by a coalition of centrist parties, defeated two other candidates, including the still-ambitious Rios Montt. The country he took over still faced overwhelming challenges. Twenty percent of the twelve million Guatemalans controlled 80 percent of the country's gross domestic product. At least seventy-five percent of the population, and by some estimates as much as ninety percent, lived in severe poverty. Taxes remained exceedingly low, allowing the rich minority to prosper while depriving the government of resources to help the poor majority. Still, the terms of public debate had shifted dramatically, with even many conservatives openly accepting the need for change in terms that would have been considered subversive only a few years back. Now began the long task of rebuilding a shattered land, not simply politically and economically but also morally. It will take all the efforts of the long-suffering Guatemalan people, and all the help the outside world can give them, to consolidate the great victory they have won and finally drive a stake through the heart of darkness that terrorized them for so many years.

STEPHEN KINZER AND STEPHEN SCHLESINGER

NOTES

All State Department, Defense Department, Federal Bureau of Investigation and Central Intelligence Agency documents cited in notes, unless otherwise indicated, have been released under the provisions of the U. S. Freedom of Information Act to Stephen Schlesinger and Stephen Kinzer. Guatemalans interviewed for this book who requested anonymity are listed under the heading "confidential communication." Throughout notes, the forthcoming book on Allen Dulles by Richard Harris Smith, author of a previous work, *OSS: The Secret History of America's First Central Intelligence Agency*, is referred to as the "manuscript" because, while completed, it was not yet published at the time this book went into print.

State Department abbreviations:

ARA   Bureau of Inter-American Affairs (principal unit in the State Department dealing with Latin America)

MID   Office of Middle American Affairs (subunit in ARA)

CHAPTER 1

1. Richard Harris Smith, "Spymaster's Odyssey: The World of Allen Dulles" (manuscript to be published, New York, 1983), Ch. 26, p. 17.

2. New York *Times*, May 28, 1954; New York *Times*, June 8, 1954; U. S. Embassy Guatemala telegram to Secretary Dulles, June 19, 1954 (translation of Guatemalan Foreign Secretary Toriello's letter to UN Security Council, June 18, 1954); David Atlee Phillips, *The Night Watch: Twenty-five Years of Peculiar Service* (New York: Atheneum, 1977), p. 43.

3. Phillips, *Night Watch*, pp. 40–46; New York *Times*, June 14, 1954.

4. "Guatemala: Battle in the Backyard," *Time*, June 28, 1954, p. 28; confidential communication with Schlesinger; *El Imparcial*, Guatemala City, June 3, 1954; U. S. Embassy Guatemala telegram to Dulles, June 19, 1954; Krieg to Department of State, Despatch 1028, June 29, 1954 (translation of President Arbenz's radio address, June 19, 1954).

5. New York *Times*, May 30, 1954; New York *Times*, June 1, 1954; New York *Times*, June 17, 1954; Richard Bissell interview, Farmington, Conn., Sept. 11, 1979; David Atlee Phillips interview, Washington, Oct. 7, 1979.

6. *Time*, June 28, 1954; Lázaro Chacón had been elected in 1921, but under a severely limited electorate; the only previous president elected under a democratic constitution was Juan José Arévalo in 1945.

7. *Time*, June 28, 1954; U. S. Department of State Translations, Messages of Guatemalan Foreign Minister Toriello to UN Security Council President, June 18, 20, 1954, Division of Language Services, Nos. 845, 864; Krieg to Department of State, Despatch 1028, June 29, 1954.

8. Guillermo Toriello, *La Batalla de Guatemala* (Mexico City: Ediciones Cuadernos Americanos, 1955), p. 121; Peurifoy telegram to Secretary Dulles, June 18, 1954, No. 1041; New York *Times*, June 21, 1954.

9. New York *Times*, May 20, 1954; New York *Times*, June 16, 1954; David Wise and Thomas Ross, *The Invisible Government* (New York: Random House, 1964), p. 189.

10. U. S. Embassy Guatemala telegram to Secretary Dulles, June 19, 1954.

11. North American Congress on Latin America (NACLA), *Guatemala* (Berkeley and New York: NACLA, 1974), pp. 20, 124;

Thomas and Marjorie Melville, *Guatemala: The Politics of Land Ownership* (New York: Free Press, 1971), pp. 51–52; Cole Blasier, *The Hovering Giant: U.S. Responses to Revolutionary Change in Latin America* (Pittsburgh: University of Pittsburgh Press 1976), pp. 55, 58; Thomas McCann, *An American Company: The Tragedy of United Fruit* (New York: Crown, 1976), pp. 13, 56.

12. For example, Peurifoy to Department of State relating Peurifoy's conversation with Arbenz, Despatch 522, Dec. 18, 1953; Henry Wallace Memorandum to *Time*, June 19, 1954.

13. Wise and Ross, *Invisible Government*, p. 177.

14. *El Imparcial*, Guatemala City, June 17, 18, 19, 1954; Phillips, *Night Watch*, pp. 40–46; New York *Times*, June 15, 1954; New York *Times*, June 21, 1954.

15. U. S. Embassy Guatemala telegram to Secretary Dulles, June 19, 1954; H. Bradford Westerfield, *The Instruments of America's Foreign Policy* (New York: Crowell, 1963), p. 436.

16. U. S. Embassy Guatemala, Weeka No. 25, to U. S. Department of State, Despatch No. 1023, June 25, 1954; confidential communication with Schlesinger.

17. Peurifoy telegram to Secretary Dulles, No. 1041, June 18, 1954; Peurifoy telegram to Secretary Dulles, No. 1036, June 18, 1954.

18. The actual figure demanded by the United Fruit Company was $15,854,849 (Weeka No. 16, April 23, 1954, U. S. Embassy Guatemala, to U. S. Department of State, Despatch No. 871); Blasier, *Hovering Giant*, p. 90.

19. Peurifoy telegram to Secretary Dulles, No. 1041, June 18, 1954; Wallace Memo, p. 6.

20. Peurifoy telegram to Secretary Dulles, No. 1042, June 19, 1954; Weeka 25, op. cit.; Toriello, Message to UN, June 20, 1954, Department of State; Wallace Memo, p. 7.

21. Toriello, Message to UN, June 20, 1954, Department of State; Peurifoy telegram to Secretary Dulles, No. 1044, June 19, 1954.

22. Peurifoy telegram to Secretary Dulles, No. 1045, June 19, 1954; Peurifoy telegram to Secretary Dulles, No. 1048, June 19, 1954; Krieg to Department of State, Despatch 1028, June 29, 1954.

23. *Time*, June 28, 1954; U. S. Embassy Guatemala, telegram to Secretary Dulles, June 19, 1954, translation of Toriello letter; Leonard McCombe, *Life* (private files), July 5, 1954.

24. Toriello, Message to UN, June 20, 1954, Department of State; David Atlee Phillips interview, Washington, Oct. 7, 1979; New York *Times*, June 21, 1954.

25. Toriello, Message to UN, June 20, 1954, Department of State.

26. Peurifoy telegram to Secretary Dulles, No. 1046, June 19, 1954; Peurifoy and Assistant Secretary of State Henry Holland, Memorandum of Telephone Conversation, June 20, 1954, recorded in Washington; Peurifoy telegram to Dulles, No. 1054, June 20, 1954; *Time*, June 28, 1954; Peurifoy telegram to Secretary Dulles, No. 1053, June 20, 1954.

27. New York *Times*, June 20, 1954, p. 4.

28. Krieg to Department of State, Despatch 1028, June 29, 1954.

29. Peurifoy telegram to Secretary Dulles, No. 1053, June 20, 1954; New York *Times*, June 21, 1954; Peurifoy telegram to Secretary Dulles, No. 1067, June 21, 1954.

30. Peurifoy telegram to Secretary Dulles, No. 1053, June 20, 1954; Peurifoy telegram to Secretary Dulles, No. 1051, June 20, 1954; Deputy Undersecretary of State Murphy to Peurifoy No. 325, June 21, 1954, Washington, D.C.

31. New York *Times*, June 21, 1954; *Time*, June 28, 1954; Wise and Ross, *Invisible Government*, p. 188.

32. *Time*, June 18, 1954; New York *Times*, June 21, 1954; Toriello, Message to UN, June 20, 1954, Department of State.

33. New York *Times*, June 21, 1954.

34. New York *Times*, June 21, 1954; Westerfield, *Instruments of American Foreign Policy*, p. 436; J. Lloyd Mecham, *The United States and Inter-American Security, 1889–1960* (Austin: University of Texas Press, 1961), pp. 445–46.

35. James Reston, "With the Dulles Brothers in Darkest Guatemala," New York *Times*, June 20, 1954.

CHAPTER 2

1. North American Congress on Latin America (NACLA), *Guatemala* (Berkeley and New York: NACLA, 1974), p. 45; Cole Blasier, *The Hovering Giant: U.S. Responses to Revolutionary Change in Latin America* (Pittsburgh: University of Pittsburgh Press, 1976), p. 28.

2. Richard Immerman, "Guatemala and the United States, 1954: A Cold War Strategy for the Americas" (unpublished Boston College Doctoral Dissertation, 1978), p. 54; Joseph Wrigley Mooney, III, "United States Intervention in Guatemala, 1954" (unpublished Northeast Missouri State University Master of Arts Thesis, 1976), p. 6.

3. Richard Adams, *Crucifixion by Power* (Austin: University of Texas Press, 1970), pp. 174–75; Amy Elizabeth Jensen, *Guatemala: A Historical Survey* (New York: Exposition, 1955),

pp. 121–37; NACLA, *Guatemala*, p. 45; Kenneth Grieb, *Guatemalan Caudillo: The Regime of Jorge Ubico* (Athens: Ohio University Press, 1979), p. 21.

4. Blasier, *Hovering Giant*, p. 28.

5. Jensen, *Historical Survey*, p. 136; Blasier, *Hovering Giant*, p. 29; José M. Aybar de Soto, *Dependency and Intervention: The Case of Guatemala in 1954* (Boulder, Colo.: Westview Press, 1978), pp. 98–99.

6. Samuel Guy Inman, *A New Day in Guatemala* (Wilton, Conn.: Worldover Press, 1951), p. 38.

7. Mario Rosenthal, *Guatemala: The Story of an Emergent Latin-American Democracy* (New York: Twayne, 1962), p. 216.

8. Jensen, *Historical Survey*, pp. 145–47; John Dombrowski et al., *Area Handbook for Guatemala* (Washington: U. S. State Department, 1968), pp. 32, 145; K. H. Silvert, *A Study in Government: Guatemala* (New Orleans: Tulane University Press, 1954), pp. 10–13, 30–31, 44–47.

9. *El Imparcial*, March 16, 1945.

10. Thomas and Marjorie Melville, *Guatemala: The Politics of Land Ownership* (New York: Free Press, 1971), p. 29; *El Imparcial*, March 16, 1945.

CHAPTER 3

1. Mario Rosenthal, *Guatemala: The Story of an Emergent Latin-American Democracy* (New York: Twayne, 1962), p. 219; Ronald Schneider, *Communism in Guatemala 1944–54* (New York: Praeger, 1959), p. 48.

2. American University, *Case Study in Insurgency and Revolutionary Warfare: Guatemala 1944–54* (Washington: Special Operations Research Office, 1964), p. 19.

3. Richard Adams, *Crucifixion by Power* (Austin: University of Texas Press, 1970), p. 445; American University, *Case Study*, p. 19.

4. Samuel Guy Inman, *A New Day in Guatemala* (Wilton, Conn.: Worldover Press, 1951), p. 13.

5. Stephen Ambrose, *Ike's Spies: Eisenhower and the Espionage Establishment* (Garden City, N.Y.: Doubleday, 1981), p. 219.

6. North American Congress on Latin America (NACLA), *Guatemala* (Berkeley and New York: NACLA, 1974), p. 53; Frederick B. Pike, "Guatemala, the United States and Communism in the Americas," *The Review of Politics*, Vol. 17, No. 2 (April 1955), pp. 236, 240. David Horowitz, *The Free World Colossus* (New York: Hill and Wang, 1965), p. 183, cites a report by the Chase National Bank, "Latin American Highlights," September, 1956.

7. Chester Lloyd Jones, *Guatemala Past and Present* (Minneapolis: University of Minnesota Press, 1966), pp. 176–79; Leo A. Suslow, *Aspects of Social Reform in Guatemala 1944–49* (Hamilton, N.Y.: Colgate University Press, 1949), p. 78.
8. NACLA, *Guatemala*, p. 47; Adams, *Crucifixion*, p. 445.
9. NACLA, *Guatemala*, p. 47.
10. *El Imparcial*, May 2, 1946.
11. American University, *Case Study*, p. 93; Schneider, *Communism in Guatemala*, pp. 25–27; Rosenthal, *Emergent Latin-American Democracy*, p. 226.
12. American University, *Case Study*, p. 94.
13. Schneider, *Communism in Guatemala*, pp. 28–29.
14. Richard Immerman, "Guatemala as Cold War History," *Political Science Quarterly*, Vol. 95, No. 4 (Winter 1980–81), p. 633; José M. Aybar de Soto, *Dependency and Intervention: The Case of Guatemala in 1954* (Boulder, Colo.: Westview Press, 1978), p. 112.
15. Schneider, *Communism in Guatemala*, pp. 30–31.
16. Rosenthal, *Emergent Latin-American Democracy*, p. 227.
17. Robert Alexander, *Organized Labor in Latin America* (New York: Free Press, 1965), p. 204; Rosenthal, *Emergent Latin-American Democracy*, p. 229; K. H. Silvert, *A Study in Government: Guatemala* (New Orleans: Tulane University Press, 1954), p. 12.
18. Schneider, *Communism in Guatemala*, p. 31.
19. Kenneth Johnson, *The Guatemala Presidential Election of March 6, 1966* (Washington: Institute for the Comparative Study of Political Systems, 1967), p. 3; Schneider, *Communism in Guatemala*, p. 186; *Newsweek*, Nov. 27, 1950.
20. Rosenthal, *Emergent Latin-American Democracy*, pp. 235–36; *El Imparcial*, March 16, 1951.

CHAPTER 4

1. Mario Monteforte Toledo, *La Revolución de Guatemala, 1944–54* (Guatemala City: Editorial Universitaria, 1971), p. 19.
2. Carlos A. D'Ascoli, "La Reforma Agraria y Estensión de las Explotaciones Agrícolas," *Trimestre Económico*, Vol. 19, No. 3 (July–Sept. 1952), p. 409.
3. David Atlee Phillips, *The Night Watch: Twenty-five Years of Peculiar Service* (New York: Atheneum, 1977), p. 36.
4. Confidential communications with Kinzer.
5. Ronald Schneider, *Communism in Guatemala 1944–54* (New York: Praeger, 1959), p. 189.

6. *El Imparcial,* March 16, 1951.
7. International Bank for Reconstruction and Development, *Mission to Guatemala* (Washington: IBRD, 1951), pp. 283, 292.
8. Mario Rodriguez, *Central America* (Englewood Cliffs, N.J.: Prentice-Hall, 1965), p. 150; North American Congress on Latin America (NACLA), *Guatemala* (Berkeley and New York: NACLA, 1974), p. 50.
9. Frederick B. Pike, "Guatemala, the United States, and Communism in the Americas," *The Review of Politics,* Vol. 17, No. 2 (April 1955), p. 240.
10. Thomas and Marjorie Melville, *Guatemala: The Politics of Land Ownership* (New York: Free Press, 1971), p. 61.
11. American University, *Case Study in Insurgency and Revolutionary Warfare: The Case of Guatemala 1944–54* (Washington: Special Operations Research Office, 1964), p. 19; NACLA *Guatemala,* p. 49; Rodriguez, *Central America,* p. 151; Nathan Whetten, *Guatemala: The Land and the People* (New Haven: Yale University Press, 1961), pp. 154–66; Melville, *Land Ownership,* pp. 51–58; Max Gordon, "A Case History of U.S. Subversion: Guatemala, 1954," *Science and Society,* Vol. 35, No. 2 (Summer 1971), p. 138.
12. John P. Powelson, *Latin America: Today's Economic and Social Revolution* (New York: McGraw-Hill, 1964), p. 55.
13. Melville, *Land Ownership,* pp. 52–53.
14. Pike, "Guatemala," p. 243.
15. Flora Lewis, "Communism in Guatemala: A Case History," *The New York Times Magazine,* Feb. 21, 1954.
16. John Martz, *Central America* (Chapel Hill: University of North Carolina Press, 1959), p. 36.
17. Schneider, *Communism in Guatemala,* pp. 57ff.
18. American University, *Case Study,* p. 45; Schneider, *Communism in Guatemala,* pp. 24ff.
19. Melville, *Land Ownership,* p. 72.
20. Richard Massock from Associated Press used slightly different figures in an article he wrote in the Washington *Post,* Nov. 15, 1953. Massock listed 4 Communists, 25 PAR, 9 PRG, 7 Renovación Nacional, 6 Independents and 5 Opposition deputies; Cole Blasier, *The Hovering Giant: U.S. Responses to Revolutionary Change in Latin America* (Pittsburgh: University of Pittsburgh Press, 1976), p. 155; Helen Simon Travis and A. B. Magil, *What Happened in Guatemala* (New York: New Century Publishers, 1954), p. 13.
21. Blasier, *Hovering Giant,* pp. 156–57.
22. Schneider, *Communism in Guatemala,* p. 41; Keith Monroe, "Gua-

temala: What the Reds Left Behind," *Harper's Magazine*, Vol. 211, No. 1262 (July 1955), p. 61.

23. Schneider, *Communism in Guatemala*, pp. 196–97, 294.
24. Robert Alexander, *Communism in Latin America* (New Brunswick, N.J.: Rutgers University Press, 1957), p. 360.
25. From *La Prensa Libre*, San José, Costa Rica, Oct. 25, 1955; quoted in Schneider, *Communism in Guatemala*, pp. 192–93.
26. John Gillen and K. H. Silvert, "Ambiguities in Guatemala," *Foreign Affairs*, Vol. 34, No. 3 (April 1956), pp. 474–75.

CHAPTER 5

1. Thomas McCann, *An American Company: The Tragedy of United Fruit* (New York: Crown, 1976), pp. 15–18; Stacy May and Galo Plaza, *United States Business Performance Abroad: The Case Study of United Fruit Company in Latin America* (Washington: National Planning Association, 1958), pp. 5–12; Embassy of Guatemala, Washington, Government Information Bureau Release, No. 8, Aug. 15, 1953.
2. McCann, *American Company*, pp. 18–20; May and Plaza, *United Fruit*, pp. 15–18; *Fortune*, March 1933.
3. May and Plaza, *United Fruit*, pp. 16–17.
4. May and Plaza, *United Fruit*, p. 17.
5. Thomas and Marjorie Melville, *Guatemala: The Politics of Land Ownership* (New York: Free Press, 1971), pp. 51–52; McCann, *American Company*, pp. 13, 56.
6. T. Harry Williams, *Huey Long* (New York: Bantam, 1976), p. 493.
7. Cole Blasier, *The Hovering Giant: U.S. Responses to Revolutionary Change in Latin America* (Pittsburgh: University of Pittsburgh Press, 1976), pp. 55–56; Ronald Schneider, *Communism in Guatemala 1944–54* (New York: Praeger, 1959), p. 48.
8. McCann, *American Company*, p. 45.
9. Melville, *Land Ownership*, p. 49.
10. Melville, *Land Ownership*, p. 50.
11. Edward Bernays, *Biography of an Idea* (New York: Simon and Schuster, 1965), p. 746; North American Congress on Latin America (NACLA), *Guatemala* (Berkeley and New York: NACLA, 1974), p. 49.
12. Blasier, *Hovering Giant*, pp. 88–90; Melville, *Land Ownership*, pp. 62–63; Richard Immerman, "Guatemala and the United States, 1954: A Cold War Strategy for the Americas" (unpublished Boston College Doctoral Dissertation, 1978), p. 146.
13. *El Imparcial*, March 16, 1954.

CHAPTER 6

1. Edward Bernays, *Biography of an Idea* (New York: Simon and Schuster, 1965), pp. 745, 761.
2. Bernays, *Biography*, pp. 757–58.
3. Bernays, *Biography*, see chapter headings; pp. 386–87.
4. Edward Bernays, *Propaganda* (New York: Horace Liveright, 1928), pp. 9, 31.
5. Bernays, *Biography*, pp. 749, 760–61; Thomas McCann, *An American Company: The Tragedy of United Fruit* (New York: Crown, 1976), pp. 45–46, 48, 50; Bernays interview, Cambridge, Mass., Sept. 15, 1979.
6. Bernays, *Biography*, pp. 349, 749, 760–61, and chapter headings.
7. Bernays, *Biography*, p. 747.
8. McCann, *American Company*, p. 46; Bernays, *Biography*, p. 749.
9. Bernays interview; McCann, *American Company*, p. 46.
10. Bernays, *Biography*, p. 749; McCann, *American Company*, p. 48.
11. Bernays, *Biography*, pp. 746, 750, 752–55.
12. Bernays, *Biography*, p. 750; McCann, *American Company*, p. 48; Thomas Corcoran interview, Washington, Oct. 6, 1979.
13. Bernays, *Biography*, pp. 746, 750, 752–55; Corcoran interview; Leon Harris, *Only to God: The Extraordinary Life of Godfrey Lowell Cabot* (New York: Atheneum, 1967), p. 300.
14. *Congressional Record*, 81st Cong., 1st Sess., Vol. 95, Pt. 1 (Feb. 14, 1949), p. 1172.
15. Bernays, *Biography*, p. 759; Bernays interview; Will Lissner, "Soviet Agents Plotting to Ruin Unity, Defenses of Americas," New York *Times*, June 22, 23, 1950; McCann, *American Company*, p. 46.
16. Samuel Guy Inman, *A New Day in Guatemala* (Wilton, Conn.: Worldover Press, 1951), pp. 36–37.
17. New York *Times*, July 18, 1950, p. 6; Inman, *New Day*, pp. 36–37.
18. Almyr Bump interview, Guatemala City, Jan. 27, 1980.
19. Inman, *New Day*, pp. 39, 44–46; Juan José Arévalo, *Guatemala: La Democracia y el Imperio* (Mexico City: Editorial América Nueva, 1954), p. 120; Cole Blasier, *The Hovering Giant: U.S. Responses to Revolutionary Change in Latin America* (Pittsburgh: University of Pittsburgh Press, 1976), p. 59.
20. Richard Immerman, "Guatemala and the United States, 1954: A Cold War Strategy for the Americas" (unpublished Boston College Doctoral Dissertation, 1978), pp. 178–80, 226.

21. Bernays, *Biography*, p. 760.

22. Bernays, *Biography*, pp. 760–61.

23. Bernays, *Biography*, pp. 761, 767; McCann, *American Company*, p. 47; Thomas McCann, letter to Nat Wartels, President, Crown Publishers, July 12, 1976, pp. 3, 5 (provided to authors by McCann).

24. McCann, *American Company*, p. 47; McCann, Wartels letter, pp. 3, 5.

25. Bernays, *Biography*, p. 761.

26. Bernays, *Biography*, p. 761; McCann, *American Company*, p. 59; Department of State "Memorandum of Conversation" between Guatemalan Ambassador to the United States Toriello, Raymond Leddy and E. W. Clark of the State Department's Inter-American Affairs section, Jan. 27, 1953; Department of State "Memorandum of Conversation" between Guatemalan Ambassador to the United States Toriello and Assistant Secretary of State for Inter-American Affairs John Moors Cabot, March 25, 1953.

27. Bernays, *Biography*, pp. 761, 763, 766; McCann, *American Company*, p. 55; Herbert Lionel Matthews, *A World in Revolution* (New York: Scribner's, 1971), p. 261.

28. McCann, *American Company*, p. 48; Thomas McCann interview, Boston, Sept. 12, 1979; North American Congress on Latin America (NACLA), *Guatemala* (Berkeley and New York: NACLA, 1974), p. 83.

29. McCann interview; NACLA, *Guatemala*, p. 83.

30. NACLA, *Guatemala*, p. 83.

31. McCann, *American Company*, p. 59; Immerman, "Guatemala," pp. 227–28, 239.

32. McCann, *American Company*, p. 59; Immerman, "Guatemala," pp. 227–28, 239.

33. Corcoran interview; Bernays, *Biography*, p. 768.

34. Corcoran interview.

35. Corcoran interview; *Fortune*, Feb. 1952, p. 142.

36. Corcoran interview; *Fortune*, Feb. 1952, p. 142; Richard Harris Smith, "Spymaster's Odyssey: The World of Allen Dulles" (manuscript to be published, New York, 1983), Ch. 25, p. 19; Dean Acheson, "Dear Boss," *American Heritage*, Feb.–March 1980, p. 48.

37. Department of State "Memorandum of Conversation" between Robert La Follette, Thomas Mann and R. R. Rubottom, Jr., of

the State Department's Inter-American Affairs section, Feb. 5, 1953.

38. Corcoran interview.

39. E. Howard Hunt, *Undercover: Memoirs of an American Secret Agent* (New York: Berkley, 1974), p. 97; Stephen Ambrose, *Ike's Spies: Eisenhower and the Espionage Establishment* (Garden City, N.Y.: Doubleday, 1981), p. 224.

40. Corcoran interview.

41. Robert Roman, "Operation Diablo," *Soldier of Fortune Magazine*, Summer, 1976, p. 19.

42. Roman, "Operation Diablo," pp. 18, 19; Douglass Cater, *Power in Washington* (New York: Random House, 1964), pp. 212–13.

43. Roman, "Operation Diablo," pp. 19, 28; McCann interview; McCann, *American Company*, p. 49.

44. Roman, "Operation Diablo," pp. 19, 28.

45. Roman, "Operation Diablo," p. 28.

46. Cater, *Power*, pp. 212–13; Roman, "Operation Diablo," pp. 28, 58.

47. Cater, *Power*, pp. 212–13; Roman, "Operation Diablo," pp. 17, 19.

48. New York *Times*, March 13, 1953, p. 14; Bernays, *Biography*, p. 765.

CHAPTER 7

1. Kermit Roosevelt, *Countercoup: The Struggle for the Control of Iran* (New York: McGraw-Hill, 1979), p. 107.

2. John Foster Dulles, "The Republican Perspective," *Foreign Policy Bulletin*, 32, No. 1 (Sept. 15, 1952); New York *Times*, Aug. 28, 1952, p. 12; New York *Times*, Sept. 4, 1952, pp. 1, 20; New York *Times*, Oct. 11, 1952, p. 14; Victor Marchetti and John Marks, *The CIA and the Cult of Intelligence* (New York: Dell, 1975), p. 49.

3. William Colby and Peter Forbath, *Honorable Men: My Life in the CIA* (New York: Simon and Schuster, 1978), pp. 72–73.

4. Roosevelt, *Countercoup*, p. 210.

5. Richard Harris Smith, "Spymaster's Odyssey: The World of Allen Dulles" (manuscript to be published, New York, 1983), Ch. 25, pp. 3A, 4; Dean Acheson, "Dear Boss," *American Heritage*, Feb.–March 1980, p. 48; Herbert Lionel Matthews, *A World in Revolution* (New York: Scribner's, 1971), pp. 262–64.

6. Smith, "Spymaster's Odyssey," Ch. 25, pp. 3A, 4; Department

of State, Memorandum on Caracas Meeting, March 1, 1953, Dulles Papers, Box 79.

7. Smith, "Spymaster's Odyssey," Ch. 25, pp. 3A, 4; U. S. Ambassador to Guatemala Rudolf Schoenfeld, Despatch 905, to Department of State, April 15, 1953, "Aftermath of Baja Verapaz Uprising"; U. S. Ambassador to Guatemala Rudolf Schoenfeld, Despatch 1002, to Department of State, May 13, 1953, "Alleged Confessions of Salamá Insurgents."

8. John Moors Cabot, *First Line of Defense* (Washington: School of Foreign Service, Georgetown, 1979), p. 87; Department of State Memorandum, W. Park Armstrong, Jr., Special Assistant to the Secretary, to John Moors Cabot, Assistant Secretary of State for Inter-American Affairs, "Effect upon Guatemala of Arms Procurement by El Salvador, Honduras and Nicaragua," June 16, 1953 (originally prepared by Division of Research for Latin America, Special Paper No. 21, June 12, 1953).

9. Adolf Berle, *Navigating the Rapids: 1918–1971* (New York: Harcourt Brace Jovanovich, 1973), pp. 616–19; Richard H. Immerman, "Guatemala and the United States, 1954: A Cold War Strategy for the Americas" (unpublished Boston College Doctoral Dissertation, 1978), p. 247.

10. Guatemalan Ambassador Toriello's meetings with the State Department occurred in 1953 on Jan. 27, March 6, March 11, March 25, June 24, June 26 and July 21.

11. Cole Blasier, *The Hovering Giant: U.S. Responses to Revolutionary Change in Latin America* (Pittsburgh: University of Pittsburgh Press, 1976), p. 89; also see State Department Memorandum of Conversation between Ambassador Toriello, Mr. Rubottom, Mr. Leddy and Mr. Fisher, March 11, 1953, "Communism in Guatemala."

12. Blasier, *Hovering Giant*, p. 89.

13. Department of Defense, Major General Richard Partridge letter to Assistant Secretary of State for Inter-American Affairs John Moors Cabot, May 20, 1953; National Security Council, Annex to NSC 144, Draft Statement of Policy, March 6, 1953, "U.S. Objectives and Courses of Action with Respect to Latin America"; Berle, *Navigating*, pp. 620–21.

14. Confidential Communication with Schlesinger; Ronald M. Schneider, "Guatemala: An Aborted Communist Takeover," in Thomas Hammond (ed.), *The Anatomy of Communist Takeovers* (New Haven: Yale University Press, 1975), p. 566.

15. Joseph Wrigley Mooney III, "United States Intervention in Gua-

temala, 1954" (unpublished Northeast Missouri State University Master of Arts Thesis, 1976), pp. 56–72; Immerman, "Guatemala," pp. 227–32; Blasier, *Hovering Giant*, pp. 89–90; Paul Hoffman, *Lions in the Street: The Inside Story of the Great Wall Street Law Firms* (New York: Saturday Review Press/ E. P. Dutton, 1973), pp. 22–23; North American Congress on Latin America (NACLA), *Guatemala* (Berkeley and New York: NACLA, 1974), pp. 164–65; Frederick J. Cook, "The CIA," *Nation*, Vol. 192, No. 25 (June 24, 1961); Paul Grabowicz and Joel Kotkin, "The CIA Puts Its Money Where Its Friends Are," *New Times*, Nov. 27, 1978, pp. 24–25.

16. Philip B. Taylor, Jr., "The Guatemalan Affair: A Critique of United States Foreign Policy," *American Political Science Review*, Vol. 50, No. 3 (Sept. 1956), p. 804; New York *Times*, May 26, 1954; Herbert Dinerstein, *The Making of a Missile Crisis: October 1962* (Baltimore: Johns Hopkins University Press, 1975), pp. 9–10.

17. Allen Dulles, *The Craft of Intelligence* (New York: Harper & Row, 1963), p. 221; E. Howard Hunt, "The Azalea Trail Guide to the CIA," *The National Review*, April 29, 1977.

18. NACLA, *Guatemala*, pp. 59–60; Immerman, "Guatemala," p. 260; L. Fletcher Prouty, *The Secret Team: The CIA and Its Allies in Control of the United States and the World* (Englewood Cliffs, N.J.: Prentice-Hall, 1973), pp. 108, 133–34; Richard Bissell, Oral History Interview, conducted by Edwin Edwin, June 5, 1967, Columbia Oral History Project; William Corson, *The Armies of Ignorance: The Rise of the American Intelligence Empire* (New York: Dial, 1977), pp. 357–58; Stephen Ambrose, *Ike's Spies: Eisenhower and the Espionage Establishment* (Garden City, N.Y.: Doubleday, 1981), p. 225; Cabot, *First Line of Defense*, p. 90.

19. David Wise and Thomas Ross, *The Invisible Government* (New York: Random House, 1964), p. 184; Immerman, "Guatemala," pp. 236, 260–61; Richard Bissell interview, Farmington, Conn., Sept. 11, 1979.

20. Smith, "Spymaster's Odyssey," Ch. 25, pp. 5–10.

21. Smith, "Spymaster's Odyssey," Ch. 25, pp. 10–11; Bissell interview.

22. Smith, "Spymaster's Odyssey," Ch. 25, pp. 11–12; Corson, *Armies*, p. 356; Blasier, *Hovering Giant*, p. 172; Ernst Halperin, "The National Liberation Movements in Latin America," Project on Communism, Revisionism, and Revolution (unpublished

paper for Center for International Studies, MIT, June 1969), pp. 54–62.

23. Corson, *Armies*, p. 357; Miami *Herald*, May 29, 1954; Smith, "Spymaster's Odyssey," Ch. 26, p. 17; Donald Grant, "Ambassador Peurifoy—The Man Who Beat the Reds in Guatemala," St. Louis *Post-Dispatch*, July 11, 1954; C. Neale Ronning (ed.), *Intervention in Latin America* (New York: Knopf, 1970), p. 32.

24. Marta Cehelsky, "Guatemala's Frustrated Revolution" (unpublished Columbia University Master's Thesis, 1967), p. 55; Richard Harris Smith, *OSS: The Secret History of America's First Central Intelligence Agency* (Berkeley: University of California Press, 1972), p. 376; Smith, "Spymaster's Odyssey," Ch. 25, p. 12; Richard Bissell interview.

25. Smith, "Spymaster's Odyssey," Ch. 25, pp. 14, 15.

26. Smith, "Spymaster's Odyssey," Ch. 25, p. 13; E. Howard Hunt, *Undercover: Memoirs of an American Secret Agent* (New York: Berkley, 1974), p. 98; Immerman, "Guatemala," p. 261.

27. Smith, "Spymaster's Odyssey," Ch. 25, pp. 16–17; Immerman, "Guatemala," p. 275; Thomas Powers, *The Man Who Kept the Secrets: Richard Helms and the CIA* (New York: Knopf, 1979), pp. 324–25.

28. Smith, "Spymaster's Odyssey," Ch. 25, pp. 18–19.

29. Smith, "Spymaster's Odyssey," Ch. 25, p. 18; Robert Roman, "Operation Diablo," *Soldier of Fortune Magazine*, Summer 1976, p. 18; Wise and Ross, *Invisible Government*, p. 185; David Atlee Phillips interview, Washington, Oct. 7, 1979.

30. Cehelsky, "Frustrated Revolution," p. 56; Smith, "Spymaster's Odyssey," Ch. 26, pp. 7A, 9A; Phillips interview.

31. Hunt, *Undercover*, pp. 97–99; Cehelsky, "Frustrated Revolution," p. 56.

32. Drew Pearson, "Washington Merry-Go-Round: Link CIA to Early Arming of Castro," New York *Mirror*, May 23, 1961; Central Intelligence Agency, Memorandum for the President, K. W. McMahan, Acting Assistant Director Current Intelligence, to President Eisenhower, June 20, 1954, Eisenhower Library; Bissell interview; Smith, "Spymaster's Odyssey," Ch. 25, p. 19.

33. Thomas Kiernan, "Primrose Yellow" (unpublished manuscript); Wise and Ross, *Invisible Government*, p. 191.

34. Roman, "Operation Diablo," p. 58; Dwight Eisenhower, *The White House Years*, Vol. I: *Mandate for Change* (Garden City, N.Y.: Doubleday, 1963), p. 426; Wise and Ross, *Invisible Government*, p. 186; U. S. Embassy Honduras telegram to Dulles, July

3, 1954; Smith, "Spymaster's Odyssey," Ch. 26, p. 1; Bissell interview; Immerman, "Guatemala," pp. 261, 272; Andrew Tully, *CIA: The Inside Story* (New York: Crest, 1963), p. 59; New York *Times*, June 18, 1954.

35. Lawrence Houston interview, Washington, Oct. 8, 1979; Roman, "Operation Diablo," p. 77; Wise and Ross, *Invisible Government*, pp. 186, 188; Paul Kennedy, *The Middle Beat* (New York: Teachers College Press, Columbia University, 1971), p. 141; Immerman, "Guatemala," pp. 261, 264–65, 272; NACLA, *Guatemala*, p. 70; U. S. Embassy Honduras telegram to Secretary Dulles, July 3, 1954; Peurifoy to Dulles, June 7, 1954; Fred Sherwood interview, Guatemala City, Jan. 28, 1980; New York *Times*, June 18, 1954; Juan José Arévalo, *Guatemala: La Democracia y El Imperio* (Mexico City: Editorial América Nueva, 1954), p. 144; Guillermo Toriello, *La Batalla de Guatemala* (Mexico City: Ediciones Cuadernos Americanos, 1955), p. 74; Memorandum from FBI Director, J. Edgar Hoover, to Miami Office, June 16, 1954.

36. Smith, "Spymaster's Odyssey," Ch. 25, pp. 20, 20A; Immerman, "Guatemala," p. 264.

37. Smith, "Spymaster's Odyssey," Ch. 25, p. 21.

CHAPTER 8

1. William Corson, *The Armies of Ignorance: The Rise of the American Intelligence Empire* (New York: Dial, 1977), p. 357; Richard Harris Smith, "Spymaster's Odyssey: The World of Allen Dulles" (manuscript to be published, New York, 1983), Ch. 25, pp. 5–10; Peter Wyden, *The Bay of Pigs: The Untold Story* (New York: Simon and Schuster, 1979), p. 24.

2. Richard Immerman, "Guatemala and the United States, 1954: A Cold War Strategy for the Americas" (unpublished Boston College Doctoral Dissertation, 1978), pp. 59, 115, 116; Samuel Guy Inman, *A New Day in Guatemala* (Wilton, Conn.: Worldover Press, 1951), p. 13; American University, *Case Study in Insurgency and Revolutionary Warfare: Guatemala 1944–1954* (Washington: Special Operations Research Office, 1964), p. 6; U. S. Embassy Honduras, John Erwin, telegram to Department of State, Nov. 5, 1953.

3. Miguel Ydígoras Fuentes, *My War with Communism* (Englewood Cliffs, N.J.: Prentice-Hall, 1963), pp. 49–50; Miguel Ydígoras Fuentes interview, Guatemala City, Jan. 25, 1980; Immerman, "Guatemala," p. 253.

4. E. Howard Hunt, *Give Us This Day* (New Rochelle, N.Y.: Arlington House, 1973), p. 117; E. Howard Hunt, *Undercover:*

Memoirs of an American Secret Agent (New York: Berkley, 1974), p. 99; Immerman, "Guatemala," p. 269; Marta Cehelsky, "Guatemala's Frustrated Revolution" (unpublished Columbia University Master's Thesis, 1967), p. 53; Department of State Office Memorandum, Mr. Burrows, Office of Middle American Affairs, to Assistant Secretary of State for Inter-American Affairs Henry Holland, June 1, 1954.

5. Thomas Corcoran interview, Washington, Oct. 6, 1979; Cehelsky, "Frustrated Revolution," pp. 43, 60.

6. Hunt, *Give Us This Day*, pp. 117, 119; Hunt, *Undercover*, p. 99; Cehelsky, "Frustrated Revolution," p. 60.

7. Confidential communication with Schlesinger; Fred Sherwood interview, Guatemala City, Jan. 28, 1980; Hunt, *Give Us This Day*, p. 117; Stephen Ambrose, *Ike's Spies: Eisenhower and the Espionage Establishment* (Garden City, N.Y.: Doubleday, 1981), p. 226.

8. Cehelsky, "Frustrated Revolution," pp. 66–67; Immerman, "Guatemala," p. 271.

9. Cehelsky, "Frustrated Revolution," p. 43; New York *Times*, June 19, 1954; Cole Blasier, *The Hovering Giant: U.S. Responses to Revolutionary Change in Latin America* (Pittsburgh: University of Pittsburgh Press, 1976), p. 160; Ydígoras, *My War*, p. 50; Robert Roman, "Operation Diablo," *Soldier of Fortune Magazine*, Summer 1976, p. 28; Thomas and Marjorie Melville, *Guatemala: The Politics of Land Ownership* (New York: Free Press, 1971), pp. 84–85; Ydígoras interview; North American Congress on Latin America (NACLA), *Guatemala* (Berkeley and New York: NACLA, 1974), p. 68.

10. Roman, "Operation Diablo," p. 28; H. Bradford Westerfield, *The Instruments of America's Foreign Policy* (New York: Crowell, 1963), p. 429; New York *Times*, June 21, 1954; Cehelsky, "Frustrated Revolution," p. 67.

11. Robert Crassweller, *Trujillo: The Life and Times of a Caribbean Dictator* (New York: Macmillan, 1966), pp. 335, 336; Blasier, *Hovering Giant*, p. 160; Cehelsky, "Frustrated Revolution," pp. 53, 54; American Embassy Guatemala, William Krieg, letter to Raymond Leddy, U. S. State Department, Nov. 10, 1953 (including attached memoranda).

12. Mario Rosenthal, *Guatemala: The Story of an Emergent Latin-American Democracy* (New York: Twayne, 1962), p. 252; Ydígoras, *My War*, pp. 50, 51; Guatemala, Secretaría de Propaganda y Divulgación, *La Democracia Amenazada: El Caso de Guatemala* (Guatemala City, 1954), pp. 15–16, 28ff.

13. NACLA, *Guatemala*, p. 69; Cehelsky, "Frustrated Revolution," p. 54; David Wise and Thomas Ross, *The Invisible Government* (New York: Random House, 1964), p. 185; Rosenthal, *Guatemala*, pp. 252–53.
14. U. S. Embassy Honduras, John Erwin, telegram to Department of State, Nov. 5, 1953.
15. Cehelsky, "Frustrated Revolution," pp. 61–62.
16. Guatemala, Secretaría de Propaganda y Divulgación, *Guatemala*, pp. 33, 46, 92.
17. Smith, "Spymaster's Odyssey," Ch. 25, p. 17; Blasier, *Hovering Giant*, p. 172; NACLA, *Guatemala*, p. 69; Miami *Herald*, Dec. 24, 1966.
18. Roman, "Operation Diablo," p. 28.
19. Krieg, U. S. Embassy Guatemala, letter to Leddy.
20. William Krieg, U. S. Embassy Guatemala, letter to John Fisher, Guatemalan Desk, U. S. State Department, Nov. 24, 1953 (including attached Memorandum of Conversation, Krieg and José Luis Arenas, U. S. Embassy Guatemala, Nov. 18, 1953).
21. Rolland Welch, First Secretary U. S. Embassy Nicaragua, cable to Department of State, Jan. 12, 1954.
22. National Broadcasting Company News, "The Science of Spying," transcript, narrated by John Chancellor, May 4, 1965.
23. Ydígoras, *My War*, p. 51; Rolland Welch, Chargé d'Affaires, U. S. Embassy Nicaragua, cable to Department of State, Feb. 12, 1954; Cehelsky, "Frustrated Revolution," p. 56; New York *Times*, Jan. 30, 1954.
24. Department of State, Mr. Smith cable to American Embassy Guatemala, Text of State Department Press Release on Guatemalan Charges re: U.S. involvement in Plot, Jan. 30, 1954.
25. *Time*, Feb. 8, 1954.

CHAPTER 9

1. Richard H. Immerman, "Guatemala and the United States, 1954: A Cold War Strategy for the Americas" (unpublished Boston College Doctoral Dissertation, 1978), p. 266; William Krieg interview, Washington, March 26, 1979.
2. Richard Harris Smith, "Spymaster's Odyssey: The World of Allen Dulles" (manuscript to be published, New York, 1983), Ch. 25, p. 13; Flora Lewis, "Ambassador Extraordinary: John Peurifoy," *The New York Times Magazine*, July 18, 1954, p. 26; Donald Grant, "Ambassador Peurifoy—The Man Who Beat the Reds in Guatemala," St. Louis *Post-Dispatch*, July 11, 1954;

H. Bradford Westerfield, *The Instruments of America's Foreign Policy* (New York: Crowell, 1963), p. 429.

3. Smith, "Spymaster's Odyssey," Ch. 25, p. 13; Immerman, "Guatemala," pp. 267, 268; William Krieg interview.

4. Lewis, "Ambassador Extraordinary"; Grant, "Ambassador Peurifoy"; William Corson, *The Armies of Ignorance: The Rise of the American Intelligence Empire* (New York: Dial, 1977), p. 357; Immerman, "Guatemala," p. 266; Paul Kennedy, *The Middle Beat* (New York: Teachers College Press, Columbia University, 1971), p. 140; Smith, "Spymaster's Odyssey," Ch. 25, p. 13; confidential communication with Schlesinger.

5. Drew Pearson, *Diaries: 1949–1959*, ed. by Tyler Abell (New York: Holt, Rinehart and Winston, 1974), pp. 298–99; Krieg interview.

6. Lewis, "Ambassador Extraordinary"; Grant, "Ambassador John E. Peurifoy"; David Wise and Thomas Ross, *The Invisible Government* (New York: Random House, 1964), pp. 182–83.

7. Allen Weinstein, *Perjury: The Hiss-Chambers Case* (New York: Knopf, 1978), pp. 21, 22, 274, 371; Immerman, "Guatemala," p. 267.

8. Lewis, "Ambassador Extraordinary"; Grant, "Ambassador Peurifoy."

9. Corson, *Armies*, p. 357; Grant, "Ambassador Peurifoy"; John Moors Cabot, *Toward Our Common American Destiny* (Freeport, N.Y.: Book for Libraries Press, 1955), p. 88. The date of Cabot's address was Oct. 14, 1953.

10. Immerman, "Guatemala," p. 268; North American Congress on Latin America (NACLA), *Guatemala* (Berkeley and New York: NACLA, 1974), p. 62.

11. William Krieg, U. S. Embassy Guatemala, telegram to Department of State, Despatch No. 378, Nov. 2, 1953 (including attached memorandum on Peurifoy-Osegueda meeting, Oct. 29, 1953); Raymond Leddy, U. S. State Department, letter to Ambassador Peurifoy, U. S. Embassy Guatemala, Nov. 6, 1953.

12. USIA Memorandum, from acting USIA Director to Operations Coordinating Board, Aug. 2, 1954 (including attached document, "Report on Actions Taken by the U. S. Information Agency in the Guatemalan Situation," July 27, 1954).

13. Peurifoy, telegram to Department of State, Despatch No. 522, Dec. 18, 1953 (including attached Memorandum of Conversation between President Arbenz, his wife, and Ambassador Peurifoy and his wife, Dec. 17, 1953); Dwight Eisenhower, *The*

White House Years, Vol. I: *Mandate for Change* (Garden City, N.Y.: Doubleday, 1963), pp. 422–23.

14. Peurifoy telegram to Secretary Dulles, Dec. 23, 1953, No. 163; NACLA, *Guatemala,* p. 53.

15. David Atlee Phillips interview, Washington, Oct. 7, 1979; David Atlee Phillips, *The Night Watch: Twenty-five Years of Peculiar Service* (New York: Atheneum, 1977), pp. 39–42; Smith, "Spymaster's Odyssey," Ch. 25, pp. 16, 17, Ch. 26, p. 24A; Marta Cehelsky, "Guatemala's Frustrated Revolution" (unpublished Columbia University Master's Thesis, 1967), p. 56; *Time,* Jan. 11, 1954; NACLA, *Guatemala,* p. 69; Immerman, "Guatemala," p. 275; Thomas Powers, *The Man Who Kept the Secrets: Richard Helms and the CIA* (New York: Knopf, 1979), pp. 324–25; Ricardo Rojo, *My Friend Ché* (New York: Dial Press, 1968), p. 55.

16. Immerman, "Guatemala," pp. 264–65; Peter Dale Scott, *The War Conspiracy: The Secret Road to the Second Indochina War* (New York: Bobbs-Merrill, 1972), p. 9; Wise and Ross, *Invisible Government,* pp. 179, 180; NBC-TV Documentary, "The Science of Spying," transcript, narrated by John Chancellor, May 4, 1965; Cole Blasier, *The Hovering Giant: U.S. Responses to Revolutionary Change in Latin America* (Pittsburgh: University of Pittsburgh Press, 1976), pp. 161, 162; U. S. Congress, Senate Committee on the Judiciary, Hearings Before the Subcommittee to Investigate the Administration of the Internal Security Act, Communist Threat to the United States Through the Caribbean, 87th Congress, July 27, 1961, Pt. 13:866.

17. Leonard Mosley, *Dulles* (New York: Dial Press, 1978), p. 270.

18. State Department, Undersecretary of State Walter Bedell Smith, Memorandum for President Eisenhower, Jan. 15, 1954 (Eisenhower Library); Guillermo Toriello, *La Batalla de Guatemala* (Mexico City: Ediciones Cuadernos Americanos, 1955), p. 56; Blasier, *Hovering Giant,* p. 164.

19. Toriello, *Batalla,* pp. 56–57; Blasier, *Hovering Giant,* p. 166.

20. James Hagerty, White House Press Secretary, Diaries 1954 (Eisenhower Library), April 26, 1954.

21. U. S. State Department, Undersecretary of State Walter Bedell Smith, telegram to American Embassy Costa Rica, Jan. 27, 1954; U. S. Embassy Costa Rica, Alex Cohen, Attaché, telegram to State Department, Despatch No. 613, Feb. 9, 1954; George Morris, *CIA and American Labor: The Subversion of the AFL-*

CIO's Foreign Policy (New York: International Publishers, 1967), pp. 80–82; Smith, "Spymaster's Odyssey," Ch. 25, p. 26.

22. David Binder, "Once 'a Declining Asset,' Guantanamo Gets New Life," New York *Times*, News of the Week in Review, Oct. 8, 1979; Dexter Perkins, *A History of the Monroe Doctrine* (Boston: Little, Brown, 1955), pp. 362–70, 390–93; C. G. Jacobsen, Acadia University, Nova Scotia, letter to New York *Times*, "The Monroe Doctrine Must Stay Dead," Oct. 9, 1979; Immerman, "Guatemala," p. 277; Blasier, *Hovering Giant*, p. 167.

23. *Time*, March 15, 1954.

24. Department of State, Office Memorandum, Mr. Burrows, Office of Middle American Affairs, to Assistant Secretary of State for Inter-American Affairs, John Moors Cabot, on "Guatemala and the Discussion of Communism at the Tenth Inter-American Conference," Feb. 10, 1954; Eisenhower, *Mandate for Change*, p. 424.

25. Guatemalan Foreign Minister, Guillermo Toriello Garido, speech to Third Plenary Session, March 5, 1954, at Tenth Inter-American Conference, Document 95 (English), entitled "A Pretext for Intervening in Our Internal Affairs," reprinted in C. Neale Ronning (ed.), *Intervention in Latin America* (New York: Knopf, 1970), pp. 72, 73, 76, 77; *Time*, March 15, 1954.

26. Blasier, *Hovering Giant*, pp. 167, 168; New York *Times*, March 7, 1954; U. S. Department of State, Tenth Inter-American Conference, Caracas, Venezuela, March 1–28, 1954, Publication 5692 (Washington, D.C., 1955), p. 8.

27. Philip B. Taylor, Jr., "The Guatemalan Affair: A Critique of United States Foreign Policy," *American Political Science Review*, Vol. 50, No. 3 (Sept. 1956), p. 791; New York *Times*, March 3, 4, 16, 1954; *Time*, March 15, 1954; USIA Memorandum, from acting USIA Director to Operations Coordinating Board; NACLA, *Guatemala*, pp. 71, 72; Kennedy, *Middle Beat*, p. 136; Daniel James, *Red Design for the Americas* (New York: John Day, 1954), pp. 300, 303; Herbert Dinerstein, *The Making of a Missile Crisis: October 1962* (Baltimore: Johns Hopkins University Press, 1975), p. 8.

28. Wise and Ross, *Invisible Government*, p. 184; NACLA, *Guatemala*, p. 64; Guatemalan Task Force, U. S. State Department, Minutes of Meetings, June 8, 16, 1954.

29. One of the reasons why Dulles removed John Moors Cabot was that Cabot wanted to expand U.S. economic help to Latin America at the Caracas Conference and Dulles did not. See Blanche Cook, *The Declassified Eisenhower* (Garden City, N.Y.: Doubleday, 1981), p. 187. Powers, *Helms*, p. 86; Smith, "Spy-

master's Odyssey," Ch. 26, p. 6; NACLA, *Guatemala*, p. 62; E. Howard Hunt, *Give Us This Day* (New Rochelle, N.Y.: Arlington House, 1973), p. 6.

30. Kennedy, *Middle Beat*, pp. 137, 138; Paul Kennedy, "U.S. Envoy Called from Guatemala," New York *Times*, April 19, 1954.

31. Hagerty, Diaries, April 26, 1954.

CHAPTER 10

1. Mario Rosenthal, *Guatemala: The Story of an Emergent Latin-American Democracy* (New York: Twayne, 1962), p. 250; Washington *Evening Star*, May 19, 1954; Andrew Tully, *CIA: The Inside Story* (New York: Crest, 1963), pp. 57, 58; Richard and Gladys Harkness, "America's Secret Agents: The Mysterious Doings of CIA," Part 1, *The Saturday Evening Post*, Vol. 227 (Oct. 30, 1954), p. 20.

2. New York *Mirror*, May 21, 1954; Richard H. Immerman, "Guatemala and the United States, 1954: A Cold War Strategy for the Americas" (unpublished Boston College Doctoral Dissertation, 1978), pp. 286, 287.

3. Juan José Arévalo, *Guatemala: La Democracia y el Imperio* (Mexico City: Editorial América Nueva, 1954), pp. 27ff.; Anthony Eden, *Full Circle* (Boston: Houghton Mifflin, 1960), p. 151; New York *Times*, May 20, 1954; New York *Times*, June 15, 1954; Statement by Guatemalan Embassy in Washington, D.C., May 21, 1954, cited in Max Gordon, "A Case History of U.S. Subversion: Guatemala, 1954," *Science and Society*, Vol. 35, No. 2 (Summer 1971), p. 145.

4. U. S. Embassy Guatemala, Weeka 21, May 26, 1954; Cole Blasier, *The Hovering Giant: U.S. Responses to Revolutionary Change in Latin America* (Pittsburgh: University of Pittsburgh Press, 1976), p. 169.

5. Central Intelligence Agency, Frank Wisner, Memorandum to Col. King, Chief, Western Hemisphere Division CIA, April 4, 1953, from C. D. Jackson Records Folder: Guatemala, Box 2, Eisenhower Library. For various theories on whom the spy might have been, see Tully, *Inside Story*, pp. 56, 57; Harkness, "Secret Agents," pp. 19, 20; Richard Harris Smith, "Spymaster's Odyssey: The World of Allen Dulles" (manuscript to be published, New York, 1983), Ch. 26, pp. 7–8A; Robert Roman, "Operation Diablo," *Soldier of Fortune Magazine*, Summer 1976,

p. 58; E. Howard Hunt, *Undercover: Memoirs of an American Secret Agent* (New York: Berkley, 1974), p. 99

6. Rosenthal, *Guatemala*, p. 250; David Wise and Thomas Ross, *The Invisible Government* (New York: Random House, 1964), p. 187; H. Gates Lloyd interview, New York, Nov. 2, 1979; James Hagerty, White House Press Secretary, Diaries 1954 (Eisenhower Library), May 20, 1954; Guillermo Toriello, *La Batalla de Guatemala* (Mexico City: Ediciones Cuadernos Americanos, 1955).

7. Wise and Ross, *Invisible Government*, p. 187; Rosenthal, *Guatemala*, pp. 249–50; Tully, *Inside Story*, pp. 57, 58; Harkness, "Secret Agents," p. 20.

8. Smith, "Spymaster's Odyssey," Ch. 26, p. 8A; Washington *Post*, May 13, 1954; *Time*, May 17, 1954.

9. Harkness, "Secret Agents," p. 20; Tad Szulc, *Compulsive Spy: The Strange Career of E. Howard Hunt* (New York: Viking, 1974), p. 68; Tully, *Inside Story*, p. 58.

10. Smith, "Spymaster's Odyssey," Ch. 26, pp. 7–8A; Peurifoy telegram to Secretary Dulles, No. 723, May 20, 1954; U. S. Embassy Guatemala, Weeka 21, May 27, 1954.

11. New York *Times*, May 18, 20, 26, 1954; Dwight Eisenhower, *The White House Years*, Vol. I: *Mandate for Change* (Garden City, N.Y.: Doubleday, 1963), p. 424; Harold Eugene Davis (ed.), *Government and Politics in Latin America* (New York: Ronald Press, 1958), p. 152; U. S. Department of State Bulletin, Vol. 30, No. 780 (June 7, 1954), p. 835.

12. Keith Monroe, "Guatemala, What the Reds Left Behind," *Harper's Magazine*, Vol. 211, No. 1262 (July 1955), p. 63; Richard Bissell interview, Farmington, Conn., Sept. 11, 1979.

13. New York *Times*, July 9, 1954; for opposing view, see *Time*, July 19, 1954.

14. Peurifoy telegram to Secretary Dulles, No. 854, June 1, 1954.

15. Rosenthal, *Guatemala*, p. 248; Department of Defense, Brig. Gen. Edward Porter, USAF, Deputy Director for Intelligence Joint Chiefs of Staff, to Joint Chiefs of Staff, May 13, 1954; H. Bradford Westerfield, *The Instruments of America's Foreign Policy* (New York: Crowell, 1963), p. 430; Edwin Lahey, "We Won't Turn the Clock Back—Maybe," *The New Republic*, July 19, 1954, p. 10.

16. *Time*, May 17, 1954; confidential communication with Schlesinger.

17. Harrison Salisbury, *Without Fear or Favor* (New York: Times Books, 1980), pp. 478–80; Sydney Gruson interview, New York, May 2, 1978; Krieg telegram to Secretary Dulles, No. 288, Feb. 2, 1954; New York *Times*, May 24, 1954.
18. Salisbury, *Without Fear or Favor*, pp. 478–80.
19. Salisbury, *Without Fear or Favor*, pp. 478–80; Flora Lewis, "Ambassador Extraordinary: John Peurifoy," *The New York Times Magazine*, July 18, 1954.
20. E. Howard Hunt, *Undercover*, pp. 98, 99; *Time* (Latin-American Edition), April 26, 1954; J. Lloyd Mecham, *The United States and Inter-American Security, 1889–1960* (Austin: University of Texas Press, 1961), p. 445; Paul Kennedy, *The Middle Beat* (New York: Teachers College Press, Columbia University, 1971), p. 137.
21. North American Congress on Latin America (NACLA), *Guatemala* (Berkeley and New York: NACLA, 1974), p. 62; Wise and Ross, *Invisible Government*, p. 194; Bissell interview.
22. Smith, "Spymaster's Odyssey," Ch. 25, pp. 21, 22.
23. Smith, "Spymaster's Odyssey," Ch. 26, pp. 10–12.
24. Richard Rovere, *Senator Joe McCarthy* (New York: Harcourt, Brace, 1959), p. 47; New York *Times*, June 3, 1954.

CHAPTER 11

1. Dwight Eisenhower, *The White House Years*, Vol. I: *Mandate for Change* (Garden City, N.Y.: Doubleday, 1963), p. 424.
2. Andrew Tully, *CIA: The Inside Story* (New York: Crest, 1963), p. 59; Key West (Florida) *Citizen*, May 28, 1954; New York *Times*, May 27, p. 30, June 3, 1954.
3. Eisenhower, *Mandate*, p. 424; U. S. State Department, Memorandum from Mr. English, Departmental Legal Adviser, to Assistant Secretary of State Henry Holland, "Interference with Shipping to Guatemala," May 20, 1954; U. S. State Department, Memorandum of Conversation between Secretary Dulles and Sir Roger Makins, British Ambassador to U.S., transcribed by Mr. Merchant, May 25, 1954.
4. U. S. State Department, Memorandum from Deputy Undersecretary Robert Murphy to Secretary Dulles, May 25, 1954.
5. New York *Times*, May 27, 1954; Operations Coordinating Board, Memorandum from Elmer Staats, Executive Officer on NSC 5419, Aug. 2, 1954; James Hagerty, White House Press Secretary, Diaries 1954 (Eisenhower Library), June 2, 1954;

Miami *Herald*, May 29, 1954; David Wise and Thomas Ross, *The Invisible Government* (New York: Random House, 1964), p. 188; U. S. State Department, Meeting of Guatemalan Group, June 7, 1954, Supplementary to Secret Minutes, transcribed by N. M. Pearson.

6. Anthony Eden, *Full Circle* (Boston: Houghton Mifflin, 1960), pp. 151–53; Leonard Mosley, *Dulles* (New York: Dial Press, 1978), p. 348; Hagerty, Diaries, June 19, 1954.

7. Eisenhower, *Mandate*, p. 424; U. S. State Department, Memorandum of Meeting Chaired by Assistant Secretary of State for Inter-American Affairs Henry Holland and six other Department officials, May 10, 1954, on "OAS Action Against Communism in Guatemala"; U. S. State Department, Memorandum of Meeting Chaired by Assistant Secretary of State for Inter-American Affairs Henry Holland and seven Department officials, May 11, 1954, on "OAS Action Against Communism in Guatemala."

8. Blanche Cook, *The Declassified Eisenhower* (Garden City, N.Y.: Doubleday, 1981), p. 191; U. S. State Department, Memorandum of Conversation between Secretary Dulles, Assistant Secretary Holland and Ambassador Carlos Muniz of Brazil, transcribed by Mr. Holland, May 27, 1954; U. S. State Department, Memorandum of Meeting Chaired by Assistant Secretary Holland and five other Department officials, on "OAS Action Against Communism in Guatemala," May 29, 1954; U. S. State Department, Memorandum of Conversation between Secretary Dulles, Assistant Secretary Holland and Ambassador Carlos Muniz of Brazil, transcribed by Mr. Holland, May 24, 1954.

9. U. S. State Department, letter from Raymond Leddy, Office of Middle American Affairs, to Ambassador Peurifoy, June 5, 1954; U. S. State Department, letter from John Hill to Ambassador Peurifoy, May 30, 1954; U. S. State Department, Office Memorandum from John Hill to Assistant Secretary Holland, "Economic Measures to Keep Guatemala Off Balance Until Proposed OAS Meeting," June 7, 1954.

10. Peurifoy telegram to Secretary Dulles, No. 860, June 1, 1954; Peurifoy telegram to Secretary Dulles, No. 866, June 2, 1954; Peurifoy telegram to Secretary Dulles, No. 870, June 2, 1954.

11. Peurifoy telegram to Secretary Dulles, No. 903, June 5, 1954; Ronald Schneider, *Communism in Guatemala 1944–54* (New York: Praeger, 1959), pp. 193–94, 316–17; Mario Rosenthal, *Guatemala: The Story of an Emergent Latin-American Democ-*

racy (New York: Twayne, 1962), p. 251; Cole Blasier, *The Hovering Giant: U.S. Responses to Revolutionary Change in Latin America* (Pittsburgh: University of Pittsburgh Press, 1976), pp. 173–74; Drew Pearson, *Diaries: 1949–1959*, ed. by Tyler Abell (New York: Holt, Rinehart and Winston, 1974), p. 323.

12. Peurifoy telegram to Secretary Dulles, No. 910, June 7, 1954; U. S. State Department, Meeting of Guatemalan Group, June 4, 1954, transcribed by N. M. Pearson; Peurifoy telegram to Secretary Dulles, No. 956, June 11, 1954.

13. *Time*, June 12, 1954; Peurifoy telegram to Secretary Dulles, No. 978, June 13, 1954; Peurifoy telegram to Secretary Dulles, No. 991, June 14, 1954; New York *Times*, June 16, 1954.

14. Richard Harris Smith, "Spymaster's Odyssey: The World of Allen Dulles" (manuscript to be published, New York, 1983), Ch. 26, p. 9; New York *Times*, May 31, 1954; Jonathan Marshall (editor, *Inquiry* magazine) interview, Summer 1977, by telephone.

15. USIA Memorandum, from acting USIA Director to Operations Coordinating Board, Aug. 2, 1954 (including attached document, "Report on Actions Taken by the U. S. Information Agency in the Guatemalan Situation," July 27, 1954); U. S. State Department, Meeting of Guatemalan Group, June 11, 1954, transcribed by N. M. Pearson.

16. David Atlee Phillips, *The Night Watch: Twenty-five Years of Peculiar Service* (New York: Atheneum, 1977), pp. 34–38.

17. Phillips, *Night Watch*, pp. 40–42; Marta Cehelsky, "Guatemala's Frustrated Revolution" (unpublished Columbia University Master's Thesis, 1967), p. 56.

18. Phillips, *Night Watch*, pp. 42–45.

19. Phillips, *Night Watch*, pp. 45–46; David Atlee Phillips interview, Washington, Oct. 7, 1979; Harry Rositzke, *The CIA's Secret Operations* (New York: Reader's Digest Press, 1977), p. 175; New York *Times*, June 21, 1954.

20. Phillips, *Night Watch*, pp. 45–46; Cehelsky, "Frustrated Revolution," p. 56.

21. Wise and Ross, *Invisible Government*, p. 189; *Newsweek*, "Damn Good and Sure," March 4, 1963, p. 19.

22. Smith, "Spymaster's Odyssey," Ch. 26, pp. 16–18; Thomas McCann, *An American Company: The Tragedy of United Fruit* (New York: Crown, 1976), p. 60.

23. *Time*, June 28, 1954; *Time*, July 5, 1954; Smith, "Spymaster's Odyssey," Ch. 26, pp. 16–18; Blasier, *Hovering Giant*, p. 172.

24. New York *Times*, June 18, 1954; *Time*, June 28, 1954; Wise and Ross, *Invisible Government*, p. 189; Smith, "Spymaster's Odyssey," Ch. 26, pp. 16–18.

25. New York *Times*, June 18, 21, 1954; Wise and Ross, *Invisible Government*, pp. 186–88, 190; *Time*, June 28, 1954; Phillips, *Night Watch*, p. 54; Phillips interview.

26. James Reston, "With the Dulles Brothers in Darkest Guatemala," New York *Times*, June 20, 1954; Central Intelligence Agency, Memorandum from K. W. McMahan, acting Assistant Director, Current Intelligence, to President Eisenhower, on "The Situation in Guatemala as of June 20th," dated June 20, 1954 (Eisenhower Library).

CHAPTER 12

1. Richard Harris Smith, "Spymaster's Odyssey: The World of Allen Dulles" (manuscript to be published, New York, 1983), Ch. 26, pp. 20–21; Richard Bissell interview, Farmington, Conn., Sept. 11, 1979.

2. Confidential communication with Schlesinger; Cole Blasier, *The Hovering Giant: U.S. Responses to Revolutionary Change in Latin America* (Pittsburgh: University of Pittsburgh Press, 1976), p. 172; U. S. State Department, Division of Language Services, translation of Guatemalan Foreign Minister Toriello's message to the UN Security Council President, June 20, 1954, No. 864.

3. New York *Times*, June 22, 1954; Peurifoy telegram to Secretary Dulles, No. 1063, June 21, 1954.

4. Smith, "Spymaster's Odyssey," Ch. 26, p. 32; U. S. State Department, Meeting of Guatemalan Group, June 22, 1954, transcribed by N. M. Pearson.

5. U. S. State Department, Meeting of Guatemalan Group, June 23, 1954, transcribed by N. M. Pearson; Paul Kennedy, *The Middle Beat* (New York: Teachers College Press, Columbia University, 1971), p. 141; New York *Times*, June 23, 24, 25, 1954 (articles by Milton Bracker).

6. David Atlee Phillips, *The Night Watch: Twenty-five Years of Peculiar Service* (New York: Atheneum, 1977), pp. 46–47; David Wise and Thomas Ross, *The Invisible Government* (New York: Random House, 1964), p. 191; *El Imparcial*, June 23, 1954.

7. Peurifoy telegram to Secretary Dulles, No. 1089, June 23, 1954; Peurifoy telegram to Secretary Dulles, No. 1079, June 22,

1954; Peurifoy telegram to Secretary Dulles, No. 1077, June 22, 1954; *El Imparcial,* June 23, 1954.

8. Wise and Ross, *Invisible Government,* p. 190.

9. *El Imparcial,* June 23, 1954; Smith, "Spymaster's Odyssey," Ch. 26, p. 23; Central Intelligence Agency, *Current Intelligence Digest,* item 2, June 25, 1954, No. 6326; Blasier, *Hovering Giant,* p. 173, *La Prensa Libre,* San José, Costa Rica, Oct. 25, 1955, pp. 9, 14; New York *Times,* June 25, 1954.

10. Smith, "Spymaster's Odyssey," Ch. 26, p. 23; Dwight Eisenhower, *The White House Years,* Vol. I: *Mandate for Change* (Garden City, N.Y.: Doubleday, 1963), p. 425–26; Wise and Ross, *Invisible Government,* pp. 178–79; Stephen Ambrose, *Ike's Spies: Eisenhower and the Espionage Establishment* (Garden City, N.Y.: Doubleday, 1981), p. 230; Thomas Ronan, "Eisenhower Finds Bay of Pigs Errors," New York *Times,* October 14, 1965, p. 2.

11. There was one other move to support Eisenhower, this one public: on June 22, Senate Democratic Leader Lyndon Johnson obtained unanimous support from Congress for a resolution attacking Communism in Guatemala and supporting U.S. policy against Arbenz; Wise and Ross, *Invisible Government,* p. 191; Bissell interview.

12. Smith, "Spymaster's Odyssey," Ch. 26, p. 21; Peurifoy telegram to Secretary Dulles, No. 1102, June 24, 1954; Peurifoy telegram to Secretary Dulles, No. 1088, June 23, 1954.

13. J. Lloyd Mecham, *The United States and Inter-American Security, 1889–1960* (Austin: University of Texas Press, 1961), p. 449; Philip B. Taylor, Jr., "The Guatemalan Affair: A Critique of United States Foreign Policy," *American Political Science Review,* Vol. 50, No. 3 (Sept. 1956), pp. 802–3; Great Britain, *House of Commons, 1953–54 Report on Events Leading Up to and Arising Out of the Change of Regime in Guatemala* (London: H. M. Stationery Office, 1954), pp. 54–55.

14. Abe Rosenthal, "Issues in Guatemala Case Troubling U.N. Delegates," New York *Times,* June 23, 1954, p. 3; Brian Urquhart, *Hammarskjöld* (New York: Knopf, 1972), pp. 92–94; Mary Margaret Ball, *The OAS in Transition* (Durham, N.C.: Duke University Press, 1969), p. 25; Mecham, *Inter-American Security,* p. 450; Robert Burr, *Our Troubled Hemisphere: Perspectives on U.S.-Latin American Relations* (Washington: The Brookings Institution, 1967), pp. 66–67; Taylor, "The Guatemalan Affair," p. 803.

15. Burr, *Hemisphere*, p. 66; Mecham, *Inter-American Security*, p. 450.

16. H. Bradford Westerfield, *The Instruments of America's Foreign Policy* (New York: Crowell, 1963), p. 444; Urquhart, *Hammarskjöld*, pp. 92–94.

17. Lodge telegram to Secretary Dulles, No. 876, June 24, 1954; Lodge telegram to Secretary Dulles, No. 870, June 24, 1954; U. S. State Department, Meeting of Guatemalan Group, June 23, 1954, transcribed by N. M. Pearson; James Hagerty, White House Press Secretary, Diaries 1954 (Eisenhower Library), June 24, 1954.

18. Hagerty, Diaries, June 26, 1954.

19. Anthony Eden, *Full Circle* (Boston: Houghton Mifflin, 1960), p. 154; Urquhart, *Hammarskjöld*, pp. 92–94.

20. U. S. State Department, Mr. Murphy telegram to American Embassies in Nicaragua and Honduras, June 21, 1954; U. S. State Department, Meeting of Guatemalan Group, June 23, 1954, transcribed by N. M. Pearson; Mecham, *Inter-American Security*, pp. 447–51; Taylor, "The Guatemalan Affair," p. 800; U. S. State Department, Meeting of Guatemalan Group, June 25, 1954, transcribed by N. M. Pearson.

21. Peurifoy telegram to Secretary Dulles, No. 1089, June 23, 1954; Ronald Schneider, *Communism in Guatemala 1944–54* (New York: Praeger, 1959), p. 311; Blaiser, *Hovering Giant*, p. 172; Peurifoy telegram to Secretary Dulles, No. 1093, June 24, 1954; U. S. Guatemalan Embassy to Secretary Dulles, Unnumbered, translation of Message by Foreign Minister Toriello to Secretary Dulles, June 25, 1954; *El Imparcial*, June 25, 1954.

22. Smith, "Spymaster's Odyssey," Ch. 26, p. 24A; NBC-TV Documentary, "The Science of Spying," transcript, narrated by John Chancellor, May 4, 1965; Richard Immerman, "Guatemala and the United States, 1954: A Cold War Strategy for the Americas" (unpublished Boston College Doctoral Dissertation, 1978), pp. 297–98; Phillips, *Night Watch*, p. 48; New York *Times*, June 26, 1954, p. 2; Eisenhower, *Mandate for Change*, p. 425, claims the three bombers hit an "ordnance depot" in Guatemala City.

23. Wise and Ross, *Invisible Government*, pp. 190–91; Phillips, *Night Watch*, p. 46; U. S. Guatemalan Embassy to Secretary Dulles, Unnumbered, translation of Message by Foreign Minister Toriello to Secretary Dulles, June 25, 1954.

24. *Time*, Aug. 8, 1960, p. 37; Daniel James, *Che Guevara* (New York: Stein and Day, 1970), pp. 76–83; Andrew Sinclair, *Che Guevara* (New York: Viking, 1970), pp. 10–12; Hilda Gadea,

Ernesto: A Memoir of Che Guevara (Garden City, N.Y.: Doubleday, 1972), pp. 54–57; *Cuba* magazine, Nov. 1967, reprint of Guevara speech, p. 67; Blasier, *Hovering Giant*, p. 178; Hugo Gambini, *El Che Guevara* (Buenos Aires: Paidos, 1968), p. 121.

25. Smith, "Spymaster's Odyssey," Ch. 26, pp. 18A–19; Phillips, *Night Watch*, pp. 46–47; *El Imparcial*, June 26, 1954; Bissell interview.

26. David Atlee Phillips interview, Washington, Oct. 7, 1979; Wise and Ross, *Invisible Government*, p. 192; Thomas Powers, *The Man Who Kept the Secrets: Richard Helms and the CIA* (New York: Knopf, 1979), p. 87; Phillips, *Night Watch*, p. 47; North American Congress on Latin America (NACLA), *Guatemala* (Berkeley and New York: NACLA, 1974), p. 69.

27. New York *Times*, June 21, 1954, p. 15; Phillips, *Night Watch*, p. 47; Peurifoy telegram to Secretary Dulles, No. 1107, June 25, 1954.

28. Clay Felker interview, New York, March 15, 1979; confidential communication with Schlesinger.

29. Donald Grant, "Ambassador Peurifoy—The Man Who Beat the Reds in Guatemala," St. Louis *Post-Dispatch*, July 11, 1954; Felker interview; William Krieg interview, Washington, March 26, 1979; confidential communication with Schlesinger.

30. Robert Roman, "Operation Diablo," *Soldier of Fortune Magazine*, Summer 1976, p. 58; Smith, "Spymaster's Odyssey," Ch. 26, p. 19.

31. Wise and Ross, *Invisible Government*, pp. 191–92; Evelyn Irons, War Dispatches, June 19, 21, 22, 23, 24, 28, 29, 1954, London *Evening Standard*; William Warner interview, Washington, April 28, 1981.

32. Tad Szulc, "Making Mischief Abroad: U.S. and ITT in Chile," *The New Republic*, Vol. 168, No. 26 (June 30, 1973), pp. 21–23; Thomas McCann, *An American Company: The Tragedy of United Fruit* (New York: Crown, 1976), p. 60.

33. Felker interview; *Life*, July 5, 1954, p. 8.

34. *Life*, July 5, 1954, p. 8; Daniel James, *Red Design for the Americas* (New York: John Day, 1954), pp. 11–13; NACLA, *Guatemala*, p. 73.

35. U. S. State Department, Mr. Burgin, Memorandum to Mr. Raine, Bureau of Inter-American Affairs, June 23, 1954, entitled "Unofficial Reactions in Latin America to the Guatemalan Situation, June 18–22."

36. Blasier, *Hovering Giant,* p. 173; Manuel Galich, *Por Que Lucha Guatemala, Arévalo y Arbenz: Dos Hombres contra un Imperio* (Buenos Aires: Elmer Editor, 1956), p. 361 (Galich was a former Minister of Education in the Guatemalan government); Smith, "Spymaster's Odyssey," Ch. 26, p. 24.

37. Thomas and Marjorie Melville, *Guatemala: The Politics of Land Ownership* (New York: Free Press, 1971), pp. 83–84; Schneider, *Communism in Guatemala,* p. 312.

38. Blasier, *Hovering Giant,* pp. 173–74.

CHAPTER 13

1. David Atlee Phillips, *The Night Watch: Twenty-five Years of Peculiar Service* (New York: Atheneum, 1977), p. 48.

2. Fred Sherwood interview, Guatemala City, Jan. 28, 1980.

3. Great Britain, *House of Commons, 1953–54 Report on Events Leading Up to and Arising Out of the Change of Regime in Guatemala* (London: H. M. Stationery Office, 1954), pp. 1–4; Richard Harris Smith, "Spymaster's Odyssey: The World of Allen Dulles" (manuscript to be published, New York, 1983), Ch. 26, pp. 25–27; *El Imparcial,* June 28 and 29, 1954.

4. Richard Bissell interview, Farmington, Conn., Sept. 11, 1979; Smith, "Spymaster's Odyssey," Ch. 26, p. 29; Peter Wyden, *The Bay of Pigs: The Untold Story* (New York: Simon and Schuster, 1979), p. 84; NBC-TV Documentary, "The Science of Spying," transcript, narrated by John Chancellor, May 4, 1965.

5. Cole Blasier, *The Hovering Giant: U.S. Responses to Revolutionary Change in Latin America* (Pittsburgh: University of Pittsburgh Press, 1976), p. 172.

6. Peurifoy cable to Dulles, June 27, 1954, No. 1121.

7. Peurifoy cable, No. 1121; *Time,* July 5, 1954.

8. Peurifoy cable to Dulles, June 27, 1954, No. 1124.

9. Peurifoy cable, No. 1124.

10. *Bohemia* (weekly magazine published in Cuba), Nov. 14, 1954; Peurifoy cable to Dulles, June 27, 1954, No. 1123.

11. Peurifoy cable, No. 1123.

12. *El Imparcial,* July 28, 1954.

13. Sherwood interview.

14. *Bohemia,* Nov. 14, 1954; Mario Rosenthal, *Guatemala: The Story of an Emergent Latin-American Democracy* (New York: Twayne, 1962), p. 258.

15. Rosenthal, *Guatemala,* pp. 259–60.

16. Rosenthal, *Guatemala,* p. 261.
17. Manuel Colom Argueta, *Una Breve Democracia en el País de la Eterna Dictadura* (Guatemala: Frente Unido de la Revolución, 1977).
18. Confidential communication with Schlesinger.
19. David Atlee Phillips interview, Washington, Oct. 7, 1979.
20. *Time,* July 26, 1954.

CHAPTER 14

1. David Wise and Thomas Ross, *The Invisible Government* (New York: Random House, 1964), p. 192.
2. David Atlee Phillips interview, Washington, Oct. 7, 1979; North American Congress on Latin America (NACLA), *Guatemala* (Berkeley and New York: NACLA, 1974), p. 72; Richard Harris Smith, "Spymaster's Odyssey: The World of Allen Dulles" (manuscript to be published, New York, 1983), Ch. 26, pp. 27–29.
3. Smith, "Spymaster's Odyssey," Ch. 26, pp. 27–29; Donald Grant, "Ambassador Peurifoy—The Man Who Beat the Reds in Guatemala," St. Louis *Post-Dispatch,* July 11, 1954.
4. Smith, "Spymaster's Odyssey," Ch. 26, pp. 27–29.
5. Peurifoy cable to Dulles, June 28, 1954, No. 1131.
6. Cole Blasier, *The Hovering Giant: U.S. Responses to Revolutionary Change in Latin America* (Pittsburgh: University of Pittsburgh Press, 1976), p. 175; Guillermo Toriello, *La Batalla de Guatemala* (Mexico City: Ediciones Cuadernos Americanos, 1955), p. 189.
7. Peurifoy cables to Dulles, June 28, 1954, Nos. 1136–38.
8. Smith, "Spymaster's Odyssey," Ch. 26, p. 30; Wise and Ross, *Invisible Government,* p. 193.
9. Peurifoy cables to Dulles, June 28, 1954, Nos. 1137 and 1138; June 29, 1954, No. 1143.
10. *Time,* July 12, 1954.
11. Peurifoy cable to Dulles, June 29, 1954, No. 1146.
12. Diary of Mrs. Peurifoy, undated, sent to authors June 5, 1981; *Time,* July 12, 1954; New York *Times,* July 1, 1954.
13. Peurifoy cables to Dulles, June 29, 1954, No. 1146, and June 30, 1954, No. 1153; Grant, "Ambassador Peurifoy."
14. Department of State Memorandum of Conversation, Peurifoy and Holland, et al., June 29, 1954; U. S. Embassy Guatemala Army Attaché to Dulles, June 30, 1954.

15. Dulles cable to Peurifoy (via Holland), June 29, 1954;
    NACLA, *Guatemala*, p. 72.
16. Department of State Memorandum of Conversation, U. S. Am-
    bassador McDermott (El Salvador) and Holland, June 30,
    1954; McDermott cable to Dulles, July 1, 1954; Department of
    State Memorandum of Conversation, McDermott and Holland,
    July 1, 1954; McDermott cable to Dulles, "Negotiations of Gua-
    temalan Peace Pact," July 5, 1954; Blasier, *Hovering Giant*, p.
    176; Marta Cehelsky, "Guatemala's Frustrated Revolution" (un-
    published Columbia University Master's Thesis, 1967), p. 63.
17. Peurifoy cable to Dulles, "Memorandum of Negotiations," July
    2, 1954; Department of State Memorandum of Conversation,
    Peurifoy and Holland, July 2, 1954.
18. Department of State Memorandum of Conversation, Peurifoy
    and Holland, July 2, 1954.
19. Peurifoy cable to Dulles, "Memorandum of Negotiations," July
    2, 1954; Department of State Memorandum of Conversation,
    Peurifoy and Holland, July 2, 1954; Blasier, *Hovering Giant*, p.
    176; Flora Lewis, "Ambassador Extraordinary: John Peurifoy,"
    The New York Times Magazine, July 18, 1954.
20. *El Imparcial*, July 2, 3, 1954.
21. Department of State Memorandum of Conversation, Holland
    and U. S. Ambassador to Mexico Daniels, July 2, 1954; Depart-
    ment of State Memorandum of Conversation, Peurifoy and
    Holland, July 2, 1954; Department of State Memorandum of
    Conversation, Holland and U. S. Ambassador to Nicaragua
    Whelan, July 2, 1954.
22. *El Imparcial*, July 3, 4, 1954; Smith, "Spymaster's Odyssey,"
    Ch. 26, p. 30.
23. *Time*, July 12, 1954; John E. Peurifoy address to Amvets, Miami
    Beach, Fla., Aug. 28, 1954, in *U. S. Department of State Bulle-
    tin*, Vol. 31, No. 793 (Sept. 6, 1954).
24. NACLA, *Guatemala*, p. 72; Cehelsky, "Frustrated Revolution,"
    p. 63; Wise and Ross, *Invisible Government*, p. 194; Peurifoy
    cable to Dulles, July 6, 1954, No. 32.
25. *El Imparcial*, July 6, 1954.
26. *El Imparcial*, July 13, 1954.
27. U. S. Department of State, *Intervention of International Com-
    munism in the Americas*, Publication #5556 (Washington, 1954),
    p. 32.
28. Philip B. Taylor, Jr., "The Guatemalan Affair: A Critique of

United States Foreign Policy," *American Political Science Review*, Vol. 50, No. 3 (Sept. 1956), p. 804.

29. Smith, "Spymaster's Odyssey," Ch. 26, p. 30; Peter Wyden, *The Bay of Pigs: The Untold Story* (New York: Simon and Schuster, 1979), p. 21; David Atlee Phillips, *The Night Watch: Twenty-five Years of Peculiar Service* (New York: Atheneum, 1977), pp. 49–50.

30. Phillips, *Night Watch*, p. 50.

31. Smith, "Spymaster's Odyssey," Ch. 26, p. 30; Phillips, *Night Watch*, p. 51.

32. Dulles cable to Peurifoy, July 17, 1954.

33. Peurifoy cable to Dulles, July 19, 1954, No. 99; Cehelsky, "Frustrated Revolution," p. 96.

34. Thomas and Marjorie Melville, *Guatemala: The Politics of Land Ownership* (New York: Free Press, 1971), pp. 100–1; *El Imparcial*, July 2, 1954; Richard Adams, *Crucifixion by Power* (Austin: University of Texas Press, 1970), p. 449; "Meeting of Guatemalan Group," State Department, July 2, 1954; U. S. State Department, Aug. 4, 1954, Bowdler to Pearson, ARA, Office Memorandum.

35. *The American Federationist*, Vol. 61, p. 27 (Sept. 1954); Cehelsky, "Frustrated Revolution," pp. 83–84; John Sloan, "The Electoral Game in Guatemala" (unpublished University of Texas Doctoral Dissertation, 1968), p. 48.

36. Paul Kennedy, *The Middle Beat* (New York: Teachers College Press, Columbia University, 1971), p. 142; *Time*, July 12, 1954, p. 31.

37. Ronald Schneider, *Communism in Guatemala 1944–54* (New York: Praeger, 1959), p. 323; private letter from Richard Adams to Schlesinger, March 8, 1979; Stokes Newbold, "Receptivity to Communist-Fomented Agitation in Rural Guatemala," *Economic Development and Cultural Change*, Vol. 5, No. 4 (July 1957), pp. 338–60.

38. Thomas McCann, *An American Company: The Tragedy of United Fruit* (New York: Crown, 1976), pp. 52–53, 62; Thomas Corcoran interview, Washington, Oct. 6, 1979; Blasier, *Hovering Giant*, p. 90.

39. Cehelsky, "Frustrated Revolution," 77–78; Wise and Ross, *Invisible Government*, pp. 194–95; Melville, *Land Ownership*, pp. 100–1; Max Gordon, "A Case History of U.S. Subversion: Guatemala," *Science and Society*, Vol. 35, No. 2 (Summer 1971), p. 149.

40. Adams, *Crucifixion*, p. 400; Cehelsky, "Frustrated Revolution,"
    p. 78; Ralph Lee Woodward, Jr., *Central America: A Nation
    Divided* (New York: Oxford University Press, 1976), p. 237;
    Time, Aug. 23, 1954; Gordon, "Case History," p. 150; NACLA,
    Guatemala, p. 75.
41. Dulles cables to Peurifoy July 9, 1954, and July 17, 1954.
42. Peurifoy cable to Dulles, No. 109, July 22, 1954; Dulles cable to
    Peurifoy, July 27, 1954.
43. Department of State Memorandum of Telephone Call, Peurifoy
    and Holland, Aug. 27, 1954; *Time*, Sept. 20, 1954.
44. Frederick B. Pike, "Guatemala, the United States and Commu-
    nism in the Americas," *The Review of Politics*, Vol. 17, No. 2
    (April 1955), p. 252; Cehelsky, "Frustrated Revolution," p. 99.
45. *El Imparcial*, Sept. 1, 1954.
46. Cehelsky, "Frustrated Revolution," pp. 78–79.
47. Adams, *Crucifixion*, p. 283, 310; New York *Times*, Dec. 12,
    1954; K. H. Silvert, *The Conflict Society: Reaction and Revolu-
    tion in Latin America* (New Orleans: Hauser Press, 1961), p.
    128; Blasier, *Hovering Giant*, p. 177.
48. Leonard Mosley, *Dulles* (New York: Dial, 1978), p. 459; Rich-
    ard Bissell interview, Farmington, Conn., Sept. 12, 1979; Ninth
    Interim Report of Hearings Before Subcommittee on Latin
    America of the House Select Committee on Communist Aggres-
    sion, *Communist Aggression in Latin America: Guatemala*
    (Washington: Government Printing Office, 1954), p. 124.

CHAPTER 15

1. Ronald Schneider, "Guatemala: An Aborted Communist Take-
   over," in Thomas Hammond (ed.), *The Anatomy of Communist
   Takeovers* (New Haven: Yale University Press, 1975), p. 576;
   William Krieg interview, Washington, March 26, 1979.
2. William R. Corson, *The Armies of Ignorance: The Rise of the
   American Intelligence Empire* (New York: Dial, 1977), p. 357;
   H. Bradford Westerfield, *The Instruments of American Foreign
   Policy* (New York: Crowell, 1963), p. 438.
3. Lawrence Houston interview, Washington, Oct. 8, 1979; Fred
   Sherwood interview, Guatemala City, Jan. 24, 1980; New York
   Times, Dec. 25, 27, 1977; confidential communications with
   Kinzer and Schlesinger; William Warner interview, Washington,
   April 28, 1981.
4. Thomas McCann, *An American Company: The Tragedy of
   United Fruit* (New York: Crown, 1976), pp. 1–3, 62, 188;

Thomas and Marjorie Melville, *Guatemala: The Politics of Land Ownership* (New York: Free Press, 1971), p. 59.

5. Confidential communications with Schlesinger and Kinzer.

6. Confidential communication with Kinzer; Arbenz interview in *La Prensa Libre*, San José, Costa Rica, Oct. 25, 1955, quoted in Ronald Schneider, *Communism in Guatemala 1944–54* (New York: Praeger, 1959), pp. 193, 313.

7. Carlos Manuel Pellecer, *Caballeros sin Esperanza* (Mexico City: Editorial del Ejercito, 1973), pp. 159–63.

8. Pellecer, *Caballeros*, p. 163; confidential communication with Kinzer.

9. Max Gordon, "A Case History of U.S. Subversion: Guatemala, 1954," *Science and Society*, Vol. 35, No. 2 (Summer 1971), p. 151; Robert J. Alexander, *Communism in Latin America* (New Brunswick, N.J.: Rutgers University Press, 1957), p. 77.

10. Richard Adams, *Crucifixion by Power* (Austin: University of Texas Press, 1970), p. 400.

11. Paul Kennedy, *The Middle Beat* (New York: Teachers College Press, Columbia University, 1971), p. 145.

12. North American Congress on Latin America (NACLA), *Guatemala* (Berkeley and New York: NACLA, 1974), pp. 74–76.

13. Miguel Ydígoras Fuentes interview, Guatemala City, Jan. 25, 1980.

14. NACLA, *Guatemala*, p. 81; Marta Cehelsky, "Guatemala's Frustrated Revolution" (unpublished Columbia University Master's Thesis, 1967), p. 109.

15. NACLA, *Guatemala*, p. 81; Kennedy, *Middle Beat*, p. 144.

16. Mario Rosenthal, *Guatemala: The Story of an Emergent Latin-American Democracy* (New York: Twayne, 1962), pp. 265–66; Robert D. Crassweller, *Trujillo: The Life and Times of a Caribbean Dictator* (New York: Macmillan, 1966), pp. 334–38; David Wise and Thomas Ross, *The Invisible Government* (New York: Random House, 1964), p. 195.

17. Ydígoras interview.

18. Rosenthal, *Emergent Latin-American Democracy*, p. 273.

19. Thomas and Marjorie Melville, *Guatemala: Another Vietnam?* (London: Penguin, 1971), p. 284; Miami *Herald*, Dec. 24, 1966.

20. Wise and Ross, *Invisible Government*, p. 195; Richard Gott, *Rural Guerillas in Latin America* (London: Pelican, 1973), p. 69.

21. Gott, *Rural Guerillas*, p. 71; Victor Marchetti and John Marks,

The CIA and the Cult of Intelligence (New York: Dell, 1975),
p. 283; Melville, *Land Ownership*, pp. 140–42; Adolfo Gilly, "The
Guerilla Movement in Guatemala," *Monthly Review*, May 1965,
p. 13; Adams, *Crucifixion*, p. 261.

22. Gott, *Rural Guerillas*, p. 72.
23. Gott, *Rural Guerillas*, p. 70.
24. Gott, *Rural Guerillas*, p. 77.
25. Gott, *Rural Guerillas*, pp. 79, 80.
26. *El Imparcial*, Jan. 4, 1963, and May 17, 1962.
27. *El Imparcial*, Jan. 26, 1963.
28. Melville, *Land Ownership*, pp. 119, 122–23, 146–48; *El Imparcial*,
    July 8, 1958.
29. Melville, *Land Ownership*, pp. 123–24; Miguel Ydígoras
    Fuentes, *My War with Communism* (Englewood Cliffs, N.J.:
    Prentice-Hall, 1963), p. 2; Georgie Anne Geyer, Miami *Herald*,
    Dec. 24, 1966.
30. Georgie Anne Geyer, Miami *Herald*, Dec. 24, 1966; Arévalo
    first hinted at his intention to return in *El Imparcial*, Jan. 3,
    1962.
31. Miami *Herald*, Dec. 24, 1966; Melville, *Land Ownership*, pp.
    148–50; Francis McNeil, Second Secretary, U. S. Embassy,
    cable to Secretary of State Dean Rusk, No. A-283, Nov. 10,
    1962; John Dreyfuss, acting for U. S. Embassy Chargé d'Affaires
    in Guatemala, cable to Rusk, No. 551, March 12, 1963.
32. The other participants not reached for confirmation on the
    meeting were the late President Kennedy, Richard Helms, re-
    tired Director of the CIA, and Theodoro Moscoso, former ad-
    ministrator of the Alliance For Progress. The original story, by
    Georgie Anne Geyer, appeared in the Chicago *Daily News* and
    was picked up and reprinted in the Miami *Herald*, Dec. 24,
    1966. Ms. Geyer's account reported that President Kennedy
    gave the green-light to the Peralta coup after a majority vote of
    his four Latin American experts recommended it; Edwin Martin,
    letter to Schlesinger, April 15, 1981; John O. Bell, letters to
    Schlesinger, May 11, June 12, 30, 1981; U. S. Embassy Gua-
    temala, cable to Secretary of State Rusk, No. 605, March 30,
    1963; Melville, *Land Ownership*, pp. 148–50.
33. Ralph Lee Woodward, Jr., *Central America: A Nation Divided*
    (New York: Oxford University Press, 1976), p. 239; Gott, *Rural
    Guerillas*, p. 119.
34. Melville, *Land Ownership*, pp. 184–86.
35. Gott, *Rural Guerillas*, p. 128; Schneider, "Guatemala," p. 578;

Jerome Levinson and Juan de Onis, *The Alliance That Lost Its Way* (Chicago: Quadrangle Books, 1970), p. 85.

36. NACLA, *Guatemala*, p. 117; Roger Plant, *Guatemala: Unnatural Disaster* (London: Latin America Bureau, 1978), p. 22; Gott, *Rural Guerillas*, pp. 124–25.

37. Daniel L. Premo, "Political Assassination in Guatemala: Institutionalized Terror" (Washington College, Chestertown, Md., unpublished), pp. 11–12.

38. Amnesty International, "Guatemala: A Government Program of Political Murder" (London: Amnesty International, 1981), pp. 3, 5; Jonathan Power, "Behind the Killings in Guatemala," New York *Times*, Feb. 17, 1981.

39. *Latin America*, Sept. 15, 1967, quoted in Gott, *Rural Guerillas*, p. 134.

40. NACLA, *Guatemala*, p. 199.

41. Gott, *Rural Guerillas*, pp. 115, 142; *Time*, Jan. 28, 1968.

42. Gott, *Rural Guerillas*, p. 144; NACLA, *Guatemala*, p. 186.

43. Premo, "Political Assassination," p. 12; Jack Anderson, "Guatemalan Tinderbox," Washington *Post*, Feb. 22, 1981.

44. Premo, "Political Assassination," p. 15; confidential communication with Schlesinger.

45. Hearings Before the Subcommittee on International Organizations of the Committee on International Relations, House of Representatives, June 8 and 9, 1976 (Washington: Government Printing Office, 1976), pp. 50–56.

46. *Newsday*, Feb. 6, 1980; Marlise Simons, "Guatemala: The Coming Danger," *Foreign Policy* (Summer 1981), p. 98.

47. Amnesty International, "Death or Exile Is the Fate of Those Who Fight for Justice in Guatemala" (New York and San Francisco: Amnesty International, 1979), p. 1.

48. *Newsday*, Feb. 6, 1980.

49. Ejército Guerrillero de Los Pobres, "The Guatemalan Revolution," *Contemporary Marxism*, No. 3 (Summer 1981), pp. 33–35.

50. The World Bank, *Guatemala: Economic and Social Positions and Prospects* (Washington: World Bank, 1978), pp. 9, 13, 18, 99.

51. Inter-American Development Bank, *Economic and Social Progress in Latin America* (Washington: Inter-American Development Bank, 1980), p. 258; Premo, "Political Assassination," p. 5.

52. Premo, "Political Assassination," p. 34.

BIBLIOGRAPHY

1. BOOKS AND MANUSCRIPTS

Adams, Richard. *Crucifixion by Power*. Austin: University of Texas Press, 1970.

Alexander, Charles. *Holding the Line: The Eisenhower Era, 1952–1961*. Bloomington: Indiana University Press, 1975.

Alexander, Robert. *Communism in Latin America*. New Brunswick, N.J.: Rutgers University Press, 1957.

——. *Organized Labor in Latin America*. New York: Free Press, 1965.

Ambrose, Stephen. *Ike's Spies: Eisenhower and the Espionage Establishment*. Garden City, N.Y.: Doubleday, 1981.

American University. *Case Study in Insurgency and Revolutionary Warfare: Guatemala 1944–1954*. Washington: Special Operations Research Office, 1964.

Aragón, Luis Cardoza y. *La Revolución Guatemalteca*. Mexico City: Ediciones Cuadernos Americanos, 1955.

Arévalo, Juan José. *Guatemala: La Democracia y el Imperio*. Mexico City: Editorial América Nueva, 1954.

——. *The Shark and the Sardines*. New York: Lyle Stuart, 1961.

Argueta, Manuel Colom. *Una Breve Democracia en el País de la Eterna Dictadura*. Guatemala: Frente Unido de la Revolución, 1977.

Aybar de Soto, José M. *Dependency and Intervention: The Case of Guatemala in 1954*. Boulder, Colo.: Westview Press, 1978.

Ball, Mary Margaret. *The OAS in Transition*. Durham, N.C.: Duke University Press, 1969.

Berle, Adolf. *Navigating the Rapids: 1918–1971*. New York: Harcourt Brace Jovanovich, 1973.

Bernays, Edward. *Biography of an Idea*. New York: Simon and Schuster, 1965.

Blasier, Cole. *The Hovering Giant: U.S. Responses to Revolutionary Change in Latin America*. Pittsburgh: University of Pittsburgh Press, 1976.

Braden, Spruille. *Diplomats and Demagogues*. New York: Arlington House, 1971.

Burr, Robert. *Our Troubled Hemisphere: Perspectives on U.S.-Latin American Relations*. Washington: The Brookings Institution, 1967.

Cabot, John Moors. *Toward Our Common American Destiny*. Freeport, N.Y.: Book for Libraries Press, 1955.

——. *First Line of Defense: Forty Years' Experiences of a Career Diplomat*. Washington: School of Foreign Service, Georgetown, 1979.

Cabot, Thomas. *Beggar on Horseback*. Boston: David Godine, 1979.

Cater, Douglass. *Power in Washington*. New York: Random House, 1964.

Cehelsky, Marta. "Guatemala's Frustrated Revolution." New York: Columbia University Master's Thesis, 1967.

Colby, William and Peter Forbath. *Honorable Men: My Life in the CIA*. New York: Simon and Schuster, 1978.

Cook, Blanche. *The Declassified Eisenhower: A Divided Legacy of Peace and Political Warfare*. Garden City, N.Y.: Doubleday, 1981.

Corson, William. *The Armies of Ignorance: The Rise of the American Intelligence Empire*. New York: Dial, 1977.

Council on Foreign Relations. *Social Change in Latin America Today.* New York: Harper, 1960.

Crassweller, Robert. *Trujillo: The Life and Times of a Caribbean Dictator.* New York: Macmillan, 1966.

Davis, Harold Eugene (ed.). *Government and Politics in Latin America.* New York: Ronald Press, 1958.

Dinerstein, Herbert. *The Making of a Missile Crisis: October 1962.* Baltimore: Johns Hopkins University Press, 1975.

Dombrowski, John, et al. *Area Handbook for Guatemala.* Washington: U. S. State Department, 1968.

Dulles, Allen. *The Craft of Intelligence.* New York: Harper & Row, 1963.

Eden, Anthony. *Full Circle: The Memoirs of Anthony Eden.* Boston: Houghton Mifflin, 1960.

Eisenhower, Dwight. *The White House Years.* Vol. I: *Mandate for Change, 1953–56.* Garden City, N.Y.: Doubleday, 1963.

Gadea, Hilda. *Ernesto: A Memoir of Che Guevara.* Garden City, N.Y.: Doubleday, 1972.

Galeano, Eduardo. *Guatemala: País Ocupado.* Mexico City: Editorial Nuestro Tiempo, S.A., 1967.

Galich, Manuel. *Por Que Lucha Guatemala, Arévalo y Arbenz: Dos Hombres contra un Imperio.* Buenos Aires: Elmer Editor, 1956.

Gambini, Hugo. *El Che Guevara.* Buenos Aires: Paidos, 1968.

Gott, Richard. *Rural Guerillas in Latin America.* London: Pelican, 1973.

Great Britain. *House of Commons, 1953–54 Report on Events Leading Up to and Arising Out of the Change in Regime in Guatemala.* London: H. M. Stationery Office, 1954.

Grieb, Kenneth. *Guatemalan Caudillo: The Regime of Jorge Ubico.* Athens: Ohio University Press, 1979.

Guatemala, Secretaría de Propaganda y Divulgación. *La Democracia Amenazada: El Caso de Guatemala.* Guatemala City: 1954.

Halperin, Ernst. "The National Liberation Movements in Latin America, Project on Communism, Revisionism and Revolution." Cambridge, Mass.: MIT Center for International Studies, 1969.

Hammond, Thomas (ed.). *The Anatomy of Communist Takeovers.* New Haven: Yale University Press, 1975.

Harris, Leon. *Only to God: The Extraordinary Life of Godfrey Lowell Cabot*. New York: Atheneum, 1967.

Herring, Hubert. *A History of Latin America: From Beginning to Present*. New York: Knopf, 1955.

Hoffman, Paul. *Lions in the Street: The Inside Story of the Great Wall Street Law Firms*. New York: Saturday Review Press/E. P. Dutton, 1973.

Hougan, Jim. *Spooks*. New York: Morrow, 1978.

Hunt, E. Howard. *Give Us This Day*. New Rochelle, N.Y.: Arlington House, 1973.

——. *Undercover: Memoirs of an American Secret Agent*. New York: Berkley, 1974.

Immerman, Richard. "Guatemala and the United States, 1954: A Cold War Strategy for the Americas." Boston: unpublished Boston College Doctoral Dissertation, 1978.

Inman, Samuel Guy. *A New Day in Guatemala*. Wilton, Conn.: Worldover Press (pamphlet), 1951.

International Bank for Reconstruction and Development. *Mission to Guatemala*. Washington: IBRD, 1951.

James, Daniel. *Che Guevara*. New York: Stein and Day, 1970.

——. *Red Design for the Americas*. New York: John Day, 1954.

Jensen, Amy Elizabeth. *Guatemala: A Historical Survey*. New York: Exposition, 1955.

Johnson, Kenneth. *The Guatemala Presidential Election of March 6, 1966*. Washington: Institute for the Comparative Study of Political Systems, 1967.

Jones, Chester Lloyd. *Guatemala Past and Present*. Minneapolis: University of Minnesota Press, 1966.

Karol, K. S. *Guerillas in Power*. New York: Hill and Wang, 1970.

Kennedy, Paul. *The Middle Beat: A Correspondent's View of Mexico, Guatemala and El Salvador*. New York: Teachers College Press, Columbia University, 1971.

Kiernan, Thomas. "Primrose Yellow" (unpublished manuscript).

Kirkpatrick, Lyman. *The Real CIA*. New York: Macmillan, 1968.

Levinson, Jerome, and de Onis, Juan. *The Alliance That Lost Its Way*. Chicago: Quadrangle Books, 1970.

Marchetti, Victor, and Marks, John. *The CIA and the Cult of Intelligence.* New York: Dell, 1975.

Martin, John Bartlow. *Overtaken by Events.* Garden City, N.Y.: Doubleday, 1966.

Martz, John. *Central America.* Chapel Hill, N.C.: University of North Carolina Press, 1959.

Matthews, Herbert Lionel. *A World in Revolution.* New York: Scribner's, 1971.

———. *The Cuban Story.* New York: George Braziller, 1961.

May, Stacy, and Plaza, Galo. *United States Business Performance Abroad: The Case Study of United Fruit Company in Latin America.* Washington: National Planning Association, 1958.

McCann, Thomas. *An American Company: The Tragedy of United Fruit.* New York: Crown, 1976.

Mecham, J. Lloyd. *The United States and Inter-American Security, 1889–1960.* Austin: University of Texas Press, 1961.

Melville, Thomas and Marjorie. *Guatemala: The Politics of Land Ownership.* New York: Free Press, 1971.

Mooney, Joseph Wrigley III. "United States Intervention in Guatemala, 1954." St. Louis: Northeast Missouri State University Master of Arts Thesis, 1976.

Morris, George. *CIA and American Labor: The Subversion of the AFL-CIO's Foreign Policy.* New York: International Publishers, 1967.

Mosley, Leonard. *Dulles.* New York: Dial, 1978.

Munro, Dana. *Intervention and Dollar Diplomacy in the Caribbean, 1900–1921.* Princeton, N.J.: Princeton University Press, 1964.

National Planning Association. *Communism versus Progress in Guatemala.* NPA, No. 85, by Theodore Geiger. Washington: NPA, 1953.

North American Congress on Latin America. *Guatemala: "And So Victory Is Born Even in the Bitterest Hours."* Berkeley and New York: NACLA, 1974.

Paddock, William. *Hungry Nations.* Boston: Little, Brown, 1964.

——— and Paddock, Elizabeth. *We Don't Know How: An Independent Audit of What They Call Success in Foreign Assistance.* Ames: Iowa State University Press, 1973.

Parker, Franklin. *The Central American Republics*. London: Oxford University Press, 1964.

Pearson, Drew. *Diaries: 1949–1959*. Edited by Tyler Abell. New York: Holt, Rinehart and Winston, 1974.

Pellecer, Carlos Manuel. *Caballeros sin Esperanza*. Mexico City: Editorial del Ejercito, 1973.

Perkins, Dexter. *A History of the Monroe Doctrine*. Boston: Little, Brown, 1955.

Phillips, David Atlee. *The Night Watch: Twenty-five Years of Peculiar Service*. New York: Atheneum, 1977.

Plant, Roger. *Guatemala: Unnatural Disaster*. London: Latin America Bureau, 1978.

Powelson, John P. *Latin America: Today's Economic and Social Revolution*. New York: McGraw-Hill, 1964.

Powers, Thomas. *The Man Who Kept the Secrets: Richard Helms and the CIA*. New York: Knopf, 1979.

Prouty, L. Fletcher. *The Secret Team: The CIA and Its Allies in Control of the United States and the World*. Englewood Cliffs, N.J.: Prentice-Hall, 1973.

Rodriguez, Mario. *Central America*. Englewood Cliffs, N.J.: Prentice-Hall, 1965.

Rojo, Ricardo. *My Friend Ché*. New York: Dial Press, 1968.

Ronning, C. Neale (ed.). *Intervention in Latin America*. New York: Knopf, 1970.

Roosevelt, Kermit. *Countercoup: The Struggle for the Control of Iran*. New York: McGraw-Hill, 1979.

Rosenthal, Mario. *Guatemala: The Story of an Emergent Latin-American Democracy*. New York: Twayne, 1962.

Rositzke, Harry. *The CIA's Secret Operations*. New York: Reader's Digest Press, 1977.

Rovere, Richard. *Senator Joe McCarthy*. New York: Harcourt, Brace, 1959.

Salisbury, Harrison. *Without Fear or Favor*. New York: Times Books, 1980.

Schlesinger, Jr., Arthur. *Robert Kennedy and His Times*. Boston: Houghton Mifflin, 1978.

Schneider, Ronald. *Communism in Guatemala 1944–54*. New York: Praeger, 1959.

Scott, Peter Dale. *The War Conspiracy: The Secret Road to the Second Indochina War.* New York: Bobbs-Merrill, 1972.

Silvert, K. H. *A Study in Government: Guatemala.* New Orleans: Tulane University Press, 1954.

———. *The Conflict Society: Reaction and Revolution in Latin America.* New Orleans: Hauser Press, 1961.

Sinclair, Andrew. *Che Guevara.* New York: Viking, 1970.

Smith, Joseph Burkholder. *Portrait of a Cold Warrior.* New York: Putnam, 1976.

Smith, Richard Harris. *OSS: The Secret History of America's First Central Intelligence Agency.* Berkeley: University of California Press, 1972.

———. "Spymaster's Odyssey: The World of Allen Dulles." To be published, New York, 1983. Manuscript.

Suslow, Leo. *Aspects of Social Reform in Guatemala 1944–49.* Hamilton, N.Y.: Colgate University Press, 1949.

Szulc, Tad. *Compulsive Spy: The Strange Career of E. Howard Hunt.* New York: Viking, 1974.

Toledo, Mario Monteforte. *La Revolución de Guatemala, 1944–54.* Guatemala City: Editorial Universitaria, 1971.

Toriello, Guillermo. *La Batalla de Guatemala.* Mexico City: Ediciones Cuadernos Americanos, 1955.

Travis, Helen Simon, and Magil, A. B. *What Happened in Guatemala.* New York: New Century Publishers, 1954.

Tully, Andrew. *CIA: The Inside Story.* New York: Crest, 1963.

Urquhart, Brian. *Hammarskjöld.* New York: Knopf, 1972.

Weinstein, Allen. *Perjury: The Hiss-Chambers Case.* New York: Knopf, 1978.

Westerfield, H. Bradford. *The Instruments of America's Foreign Policy.* New York: Crowell, 1963.

Whetten, Nathan. *Guatemala: The Land and the People.* New Haven: Yale University Press, 1961.

Williams, T. Harry. *Huey Long.* New York: Bantam, 1976.

Wise, David, and Ross, Thomas. *The Invisible Government.* New York: Random House, 1964.

Woodward, Ralph Lee. *Central America: A Nation Divided.* New York: Oxford University Press, 1976.

Wyden, Peter. *The Bay of Pigs: The Untold Story.* New York: Simon and Schuster, 1979.

Ydígoras Fuentes, Miguel. *My War with Communism.* Englewood Cliffs, N.J.: Prentice-Hall, 1963.

2. ARTICLES

Acheson, Dean. "Dear Boss." *American Heritage,* Feb.–March 1980.

Alexander, Robert. "Communists and the Guatemalan Revolution." *Hemispherica,* Vol. 3, No. 2 (March–May 1954), pp. 2–4.

———. "Revolution in Guatemala." *The New Leader,* Jan. 5, 1953, pp. 6–8.

———. "The Guatemalan Revolution and Communism." *Foreign Policy Bulletin,* April 1, 1954, pp. 5–7.

Anderson, Jack. "Guatemalan Tinderbox." Washington *Post,* Feb. 22, 1981.

Bernstein, Carl. "The CIA and the Media." *Rolling Stone,* No. 250 (Oct. 20, 1977), pp. 55–67.

Bracker, Milton. "The Lessons of the Guatemalan Struggle." *The New York Times Magazine,* July 11, 1954.

Brown, Cynthia. "Guatemala–The Next Nicaragua." *The Nation,* Aug. 25–Sept. 1, 1979, pp. 138–42.

Contemporary Marxism, No. 3 (Summer 1981). "Revolution and Intervention in Central America."

Cook, Frederick J. "The CIA." *Nation,* Vol. 192, No. 25 (June 24, 1961).

Crewsdon, John, and Treaster, Joseph. "The CIA's 3-Decade Effort to Mold the World's Views." New York *Times,* Dec. 25, 27, 1977.

D'Ascoli, Carlos A. "La Reforma Agraria y Estensión de las Explotaciones Agrícolas." *Trimestre Económico,* Vol. 19, No. 3 (July–Sept. 1952), p. 409.

Fortune, Feb. 1952. "Lawyers and Lobbyists."

Gillin, John, and Silvert, K. H. "Ambiguities in Guatemala." *Foreign Affairs,* Vol. 34, No. 3 (April 1956), pp. 469–82.

Gilly, Adolfo. "The Guerilla Movement in Guatemala." *Monthly Review,* May 1965, p. 13.

Gordon, Max. "A Case History of U.S. Subversion: Guatemala, 1954." *Science and Society,* Vol. 35, No. 2 (Summer 1971).

Grabowicz, Paul, and Kotkin, Joel. "The CIA Puts Its Money Where Its Friends Are." *New Times*, Nov. 27, 1978, pp. 24–25.

Grant, Donald. "Ambassador Peurifoy—The Man Who Beat the Reds in Guatemala." St. Louis *Post-Dispatch* July 11, 1954.

——. "Guatemala and United States Foreign Policy." *Journal of International Affairs*, Vol. 9, No. 1 (1955).

Harkness, Richard and Gladys. "America's Secret Agents: The Mysterious Doings of CIA." *The Saturday Evening Post*, Vol. 227 (Oct. 30, 1954).

Hunt, E. Howard. "The Azalea Trail Guide to the CIA." *The National Review*, April 29, 1977.

Immerman, Richard. "Guatemala as Cold War History." *Political Science Quarterly*, Vol. 95, No. 4 (Winter 1980–81).

Lahey, Edwin. "We Won't Turn the Clock Back—Maybe." *The New Republic*, July 19, 1954, p. 10.

Lewis, Flora. "Ambassador Extraordinary: John Peurifoy." *The New York Times Magazine*, July 18, 1954.

——. "Communism in Guatemala: A Case History." *The New York Times Magazine*, Feb. 21, 1954.

Life, June 14, 28; July 5, 12, 19; Aug. 16, 1954.

Lissner, Will. "Soviet Agents Plotting to Ruin Unity, Defenses of Americas." New York *Times*, June 22, 23, 1950.

Monroe, Keith. "Guatemala: What the Reds Left Behind." *Harper's Magazine*, Vol. 211, No. 1262 (July 1955), pp. 60–65.

Newbold, Stokes (Richard Adams). "Receptivity to Communist-Fomented Agitation in Rural Guatemala." *Economic Development and Cultural Change*, Vol. 5, No. 4 (July 1957), pp. 338–60.

Pearson, Drew. "Washington Merry-Go-Round: Link CIA to Early Arming of Castro." New York *Mirror*, May 23, 1961.

Pearson, Ross. "Land Reform Guatemalan Style." *American Journal of Economics and Sociology*, Vol. 22, No. 2 (April 1963), pp. 225–34.

Pike, Frederick B. "Guatemala, the United States and Communism in the Americas." *The Review of Politics*, Vol. 17, No. 2 (April 1955), pp. 232–61.

Power, Jonathan. "Behind the Killings in Guatemala." New York *Times*, Feb. 17, 1981.

Premo, Daniel. "Political Assassination in Guatemala: Institutionalized Terror." Washington College, Chestertown, Md., unpublished.

Reston, James. "With the Dulles Brothers in Darkest Guatemala." New York *Times*, June 20, 1954.

Rey, Julio Adolfo. "Revolution and Liberation: A Review of Recent Literature on the Guatemalan Situation." *The Hispanic American Historical Review*, Vol. 38, No. 2 (May 1958).

Roman, Robert. "Operation Diablo." *Soldier of Fortune Magazine*, Summer 1976, pp. 1–19ff.

Ronan, Thomas. "Eisenhower Finds Bay of Pigs Errors," New York *Times*, October 14, 1965, p. 2.

Rosenthal, Abe. "Issues in Guatemala Case Troubling U.N. Delegates." New York *Times*, June 23, 1954, p. 3.

Simons, Marlise. "Guatemala: The Coming Danger." *Foreign Policy Magazine*, Summer 1981, pp. 93–103.

Stone, I. F. "The Return to Dollar Diplomacy," *I. F. Stone's Weekly*, Vol. 2, No. 22 (June 21, 1954).

Szulc, Tad. "Making Mischief Abroad: U.S. and ITT in Chile." *The New Republic*, Vol. 168, No. 26 (June 30, 1973), pp. 21–23.

Taylor, Philip B. "The Guatemalan Affair: A Critique of United States Foreign Policy," *American Political Science Review*, Vol. 50, No. 3 (Sept. 1956), pp. 787–806.

Trento, Joe, and Roman, David. "The Spies Who Came In from the Newsroom." *Penthouse*, Vol. 8, No. 12 (Aug. 1977).

3. PUBLISHED GOVERNMENTAL RECORDS AND OTHER SOURCES

Beaulac, Willard L. "The Communist Effort in Guatemala." *The Department of State Bulletin*, Vol. 31, No. 790 (Aug. 16, 1954), pp. 235–37.

Cabot, John Moors. "Inter-American Cooperation and Hemispheric Solidarity." *The Department of State Bulletin*, Vol. 39, No. 748 (Oct. 26, 1953), pp. 554–59.

Carrollton Press, Inc. *The Declassified Documents Quarterly*, Vol. 1, Nos. 1–4 (Jan.–Dec. 1975). Washington: Inverness.

———. *The Declassified Documents Retrospective Collection*, Vols. 1–2. Washington: Inverness, 1976.

Central Intelligence Agency. *Review of the World Situation as It Relates to the Security of the United States, 1948–1950*. Truman Papers, Truman Library.

Congressional Record, 1944–54, Washington.

Curl, Peter V. (ed.). *Documents on American Foreign Relations, 1954.* New York, 1955.

Dreier, John C. "The Guatemalan Problem Before the OAS Council." *The Department of State Bulletin,* Vol. 31, No. 785 (July 12, 1954), pp. 45–47.

Dulles, John Foster. "Communist Influence in Guatemala." *The Department of State Bulletin,* Vol. 30, No. 780 (June 7, 1954), pp. 873–74.

———. "General Strike in Honduras." *The Department of State Bulletin,* Vol. 30, No. 778 (May 24, 1954), p. 801.

———. "International Communism in Guatemala." *The Department of State Bulletin,* Vol. 31, No. 785 (July 12, 1954), pp. 43–45.

———. "Intervention of International Communism in the American Republics, Statement at Caracas." March 8, 1954, Press Release No. 121. Dulles Papers, Box 79.

———. "The Republican Perspective." *Foreign Policy Bulletin,* 32, No. 1 (Sept. 15, 1952).

———. "U.S. Policy on Guatemala." *The Department of State Bulletin,* Vol. 30, No. 782 (June 21, 1954), pp. 950–51.

Key, David. "The Organization of American States and the United Nations: Rivals or Partners." *The Department of State Bulletin,* Vol. 31, No. 787 (July 26, 1954), pp. 115–18.

Lodge, Henry Cabot, Jr. "The Guatemalan Complaint Before the Security Council." *The Department of State Bulletin,* Vol. 31, No. 784 (July 5, 1954), pp. 26–31.

Morton, Thurston B. "Foreign Policy in Perspective." *The Department of State Bulletin,* Vol. 31, No. 787 (July 26, 1954), pp. 119–21.

NSC-68: A Report to the National Security Council by the Executive Secretary on United States Objectives for National Security, 14 April 1950.

Organization of American States. *Agenda of the Tenth Inter-American Conference.* Washington, 1953.

———. *Annals,* Vols. 5–6 (1953–54). Washington, 1953–54.

Peurifoy, John E. "The Communist Conspiracy in Guatemala." *The Department of State Bulletin,* Vol. 31, No. 802 (Nov. 8, 1954), pp. 690–97.

——. "Meeting the Communist Challenge in the Western Hemisphere." *The Department of State Bulletin*, Vol. 31, No. 793 (Sept. 6, 1954), pp. 333–36.

United States Department of Commerce. *Investment in Central America*. Washington, 1956.

United States Department of State. *A Case History of Communist Penetration: Guatemala*. Washington, 1957.

——. *American Foreign Policy, 1950–1955, Basic Documents*. Washington, 1957.

——. "Arms Shipment to Guatemala from Soviet-Controlled Area." *The Department of State Bulletin*, Vol. 30, No. 779 (May 31, 1954), pp. 43–85.

——. "Declaration of Caracas." *The Department of State Bulletin*, Vol. 30, No. 769 (March 22, 1954), p. 420.

——. "Expropriation of United Fruit Company Property by the Government of Guatemala." *The Department of State Bulletin*, Vol. 29, No. 742 (Sept. 14, 1953), pp. 337–60.

——. *Papers Relating to the Foreign Relations of the United States, 1944–50*. Washington.

——. *Penetration of the Political Institutions of Guatemala by the International Communist Movement*. Washington, 1954.

——. *Tenth Inter-American Conference: Report of the Delegation of the United States of America with Related Documents*. Washington, 1955.

United States House of Representatives, Committee on Foreign Affairs (92nd Cong., 2nd Sess.). *Inter-American Affairs*. Washington, 1972.

United States House of Representatives, Committee on Foreign Affairs (85th Cong., 1st Sess.). *Report of the Special Study Mission to Guatemala*. Washington, 1957.

United States House of Representatives, Subcommittee on Latin America of the Select Committee on Communist Aggression. *Ninth Interim Report of Hearings: Communist Aggression in Latin America*. Washington, 1954.

United States House of Representatives, Select Committee on Communist Aggression. *Report of the Subcommittee to Investigate Communist Aggression in Latin America*. Washington, 1954.

United States Senate, Committee on Appropriations. *Review of the United States Government Operations in Latin America, 1958*, by Allen J. Ellender, Feb. 19, 1959. Washington, 1959.

United States Senate, Committee on Foreign Relations. *Executive Sessions of the Senate Foreign Relations Committee* (Historical Series), Vol. 2 (81st Cong., 1st and 2nd Sess.), 1949–50. Washington, 1976.

United States Senate, Committee on Foreign Relations. *Executive Sessions of the Senate Foreign Relations Committee* (Historical Series), Vol. 3 (82nd Cong., 1st Sess.), 1951. Washington, 1976.

United States Senate, Judiciary Committee. *Report of the Subcommittee to Investigate Administration of the Internal Security Act and Other Internal Security Laws.* Washington, 1962.

United States Senate, Special Committee to Study the Foreign Aid Program. *Compilation of Studies and Surveys: Survey #9, Central America and the Caribbean Area.* Washington, 1957.

4. INTERVIEWS AND CORRESPONDENCE

Adams, Richard. Letter to Schlesinger, March 8, 1979.
Bell, John O. Letter to Schlesinger, May 11, June 12, 30, 1981.
Bernays, Edward. Cambridge, Massachusetts. Sept. 15, 1979.
Bissell, Richard. Farmington, Connecticut. Sept. 11, 1979.
Bump, Almyr. Guatemala City, Guatemala. Jan. 27, 1980.
Confidential correspondence (Schlesinger and Kinzer).
Corcoran, Thomas. Washington, D.C. Oct. 6, 1979.
Felker, Clay. New York City. March 15, 1979.
Gruson, Sydney. New York City. May 2, 1978.
Houston, Lawrence. Washington, D.C. Oct. 8, 1979.
Krieg, William. Washington, D.C. March 26, 1979.
Lloyd, H. Gates. New York City. Nov. 2, 1979.
McCann, Thomas. Boston, Massachusetts. Sept. 12, 1979.
———. Letter to Nat Wartels, July 12, 1976.
Miller, Edwin. Letter to Schlesinger, April 15, 1981.
Phillips, David Atlee. Washington, D.C. Oct. 7, 1979.
Sherwood, Fred. Guatemala City, Guatemala. Jan. 28, 1980.
Stewart, Mrs. Arthur C. (formerly Mrs. John Peurifoy). Letter to Schlesinger, June 2, 1981.
Warner, William. Washington, D.C. April 28, 1981.
Ydígoras Fuentes, Miguel. Guatemala City, Guatemala. Jan. 25, 1980.

5. TELEVISION DOCUMENTARY

NBC-TV Documentary. "The Science of Spying." Narrator, John Chancellor. Producer, Robert Rogers. May 4, 1965.

INDEX